A WORLD
CONTRIBUTIO...

This is the first detached and authoritative American attempt to review three decades of the most profound turbulence and change in the relations between the Western powers and the Soviet Union, from the deposition of the Tsar in 1917 to the day of summit meetings and the cold war.

Mr. Kennan, an eminently qualified observer, traces the diplomatic dilemmas that grew out of ignorance and mutual distrust. He begins with the Allied intervention in Russia in 1918, through World War I, the Versailles conference, the bloody purges of 1934-1938, the Soviet-German Nonaggression Pact of 1939, the end of World War II, and the meeting in Yalta between Churchill, Stalin, and Roosevelt. His book is a history of illusion and error that has expanded from misunderstanding to hostility . . . and to the power-conflict of East and West.

"Superbly concise, meaty, and lucid. It surveys the whole fascinating, involved drama of Communism's rise to world power."
—*Newsweek*

Thoughtful Reading from SIGNET and MENTOR

RUSSIA
AND THE
WEST
UNDER LENIN AND STALIN

George F. Kennan

A MENTOR BOOK
NEW AMERICAN LIBRARY

NEW YORK AND SCARBOROUGH, ONTARIO

*This book is dedicated to
my wife Annelise,
on whose energies and good will,
no less than on my own,
academic lecturing
has levied its exactions*

*Published as a MENTOR BOOK
by arrangement with Little, Brown and Company,
by whom the work is published in association
with the Atlantic Monthly Press.*

Chapters 9 and 10 first appeared in the *American Scholar*,
and Chapter 18 in the *Atlantic Monthly*.

 MENTOR TRADEMARK REG. U.S. PAT. OFF. AND FOREIGN COUNTRIES
REGISTERED TRADEMARK—MARCA REGISTRADA
HECHO EN CHICAGO, U.S.A.

SIGNET, SIGNET CLASSICS, MENTOR, PLUME AND MERIDIAN BOOKS
are published *in the United States* by
The New American Library, Inc.,
1301 Avenue of the Americas, New York, New York 10019,
in Canada by The New American Library of Canada Limited,
81 Mack Avenue, Scarborough, 704, Ontario

12 13 14 15 16

PRINTED IN THE UNITED STATES OF AMERICA

Preface

THE MATERIAL contained in this book is drawn from lectures, some of which were delivered in 1957-1958 in the schools at Oxford University, others—in the spring of 1960—at Harvard University.

When one thinks of the importance of the relations between Soviet Russia and the West today, and when one considers that the present nature of this relationship is something that has been formed by experiences and reactions running back over forty years, one wonders that the history of Soviet foreign relations has attracted so little attention on the part of Western scholars. There have been two excellent books—one by Louis Fischer, the other by Max Beloff—dealing with limited periods in the history of Soviet foreign relations. There have been valuable documentary collections, fascinating memoirs, and able secondary works devoted to individual phases or episodes within this field. But there has been as yet no comprehensive work addressed to the entire span of Russia's relations with the outside world, or even with the West, from the foundation of the Soviet regime down to the point where history merges with contemporary affairs; and it was with a view to filling a part—by no means all—of this gap that these lectures were conceived and delivered.

The lack of a strong and firm Western historiography in this subject is particularly unfortunate for the reason that Soviet historians have recently been giving elaborate attention to certain of its phases. The tendency of their labors has been to establish an image of this historical process which they conceive to be useful to the present purposes of the Soviet Communist Party but which is deeply discreditable to Western statesmanship and to the spirit and ideals of the Western peoples generally—so discreditable, in fact, that if the Western peoples could be brought to believe it, they would have no choice but to abandon their faith in themselves and the traditions of their national life.

Either because these Soviet materials are seldom available in Western languages or because, when seen, they have seemed to the Western eye too obviously and absurdly tendentious to be taken seriously, Western people have tended to ignore this outpouring of Soviet historiography and to doubt its importance. In this, I am convinced, they are wrong. There could be no greater error than to suppose that historical myths cannot be actually created by design, or that the crudity of such special pleading necessarily always militates against its effectiveness. The image of Soviet-Western relations now being cultivated by Soviet historians is an important part of Moscow's contemporary political appeal to the peoples of countries just emerging to national consciousness and independence. Much of it appears to these people entirely plausible and creditable. Western scholarship owes it not only to its own ideals of historical truth but also to the need for clarity and sanity in contemporary international relations generally to see that the record of this vital phase of diplomatic history is correctly established and made available to whomsoever is interested. This task, as the present volume should illustrate, does not involve concealing or understating the many failings and errors of which Western statesmanship has been guilty in its dealings with Soviet Russia over the decades. It does involve seeing to it that these failings and errors are not given so exaggerated and one-sided an interpretation as to deprive the world public of the true picture on which alone a correct understanding of some of the greatest problems of international life in our time can be founded.

Contents

1   Conflict of the Two Worlds

THIS IS A STUDY of the relationship between the Soviet Union and the major Western countries, from the inception of the Soviet regime in 1917 to the end of World War II. It is not intended as a chronological account of the happenings in this phase of diplomatic history, but rather as a series of discussions of individual episodes or problems. I think it might be useful, before we get into details, to note one or two things about the states of mind prevailing on the two sides of this relationship at the time it came into existence in 1917 and 1918.

No one can hope, I think, to unravel the confusions of this period unless he understands that two wholly separate conflicts were involved. The Soviet leaders cared about one of these; the Western powers cared about the other. Each side was inclined to make light of the importance of the conflict which it did not care about and to exaggerate the importance of that which it did.

On the one side—the Communist side—you had a social theory (let us call it Marxism-Leninism) conceived to be general, even universal, in its relevance. You also had a political faction, the Bolsheviki, dedicated to the purpose of putting this theory into practice wherever and whenever this might be possible. Russia was, as it happened, the political home of these people. It was in Russia, as it also happened, that the first possibilities opened up for a seizure of power in the name of this doctrine.

This was not the choice of Lenin and his associates. They would probably have preferred it had this opening appeared in Germany rather than in Russia. Germany was the orig-

inal home of Marxism. It was in Germany that the preconditions for the transition from capitalism to socialism,
as Marx had defined them, seemed to be farthest advanced.
It was Germany that had the highly developed industry and
the politically conscious and mature proletariat. The German
Social Democratic Party was the greatest Marxist political
organization in the world, far outshadowing its weak Russian counterpart.

But Russia was the first great country to crack under the
strain of the World War. This meant social and political
instability. And the Bolsheviki, being a Russian party, starved
for power and success, could not resist the temptation
to take advantage of this instability and to make the bid
for power. They knew that Russia was scarcely ripe for
socialism, in Marxist terms; but they rationalized their action by persuading themselves that a successful seizure of
power by Communists in Russia would ignite the smoldering
tinder of social revolution in Germany as well.

The Bolsheviki were, of course, by no means the only
faction struggling for exclusive power in Russia in 1917.
The sudden disintegration of the Tsarist regime had roused
to frantic and desperate activity every other political faction
active on the Russian scene. In view of the narrow intoler-
ance which has always characterized Russian political thought
and activity, the penalty for failure in Russian political life,
at crucial moments, can very well be destruction at the
hands of others. Once the disintegration of Tsarist power set
in, conditions of self-preservation alone would thus have
forced every one of these Russian factions to exert its utmost
effort, even had ambition for predominance not had this
same effect. The result was that Russia was plunged, from
the beginning of 1917, into a tremendous domestic-political
crisis: probably the greatest that country had ever experienced—certainly the greatest since the so-called "time of
trouble" at the end of the sixteenth century. The struggle
of the tiny, fanatical Bolshevik faction against all the others
was at first only one portion of this huge upheaval.

The things involved in this crisis were of greatest conceivable importance to every individual Russian. The social
structure, the system of land ownership, the privileges and
property interests of entire classes, were now at stake.
There was not a single Russian for whose fate the outcome of this crisis would not have momentous, intimate personal significance.

This being so, it was, of course, the internal crisis which preoccupied the individual Russian from the beginning of 1917 on. The World War had nowhere near the same significance in his eyes. It is difficult, in fact, to see what stake the common people of Russia ever did have in the outcome of the war. A Russian victory would presumably have meant the establishment of Russia on the Dardanelles. For this, the Russian peasant could not have cared less. A German victory would obviously have affected the prestige of the Tsar's government. It might have led to limited territorial changes, and to some German commercial penetration. That any of this would have affected adversely the situation of the Russian peasant is not at all clear; in any case, he was not convinced that it would. Not only this, but he was by now, as a rule, heartily tired of the struggle: of the losses, the hardships, the deprivation. And if this detachment from the issues of the war was true of the ordinary people, how much more true it was of the Bolsheviki, for whom this was the great moment of political existence. They had never had anything but contempt, anyway, for the issues over which people claimed to be fighting in this imperialist war in the West.

How different all this was in the Western countries! Here, war fervor had by 1917 attained a terrific intensity. The Western democracies had by this time convinced themselves, as embattled democracies have a tendency to do, that the entire future of civilization depended on the outcome of the military struggle.

There is, let me assure you, nothing in nature more egocentrical than the embattled democracy. It soon becomes the victim of its own war propaganda. It then tends to attach to its own cause an absolute value which distorts its own vision of everything else. *Its* enemy becomes the embodiment of all evil. *Its* own side, on the other hand, is the center of all virtue. The contest comes to be viewed as having a final, apocalyptic quality. If *we* lose, all is lost; life will no longer be worth living; there will be nothing to be salvaged. If we win, then everything will be possible; all problems will become soluble; the one great source of evil—*our* enemy—will have been crushed; the forces of good will then sweep forward unimpeded; all worthy aspirations will be satisfied.

It will readily be seen that people who have got them-

selves into this frame of mind have little understanding for
the issues of any contest other than the one in which they
are involved. The idea of people wasting time and substance
on any *other* issue seems to them preposterous. This explains why Allied statesmen were simply unable to comprehend how people in Russia could be interested in an
internal Russian political crisis when there was a war on
in the West. Did the Russians not realize, it was asked in
Paris and London, that everything depended on the defeat
of the Germans, that if Germany was successful, no one
could ever conceivably be happy again, whereas if Germany lost, everyone would somehow or other receive what
he wanted?

You saw this well illustrated in the first reaction of
President Woodrow Wilson to the news of the seizure of
power in Russia by the Communists, in November 1917. "It
is amazing to me"—he said—

...that any group of persons should be so ill-informed as
to suppose, as some groups in Russia apparently suppose,
that any reforms planned in the interests of the people can
live in the presence of a Germany powerful enough to undermine or overthrow them by intrigue or force....[1]

There was, of course, an important substantive difference
between the issue that interested the early Bolsheviki and
that which interested the warring powers in the West. The
first was ideological, with universal social and political implications. The Bolsheviki believed that questions of social
organization—in particular the question of ownership of the
means of production—had an importance transcending all
international rivalries. Such rivalries were, in their eyes, simply the product of social relationships. This is why they
attached so little importance to the military outcome of the
struggle in the West.

The conflict in which the Western peoples were interested
was, on the contrary, overwhelmingly a national one. It
was almost devoid of ideological overtones. It had begun
in large part as a struggle between the Russian and Austro-
Hungarian empires for succession to the declining power of
Turkey in the Balkans. By 1917 this issue had been largely
fought to death, in the sense that both of these empires
had now weakened themselves so seriously by the military
exertion that they were beyond the point of caring much

about the original points of difference. With their exhaustion, the center of gravity of the war had moved northward, and had settled on the German problem. To the extent that a real issue was still involved during the last two years of the war, as distinct from the emotional states into which people had now worked themselves, it was simply the question of the position Germany was to occupy in the future Europe and on the trade routes of the world.

There was, to be sure, an effort on the Allied side, increasing as the war ran its course, to portray the contest as one of political ideology: as a struggle between democracy and autocracy. To this, I think, we Americans were particularly prone. The effort was, in retrospect, unconvincing. Wilhelminian Germany at its worst was much closer to Western parliamentarianism and to Western concepts of justice than was the Tsarist Russia whose collaboration the Western Allies so gladly accepted in the early stages of the war. The truth is that the war was being waged against Germany, not because of the ideology of her government, but because of her national aspirations. The ideological issue was an afterthought.

We can see, today, that in the overriding significance they attributed to their respective conflicts, both Allies and Bolsheviki were largely wrong. Both were pursuing illusions which time was destined to correct.

The Bolsheviki were right, of course, in believing that their victory would have far-reaching international effects. But the nature of this impact was destined to be quite different from what they anticipated. The future was to reveal that the socialist revolution to which they so fervently aspired would not take place in the major industrialized countries of the West, where they confidently expected it. The success of their diplomacy toward the West in the coming decades would be derived, as time would show, not from the strength of their ideas: not from the workings of the laws they conceived Marx to have discovered, not from the economic rivalries among the Western countries to which the Marxists looked as the guarantee of the collapse of the capitalist system. It would be derived from the weaknesses of the Western community itself: from the social and spiritual exhaustion of the Western peoples by the two great wars of this century, from the deficiencies of the Versailles settlement, from the failure to find an answer to the German problem, from the disintegration of Europe's overseas relationships.

But even these weaknesses, while giving valuable opportunities to Soviet diplomacy and eventually placing half of Europe under Russian Communist power, would not produce the European revolution for which the Russian Communists hoped. Insofar as their political impulses had an exciting, important future, this would not be with direct relation to the highly industrialized countries of the West to which Marx's calculations were supposed to be relevant but, rather, with relation to the awakening peoples of Asia and Africa. And even here, the power of Communist inspiration would prove to reside not in anything essential to the structure of Marxist thought, but in the infectious example of a political movement successfully contemptuous and defiant of old Europe; in the identification of the Marxist slogan of imperialism with the national and racial resentments of peoples emerging from colonialism in many parts of the world; in the political fascination inevitably radiated by any effective despotism in an age of change and uncertainty; in the inacceptability, to many ruling groups, of the liberal freedoms of the West; and, finally, in a pervasive illusion that the devices of Communist dictatorship in Russia represented a short cut, available to any people, to the glories of industrial and military power. These were to prove the real sources of future Russian Communist strength in the world arena; and precious little any of them had to do with Marxism.

As for the Western peoples and their passionate preoccupation with the issues of World War I, I would not wish to wander too far into the realm of controversy. What is at issue here is, of course, the soundness of the Allied cause in the latter stages of that war, as the Allied peoples and governments then conceived it. There can of course be many views about this. No one would wish to belittle the huge fund of idealism, courage, and good faith that was invested in the war on the Allied side in those final months. Nor would I wish to suggest that the German problem was not an important problem in its own right. It was then; it still is today.

But I wonder whether anyone can read today the literature emanating from the Western countries in the final year of World War I without feeling that he is in the presence of a political hysteria so violent that the real outlines of right and wrong, insofar as they may ever have existed at all, are largely lost in the turmoil. In the bewilderment that accompanied this hysteria, two mistakes were made. First, the significance of the German problem was inflated out of all semblance of reality. The Germans were a problem in Europe—yes; but they were not as awful a problem as all this: their guilt for the outbreak of the war was not *so* great, their victory would not have been quite *such* a catastrophe, nor would *so* many problems be solved by their defeat. But an even more serious error was the failure to recognize the limitations of modern war generally as a means to an end—the failure to realize to what extent prolonged warfare in the industrial age, with its fearful expenditure of blood and substance, was bound to be self-defeating.

The things people thought they were trying to achieve by the long and terrible military exertion in Europe were simply not to be achieved by this means. The indirect effects of that war—its genetic and spiritual effects—were far more serious than people realized at the time. We can see, today, that these effects penalized victor and vanquished in roughly equal measure, and that the damage they inflicted, even on those who were nominally the victors, was greater than anything at stake in the issues of the war itself. In other words, it did not take the atom to make warfare with modern weapons a fruitless and self-defeating exercise. This was already a reality in 1918; and the recognition of this offers, in my opinion, the key to the understanding of a great deal of the subsequent history of the Western peoples.

This is what I mean when I say that the conflict the Allies were interested in at the time of the Russian Revolution was one about which they were largely wrong, just as the Bolsheviki were wrong about theirs. The same could, of course, be said of the Germans, though in lesser degree. In the later stages of the war the Germans, I think, saw things somewhat more clearly than did people in the Allied countries, partly because they had never had such a sense of virtue about the war from the beginning, partly because they were now more disillusioned with it and hoped for less from it. But both sides hoped for more than could really be achieved. Both underestimated the seriousness of the damage they were doing to themselves—to their own spirit and to their own physical substance—in this long debauch of hatred and bloodshed.

I say these things because I think it important that you
should have clearly in mind, as we move into this subject,
the image of these two groups of men—the Russian Communist leaders on the one hand, and the responsible Western
statesmen on the other—each preoccupied with a different
issue, each moving earnestly forward in pursuit of its particular goal, each to some extent deceived as to the feasibility
of that goal and the values implicit in it, each nevertheless
endowed with a sense of total self-righteousness, having no
understanding or respect or tolerance for the issue that
preoccupied the other.

It is also of importance to recognize that these two goals
were not necessarily even in direct conflict. Each could,
theoretically, have been realized in the same world without
the other being vitiated. The international socialist revolution would not necessarily have precluded victory over
Germany. The same would have been true conversely. The
two goals were simply irrelevant to each other. Their impact on each other was tangential, not direct. Only this
explains the curious kind of exasperation both sides inflicted on each other in 1917 and 1918, by their insistence
on talking about the wrong things. People simply talked
past each other. The contacts between the two sides, for
this reason, tended to have a distracted, absent-minded
quality. The words they addressed to each other were usually
shining examples of irrelevance. I hesitate to be vulgar about
a subject as solemn as this; but I can think of no better illustration of the manner in which the Western democracies
and the early Bolsheviki encountered each other in the years
from 1917 to 1920 than the hoary American anecdote
about the two cross-eyed men who bumped into each other
on the street in Philadelphia. The one said: "Why in hell
don't you look where you're going?" To which the other
replied: "Why in hell don't you go where you are looking?"

This was the manner in which our present two worlds
first collided in 1917; and this was about the degree of
relevance you must expect from many of the terms in
which they discussed their differences. It is particularly
important that you understand this, because if you read the
Soviet historical material of the present day you will find
the Soviet historian very concerned to persuade you that it
was not this way at all: that, on the contrary, the Western
world in 1917, under the influence of its own capitalists,
had no greater concern than the challenge raised for it by

the Russian Revolution—that it was wholly absorbed with the problem of how it could counter and destroy this tremendous force of justice and truth—namely, the Russian Communist movement—which had just appeared on the world horizon and was threatening to destroy everything dear to the selfish interests of world capital. To read much of this Soviet material, you would never suspect that there was a World War in progress at that time and that its issues seemed of real importance to Western statesmen.

Such is the egocentricity which has characterized the Russian Communists down to the present day. What they did in 1917 appeared to them then, as it does now, the most important of world happenings. They cannot believe that it could have appeared otherwise to anybody else.

So much for the introductory remarks. Let me now, before we go on to the substance of this discussion, remind you of certain basic dates that ought to be borne in mind.

The first is that of the so-called "February Revolution." This was the upheaval that occasioned the deposition of the Tsar, and inaugurated the eight months' rule of the relatively moderate and liberal Provisional Government. Although it is called the "February Revolution," this development actually took place in March 1917, our time—the difference being attributable to the difference between our calendar and that which was at that time in effect in Russia.

The second date is that of what is usually known as the "October Revolution": namely, the suppression of the Provisional Government and seizure of power by the Communists—the Bolsheviki. This took place, by our calendar, in November of the same year, 1917.

The third date to remember is the end of World War I. This came in November 1918, just one year after the Communist seizure of power, so that the first year of Soviet power in Russia coincided precisely with the last year of the World War.

Finally, it will be useful for you to recall that America's entry into World War I occurred in April of 1917, less than a month after the first Revolution in Russia. Thus the final year and a half of the war, beginning with the spring of 1917, saw both the Russian Revolution and the dying-out of Russia's effort of participation in the war, and the gradual replacement of Russia by the United States as a major factor in the struggle.

You will recall, perhaps, that it was in the latter part of 1916, some weeks before the February Revolution, that the signs of the political disintegration of the old Tsarist regime first became marked and menacing. The disintegration found its expression primarily in the most sinister sort of court intrigue, in an increasing political isolation of the royal family, in a growing restlessness and despair throughout all moderate Russian political circles, and in a creeping paralysis of the Russian war effort. It was in December of that year that Rasputin was murdered. The fact that the murder was carried out by a group of noblemen which included one of the Grand Dukes emphasized the degree to which the disintegration of the regime had advanced; and there was perhaps a deep political logic in Rasputin's own prediction—that when he died the dynasty would not long survive him.

While the French and British governments were vaguely aware at this time that things were not quite as they should be in the camp of their Russian ally, they did not realize how far the disintegration had gone and how deeply the Russian capacity to wage war was already undermined. This was not for lack of warning. Both the French and British ambassadors in Russia had done their utmost to point out to the Tsarist court and to their own governments the menacing direction in which developments were tending. The British ambassador, Sir George Buchanan, had even had the unpleasant experience of trying to warn the Tsar in person. The Tsar had received him with glacial frigidity, in an anteroom, and had kept him standing throughout the interview. The French ambassador, Maurice Paléologue, a man of wide intellectual and aesthetic interests and deep historical knowledge, was particularly sensitive to the signs of the times. In the cautious and indirect manner to which diplomatists are often condemned when they try to warn about future cataclysms, Paléologue did what he could to make Paris understand the real dimensions of the danger; but, like his British colleague, he found it hard going.

We encounter right here, at the very start, a vivid example of the way in which the unbalanced preoccupation of the Allied chanceries with the war against Germany interfered with their ability to get a clear and useful view of what was happening in Russia. To the extent they took note of the disturbing signs of disintegration in Russia's capacity to

make war and of the growing crisis of the dynasty, they
tended to attribute these phenomena primarily to German influence. The Germans, as they saw it, had to be the
source of all evil; nothing bad could happen that was
not attributable to the German hand. From this fixation
flowed the stubborn conviction in Paris and London that
the troubles in Petrograd in late 1916 were merely the
result of German influence and intrigue at the Russian court.
Allied statesmen were unable to understand that it was
not German intrigue, but precisely the strain of the war
against Germany, which had brought Russia to this deplorable state. In their belief in the predominance of German
influence they were encouraged by moderate Russian political
factions, particularly the Kadet (Constitutional Democrat)
Party, who were eager to enlist the influence of the Allies
in their own struggle against the reactionary clique surrounding the Tsar, and were not above invoking the Allied fear
of Germany for this purpose. In this way there grew up
and was confirmed in the West the highly misleading image
of a Russia thirsting to fight for the Allied cause, but
lamed by the influence of a pro-German court.

The recently captured German documents reveal that
there was very little substance for such suspicions. The
Germans made their efforts at political warfare and penetration of the Tsarist court, as every warring power would.
But they were not nearly so successful as the Allies thought.
Their agents in Petrograd society were few, and shabby
ones at that. The unfortunate Tsarina, foolish woman
though she was, was quite innocent of any illicit dealings
with the Germans. So was the Prime Minister, Boris Stür-
mer, who attracted suspicion because of his German name.
These exaggerated suspicions served mainly to mislead the
Allies themselves, and to cause them to underrate the
depth and nature of the real problem.

The myopia of the Western capitals in the face of
Russia's growing agony was well illustrated by the Allied
diplomatic conference which took place in Petrograd in
January 1917, just one month before the first Revolution.
The purpose of this gathering was to stimulate the Russians
to new efforts on the eastern front and to co-ordinate these
efforts with Western war strategy. Lord Milner and Sir
Henry Wilson attended for Great Britain. The French Minister of Colonies, Gaston Doumergue, was there for the

French. The Americans were of course not represented, being not yet in the war.

The conference afforded an excellent opportunity for the Allied statesmen to acquaint themselves with the seriousness of the situation in Russia and to take measures betimes to mitigate its effects. Had they looked carefully at the Russian scene at that moment, they could have discerned in it the dilemma that was to be basic to their problem of policy toward Russia throughout the following two years. This dilemma consisted in the fact that not only had Russia become involved in a great internal political crisis, but she had lost in the process her real ability to make war. The internal crisis was of such gravity that there was no chance for a healthy and constructive solution to it unless the war effort could be terminated at once and the attention and resources of the country concentrated on domestic issues. The army was tired. The country was tired. People had no further stomach for war. To try to drive them to it was to provide grist to the mill of the agitator and the fanatic: the last people one would have wished to encourage at such a dangerous moment. The sad fact is that from 1916 on, the demands of the political situation in Russia were in conflict with the demands of the Allied war effort.

At the time of the inter-Allied conference in January 1917, the Russian bureaucracy, themselves partially blind to these realities, had no desire that the Allied Governments should pry too deeply into Russia's weaknesses and embarrassments. They were reluctant, in particular, to admit to the real exhaustion of their war effort, being fearful of losing Allied military aid and future support at the peace conference. Instead, therefore, of confessing their real plight, they made efforts to conceal it. They defended themselves against Allied curiosity and Allied demands in the traditional manner: by a combination of extravagant promises of military performance, on the one hand, and a formidable barrage of banquets and other social ordeals on the other. This was a combination guaranteed, by the experience of centuries, to get even the most sanguine Western visitor out of town—exhausted, bilious, empty-handed, but grateful for his escape—within a matter of weeks, if not days. It is a technique, incidentally, which the Soviet government has not hesitated to borrow from its predecessors.

In January 1917 this technique, superimposed on the general pallidness of Western curiosity, worked very well.

Some of the Allied visitors, polite, ill-informed, and poorly instructed after the manner of Western statesmen in multilateral conferences with the Russians, were vaguely aware that they were being had in this fashion. "We are wasting time," Milner kept muttering to Paléologue as the talks progressed.[2] But they had no defense. They saw no choice but to content themselves with the fulsome promises they received. (Shortly after their departure, incidentally, the Russian commander in chief at the front, in a private letter to the Russian Cabinet, complained that he had not the faintest ability to live up to what had been promised to the Allies in the way of Russian military performance during the forthcoming campaign of 1917.)

Paléologue tried in vain, during the course of the conference, to impress on Doumergue the seriousness of Russia's internal situation. Russia, he insisted, was nearing the abyss. "Time," he said, "is not working for us, at least not in Russia . . . we must be prepared for the default of our ally, and must draw the necessary consequences."[3] He took Doumergue to see two of the moderate-liberal leaders, Milyukov and Maklakov. They both confirmed Paléologue's anxiety; the existing state of affairs, they said, could not go on—something must be done at once.

Doumergue's answer could be taken as symbolic of the Western response to the Russian Revolution. The Russians, he said, should be patient and forget these internal problems. "Think of the war," was the best advice he found to give them.[4]

And to the correspondent of *Le Matin,* who interviewed him at the close of his visit to Russia, he said:

I have brought back an excellent impression from my journey. It is clear from all the conversations I had and all that I saw that Russia is filled with a unanimous will to pursue the war to a complete victory.[5]

Similar efforts were made to warn Lord Milner. Mr. R. H. Bruce Lockhart[6] has described his own effort in this direction. Here, again, the warnings were futile. Milner returned to London to report to the War Cabinet, according to Lloyd George, that there was "a great deal of exaggeration in the talk about revolution, and especially about the alleged disloyalty of the army."[7]

Less than three weeks after these two statements were

made, the structure of Tsarist power came crashing to the ground, carrying with it the traditions of centuries, putting an early end to Russia's war effort, and saddling the Russian people of that day with the enormous task of creating a new political edifice to take the place of the old.

I shall not attempt to describe to you the dramatic circumstances of the February Revolution. I should like only to tell you of two incidents which to my mind reveal the deficiencies of the Allied reaction to what was going on and illustrate the extent to which, as I said earlier, the Russians and the Westerners were preoccupied with different things. Both concern the French ambassador, Paléologue. While he was, as I say, an intelligent man, with much understanding for what was happening, he was first and foremost the representative of his government; he had to follow in his utterances the line his government had laid down for him; and like all Frenchmen he felt very strongly about the war in Europe.

At one point, walking through the streets amid the kaleidoscopic events of the February Revolution, Paléologue found himself surrounded by a group of celebrating students, half-curious, half-suspicious. They evidently first thought him to be some distinguished member of the old regime, and took a hostile attitude. On learning that he was the French ambassador, they called upon him to accompany them to the Tauride Palace, the home both of the Duma and of the Petrograd Soviet, and to do homage there to the red flag of the Revolution which now waved over the building. His answer was eloquently revealing: "I can render no better homage to Russian liberty," he said, "than by asking you to join me in shouting *'Vive la Guerre.'*"[8] In other words, "Forget about your Revolution; think of the war."

The second incident took place a few days later. The head of the Russian Duma, Mikhail Rodzyanko, appealed to Paléologue for advice as to the course the Russian moderates should now adopt. Rodzyanko and his friends were men deeply attached to the Allied cause. They really needed advice and help. But Paléologue had to evade the issue. No one in Paris, he realized, would have much understanding for the problems of these men. The words with which he put them off were again revealing. "As ambassador of France," he said, "the war is my principal preoccupation."[9]

In these simple words the principal reason for the bankruptcy of Allied policy in the face of the Russian Revolution—namely, the inability to believe that anything other than the war in Europe could be of real importance—became visible at the start.

2 The Provisional Government

THE REACTION in the Western capitals to the February Revolution was mixed. In London and in Paris there was great surprise, mingled with a guarded hopefulness. There was some apprehension in conservative circles over the ideological implications of the Revolution; but it was moderated by the reflection that if, as was so widely believed, it was really German intrigue which had been impeding the Russian war effort, and if the channel of German influence had really been the Tsar's entourage, then the elimination of the Tsar's regime might open the path to a renewed Russian enthusiasm for the conduct of the war. This reasoning could not, of course, have been more erroneous.

In America there was general rejoicing over the change, both in the government and among the public. The ideological complexion of the Tsar's government had already caused uneasiness to Americans as they contemplated their own imminent entrance into the war on the side of the Entente. They had no desire to become the allies of Tsarist autocracy, and would have been hard put to it to find an appealing rationale for their own war effort had the Russian Revolution not occurred. What happened in Russia in mid-March 1917 thus came as the answer to a prayer. It seemed initially to Americans to be a political upheaval in the old American spirit: republican, liberal, antimonarchical. Americans eagerly accepted the change as a sign of the sort of progress in which they themselves so confidently believed.

American feeling was well reflected in the eloquent and excited words in which Wilson, in his speech to the Congress asking for the declaration of war, took note, for the first time in a public statement, of the Russian Revolution:

> Does not every American feel that assurance has been
> added to our hope for the future peace of the world by the
> wonderful and heartening things that have been happening
> within the last few weeks in Russia? Russia was known
> by those who knew it best to have been always in fact
> democratic at heart, in all the vital habits of her thought,
> in all the intimate relationships of her people that spoke
> their natural instinct, their habitual attitude towards life. The
> autocracy that crowned the summit of her political structure,
> long as it had stood and terrible as was the reality of its
> power, was not in fact Russian in origin, character, or pur-
> pose; and now it has been shaken off and the great, generous
> Russian people have been added in all their naïve maj-
> esty and might to the forces that are fighting for freedom
> in the world, for justice, and for peace. Here is a fit part-
> ner for a league of honour.[10]

I need scarcely remind you that practically every element
in this moving statement—the belief in the democratic traditions and instincts of the Russian people, the belief that
the Tsar's government had been an alien regime, the belief
that the common people of Russia saw the war (rather
than internal revolution) as the means whereby freedom,
justice, and peace were to be attained—reflected a complete
misunderstanding of the real situation in Russia. The statement did honor to Wilson's generous ideals, not to his
knowledge of the outside world.

Despite some misgivings in England, where the overthrow
of another crowned head was not greeted with universal enthusiasm, diplomatic recognition was promptly accorded to
the new regime by the leading Allied governments. But now
the question at once arose of the relationship of the new
Russia to the war.

You may recall the domestic-political situation that ensued in Russia as a result of this first revolution. Power was
dangerously divided between the Provisional Government,
drawn exclusively at the outset from nonsocialist elements, and the Petrograd Soviet, an *ad hoc* body representing
the workers and military garrisons of the Petrograd area.
The Soviet was exclusively socialist in its composition. Its position was comparable to that of the Workers' Council in
Budapest during the abortive Hungarian revolution in 1956.

The Provisional Government had the formal responsibilities and outward emoluments of power, and direct control over foreign affairs; but it was the Petrograd Soviet which commanded, insofar as anyone could be said to do this, the obedience of the workers and soldiers, and thus controlled the streets of the capital. An American scholar has well described the resulting confusion by saying that, in this arrangement, "responsibility without power confronted power without responsibility."[11]

One cannot understand this situation unless one understands the immense and hopeless bitterness by which these various Russian political factions were divided from one another. Between the nobility, the monarchists, and the officer class on the one hand, and the Socialists on the other, there was a gulf so profound, a hatred so deep, that one can describe the situation only as one of latent civil war. Russian society had really come apart—in the most serious way. The liberal-democratic element—the so-called Kadets (Constitutional Democrats), a party led by professors and liberal businessmen—tried to stand somewhere in the middle; but they were rejected by the Socialists no less brutally than were the Conservatives. Among these various elements, there was simply no bond of confidence whatsoever. Even the fact that all were Russians appears to have meant nothing, except insofar as it made the treachery and duplicity of the other fellow seem even more heinous than would otherwise have been the case. It is a disturbing experience to read the memoirs of various Russians who were politically active at that time. Such a thing as charity or sympathy or human understanding in the judgment of others simply doesn't enter into the picture. Political opponents are invariably portrayed as fiends in human guise, devoid of redeeming characteristics. The author is left as the sole repository of decent instinct, clear vision, and a love of humankind.

It was by precisely this sort of a gulf that the socialistic Petrograd Soviet was divided from the "bourgeois" Provisional Government. The two met, not as partners in the effort to save Russia in her hour of need, but as mortal enemies. And the picture is not complete unless one also bears in mind the Bolsheviki, politically the most violent and extreme of all these groups, a small faction at first within the Soviet, but growing larger as the summer progressed, bearing at all times a deadly, implacable, snakelike

enmity toward every other group and every other individual
on the entire political scene.

The Bolsheviki had been taken completely by surprise by
the February Revolution. After decades of endeavoring in
vain to produce just this result, it was both annoying and
immensely encouraging to them to have the Revolution
suddenly occur all by itself at a moment when most of
the Bolshevik leaders were all nodding in the dreary routine
of exile life, either in Switzerland or in Siberia. But, like everyone else, they were at once galvanized into action. I do not
need to repeat for you the familiar tale of how Lenin and a
number of others were permitted by the German government
to pass through Germany in the famous sealed train, and
were gently inserted in this way into the Russian political
situation, as one might gingerly insert a deadly bacillus into
the body of an unsuspecting enemy. Suffice it to say that, by
the end of April, Lenin was back in Russia and in full
operation, and he had already set the course of the Party
on the effort to turn the liberal February Revolution into
a full-fledged proletarian revolution at the earliest possible
moment.

To the hostility of the Russian Socialists toward the liberal
and conservative elements there was now added the relentless enmity of the Bolsheviki toward all the rest. You must
be careful, generally, when thinking about Russian political
life of the Provisional Government period, not to equate it
with the relatively decorous and bloodless exercise that
we know as politics in our English-speaking countries. There
was no similarity. In Russia, politics was a mortal exercise—
it was played for keeps.

There was, at first, no question of any complete and formal
departure of Russia from the war and from her obligations
of alliance. It was only the left wing of the Petrograd Soviet,
to which the Bolsheviki belonged, who in the immediate
aftermath of the February Revolution favored so drastic a
step; and even many of these left-wingers hesitated to say so
openly. The argument revolved initially not over the possibility of a complete departure from the war but merely over
the question of the objectives for which Russia should now
conceive herself to be fighting. The secret treaties by which
Tsarist Russia had been bound to the Allies in the war effort had not yet been made public; but their general tenor
was fairly well known. They obligated Russia to support var-

ious territorial aspirations of the Western powers, in return for which Russia was to receive control of the Dardanelles.

Paul N. Milyukov, the first Foreign Minister of the Provisional Government, unwisely took the position that Russia ought to adhere in full to the obligations of these treaties, and to carry on the war as before, for the purposes which the treaties envisaged. In the Petrograd Soviet, on the other hand, among the Socialists, a war for the purposes set forth in the secret treaties appeared as the epitome of what was called, in Socialist parlance, an "imperialist" war, and it was indignantly rejected. The Russian Socialists had no interest in fighting for the Dardanelles. The initial consensus in the Petrograd Soviet was that while Russia should not at once make a separate peace, she should join with the Socialists of the Western countries in compelling the Entente governments to abandon their imperialistic war aims and to make peace on the basis of the formula "no annexations and no indemnities" —on the basis, that is, of the *status quo ante*. Russia, in other words, should not leave the war unilaterally, but she should exploit the huge emotional appeal of the Russian Revolution as a means of bringing hostilities to an end at once on the basis of a nonimperialistic, nonannexationist, compromise peace.

The French ambassador, Paléologue, acting no doubt on the instructions of his government, supported Milyukov in his uncompromising and unpopular position in favor of a continuation of the war on the basis of the old treaties. The British ambassador, Buchanan, on the other hand, believed that there could be no vigorous Russian war effort unless the Socialists wholeheartedly supported it. He therefore favored an attempt to meet the feelings in the Russian Socialist camp by modifying and restating Allied war aims in such a way as to command more general confidence in liberal opinion throughout the world. The Allied representatives were thus split from the start in their attitude to the problem of Russia's future relationship to the war.

Thinking that they might by this means arouse greater enthusiasm for the war among the Russian Socialists, both the British and French governments sent to Russia, in the weeks immediately following the February Revolution, prominent Socialists of their own who had taken positions in support of the war effort, even to the point of participating in the war cabinets. The British sent Mr. Arthur Henderson, Minister without Portfolio in Lloyd George's Cabinet. The

French government sent the Socialist Minister of Munitions, M. Albert Thomas. Other Socialist and Labour representatives were sent by the British trade-unions, by the Socialists in the French Parliament, and by the Belgian government.

These visits were not much of a success in their primary purpose of promoting Russian enthusiasm for the war. The Western visitors were coldly received in the Petrograd Soviet. They were viewed by the Russian Socialists as unprincipled opportunists who had sold out to their own imperialists. This coolness was, incidentally, cordially reciprocated by the British labor union representatives. These latter did not fail to notice that the intellectuals of whom the Petrograd Soviet was exclusively composed had lily-white hands which had obviously never touched lathe or plow. Thus the contempt which the Russian Socialists bore towards their Western confreres for their lack of ideological sharpness and their support of the Allied war effort was balanced by the disgust with which the latter noticed that the Russian Socialists had literally no personal experience with that "toil" about which they talked so much and in the name of which they proposed to revolutionize society.

You had right here, at the outset, the conflict that was to mark the relations between the Russian Communists and the Western labor movement for decades to come: the conflict between the theoretical, dogmatic character of Russian Socialism, born of the intellectuals who opposed Tsardom, and the pragmatic, moderate, practical spirit of Western labor, founded on the experience of "toil" itself.

However, the visits of these Western Socialists to Russia did have one important effect. Some of the Western representatives, instead of spurring the Russians on to a greater enthusiasm for the war, themselves became infected with the Russian Socialist view of the war aims question. The French visitors, in particular, were soon won over to the opinion that the Allies must make adjustments in the matter of war aims to meet the feelings set in motion by the Russian Revolution. They came to accept the conclusion that the annexationist war aims of the Entente were a burden on the Allied cause, and must be abandoned. "We must jettison the ballast," Albert Thomas said to Paléologue.[12]

In this way a portion of the French Socialists found themselves supporting the position taken by Buchanan, rather than that taken by their own government; and they helped to cut the ground from under the feet of Milyukov and Paléologue, who had been trying to tell people in Russia that there was no chance of persuading the Entente to alter its objectives in the war. This led to the first serious political crisis in the Provisional Government. Milyukov and the conservative Minister of War, Guchkov, were forced out. Paléologue, humiliated and discouraged, left Russia the night before the Cabinet change, never to return. He left convinced (quite erroneously) that he was the victim of a conspiracy between Buchanan and the Russian Socialists. From this time on, governmental power in Russia gravitated increasingly to the left.

Kerensky, who was a Socialist of sorts, though not really powerful in the Petrograd Soviet or very representative of it, now took on the impossible task of trying to reconcile Russian governmental policies both with the demands of the Allies and with those of the Soviet. He based his plea for Allied support on the claim that it was only the Socialists, under his leadership, who could stir the war-weary Russian army to a new military effort. Having taken this position, he felt obliged to make good on it. Entering the Cabinet initially as Minister of War, he at once set about to reactivate military operations and even to launch an offensive on the Galician front. This was a ghastly error. The deterioration of army morale and discipline had already gone beyond the point where successful offensive operations were possible. The effort to conduct them could only bring the latent disciplinary crisis to the surface. Such as it was, the offensive was really a *tour de force*, designed only to impress the Allies. It was launched at the end of June in 1917. It petered out within a few days, leaving the Russian army once more in full retreat, and in a state of advanced and hopeless dissolution.

I think we should note that it was not only the British and French to whom this misguided military effort had been meant to appeal. America was now in the war, and it was to America, in the first instance, that the Russians had to look for economic and military assistance.

The United States government had dispatched to Russia in June a high-powered good will mission under the chairmanship of the distinguished Republican elder statesman, Elihu Root, former Secretary of State and Secretary of War. The function of this mission was both to spur the Russians on to a new enthusiasm for the war and at the same time to find out more about the situation there. It was to be assumed

that future American support would depend to some extent
on the impressions gained by this mission.

It is characteristic that whereas the European countries sent
Socialists to Russia, the United States sent people supposed to
represent all walks of American life. Wilson himself would
have liked the mission to have had a more liberal coloring;
but he had difficulty in finding anyone who would confess
to a Socialist persuasion and yet would be eligible, in the
view of respectable American opinion, for inclusion in the
group. The choice finally fell on a mild parlor-Socialist,
Mr. Charles Edward Russell, and on the elderly vice-president
of the American Federation of Labor, Mr. James Duncan. The
political complexion of these two gentlemen would have been
several degrees to the right of that of Mr. Attlee. The other
members of the mission represented business, finance, the
army, and philanthropy.

The Root Mission spent the latter part of June and the
beginning of July in Petrograd. Most of its time was taken up
with an endless round of dinners and speeches. Nothing in
Elihu Root's rich experience of American political life and
the law had fitted him to fathom the violent and desperate
depths of Russian politics; nor was he in any way aware of
the political dangers that might be involved for the Provisional
Government in a renewed effort to carry on the war. His
position on this whole subject was summed up by himself, in
Petrograd, in the simple formula: "No fight, no loan."

Being in Petrograd precisely in those days when the Galician offensive was being launched to the tune of a tremendous propaganda campaign, Root gained the impression that
everything was in order, that the Provisional Government
proposed to carry on the war, and could do it successfully
if only it received adequate support in the West. He was
also affected by that curious trait of the American political
personality which causes it to appear reprehensible to voice
anything less than unlimited optimism about the fortunes
of another government one has adopted as a friend and
protégé. Having concluded that America's best bet was to support the Provisional Government, he would now listen
to no warning about its political difficulties.

The upshot of all this was that the Root Mission returned to the United States breathing sweetness and light,
confidence and reassurance, about the situation in Russia. And
although this optimism was questioned by the Secretary of

State, Robert Lansing, it was enough to make a decisive imprint on Washington opinion and to commit the United States government from that time on to a policy of financial support of the Provisional Government and publicly professed confidence in its political and military prospects.

Actually, the failure of the July offensive was followed immediately by a drastic deterioration in Kerensky's political situation, both to the Left and to the Right. Only a few days after this failure became evident, segments of the Petrograd garrison and of the industrial worker element in the capital, all very much under Bolshevik influence, attempted to stage what amounted to an uprising against the Provisional Government. It does not appear that the Bolsheviki ordered this action; they were not yet ready for an attempt to seize power, and were actually embarrassed by what occurred. But the elements who carried out the action were the very people on whom the Bolsheviki were relying for support when the moment was ripe. Lenin and those around him dared not antagonize these people, nor lose leadership among them. They were therefore obliged to associate themselves politically with the insurrectionary effort and to give it moral support. This, in turn, led the Provisional Government to take action against them. The insurrection was suppressed. Some of the Bolshevik leaders were arrested. Lenin was forced to go into hiding. The Party had to shift to an underground status. It did continue, however, to enjoy favor among the more radical of the workers and soldiers of the Petrograd area. And Kerensky's position became that much weaker by the loss of support in this quarter.

Meanwhile, the right wing of the Russian political spectrum had also become completely alienated from Kerensky by the effects of the unsuccessful military offensive. I have noted that the effort to continue the war was bound to stir up and bring to the surface the whole problem of discipline in the armed forces. This was the most troublesome and dangerous issue the Provisional Government had to face.

One of the first acts of the Petrograd Soviet, after the Revolution, had been to issue the famous Order No. 1, which in effect deprived the officers' corps of real disciplinary power over the troops. This was, of course, an impossible arrangement from the standpoint of conducting a war; but the Order acquired a sort of symbolic value in the eyes of the troops. Its reversal would have meant, as they saw it, the sacrifice of the gains of the Revolution and the virtual restoration of the old order. Had the attempt not been made to renew the war effort in the summer of 1917, and had it been possible to proceed at once with large-scale demobilization, this problem of military discipline might have been permitted to simmer down until some sort of a new start could be made. But the effort to renew hostilities, demanding as it did an attempt to reimpose discipline, forced the issue to the fore. This, together with the unsuccessful outcome of the offensive, completed the demoralization of the rank and file, and sent the officers' corps into a state of highest alarm and indignation.

The officers saw not only the honor of their profession but the glory and dignity of the country being dragged into the dust. They blamed the Socialists, beginning with Kerensky, for this fact. They were now reduced to a state of complete desperation. The result was that General L. G. Kornilov, formerly commander in chief on the southwestern front, mounted in the latter part of August an effort to march on Petrograd and to unseat Kerensky in favor of a military dictatorship. This effort, in addition to being fouled up with a confused welter of political intrigue, was clumsily prepared, and quite unsuccessful. Kornilov had no more real authority than anyone else over the rank and file, and could get few troops to follow him. The expedition petered out before it ever reached the city. Kerensky need not, in these circumstances, have been frightened. Perhaps he really wasn't. But he saw in this episode, which threw a certain momentary alarm into the entire Socialist camp, a chance to repair his political fences on the Left and to gain a new intimacy with the extreme element among the workers and soldiers, on the basis of a common defense against the intrigues of reactionary generals. He therefore made his peace, after a fashion, with the Bolsheviki, relaxed the measures taken against them, and permitted them to arm their followers, under the guise of participation in a workers' defense of the regime from the menace of the right-wing elements.

This, again, was a tremendous mistake. To accept the armed aid of the Bolsheviki was, under the circumstances, to entrust oneself to the protection of a boa constrictor. Things now moved inexorably, in the course of a few weeks, to the demise of the Provisional Government. Abandoned and opposed by the Right, helpless in the face of growing Bolshevik power in the capital, Kerensky tried many desperate expedients, but all to no avail. The Bolsheviki soon advanced to a position where they controlled the Petrograd Soviet. They could in fact have seized the capital even earlier than November; but they feared to take this step before they had completed their preparations for seizing power in the provinces and among the troops at the front as well. On the other hand, they also feared that if they delayed too long, the elections to the Constituent Assembly, scheduled to take place in November, might yield results that would complicate their situation. For this reason, they chose the first days of November to act; and we are all familiar with the consequences. In two days' time they succeeded, with an almost total absence of bloodshed, in seizing power in Petrograd. Another ten days saw the process completed, though by no means so peacefully, in Moscow and other parts of the country. Kerensky was forced to flee. The Provisional Government was at an end. The era of Soviet power had begun.

Aside from its ideological implications, the Bolshevik seizure of power was, of course, a complete disaster from the standpoint of the Allied war effort. The Bolsheviki were committed to taking Russia out of the war—committed to this not just by their own promises but by the very methods they had used to come into power. They had worked hard and successfully at the demoralization of the armed forces. They had done this in order that the Provisional Government should not have under its control at the crucial moment any sizable body of armed men which could be used as a defense against the violent usurpation of power by the Communists. To this end the Bolsheviki had played for all it was worth the purely demagogic card of land reform, promising the peasant soldier the division of the larger farms and estates and encouraging him to leave the trenches and go back to the village to get his share. This agitation had begun to take effect well before the Bolshevik seizure of power. For days and weeks, the army had been streaming away from the trenches and making its way home as best it could. It was this that caused Lenin to say triumphantly that the army had voted against the war with its feet. By mid-November, when the Communist seizure of power in the main centers was complete, it would have been physically impossible and politically suicidal for the Bolshevik leaders to do anything else but sue for peace. It was therefore natural that the first act of foreign policy of the new regime, taken on the very day of the Revolution, should have been the issuance of the Decree on Peace, calling on all the belligerent peoples and their governments to open negotiations for an immediate cessation of hostilities on the basis of no annexations and no indemnities. With this act, the departure of Russia from the war was really sealed.

Please note how intimately the causes of Kerensky's failure were connected with his effort to continue Russia's participation in World War I. Had he been able to demobilize the Petrograd garrison, and to get its members out of town, he presumably would never have been faced with the July insurrection; nor would the Bolsheviki have been able to organize the final seizure of power in November. But the fact that there was a war on prevented this. Had he not undertaken the summer offensive, he might have permitted the army to demobilize peacefully without raising the fateful problems of military discipline and authority by which he and his regime were bound to be crushed. Had he not endeavored to hold the armed forces together for a military purpose, he might have been able to compete with the Bolsheviki in encouraging the soldiers to return to their villages and in carrying out a prompt and politically effective land reform. The Bolsheviki had, after all, largely stolen the agrarian program of the Socialists-Revolutionary Party,* to which Kerensky himself nominally belonged. The only reason they were able to exploit this issue successfully was that they, uninhibited by any loyalty to the war effort, were willing to put this agrarian program into effect at once, whereas Kerensky and his associates felt obliged to ask for delay in deference to the needs of the war effort. In every respect Kerensky's political position would have been eased, and his prospects for resistance to Bolshevik pressure would have been improved, had he been able to take the country out of the war at once.

The question may legitimately be asked: If all this was so, why did Kerensky attempt to continue the war at all? Why did he not flout the wishes of the Allies and address himself exclusively to his internal political problem? I am not

* In subsequent references, the name of this party will be abbreviated, as it was in common Russian parlance, to S-R.

sure that I can answer this question. Trotsky alleges that the Provisional Government clung to the tie with the Allies as a means of protecting themselves against the full sweep of the Revolution. This sounds to me forced and unconvincing. Kerensky and other members of the Provisional Government felt themselves bound to the Allies by many bonds. They had no sympathy for the Germans. Feelings of national pride made them reluctant to abandon outright the coalition with which they had been associated. They were urged to continue the war not just by conservative circles in the West but also by the Western Socialists and the representatives of Western labor. Finally, they were well aware that the country over which they presided was at the end of its economic and financial rope; and I am sure that they hesitated to face the future without the assurance that they would have some claim on Western economic assistance after the war.

Like everything else that had to do with the Russian Revolution and Soviet power, Kerensky's final defeat exercised a highly divisive effect on Western opinion. The French and British governments, still swayed predominantly by their interest in the war, tended to sympathize with Kornilov and to blame Kerensky for frustrating what they felt to be the only serious attempt to restore the discipline and fighting capacity of Russia's armed forces. American circles in Russia, on the other hand, had less natural sympathy for the upper classes, and appreciated dimly the fact that the old Humpty Dumpty of Tsarist Russia could never be put together again. They thought Kornilov's venture doomed to failure in any case. They considered it the height of folly for the Allies to support it: this, they considered, only estranged the workers and peasants without whose support a war effort was unthinkable.

If history has any comment to make on these arguments, from the perspective of forty years, it is that all the parties to these disputes were wrong. The premise from which they all departed—namely, that Russia could and should be kept in the war—was an impossible premise. The sad fact is that by the spring of 1917 nothing the Allies might have done could have made Russia once more a serious factor in the war. The entire Russian economic and political system had by this time been overstrained by the military effort. The prerequisites for a continuation of this effort—spiritual, psychological, and political as well as economic—were simply

no longer there. From this standpoint the policies of Paléologue, of Milyukov, and of Kerensky were as futile as those of
Buchanan, President Wilson, or Elihu Root. Whichever had
been adopted, the results would have been substantially the
same, so far as the Russian war effort was concerned. The
only point at which Allied statesmanship might, with different
policies, have produced a different result was in the political
field. It was inevitable that Russia should leave the war in
1917. It was not inevitable that this should have occurred
under the chairmanship of the Bolsheviki. This, surely, was
at least in part the effect of the blunders of Western statesmanship.

When we inquire, then, into the causality of the Russian
Revolution—when we ask ourselves why it was that the
Russian political structure broke down in 1917 and why the
ensuing situation degenerated within a few months into
the rigidities and extremisms of Bolshevism—we see that in
each case it was the World War, and specifically the Allied
cause in the World War, which was the determining factor.
Whatever it may be said to have been that the Western
Allies were fighting for, it was this to which the real needs
of Russia in these crucial years were sacrificed. The Russian Revolution and the alienation of the Russian people from
the Western community for decades to come were only a
part of the staggering price paid by the Western people for
their insistence on completing a military victory over Germany in 1917 and 1918.

Can it conceivably have been that the end in view was
worth this price? I should like to let the discussion of Allied
policies toward the Provisional Government rest with this
question. The impression I gain after three or four years of
immersion in these problems is that in attaching such enormous value to total military victory in 1917 and 1918, the
Western peoples were the victims of a great misunderstanding
—a misunderstanding about the uses and effects of the war
itself. And I suspect that this misunderstanding also lies at
the heart of those subsequent developments which have carried the Western community in the space of forty years
from a seemingly secure place at the center of world happenings to the precarious and isolated position it occupies today,
facing a world environment so largely beyond its moral and
political influence.

3 Brest-Litovsk

THE FIRST official act of the Soviet government, performed on the very day of the Revolution, was the issuance of the Decree on Peace. In this document the All-Russian Congress of Soviets (of whose claim to be the sovereign governing body of Russia the Allied governments, incidentally, had had no prior notification) proposed to all belligerent peoples and their governments the immediate opening of negotiations for what was called "a just and democratic peace." This, it was said, meant a peace without annexations or indemnities. The Decree went on to define these terms. "Annexations," it was said, meant not just acquisitions of territory resulting from the outcome of the war. It also included any existing relationships by virtue of which any small or weak nationality might be held without its consent within the composition of a large and powerful state. It was stipulated that this consent must be "definitely, clearly, and voluntarily expressed." The proposal thus amounted to this: that the peace should not only involve an abandonment by the Allied governments of whatever plans and aspirations they might have had for territorial or colonial aggrandizement as one of the fruits of victory in the war, but that they should also give a solemn undertaking to relinquish at once their existing colonial possessions, unless the colonial peoples should specifically request otherwise. As for the secret treaties by which the Tsar's government had been bound to the Allies: the Congress proposed to begin at once the publication of their provisions, which it roundly denounced. It proposed an immediate armistice. It called, finally, on the class-conscious workers of England, France, and Germany to understand their duty not only to rescue mankind from the horrors of war and to help in bringing about a peace on the basis suggested, but also to liberate from every kind of slavery and exploitation the toiling masses of the world. It was thus an appeal addressed to peoples, rather than to governments; it implied a clear desire to play peoples off against governments; and it hinted that social revolution was a part of what was really meant by "peace."

In my book *Russia Leaves the War,* in describing the first few months of the Soviet-American relationship, I expressed doubt that such proposals were made in good faith. It seemed to me implausible that the Soviet leaders could really have expected that proposals so formulated and so presented would be seriously entertained by the Allied governments. I cited the Decree on Peace as an example of what the Communists themselves call "demonstrative diplomacy"—diplomacy, that is, "designed not to promote freely accepted and mutually profitable agreement as between governments, but rather to embarrass other governments and to stir up opposition among their own people."[13]

This statement of mine seems to have stung the Soviet historical fraternity. In a review of my book which appeared in one of the Soviet historical journals,[14] the reviewer indignantly rejected the suggestion that the Decree on Peace was not a step taken in good faith. In support of this view, he merely cited evidence that President Wilson was disturbed by the reports of the effect the Soviet peace move had in Italy and had felt compelled, in consequence, to come out with his Fourteen Points speech. But this was precisely my point. The Decree was published not with a view to arriving at any freely accepted agreement with the Western governments, but with a view to putting these governments in an awkward position and forcing them, in this way, to abandon the war effort.

The Soviet reviewer was also annoyed at my suggestion that the formula "no annexations and no indemnities" was only a paraphrase of the words Wilson himself had used seven months earlier (on April 2, 1917) in his message to the Congress calling for the declaration of war. Here Wilson had said: "We desire no conquest, no dominion. We seek no indemnities for ourselves. . . ."[15] The Soviet reviewer referred to Wilson's words as a "banal and mendacious phrase," which "obligated no one to anything." "What could there be in common," he asked, "between the cloudy phraseology of empty Wilsonian irrelevancies and the hard precision of Lenin's decree?"

It just goes to show how differently people's minds work. I had thought there was a similarity between Lenin's phrase "without annexations" and Wilson's reference to "no conquest, no dominion." And the phrase "no indemnities," after all, was identical in each case.

I cannot leave this subject of the Decree on Peace without drawing attention to the contemporary relevance of certain of its passages. The decree was written by Lenin himself; and his mind was strongly occupied, at that moment, by the problem of self-determination for the peoples of central and eastern Europe. It was partly this that he had in mind when he called for an end to "annexations"; and he went out of his way to make clear that by "annexations" he meant not only the formal appropriation of the territory of other peoples but also its concealed domination. This being the case, I think we should note the following passage from the Decree on Peace, with particular relation to the situation of Hungary since 1956:

If any people is held by force within the borders of a given state, if such a people in defiance of its expressed wish—whether this wish be expressed in the press, in meetings of the populace, in the decisions of a party, or in uprisings against the national yoke—is not given the right of deciding, free of every form of duress, by free elections, without the presence of the armed forces of the incorporating state or any more powerful state, what form of national existence it wishes to have—if these circumstances prevail, then the incorporation of such a state should be called annexation, i.e., an act of seizure and force.[16]

If the continuation of the Soviet domination of Hungary does not constitute "annexation" within the terms of this definition, then I do not know what the words mean.

However, to return to 1917: None of the warring governments paid any formal attention to the Decree on Peace. It was not addressed directly to them. It emanated from a body of whose authority and legitimacy they had no clear evidence. But in spite of this indifference in the West, the Soviet leaders were in no position to delay making good on their commitment to give peace to the Russian people. As soon as they had consolidated their power in Petrograd and Moscow, and had collected themselves sufficiently to make a beginning at the conduct of foreign affairs, the first thing they did was to address themselves directly to the Allied governments through their representatives in Petrograd, asking the

Allies to join in negotiations for a general armistice. Simultaneously, without waiting for an answer to this appeal, they dispatched parliamentarians across the German lines to ask for armistice talks. In all of this they were at great pains to emphasize that it was precisely a *general, multilateral* armistice, affecting all parties in the war, for which they were calling; that they had no desire to conclude a separate peace; and that if they were compelled to conclude one, it would be the fault of the Allies for failing to respond to their initiative.

I have been somewhat at a loss to explain this reluctance on the part of Lenin and his associates to admit that they were asking for a separate peace. If the war was really an imperialistic one, as they claimed it was, then there would seem to have been no shame involved in retiring from it unilaterally. I suspect that their real concern was to associate the European socialists with the peace move, in order that the Western governments might be compelled to end the war and the new Soviet regime might be spared the necessity of facing the Germans alone over the negotiating table. They seem to have sincerely believed that all that was necessary was for the socialist revolution to succeed in a single country, and for the socialists of that one country to ask for peace, in order to bring down upon the heads of all the warring governments an irresistible pressure of working-class opinion in favor of the ending of hostilities. Not until every conceivable possibility for support in Western Europe had been probed and had failed could the Bolshevik leaders bring themselves to face the bitter fact that, having ruined their country's army and forced its withdrawal from the war, they must now face the consequences of their action and come to terms, alone and unaided, with the formidable power of the German High Command.

The Germans were surprised but delighted to receive the Soviet bid for an armistice. Earlier in the war, the German government had maintained clandestine contacts—of which the Allies were suspicious—with the extreme Right of the Russian political spectrum, and had used the contacts with a view to stimulating sentiment for a separate peace between Germany and Russia. Possibly the Germans could have had such a peace in 1916, had it not been for the far-reaching demands of the German High Command with respect to the future of Poland, and the fears of the Tsar's government as to what the Japanese would do if Russia failed in her obligations to the Entente. After the February Revolution occurred, the Germans consented, as I have mentioned, to transport across Germany to Russia Lenin and some of the other political exiles in Switzerland, thus enabling them to regain their own country and to participate in the great political fermentation unleashed there by the fall of Tsardom. In addition to that, there is evidence to show that the Germans went ahead, during the period of the Provisional Government, to give secret subsidies to the Bolshevik faction, thus aiding it in its competition with other Russian groups. They did this, of course, not because they had any liking or sympathy for the Russian Communists, but quite simply because the Bolsheviki were the only Russian faction which flatly opposed the Russian war effort. It was naturally regarded as desirable, from the German standpoint, that Bolshevik influence should become as strong as possible on the Russian political scene.

This subsidizing of the Bolsheviki was done by the Germans in a routine way, as a small part of the secret operation in which governments normally engage in wartime. The Bolsheviki were by no means the only Russian group aided in this manner. This particular operation was apparently known to few people in the German government, and was not regarded in Berlin as of very great importance. There is no reason to suppose, in particular, that the Germans expected, in financing the Bolsheviki, that the latter would ever actually come into power. It was simply thought that it would be useful to the German cause to keep them in the running, politically. Actually, these German subsidies succeeded too well. I suspect that the Germans themselves were a bit appalled when they realized what they had done.

I said the Germans were surprised to receive the Soviet bid for an armistice. This may seem odd, in view of the fact that they had just been sending secret subsidies to the Bolsheviki. But it is not really surprising. The subsidies had gone through an elaborate system of cut-outs. They had involved no secret understandings, and had implied no obligations of communication or information from the Bolshevik side. From July 1917 until the eve of the seizure of power in November, furthermore, the Bolshevik leaders had been in a semi-underground situation. During this period, in particular, they were certainly not communicating their plans to anyone outside the family. The Germans, of course, had no official representative in Russia, being still technically at war with that country. Their former secret agents there, mostly people who had circulated in high Russian society, were of little value to them now. Thus the Germans seem to have been as little aware as were the Entente governments of the full extent of the deterioration of Kerensky's position in the weeks just prior to the November uprising; and when their radios picked up the first armistice bid, signed by Trotsky, they had to scramble around to find out what it was all about. Trotsky was not one of those with whom they had dealt; they didn't even know his name. Once they realized what had happened, and once they had established the genuineness of the Soviet offer, they of course seized on it with alacrity. They were just then engaged in planning the tremendous offensive they proposed to launch the following spring on the western front. Russia's withdrawal from the war meant for them a gift of about one million men, not to speak of transport and supply, available for transfer to the western front and for use in this offensive.

The German-Soviet negotiations were strung out, with various interruptions, during the winter months from December 1917 to March 1918. It will suffice for our purpose to recall the highlights of the talks and the crisis to which they led.

The separate German-Soviet armistice was negotiated at the beginning of December and was formally signed by the middle of the month. The negotiations for a final peace treaty were inaugurated just before Christmas at Brest-Litovsk, the headquarters of the German command for the eastern front. They were interrupted for a few days at the end of December when the Bolsheviki learned, to their surprise and anger, that the Germans intended to keep the Baltic States and Russian Poland under their own control. The Russians were now seriously alarmed at the predicament in which they had involved themselves. Contrary to their expectations, the Western governments had *not* been obliged to leave the war, nor had there yet been any revolution in the West. They realized, therefore, that they were really now in serious difficulty. They suspended the talks temporarily, and tried to get the scene of negotiations moved to Stockholm, in the hopes that from there it would be easier for them to work on Socialist opinion in the West. But the Germans were having none of this. In January the talks were renewed at Brest.

For about a month the Russian negotiators, now headed by Trotsky in person, were permitted by the Germans to make inflammatory political speeches instead of getting down to serious talk at the negotiating table. The reason for this patience was that the Germans were busily negotiating with a delegation of the non-Communist Ukrainian separatists, the so-called Rada, for a separate peace treaty with the Ukraine. This was, of course, a bitter blow to the Bolsheviki. Not only did it deprive them of the food resources of the Ukraine, but it implied German recognition of the Ukraine as an independent political entity, not under Soviet power, and thus weakened greatly their prestige. As soon as the Ukrainian Treaty was signed, on the 8th of February, 1918, the German negotiators at Brest-Litovsk, who were by this time thoroughly fed up with the argumentative and insulting tactics of the Bolsheviki delegation, prepared to get down to brass tacks with the Russians and to deliver to them the ultimatum which they had had it in their power, all along, to give. It was at this point that Trotsky, sensing what was coming, laid down his famous formula, "no war, no peace," broke off the negotiations, and took the Soviet delegation home. His position was: We will not sign your terms, but we will not fight you either.

For a couple of days there was great glee in Soviet circles over the effect of this move. It was supposed that Trotsky's action had left the Germans in a helpless and ridiculous position. Actually, the Germans were not at a loss to know what to do in such a situation. They simply re-opened hostilities, and continued to advance into Russian territory, until the Bolsheviki had had enough and once more asked for terms. This was the occasion on which Lenin had to bring his entire prestige and authority to bear—he, in fact, threatened to resign—in order to force his hotheaded colleagues to recognize superior military force when they saw it, and to take the consequences realistically. A new Soviet delegation was sent, in the beginning of March, to effect the capitulation. They found the German terms, as might have been expected, considerably stiffer than those they had declined to sign in early February. But they were helpless. After checking with Petrograd, they finally signed what was put before them. In doing so, they demonstratively refused to read the final draft of the document, as a way of emphasizing that it was a *Diktat* and not a negotiated peace.

Incidentally, Soviet historians have had the effrontery to

suggest that the military difficulty experienced by the Soviet
government at the time of the renewed German offensive in
February, 1918, was occasioned by the fact that the Entente
had practically ceased to do any serious fighting on the
western front and that this had given to the Germans the
opportunity to move the Bavarian Corps from west to east
and thus to strengthen German forces in the east. In many
years of acquaintance with historical falsification, I cannot
recall seeing any statement more shameless than this. During the winter of 1918 the Germans moved approximately
forty divisions and something close to one million men from
east to west. If any German units were actually moved the
other way, it was part of a reshuffle of the German forces
enormously to the disadvantage of the Western Allies and
occasioned entirely by the collapse of Russian resistance.
No one, futhermore, had done more to demoralize and destroy the Old Russian army than the Bolsheviki themselves.
The Germans encountered almost no resistance when they
resumed the offensive. The speed of their advance was determined primarily by problems of terrain and supply. To
suggest that this German advance was due to inactivity on
the western front, that this inactivity enabled the Germans
to *strengthen* their forces in the east at the time of the
Brest-Litovsk talks, and that without this strengthening the
German advance in Russia would have been repulsed, is
simply to turn the facts of history upside down and to evoke
an image in which the actual occurrences of this time become wholly unintelligible.

The Brest-Litovsk Treaty has usually been regarded as an
extremely onerous settlement—a prize example, in fact of
the ruthless brutality of the German mailed fist. I think this
assertion deserves some modifications. In comparison with
the settlements the Western Allies themselves imposed, on
the basis of unconditional surrender, after two world wars, the
Brest-Litovsk Treaty does not strike me as inordinately severe.
No reparations were originally demanded in the treaty itself. The territories of which the Bolsheviki were deprived
were ones the peoples of which had no desire for Russian
rule, least of all Russian Communist rule. The Bolsheviki
themselves had never at any time had authority over these
territories. It was a hope, rather than a reality, of which
they were deprived by the terms of the treaty. The settlement accepted by the Allies at the end of the Russian civil

war—the arrangement, that is, that prevailed from 1920 to 1939—was considerably less favorable to Russia, territorially, in the Baltic-Polish region than that which the Germans imposed on Russia in 1918.

The greatest hardship inflicted on the Russians at Brest-Litovsk was not anything embraced in the treaty concluded with them but rather the fact that the Ukraine was excluded from the German-Soviet settlement, that a separate agreement was concluded with the representatives of the Ukrainian Rada, and that this left the Germans free to occupy and exploit the Ukraine for purposes of their own war effort. This was what really hurt. The inability to seize the Ukraine by force of arms, which is what they would have done in the absence of German interference, and the abandonment of this area to economic exploitation by the Germans: this was the real price the Bolsheviki paid for a separate peace.

The fact is that Russia had endeavored to fight a war and her armies had collapsed in the midst of it. Militarily, she was defeated. There is usually a price to be paid for that. Her enemy, still engaged on another front, now needed the resources to be found in the Ukraine, particularly the food. The grain of the Ukraine was vital, at this point, to a continuation of the war effort of the Central Powers, particularly the Austrians. I find it difficult to believe that the Allied High Command, confronted with similar necessities and similar opportunities, would have behaved much less forcefully than did the Germans.

Actually, it would be wrong to attribute excessive importance to the instruments signed at Brest-Litovsk. Neither side took too seriously the letter of the agreements. For this, I find it difficult to blame exclusively the Germans. The Bolshevik negotiators made no effort during the negotiations to conceal their contempt for the German government and their determination to bring about its overthrow at the earliest possible moment by agitation among the rank and file of the German army and the German working class. When the train bringing the Bolshevik delegation pulled into Brest-Litovsk, one of the Soviet delegates, Karl Radek, calmly stood at the train window throwing revolutionary pamphlets out to the German guards along the tracks. Later, at the negotiating table, Radek took special delight in a procedure which involved blowing pipe smoke into the face of the German commander, Major General Max Hoffmann, following this with long, silent, beady stares, and then saying deliberately insulting things. This may be a way in which one indulges personal feelings. It is not a way in which one promotes international agreement in good faith.

I have read somewhere that when, one or two days after ratification of the treaty in March, Lenin was assailed by an indignant comrade who had opposed ratification of the treaty, and who now said he hoped at least they wouldn't observe it, his reply was to throw up his hands in pious horror and to say, in substance: "My dear fellow, what do you take us for? We have already broken it forty times." This was the attitude of the Soviet leaders toward the Brest-Litovsk settlement. The Germans were well aware of it. It is not surprising that the Germans were cynical, too.

While all these things were happening between the Russians and the Germans, the Allied governments hovered nervously on the edge of events, wringing their hands, trying to find some way to moderate the dismal setback which Russia's departure from the war and the German access to the Ukraine spelled for them. The thought that immediately presented itself to a great many minds in Allied officialdom, particularly to the French and to the Allied military planners at the Supreme War Council in Versailles, was that of restoring an eastern front by the direct intervention of an Allied expeditionary force, operating together with such of the Russian factions and military units which had not yet recognized Soviet authority and still professed loyalty to the Allied cause. In this thought you had, of course, the kernel of the rationale for what was later to become the Allied military intervention in Russia.

Two major difficulties lay along the path of the realization of this idea. One was the desperate need for the maximum number of troops on the western front, in view of the virtual certainty, now, of a great German offensive in the coming spring of 1918. The other, as we shall have ample occasion to see, was the extreme instability of the Russian White cause—that is, the anti-Bolshevik cause—with which it was proposed to collaborate: the woeful disunity among its various components, the confusing, kaleidoscopic quality of the changes that were constantly taking place in the political and military fortunes of these various groups. It was very difficult, the future would prove, to help people who themselves had little popular support, who were always at each other's throats, who were there one day and gone the next.

It was the latter part of November of 1917, before it

became fully clear to the Allied chanceries that the Bolsheviki had really succeeded in their bid for power, and that they were, at least for the moment, in command of the key positions of administrative authority in the Russian centers. It was natural, in these circumstances, that the Russian question should come up for discussion at the first great inter-Allied conference for the co-ordination of the war effort, which convened in Paris at the end of November. Lloyd George was there; so were Clemenceau and Balfour. Colonel Edward M. House attended for the Americans. The Russian question was not on the agenda of any of the formal gatherings, but the senior statesmen could scarcely fail to talk about it among themselves.

At one of the informal meetings of these statesmen in Paris, Marshal Foch came up with a scheme for Allied military intervention in Russia, with a view to bringing the Trans-Siberian Railway under Allied control and by this means assuring the restoration of an eastern front. This scheme was wholly unacceptable to the Allies. Colonel House was dead against it; so were Lloyd George and Balfour. Only a few days later, in a memorandum written for his colleagues in the Cabinet, Balfour remonstrated against any policy that would tend to drive Russia into the arms of Germany. "No policy," he wrote, "would be more fatal than to give the Russians a motive for welcoming into their midst German officials and German soldiers as friends and deliverers."[17]

In November 1917, therefore, the Allies rejected, for the moment, the thought of military intervention. Instead, the senior statesmen at Paris contented themselves with discussions of the diplomatic problems created by Russia's departure from the war. There was general agreement that no recognition should be accorded to the new regime in Petrograd, which had as yet no visible sanction in public opinion. As for the violation of Russia's wartime obligations which was implicit in the bid for a separate peace, some consideration was given to the sensible suggestion of Sir George Buchanan, the British ambassador at Petrograd, that the Allied governments, instead of protesting the Bolshevik action, should release Russia from her formal bond and accept the inevitable with some semblance of good grace. But this was wholly unacceptable to Clemenceau, who declared that "if . . . all the celestial powers asked him to give Russia back her word, he would refuse."[18]

No agreement being possible on this question, talk then turned to the matter of war aims. The diplomatic representatives of the defunct Provisional Government, together with such of Kerensky's former associates as had already escaped to western Europe, had been maintaining that if only the Allied governments would make concessions in the matter of war aims, it might still be possible for the anti-Bolshevik factions, which favored Russia's continuing the war, to make headway against the Bolsheviki. Colonel House, with President Wilson's backing, was strongly in favor of meeting these suggestions halfway. He would have had the Allied governments renounce the secret treaties and state flatly, then and there, that they were not waging war for purposes of aggression or indemnity. He would have had the Allies, in other words, accept Lenin's slogan of "no annexations, no indemnities." But this view foundered, again, on French and Italian opposition. The French and Italian governments, especially now that their military prospects were improved by the entry of the United States into the war, had no intention of moderating their war aims or renouncing anything they could hope to get out of a total victory. If this meant the defection of Russia, so much the worse for Russia for her betrayal of the Allied cause. To have had any chance of moderating French and Italian aspirations, Wilson would have had to negotiate with those governments *before* America entered the war, not *after*. Once the United States government had declared war, it lost much of its diplomatic bargaining power vis-à-vis the French and Italians.

It thus became apparent, within less than a month after the November Revolution, that the Allied governments were hopelessly divided on everything that had to do with a positive policy toward Russia. The British and Americans vetoed a military intervention. The French and Italians vetoed any liberalization of war aims. There was simply no intimacy of outlook or purpose among them, particularly as between the Continental allies, on the one hand, and England and the United States, on the other. The only proposition on which they were able to agree was the negative one of no recognition of the Soviet regime. This, I may say, is characteristic of coalition diplomacy. Coalitions find it possible to agree, as a rule, only on what *not* to do. This is the reason why their tendency is so often to do nothing at all.

The initial aversion in London to the idea of direct mil-

itary intervention in Russia by Allied forces did not preclude the extension of financial aid to such anti-Bolshevik
factions in Russia as still professed loyalty to the Allied cause.
In the weeks immediately following the November Revolution,
there were three regions that still held out against Bolshevik domination. All were in the south of Russia. One was
the Ukraine, where the so-called Rada—a weak, autonomous
regime, consisting mostly of a few romantic intellectuals in
Kiev—was feebly struggling for existence. Another was the
Cossack country of the lower Don, where a local Cossack
ataman, A.M. Kaledin, continued to defy Communist authority by force of arms. A third was the Transcaucasus, where
the Bolsheviki had almost no popular support, where even
the Socialist movement was largely in the hands of their
Menshevik rivals, and where the breakdown of the Russian
front against Turkey had led to chaotic conditions. None of
the leaders of these various anti-Bolshevik regimes really
cared very much, I fear, about the Allied cause in the war.
But they were at least not committed, as were the Bolsheviki,
to seeking a separate peace. And they all cared enough about
the possibility of receiving Allied support to make a few pro-
Allied noises from time to time.

By a secret convention concluded in mid-December, the
French and British governments agreed on a rough division
of labor, by geographic area, in the clandestine financing and
supporting of these South Russian factions. The French took
the Ukraine; the British took the Caucasus, both north and
south of the mountains.

Actually, the effort to revive resistance to the Germans
in this manner was a dismal failure. The Ukrainian Rada,
after pocketing some fifty million rubles of French money,
tricked the French in the most heartless manner, went over
to the Germans, rubles and all, and concluded with the
Germans the separate treaty that placed the Ukraine at
German disposal. Kaledin failed militarily before any actual
aid could be got to him, and he committed suicide in early
February. Only the Caucasus continued to resist Bolshevik
rule.

This abortive Anglo-French agreement could not fail, in
time, to draw the fire of Soviet historiography. Although
the main purpose of the convention was to stimulate military
resistance to Germany, and although it involved no more than
the continuation on a local basis of the aid the Allies had
been giving to the Russian war effort for years past, it has

been hailed by the official Soviet historians as a scheme for the division of Russia into spheres of influence—her dismemberment, in fact, at the hands of the imperialists. As is so often the case with Soviet propaganda, there is a tiny ingredient of truth in these elaborate distortions. It was the concept underlying this convention which seems first to have given rise in the minds of some of the British military planners to a scheme for linking Allied military predominance of South Russia with a similar predominance in Siberia, thus confining German penetration to the northern part of European Russia, a region poor in natural resources. The Anglo-French convention thus had in it the seed of the subsequent Allied intervention. There is, however, no reason to suppose that it was conceived at the time as anything more than a military measure, designed to check German military penetration into areas of Russia where, it was believed, orderly government had broken down altogether.

Now a word or two, in conclusion, about the broader historical significance of these events.

The official Communist thesis is that the Bolsheviki, immediately on their assumption of power in Russia, offered to all the warring powers a general peace on a decent basis; that the Allied governments, intent on their various imperialistic designs, selfishly rejected this offer, caused the slaughter to endure for another year, and abandoned Russia to plunder and oppression at the hands of the Germans.

I should like to make my own position clear. I hold the First World War to have been *the* great catastrophe of Western civilization in the present century. I think it an endless pity that it did not cease in November 1917, when the Bolsheviki called for its termination. It was just at this time that Lord Lansdowne published his well-known letter, pleading for an early end of the war on the basis of compromise with the Germans rather than unconditional surrender. Lansdowne was a man whose patriotism was unchallengeable, who had suffered keenly from the war in the personal sense, and who wrote from great depths of sadness and reflection. His letter has always seemed to me one of the most moving and penetrating documents of the time; and I consider that the Western governments would have done well to be guided by it instead of rejecting it out of hand, as they did.

But to say that this war ought to have ended in 1917 is not to say that the Soviet Decree on Peace was a proper or feasible basis for its termination. The Russian Communists, determined as they were to tear the social structure of old Europe stone from stone in the name of a doctrine whose actual relevance to the development of Western society was even then on the wane, were not the people under whose auspices Europe was suitably to be rescued from the madness in which it was then engaged. If Allied statesmanship was at fault in the autumn of 1917, it was at fault in its failure to see the tragedy and futility of the war itself and to bring the struggle to an end by its own efforts, on a basis of compromise. It was not at fault in its failure to accept the political initiative of Communist Petrograd, which viewed Western society through an ideological lens as distorted as any men have ever used, which had no understanding for the deeper values of Western civilization as most of us see them, and the motive of which, in calling for a cessation of hostilities in the war, was not to end violence and bloodshed but only to transfer them from the arena of formal international conflict to that of civil strife within the warring countries.

4 Unofficial Allied Agents

THE TREATY of Brest-Litovsk which sealed Russia's withdrawal from the war prompted, as I have said, various reactions among the Western governments. There were those who wanted to send armies into Russia; there were others who wanted to try to re-enlist the enthusiasm of the Russians for the war by formulating a more inspiring pattern of Allied war aims; there were still others who wanted to release Russia from her bond and to adjust in this way to the inevitable.

There was one more Allied reaction, however, which I think I ought to tell you about, not because it was very widely entertained in the Allied chanceries or because it led to any concrete results (actually, it didn't), but because it represented the first instance of another phenomenon destined in later years to play a very important part in the relations between the Soviet government and the West, namely, the phenomenon of what we might call "bourgeois pro-Soviet-ism." By this I mean the adoption of pro-Soviet attitudes by people who would not have been prepared to share to the full, or even in its main outlines, the Soviet ideology, but who, nevertheless, made themselves in some ways spokes-men for the Soviet leaders and advocated policies friendly toward them on the part of the Western governments.

At the time of the November Revolution there were, in the Russian capital, large wartime missions, diplomatic and military, of the Western Allied governments. These had, of course, been accredited to the Provisional Government. Strictly speaking, they should not have remained after the November Revolution, since their governments did not recognize the Soviet government. But remain they did, for various reasons; and they were tolerated on the Soviet side for some months, for various other reasons.

Sir George Buchanan, the British ambassador, left Petrograd two months after the Revolution, an exhausted, discouraged man. Britain was represented thereafter by a chargé d'affaires.

As for the French, Paléologue had been replaced as am-bassador, in the summer of 1917, by Joseph Noulens, one of the leaders of the Radical Party, and formerly a cabinet minister. Vigorous, shrewd, and politically skillful, Noulens soon conceived a violent antipathy to the new Soviet power. He eventually became one of its most dangerous and persistent opponents in the Western camp.

The American government had, as its ambassador in Petrograd, an elderly businessman and politician from St. Louis, Mr. David R. Francis. Despite the fact that he had held a number of high positions in American political life, having been Mayor of St. Louis and Governor of Missouri and even, for a year or two, a member of the Cabinet under President Grover Cleveland, Francis was not what you would call a cosmopolitan person. He was a product of the old West, a "provincial" in the best sense of the term, in whose character there was reflected something of the "showboat" Mississippi: the vigor, the earthiness, the slight-ly flamboyant elegance, and the uninhibited enjoyment of the good things of life. His values and opinions were, at his age of 67, firmly established, and were not to be essentially shaken even by the experience of residence in a foreign

capital in dramatic times. He clung to them with vociferous
fidelity throughout the period of his ambassadorship. Serving
in Russia continuously from mid-1916 until the autumn of
1918, he bore with conspicuous personal courage the strains
and dangers of life in such a country at such a time; and
he pursued his duties with great fidelity and persistence.
If, as was the case, he was poorly prepared in many ways
for this unusual task, one cannot deny him a certain admiration for the spirit in which he accepted and performed
it. His political role was not a great one, but his simple,
outspoken, American pragmatism provided a revealing contrast to the intensely theoretical controversies that raged
around him, and one comes away from the reading of his
memoirs with the feeling that America could have been in
some ways much worse served, if in other ways better. It
need hardly be added that he viewed the new Soviet
regime, at all times, with distaste and suspicion.

Since the Allied governments did not recognize the Soviet
government, the Allied ambassadors refused, as a rule, to
have any dealings with it personally, but if there is any one
thing we have been taught in these forty years of the existence
of Soviet power, it is that it is useful and necessary, in a
complex world, to have dealings with enemies as well as
with friends. Partly for this reason, and partly by coincidence, each of the three diplomatic missions soon developed
unofficial, back-door channels of contact with the Soviet
leaders.

On the French and American sides, the arrangement grew
up by chance. In the case of the French, the person in
question was a liberal lawyer, M. Jacques Sadoul, who
was attached, by virtue of a wartime commission, to the
large French Military Mission in Russia. Sadoul was a
Socialist. His presence on the mission was presumably the
result of the influence of the Socialist Minister of Munitions, M. Albert Thomas, whose visit to Russia in the summer of 1917 I have referred to earlier. Sadoul's memoirs
of this period have survived, in the form of two published
volumes of the letters which he wrote to Thomas from
Russia in the 1917-1918 period. His sympathies for the
Soviet regime grew steadily as his disgust mounted for the
Russian policy of his own government. He eventually became a full-fledged member of the French Communist
Party and a stout Stalinist. If anyone wishes to see an
example of what twenty-five years of participation in the

Communist movement can do to a first-class mind, I suggest
he look up Sadouls brilliant letters, written in 1918, full of
subtlety and warmth and sincerity, and compare them with
the book he published twenty-seven years later, in 1945,
on the same subject: a typical Stalinist document, wooden
and jerky in style, full of the crudest, most routine distortions of the historical record.

On the American side, the unofficial contact with the
Soviet government was conducted by a man so colorful that
I shrink from attempting to introduce him, as I must, in a
few inadequate words. This was Raymond Robins—*Colonel*
Raymond Robins, as he was then known, for he had inherited the command of America's wartime Red Cross
Commission to Russia, and had thereby, like Sadoul, as-
similated military rank. The biography of Robins remains
to be written; and if the pen that writes it is in any way
worthy of the subject, it will be a fascinating story.

Robins was a romanticist, a mystic, and something of
an evangelist, and withal a man of great physical vigor and
power of personality. He seemed a character out of Jack
London. He had received his religious conversion while
participating in the Alaska gold rush of the turn of the
century. Now, in Russia, he was at the peak of his
strength, and undergoing the greatest experience of a life
by no means poor in experiences. Magnetic, vibrant, somewhat lonely, given to fierce loyalties and equally fierce suspicions, Robins's figure dominates the history of the first
months of the Soviet-American relationship, romanticizing—
not without a touch of genius—itself and everything with
which it came into contact, communicating a curious un-
reality to the whole story, lending to it all, for the historian,
a tinge of fiction instead of history.

It might be interesting, before we leave Robins, to compare him with another colorful American figure who was
very much on the Petrograd scene at the time of the Revolution and who, even more than Robins, was on the pro-
Soviet side of the fence. This was the young intellectual-
socialist, John Reed, whose book about the November Revolution, *Ten Days That Shook the World*,[19] remains a classic
of political reporting and the most vivid, outstanding eye-
witness account of that stirring time. Reed, who was in
Russia as the correspondent for American Socialist papers,
was a very young man. He was a Harvard graduate and a
thorough-going rebel against the upper-class American so-

ciety in which he had been reared. A man of magnificent literary talent, a poet rather than a political thinker, knowing very little (one suspects) about the capitalism he so contemptuously attacked, he had swallowed a good portion of standard Marxist dosage of concept and phraseology. In contrast to Robins, who for all his sympathy with the Soviet leaders regarded himself as an intermediary between two worlds, Reed threw himself wholeheartedly into the Bolshevik cause. The Soviet Foreign Office was even induced, at one point, to take the bizarre step of trying to appoint him as Soviet Consul General in New York.

Reed knew nothing about practical affairs and never played any role in the foreign relations of the Soviet government. He left Russia in February 1918, to return a year or so later, and to die of disease in Russia in 1920. His influence on the course of events was exerted less by his activity in Russia than by the effect on American liberal opinion of his eloquent literary descriptions of the Russian political scene.

The only one of the three Western governments to send a man to Russia expressly for the purpose of maintaining this backstairs contact with the Soviet leaders was the British. It selected for this purpose a young man who had until recently been British Consul General in Moscow and was well acquainted with the Russian scene. This was Mr. R. H. Bruce Lockhart. Mr. Lockhart has made a distinguished contribution to the written record of the period by the memoirs which he published some years ago under the title of *British Agent*.[20]

These three men—Lockhart, Sadoul, and Robins—worked, so to speak, in the same direction—Lockhart and Robins bound by a mutual liking and respect and keeping in close touch with each other; Sadoul going rather his own way. All three had frequent contact with the Soviet leaders—primarily with Leon Trotsky, who was Commissar for Foreign Affairs throughout the period of the Brest-Litovsk talks; then, subsequently, with his successor, Georgi Chicherin.

The renewal of the German offensive at the end of February drove not only the Soviet government but the Allied missions as well out of Petrograd, and caused the abandonment of that city as a captial. The Soviet government moved to Moscow. Ambassador Francis, who, since Buchanan's departure, was dean of the diplomtaic corps, betook himself at that time to the provincial town of Vologda, three or four hundred miles east of Petrograd, on the line to Siberia and Vladivostok. The place was well selected strategically from the standpoint of making a getaway if things became hotter still. Some of the other diplomats went with him to that point; and a little diplomatic corps accumulated there. The French and British embassies, instead of going at once to Vologda, set off in special trains to try to make their way through Finland, then torn with civil war. The French failed to get through, were shunted uncomfortably about for many days, and finally ended up back in Russia. The British, to the intense resentment of the French ambassador, succeeded in wangling their way through Finland and thus getting out to England.

Instead of accompanying the Allied diplomatic missions when the latter left Petrograd, Lockhart, Robins, and Sadoul all chose to follow the Soviet government to Moscow. Here, unencumbered by the presence of the hesitant, inhibited, and somewhat jealous ambassadors, they were able to cultivate their contacts with the Soviet leaders even more freely than was the case in Petrograd.

These three unofficial agents became, as I said, the initiators and the protagonists of another concept of what one might do about the triumph of Soviet power in Russia—a concept that seems not to have occurred to the Allied chanceries in the West. This was the idea of restoring resistance to Germany by supporting the Soviet government, by working through it rather than against it, by strengthening it and encouraging it in its resistance to German pressures.

Let us consider how much reality lay behind this suggestion. From the time when the first difficulties developed in the Brest-Litovsk talks, the Soviet leaders were frightened men. I do not mean to impugn their personal courage. Of that they had plenty. But they were genuinely alarmed at the situation in which they had involved themselves, at their complete military helplessness, their lack of any sort of regular armed force, and the possibility that the Germans might at any time decide to go all out: to occupy Petrograd and Moscow, and to destroy Soviet power entirely. For this reason they began, as early as February 1918, at the time of the renewal of the German offensive, to build up a new Red army to replace the Tsarist army which they had deliberately wrecked as a fighting force. At the time of the signing of the Brest-Litovsk Treaty, Trotsky, theretofore

Commissar for Foreign Affairs, became Commissar for War, and set about, with great administrative ability and energy, to build up this new force.

There were three ways in which the Allies could have given military assistance to the Soviet government at this time. First, there was the possibility of shipment of arms and supplies to Russia. This became a subject of discussion between the Soviet government and the unofficial envoys during the period of renewed military operations by the Germans at the end of February. Please remember that no one knew, at that moment, whether the Germans would consent to stop on any terms, or whether they would simply push on and attempt to overthrow Soviet power entirely. In their desperation, Lenin and Trotsky were ready at that moment to clutch at any straw. In these circumstances the possibility of accepting Allied aid came before the Central Committee of the Russian Communist Party as a question of principle. Was it thinkable, it was asked, that a workers' government should accept aid from capitalist governments? There were many members of the Central Committee who thought anything of this sort wholly impermissible. Lenin was not present at the session of the Central Committee where the matter was discussed. He was tied up in some other sort of meeting. His comrades sent a note to him, asking his opinion. His one-sentence reply, scrawled on a little chit of paper, has become famous. "I request that my vote be added," he wrote, "in favor of the acceptance of potatoes and arms from the bandits of Anglo-French imperialism."[21] Lenin's view prevailed, and it thus became the official Party policy that such aid *could* be accepted, if there were no other alternative but destruction at the hands of the Germans, and if it could be obtained on favorable terms.

Actually, nothing came of the suggestion. The Germans did not continue the offensive. And the Allied governments would never have extended such aid at that time on terms acceptable to the Soviet government, even had the emergency arisen. But the discussion of this possibility gave rise to some rather enduring legends and misunderstandings.

Robins and Lockhart really believed, and were apparently encouraged by Trotsky to believe, that if the Allies had been willing, in these last days of February and first days of March, to promise that there would be no Japanese intervention in Siberia and to make a handsome offer of military aid, the Soviet government might have been induced not to ratify the treaty but to attempt to continue hostilities against the Germans.

On March 5, two days after signature of the treaty but before its ratification, Lockhart, who had just had interviews with some of the Soviet leaders at their headquarters, wired to London pointing out that the problem of ratification of the treaty would be up for consideration by the Congress of Soviets in a few days. He then went on to say:

> Empower me to inform Lenin that the question of Japanese intervention has been shelved . . . that we are prepared to support the Bolsheviks in so far as they will oppose Germany and that we invite his suggestions as to the best way in which this help can be given. In return for this there is every chance that war will be declared. . . .[22]

On that same day, Trotsky received Robins and asked him a number of questions about what the United States attitude would be and what help might be expected in case ratification of the treaty should be refused by the Congress of Soviets or in case there should be a renewal of hostilities. Robins suggested Trotsky put these questions in writing. Lenin was consulted, and Robins was then supplied with a piece of paper setting forth the questions. Greatly excited over the possibilities that seemed to him implicit in this evidence of Soviet interest, Robins at once turned the document over to the American Military Attaché for transmission to the War Department in Washington. He was sure that if an encouraging response were forthcoming from Washington, the Brest-Litovsk Treaty would never be ratified, and the war would be resumed.

Robins later told a senatorial investigating committee a dramatic tale of how the Congress of Soviets, called to ratify the treaty, was postponed for two days by Lenin in the hope that the American reply would come through, of how Lenin then let the others debate for two extra days in order to give the Americans more time to answer, and of how, finally, the fatal moment arrived when Lenin could wait no more.

"About an hour before midnight on the second night of the conference"—Robins told the Senators—

. . . Lenin was sitting on the platform; I was sitting on a step of the platform, and I looked at this man, and he motioned

to me. I went to him. He said, "What have you heard from
your Government?" I said, "Nothing." I said, "What has
Lockhart heard?' He said, "Nothing." He said, "I am now
going to the platform and the peace will be ratified"; and
he went to the platform, and he made a speech of an
hour and twenty-odd minutes or so, in which he outlined
the economic condition, the military condition, the absolute
necessity after three years of economic waste and war
for the Russian peasant and workingman to have the
means, even by a shameful peace, for the reorganization of
life in Russia and the protection of the revolution, as he
said; and the peace was ratified by two and a half to one
in that vote.[23]

This makes a wonderful story, with the United States government gnashing its teeth, as usual, in the role of the
villain. Robins was wholly sincere in telling it this way, and
one feels cruel in puncturing it. But a careful study of the
Soviet documents does not bear it out in any way. The
Congress *was* put off for two days, but *not* for reasons having anything to do with Trotsky's questions to Robins. Lenin
did speak at the conclusion of the debate, and he *did* call
for ratification of the treaty; but this was something he had
been insisting on all along in the private counsels of the
Central Committee; the possibility of aid from the American imperialists had never even entered into these internal
discussions. And as for the telegram to Washington, it has
recently been established, after the lapse of nearly forty
years, that the Military Attaché, being a timid and inexperienced man—he had been sent to Russia, actually, as a result
of confusion of names in the War Department—put the
document in his pocket and neglected entirely to hand it in
at the telegraph office until the whole crisis was over, so
that the United States government was innocent of any
knowledge of the whole affair.

The second possibility which was involved in this idea of
working through the Bolsheviki to defeat Germany was
that of technical military assistance: the idea that Allied
officers might participate in the training of the new Red army
or might serve the Soviet government as military experts.
Discussions along this line took place just before and just
after the signing of the Treaty of Breast-Litovsk. I think
these discussions were taken much more seriously by the
unofficial Allied representatives than they ever were by the

Soviet leaders. Trotsky doubted initially that many of the old Tsarist officers would consent to serve in the new Red army. When it developed, as it did very quickly, that it would not be too difficult to find ones who would serve, Trotsky's interest in Allied military technicians rapidly flagged. The Soviet leaders were, for obvious political reasons, not anxious to use Allied officers if there were any way to avoid doing so. The whole idea was soon killed, in any case, on the Allied side, by the opposition of the French ambassador, Noulens; and nothing ever really came of it.

It is possible that one or two French officers may have helped with the demolition of the Russian railways at the time of the German renewal of hostilities in February. Lenin later made a reference to this in his so-called "Letter to the American Workingmen," of August 1918. But it is significant that he referred to it simply as an illustration of the unlimited opportunism by which, in his opinion, militant socialism had a right to be guided. It will be useful to note his words, for they are revealing of Soviet policy generally. "The French Captain, Sadoul"—he wrote—

... making a pretense of sympathy for the Bolsheviki, but actually serving French imperialism in word and deed, brought to me a French officer, de Lubersac. "I am a monarchist, my only purpose is the defeat of Germany," de Lubersac said to me. "That goes without saying," I replied. This in no way prevented me from "agreeing" with de Lubersac about the services which certain French officers, demolition specialists, wanted to render to us in blowing up railway tracks in order to delay the German advance. . . . The French monarchist and I shook hands, knowing that each of us would gladly have hung the other. But at the moment, our interests coincided.[24]

This passage does not sound as though Lenin attached much importance, in retrospect, to the substantive part of these discussions; and there is no reason to suppose that the collaboration implied lasted for more than two or three days.

There was also a third possibility: namely, that the Soviet government might actually be brought to request the intervention by Allied military forces on Russian territory to give aid against the Germans. The idea arose just at the time of the final Brest-Litovsk crisis, and was actively pursued by the unofficial envoys for two months following that event, from roughly the middle of March to the middle of May in 1918. There seems to be no question but that the three unofficial agents were encouraged by Trotsky to believe that there was a possibility of some such arrangement, if suitable conditions could be worked out.

How much reality was there in this suggestion? Did the Bolsheviki ever seriously contemplate inviting the Allies in? Available records of the inner-Party discussions reveal that there was only one contingency on which the Bolsheviki would ever have considered doing this, and that was in the event of an all-out attempt by the Germans to occupy Petrograd and Moscow and overthrow Soviet power. Never at any time did they even consider inviting or agreeing to the movement of Allied forces onto Russian territory except as a measure of last resort, if the alternative appeared to be the complete destruction of Soviet power. Since such a situation never arose, the matter was never actually considered as a policy question by the Central Committee, and no formal position was ever taken along these lines.

The main reason, in my opinion, why Trotsky for a time encouraged Lockhart and Robins to believe that such a possibility existed was that he hoped in this way to cause the Western Allies, in deference to these hopes, to put a damper on the Japanese and to cause the latter to refrain from intervening in Siberia. Trotsky calculated that if the Allies still thought there was a possibility that the Soviet government might invite them to intervene, they would use their influence to prevent the Japanese from spoiling this possibility by intervening without invitation.

This maneuver was not entirely unsuccessful. Lockhart's reports to London along these lines did cause the British government to believe that there might be something in this suggestion, and for roughly two months the discussions among the Allied chanceries about the intervention problem revolved around this possibility. The American ambassador, Mr. Francis, confessed that he waited for six weeks before recommending Allied intervention, in the hope that perhaps an invitation might be forthcoming from the Soviet government. By this means, the Soviet government did succeed in diverting the Allied discussion of the intervention problem, for a period of six weeks, into what was actually a blind alley.

But it would be wrong to exaggerate the significance of this fact. The American and Japanese governments, whose

decisions had the greatest importance for the Siberian intervention, never warmed at all to this suggestion of a Soviet
invitation, and it had no appreciable effect on their policies.
For a variety of reasons, it was never a very real alternative to what actually occurred.

All in all, we see, then, that the possibilities for stimulating resistance to the German government by working
through the Soviet government were very slender indeed,
and the tentative discussions along these lines that took place
in Moscow in the early months of 1918 were, in the
substantive sense, a tempest in a teapot. Yet in other respects, these contacts between the unofficial Allied agents and
the Soviet leaders were of considerable importance; and I think
we should note, before we leave this subject, why this was so.

First of all, Robins and Sadoul, and to some extent Lockhart, came away from this episode convinced that the failure to realize these possibilities had been largely the result
of the shortsightedness and stupidity of the Allied governments themselves. We have already seen Robins's misinter-
pretation of the reasons for the Soviet ratification of the
Brest-Litovsk Treaty. Robins and Sadoul, in particular, were
never disabused of this impression—that the Allies had
struck down the proffered hand of Soviet friendship in the
first months of Soviet power, and had, by so doing, not only
forfeited real opportunities for collaboration with the Soviet
regime, but had permanently embittered the Soviet leaders
against the West. Soviet propagandists have naturally not
been loath to let this impression stand. The result is that it
has gained a respectable place in liberal thinking in England
and America. It still finds reflection from time to time in
Western historical literature. It has entered, in other words,
into what I might call "the mythology" of the Russian Revolution.

But the second reason why these backstairs contacts were
important was that the unofficial Allied agents carried away
from these contacts an impression of the Soviet leadership
quite different from that which had been gained by Allied
officialdom as a whole. They saw the Soviet leaders not as
ogres or monsters of sorts, but as human beings, and in
many ways impressive human beings at that. It was a start-
ling experience for these men, after long immersion in the
Western society of that day—where the accent was so
extensively on individualism, on personal vanity, on social
rivalry and snobbishness—to encounter men who had a burn-

ing social faith, and were relentless and incorruptible in the pursuit of it.

The image of reality against the background of which the political fanatic plays his part is always largely artificial. He creates it for himself; but he believes in it implicitly, and in part he generally succeeds in making it seem real to others as well. And his role, as he plays it, may be none the less heroic and impressive for this artificiality of the scenery.

The Soviet leaders knew what they wanted; they worked day and night to carry it into effect; they gave no thought to themselves. They demanded discipline from others; they accepted it for themselves. In their seriousness of purpose, in the forthright simplicity of their behavior, in their refusal to bother about nonessentials, in their contemptuous rejection of personal considerations to the needs of the movement, in their willingness to get their hands dirty in the interests of the cause—in these manifestations of the early Bolshevik personality, a thousand outworn affectations and pretenses of the era of the turn of the century seemed to go crashing to the ground. For those who saw this at first hand, the impression was unforgettable.

Neither Robins nor Lockhart was a Socialist. Neither was converted to Socialism by these experiences. But they were pressed by what they had seen into taking a larger view of Soviet power than was taken by a great many of their compatriots. Their firsthand knowledge could not fail to make them impatient of the stupid and prejudiced views about Russian Communism that were beginning to find currency in Western officialdom and respectable Western opinion. It fell largely to them to combat such silly and ineradicable legends as the belief that the Bolsheviki were paid German agents or that they had nationalized women. In their effort to combat these impressions, Robins and Lockhart ran the risk of sounding like Communist apologists.

Robins, to be sure, did make mistakes. Above all, he made the mistake of drawing general conclusions from too small a selection of particular phenomena. Because the Soviet leaders proved, or appeared, to be co-operative in one particular set of circumstances, and in one single field of activity, he allowed himself to suppose that they could easily be brought to respond the same way in other situations, if only they could be approached in the proper, sympathetic manner. In this, he was only the first of a long series of respectable Western sympathizers and fellow travelers who would insist on drawing general conclusions from similar partial manifestations of Soviet behavior. I have seen businessmen, technicians, scholars, and military men in abundance (during the recent war), even churchmen, who made this mistake. The consequences could, on occasion, be quite serious.

But there were two appreciations to which these early unofficial agents were brought which seem to me to have been of a great and prophetic value.

The first of these was the realization that just because a given political movement is hostile and provocative and sometimes insulting is no reason why it should not be carefully and attentively and dispassionately studied from our side. With a pathetic patience and earnestness, Robins labored, in the subsequent congressional hearings, to make the Senators understand the difference between a partiality to the Soviet ideology, on the one hand, and a desire to learn the truth about it, on the other. "I would like"—he said—

... to tell the truth about men and about movements, without passion and without resentment, even though I differed from men and from movements. I think that is the essential thing . . .[25]

"I believe," he said at another point—in reference to the Russian Revolution—

... that when we understand what it is, when we know the facts behind it, when we do not libel it nor slander it or do not lose our heads and become its advocates and defenders, and really know what the thing is, and then move forward to it, then we will serve our country and our time.[26]

I should like to say that in these words Robins was almost as close, in my opinion, as one could get to the best answer Western society can find to the problem of Russian Communism. Our success in dealing with this problem will begin on the day when we recognize it as primarily a problem of understanding, rather than one of the physical repulsion of an external force. But then we must go one step further than Robins went, and we must realize that this is at least as much a matter of understanding ourselves and our own society as it is of understanding those on the other side of the Iron Curtain.

The second appreciation to which these men were brought was the realization that just because the leaders of another regime were hostile and provocative and insulting, if you will, in their approach to the countries of the West, that did not mean that one could afford the luxury of having no dealings whatsoever with them or that there was nothing to be gained by meeting them face to face and talking about this question or that. I think that Robins and Lockhart may have been the first to see that our world had become too small, and our dependence on each other too great, to permit of the luxury of ignoring one's enemies. They were perhaps the first to sense the reality which the atomic bomb is finally bringing home to all of us today; namely, that we cannot divide our external environment neatly and completely into friends and enemies—that there must be a certain relativism about enmity, as I suppose there must be about friendship—that we must learn to recognize a certain duality in our relationship to all the rest of mankind, even those who hate us most.

These appreciations were the more lasting fruits of the hectic and abortive discussions of Allied aid that were conducted in Moscow in the early months of 1918. The men who conducted these discussions deserve to be remembered for this, if not for the political will-o'-the-wisps which circumstances moved them to pursue.

5 The North Russian Intervention

IN MY discussion of the Brest-Litovsk negotiations, I mentioned the fact that only some three weeks after the second Russian Revolution and the issuance of the Decree on Peace, Marshal Foch, at a meeting of Allied statesmen in Paris, proposed the dispatch of Allied forces to Russia as a means of restoring resistance to Germany on the eastern front; and I told you that this suggestion was firmly rejected, at that moment, by both Lloyd George and Colonel House.

It now becomes necessary for me to explain how the British and American governments nevertheless contrived within the space of a few months to involve themselves in the trials and responsibilities of military intervention in Russia. Since the expeditions to different parts of Russia proceeded from quite different patterns of motivation, I shall have to speak about them separately. The first is the expedition that was dispatched to the northern ports of European Russia.

I think it well to begin with the interpretation placed on these events by Soviet leaders and historians today.

On September 15, 1957, *Pravda* devoted the first four and a half pages of its six-page issue exclusively to a single document. This document represented the propaganda theses of the Soviet Communist Party to be used in connection with the forthcoming fortieth anniversary of the November Revolution.

In the course of these theses, the following statements were made concerning the Allied intervention of 1918-1920:

Having taken power into their hands, the workers and peasants of Russia entered, under the leadership of the Bolshevik party, on peaceful creative work. But the exploiting classes overthrown by the revolution mounted a civil war against the power of the workers and the peasants. . . .

The organizer and inspirer of armed struggle against the Soviet Republic was international imperialism. The tremendous revolutionizing effect of the first republic of workers and peasants in world history aroused fear and bitter anger in the ranks of the imperialists of all countries. They saw in the victory of the Socialist Revolution a threat to their own parasitical existence, to their profits and their capital, to all their privileges. In the effort to throttle the young republic of the Soviets, the imperialists, led by the leading circles of England, the U.S.A., and France, organized military campaigns against our country. From all sides—from north and south, east and west—the attacking hordes of interventionists and White Guards poured onto our territory.

In these difficult circumstances, the Communist Party and the Soviet government summoned the people to a just, revolutionary, and patriotic war against the foreign interventionists and the internal counterrevolution. For over three years the Soviet Republic was obliged to fight off the mad armed attack of the combined forces of the imperialist beasts of prey and the internal revolution. . . .[27]

This document then went on to tell of the decisive resistance said to have been met by the imperialist governments at the hands of their own workers, in their effort to conduct the war against Russia. The workers of all countries, it was stated, regarded the defense of the Russian Revolution as their own most intimate affair and as a part of their international duty in the struggle against capitalism. The reader was encouraged to infer that this, as much as the heroic resistance of the Soviet people, frustrated the imperialistic design that lay behind the intervention. The final victory of the Soviet people over the interventionists and the White Guards was accordingly described as "the most tremendous military and political defeat of world imperialism" and "a demonstration of great vitality and unconquerableness of the young Soviet state."[28]

These represent the things the Soviet government wishes people in Russia and abroad to believe today about the intervention of 1918. This thesis has been repeatedly reinforced by personal statements of Khrushchev and other individual Soviet leaders on this subject. Please note the two main elements of this Soviet thesis, as it concerns the origins of the Allied action. First, it says the intervention occurred because the Western capitalists were enraged by the triumph of the Revolution in Russia and its political effect abroad, and were frightened lest they lose their profits, their capital, and their privileges; therefore, it is suggested, they attempted to crush the Revolution. Secondly, the Soviet thesis fails to mention in any way *the fact that there was at that time a world war in progress.* The Soviet student who is guided by this official line of historical interpretation could only assume that the war had nothing whatsoever to do with the intervention.

With this in mind, let us have a look at the facts.

During the years when Russia was still carrying on as a member of the Entente in World War I, access to Russian ports for the Western Allies was blocked in the Baltic Sea by the Germans and in the Dardanelles by the Germans and the Turks. The only access was either through Vladivostok, which meant a journey halfway around the world and then 5000 miles of rail haul across Siberia to European Russia, or around the North Cape to the north of Russia. At the beginning of the war, the only port in the Russian North of any size, connected with the main Russian railway system, was Archangel. Situated on the southern shore of the White Sea, in the delta of the Northern Duna River, Archangel was, even then, a fine port; but for six or seven months of the year it was frozen tight as a drum. To obviate this difficulty, a new port was constructed during the war on the shore of the Murmansk inlet, adjacent to the Finnish and Norwegian borders. This was closer to England and the Atlantic, and it was, although several hundred miles farther north than Archangel, ice-free all the year round, thanks to the effects of the Gulf Stream. To connect this port with the Russian railway system, a new railway line of some 800 miles had to be constructed, linking it to a point on the Trans-Siberian Railway not far east of Petrograd. Largely under the prompting of the British, all this was done during the war against heavy obstacles and at considerable cost in effort and human life. The new port was just being completed when the Revolution occurred, and the new railway was ready to be put seriously to use for the first time in the winter of 1917-1918.

The shipping route from England to the North Russian ports had to be protected against German submarines during the First World War, just as it had to be during the second. The British provided from the start the major portion of this naval effort; and as the Russian armed forces disintegrated at the time of the Russian Revolution, the role of the British as the protectors of this supply route increased. Not only were they obliged to protect the ships moving to Archangel and Murmansk, but they became in large measure the suppliers of Murmansk, in particular, with food and necessities of all sorts. At the time of the November Revolution they had a naval squadron there, commanded by Rear Admiral Thomas W. Kemp. Kemp was ordered to keep his force there during the ensuing winter as a protection to Allied interests in that region.

In the months just preceding the November Revolution—during the period, that is, of the Provisional Government—the Allies had sent great quantities of war matériel to Archangel for use in the Russian war effort. Owing to the inefficiency and the near-breakdown of the Russian railway

network, much of this matériel could not be moved during
that summer season. At the time of the November Revolution, great quantities of it, something in excess of 160
thousand tons, lay strewn along the riverbank in the great military dumps across from the city. This was extremely valuable matériel. It included priceless stocks of metals made
available from the short supplies of the Western Allies as a
contribution to the Russian war effort. It had been sent to
Russia in shipping which the Allies could very well have
used in other theaters of war, and which was made available only with great difficulty. The Russians had not, as yet,
paid a penny for these materials. They had all been covered
by· credits extended to the Russian government in London
and New York—credits, incidentally, for which the Soviet
government had just renounced all responsibility, proclaiming
its intention to make no reimbursement at all.

Not until February 1918 did the Bolsheviki move in on
the Archangel scene, establish a majority in the Archangel
Soviet, and thereby gain control of the city. Their first act,
on acquiring local power, was to mount an intensive effort
to move the accumulation of war stores into the interior. Please
bear in mind that they now had no ostensible use for these
stores in any military effort against Germany. This was just
the time when they were making peace with the Germans
at Brest-Litovsk. They did not consult with the Allies before
moving this accumulation, nor were they at all communicative
about the disposition of the stores once they had been hauled
away from the Archangel waterfront.

The population of Archangel was already seriously threatened at this time with shortage of food. The British government offered to supply food in exchange for the release of
the stores for removal by the Allies. The offer was never
accepted by the Bolsheviki; and two British food-ships dispatched to Archangel for this purpose lay for many weeks at
anchor in the channel without unloading, while the trains
bearing the war supplies continued to rumble off into the
interior.

Throughout the spring of 1918 there was nothing the
Allies could do. The port was still frozen and not accessible
even to naval action. But one can understand the indignation
many Allied officials felt at this highhanded appropriation
by the Soviet government of war stores for which that government had paid nothing, which were desperately needed for
the war effort in the West, and which the Soviet authorities

had no intention of using for the purpose which had prompted their original dispatch to Archangel.

At Murmansk, the local Soviet was also not under the control of the Bolsheviki in the period immediately after the November Revolution. It was of a moderate-socialist complexion, and remained in a relationship of friendly collaboration with the British naval force stationed in the port. Strenuous efforts were made by the Bolsheviki to gain control of the situation there, just as at Archangel. But these efforts were clumsy. They included the assassination of the very liberal and popular Russian admiral who commanded the Russian naval base. The result was only to drive the local Soviet into an even closer association with the Allied authorities.

At the end of February 1918, at the height of the Brest-Litovsk crisis and just before the Soviet capitulation, there was considerable alarm in Murmansk lest the advancing Germans, together with the Finnish Whites, should move against the Murmansk Railway and attack the city from the south. The Murmansk Soviet consulted the central Soviet government about the desirability of accepting military aid, in such a contingency, from the Allied units in the port. They received in reply, on March 2, a telegram from Trotsky which has subsequently been the subject of much controversy and recrimination. It contained the sentence: "You must accept any and all assistance from the Allied missions and use every means to obstruct the advance of the plunderers."[29]

The circumstances in which this telegram was sent were curious ones. It was really meant to relate only to the crisis of that particular moment, and it was out of date a few hours after it was sent. But it was never specifically canceled; and it became the formal basis for a very intimate military collaboration between the Murmansk Soviet and the Allied naval authorities in the port. A few days after it was sent, Admiral Kemp landed a couple of hundred British marines to help in the defense of the port. From that time on, the whole defense of the Murmansk region against the Germans was a joint undertaking of the Allies and the local Soviet authority. As late as May and June 1918, it was still the understanding in Washington that the Soviet government had given its blessing to the idea of a joint defense of Murmansk.

This collaboration was stimulated by the constant exaggeration on the Allied side of German intentions with respect to Finland and of the degree of intimacy between the Germans and the White side in the Finnish Civil War. The Finnish Civil War had a tendency to spill over now and then into the neighborhood of the Murmansk Railway. The Allied representatives in Russia saw in each of these very minor incursions and skirmishes the beginning of a German attack on the railway and on Murmansk, and took them much more seriously than they need have done. The Germans, on the other hand, receiving equally exaggerated reports about what the Allies were up to at Murmansk, naturally saw in this a violation of the Brest-Litovsk Treaty and the beginning of an Allied military action on the eastern front. As time went on, they became more and more indignant about this, and therefore gradually increased their own attention to the Murmansk area. In this way both sides worked each other into a state of military tension over an area in which neither really had more than a secondary interest.

While these things were happening on the spot, the Allied military planners at the Supreme War Council at Versailles were giving anxious attention to the situation. How much they knew, at any given time, as to what was actually occurring in this part of Russia is an intricate and difficult question to answer. A portion of the situation I have just described was covered by the information they received; but this information had many gaps, and it included a good deal of direct misinformation. Their thinking was therefore conditioned at all times by a spotty and in some respects seriously inaccurate picture of the situation. They were particularly concerned, just at the time of the Brest-Litovsk crisis, by the reported German move in Finland and the threat to the security of the Archangel war supplies. They knew that they could not spare any sizable forces for use in that part of the world, but they were determined to find means at least to keep the two North Russian ports out of German hands and to create a diversion which would tie up some of the German forces in the east. They therefore worked out a scheme for a combined Siberian and North Russian intervention which involved the use of very few British or French forces but did assume the help of the Japanese in Siberia and the utilization, both in Siberia and the Russian North, of members of the so-called Czechoslovak Corps. This was a pro-Allied force, numbering forty to fifty thousand men, which was at that time trying to make its way out of Russia via Siberia. I shall have more to say below about this Czech Corps. Suffice it to say that the scheme evolved by the military planners at Versailles at the end of March, in 1918, envisaged that a portion of these Czechs would be routed to Murmansk and Archangel, where they would be used for garrison purposes and given further combat training by British officers. It was hoped that this group of Czechs would later join with anti-Bolshevik Russian forces in the north, and that together they would strike into the interior, in the direction of the Urals, and link up with the Japanese intervention in Siberia.

This was, please let me explain, not yet a decision to intervene. It was at first merely a recommendation of the British staff planners. They pressed it behind the scenes, with great energy and persistence, but they could not themselves make the decision. This required consent of the Allied governments themselves and of the Czechoslovak National Council in Paris; and here there were difficulties. The Czechoslovak National Council wanted the Czech Corps evacuated as rapidly as possible to the western front. It did not want to see the Corps detained in Russia as part of an Allied intervention. This view was supported by Clemenceau, who also wanted to see the Czechs added to the forces on the western front.

The matter dragged on until the Abbeville meeting of the Supreme War Council, at the beginning of May, when a rather fuzzy compromise was worked out. This compromise involved splitting the Czech Corps, bringing part to Murmansk and Archangel and letting the rest continue on through Siberia. It was still the stated purpose that the Corps should eventually be evacuated to France; but it was left extremely obscure when and how this would occur. I am afraid we cannot describe the whole arrangement as other than an evasion, designed to assure the use of these Czechs for purposes of a military intervention in Russia without actually saying so, while permitting the French and the Czechoslovak leaders to think they were going to be evacuated to France.

For reasons that I shall again have to talk about in connection with Siberia, this scheme was never implemented. The Corps, as it turned out, was never split, and no Czechs ever came to Murmansk and Archangel. But this appears to have remained concealed for a long time from the Allied military planners at Versailles. They thought, the decision having been taken, that the Czechs were on their way to the northern ports, and they proceeded to press their plan with all due vigor. At the next meeting of the Supreme War Council, in June, they asked for and received the approval of the senior statesmen to a paper which now made detailed provision for the Allied occupation of the northern ports, for the retention of the expected Czech units there as part of the Allied occupying force, and for the dispatch of some four to six Allied battalions—English, French, American, and Italian. While this paper was accepted by the senior French and British statesmen, it was conditional, so far as American participation was concerned, on the agreement of the United States government. A request for the necessary American support was therefore at once dispatched to Washington. Nothing was said to the American government about the idea of a later penetration into the interior of Russia, and nothing was said about a linking up of this action in the Russian north with a similar action in Siberia. The United States government was still known at this time to be violently averse to any sort of a Siberian expedition. In the request for the assignment of American battalions to the Russian north, it was simply put to the United States government that the forces were needed for the occupation of the two ports, in order to secure the war supplies against German seizure and to protect Allied military interests generally.

The month of May 1918 brought growing tension among the Soviet government, the Germans, the Murmansk Russians, and the Allied authorities in Murmansk over the situation there. The Germans were becoming increasingly resentful of Allied activity at Murmansk. The Soviet government was becoming increasingly impatient over the independence and pro-Allied tendencies being shown by the Murmansk Soviet. The Murmansk Soviet was becoming increasingly apprehensive about its own position. And the Allied representatives at Murmansk were becoming nervous about the signs of German pressure on the Soviet government and of growing hostility in Moscow toward the whole arrangement.

Moscow began at the end of May to try to reassert its authority in Murmansk. It sent to that port a special commissar, who spent a few days there, talked with local Russians and the Allied officers, and returned with a report that things were very bad indeed and that the Soviet government must take vigorous action to establish its authority and combat Allied influence. This commissar, a Lithuanian Communist by the name of S. P. Natsarenus, was accordingly given a small armed force of several hundred members of the Cheka, the forerunner of the GPU and the NKVD, and was told to move up the Murmansk Railway and to bring the Murmansk Soviet under control. Ostensibly, this was not a move against the Allies but merely an attempt to assert Moscow's authority in Murmansk. Actually, of course, it threatened the position of the Allies. Had it succeeded, there can be no question but that the intimate collaboration between the Allies and the Murmansk Soviet would have been promptly terminated. It was, let me add, just after the middle of June that Natsarenus's unit began its advance up the railway.

The British military authorities, meanwhile, had not waited for President Wilson's reply before proceeding to put their scheme into operation. As early as mid-May, before the scheme was even adopted at the Supreme War Council, they had confidently sent to Murmansk Major General F. C. Poole, whom they had selected to command the whole projected northern operation. Now, in June, they dispatched a force of six hundred men (all ones who had been declared physically unfit for service on the western front) under the command of Major General Charles C. M. Maynard. This was to be their initial contribution to the Allied force supposed to participate in the occupation of the northern ports.

Maynard and his men reached Murmansk on June 23. The forces at Poole's disposal at that time were still wholly inadequate for an attack on Archangel, which was under full-fledged Soviet control. But Maynard, being eager for some sort of action, as any military man would be, took a few of his men, fitted up a special train, and set off on a reconnaissance trip south down the Murmansk Railway. At a point about a hundred miles south of Murmansk, he encountered, to his astonishment, the first trainload of Natsarenus's Red Guards, moving north. It would be hard to say which of the two commanders was the more bewildered by this encounter—presumably the Soviet commander, because, in addition to having no idea who Maynard and his men were, he was allegedly drunk. It was a rather ticklish situation. The two trains found themselves standing parallel to each other at a passing siding. The railway personnel did not conceal their hostility to the British force. It was obvious that they proposed to throw the switches in such a way as to let the Russian force proceed to Murmansk. Maynard realized that, if this happened, the Soviet force would descend on Murmansk without warning, and the consequences might jeopardize the security of the Allied position there. He therefore acted boldly and swiftly. His men immediately surrounded the Soviet train, disarmed its occupants, and packed it off southward, following along behind as it went. On their further journey southward, they encountered two more trainloads of Red Guards, to whom they did the same thing. In this way they secured the entire railway as far south as Kem.

The effect of this action was to bring things to a head and to produce a complete political break between Moscow and Murmansk. The Soviet government, infuriated by Maynard's action and alarmed by the sharp protests they were now receiving from the Germans, ordered the Murmansk Soviet to break off its ties with the Allies and to insist on immediate departure of the Allied forces.

I wish I had time to tell you in detail the story of what ensued. It was quite impossible for the Murmansk Soviet to force the Allies to leave. The Allied forces in the port were much stronger than the local garrison. The head of the Murmansk Soviet was a simple man—an oiler or a fireman, it is said—off one of the Russian merchant vessels. His name was Aleksei Mikhailovich Yuryev. We have the record of the telegraphic exchanges between him and the giants of Soviet power in Moscow in those final days. Yuryev stood up manfully to the Moscow pressures. Never, surely, have the heads of the Russian Communist Party been talked to in this way by a subordinate. Lenin at one point sent to him a personal warning in the following words: "If you still refuse to understand Soviet policy—a policy equally hostile to the English and to the Germans—you have yourself to blame."[30] To this, Yuryev replied: "It is all very well for you to talk that way, sitting there in Moscow."[31] In a final violent altercation with Foreign Commissar Chicherin, Yuryev said at one point:

Comrade, has life not taught you to view things soberly? You constantly utter beautiful phrases, but not once have you told how to go about realizing them. Russia has been reduced to a mere shadow as a result of these phrases. ...If you know a way out of our condition please tell it to us. . . . We ourselves know that the Germans and the Allies are imperialists, but of two evils we have chosen the lesser. . . .[32]

Chicherin, infuriated by Yuryev's obstinacy, finally said to him: "Tell the Admirals who put you up to this" (meaning of course the British admirals in the port) "that in the event of an armed intervention onto the territory of revolutionary Russia, they will encounter a popular uprising. . . ." Undaunted by this reproach, Yuryev came right back. "Comrade Chicherin"—he replied—

. . . you said that some sort of admirals put me up to this, but this is not true—they did nothing of the sort . . . and if you persist in thinking of me in this way, then I can say that I have the impression that Count Mirbach [the German ambassador in Moscow] is standing behind your back and suggesting these thoughts to you. . . .[33]

This was too much for the Soviet government. It responded by denouncing Yuryev as an enemy of the people and severing all relations with the Murmansk Soviet. The Soviet commander on the southern stretch of the railway received instructions to burn the bridges north of him, break the telegraph line, and establish a regular military front. A few days later the Allies entered into a formal agreement with the Murmansk Soviet, recognizing it as the provisional sovereign authority in that whole region. Further Allied action at that point was carried out in complete formal agreement with what might be called an anti-Soviet Soviet.

While all this was happening in Murmansk, President Wilson, quite ignorant of these events, was wrestling with the British request that he make available American forces for the occupation of the two northern ports. The request was a secret one, and I cannot find that Wilson, in making his decision on it, consulted anyone other than the American Chief of Staff and two or three members of his own cabinet. Neither he nor Secretary of State Lansing, nor the Secretary of War, Newton Baker, nor the Chief of Staff, General Peyton C. March, had the slightest confidence in this scheme or any desire to contribute American troops to its accomplishment. Time after time, they voiced and recorded their disbelief in the soundness of the entire venture. But Wilson had by this time, as we shall see when we come to

talk about Siberia, turned down so many French and British
requests concerning the Siberian intervention that he hesitated now to turn down a similar one for North Russia. He
was afraid, Baker later wrote, that the French and British
were "beginning to feel that he was not a good associate,
much less a good ally."[34] After some delay, he finally agreed
in early July to make available three American battalions,
provided Marshal Foch, the Supreme Commander in Europe, would confirm in writing that these troops were more
needed in North Russia, from the standpoint of the war
against Germany, than they were in France. Only when this
assurance was received did Wilson consent, on July 17, to
make available the American battalions.

We might note the language Wilson actually used in this
connection. The United States government—he stated—

... yields, also, to the judgment of the Supreme Command
in the matter of establishing a small force at Murmansk, to
guard the military stores at Kola, and to make it safe for
Russian forces to come together in organized bodies in the
north. But ... it can go no further.... It is not in a
position, and has no expectation of being in a position, to
take part in organized intervention in adequate force from
... Murmansk and Archangel. It ... will ... feel obliged to
withdraw these forces, in order to add them to the forces at
the western front, if the plans ... should develop into others
inconsistent with the policy to which the Government of the
United States feels constrained to restrict itself.[35]

You will see from this wording that Wilson was somewhat confused, as busy senior statesmen are apt to be, about
the facts. He speaks of guarding the military stores at
"Kola." This was the old name for the fjord on which Murmansk is situated. But there was no appreciable quantity of
war stores there. Wilson was apparently ignorant of the fact
that the accumulation had been in Archangel and that the
greater part of these stores had now been removed by
the Bolsheviki. His reference to making it possible for Russian forces to come together in an organized body in the
north reflects either his exaggerated idea of German activity
in that area—so characteristic of Allied statesmanship at
that time—or his own inability or reluctance, whichever it
may have been, to recognize the full bitterness of Russian
civil strife. His language indicates only that he was suspicious of British and French intentions, and did not intend

that American forces should be used for any intervention into the interior or any direct interference into Russian internal affairs.

The British command, once again, did not wait for the American contingent to arrive before launching the attack on Archangel for which it had long been itching. A French colonial battalion, representing the French contribution to the North Russian scheme, arrived in Murmansk in early July. With this reinforcement, General Poole now assembled a little amphibious expedition for the seizure of Archangel. It left Murmansk on July 30 and arrived off Archangel on August first. The city was delivered into the Allied hands without bloodshed by a few anti-Bolshevik figures, who staged a successful uprising on the eve of the arrival of the Allied force. But the Bolsheviki mounted more serious resistance in the outskirts, and soon formed an encircling front at a certain distance from the city. Within a very short time the tiny Anglo-French force found itself, in view of the nature of the terrain and the enormous distances involved, seriously overextended.

The American battalions meanwhile had been duly turned over to British command in England. Fitted out with British clothing and old Russian rifles, they were packed onto three old transports and sent off to Murmansk. They were mostly young Polish-American boys from Michigan and Wisconsin. They had very little training and were of course quite without combat experience. While this contingent was en route to Murmansk, the British command, worried about the Archangel situation, rerouted them, without further ado, to Archangel. They arrived there on September 4, on a cold and rainy afternoon. Of those who were healthy (many had been taken by the Spanish influenza during the journey) two battalions were packed off to the front directly from the boat. Some of them found themselves the following morning occupying front positions deep in the interior, in the vast swampy forests of North Russia, confronting an adversary whose identity and nature were as much a mystery to them as were the reasons why they were fighting at all. The adversary was, of course, the Soviet Red army; and these men were, unbeknownst to themselves and to the President who had authorized their use, virtually participating in the Russian civil war.

Reports of all this, of course, reached Washington; but

they did so very indirectly, in view of the fact that the men were under British command. By the time the senior figures in Washington got any real idea of what dispositions were being made of these units, the German army was collapsing, the World War was coming to an end, and there were many more important things for people in Washington to think about. It was no time now for protests or questions to the British about the uses to which the American battalions were being put.

I have concentrated here on the *American* motives for the Archangel expedition because the Americans did provide, initially, the bulk of the force, and because it is mainly against the "American imperialists" that Soviet charges have been advanced. In presenting to you this picture of the origin of the North Russian expedition, I have no desire to paint the lily. The driving impulse of this entire action came from the British military planners. The expedition was at all times under British command. The origins of the expedition were strung out over a period of five months, during which there were many changes and fluctuations in the background situation, in the relations between the Allies and the Soviet government, and in the motives and calculations of people on the Allied side. Dislike of the Bolshevik regime, a recognition of the boundless hatred of this regime for Western society, suspicion of the degree of its subservience to Germany, and a desire to see it replaced with a Russian regime which would make an effort to carry on the war, all certainly played a part in the Allied policies and motives that led to the North Russian intervention. This was, as you will see, a very complex matter.

But to picture the action as deriving only from a desire to overthrow the Soviet government for reasons of social ideology is to ignore a host of factors, including World War I itself, the highhanded removal of the war stores from Archangel, the friendly attitude of the Murmansk Soviet, and the express desire of the main military contributor, the United States government, to avoid anything like a direct interference in Russian internal affairs. At what point the greed of the Allied capitalists had anything to do with the course of these events is something that escapes me entirely. The decisions were military decisions, taken in strict wartime secrecy; and I doubt that any "capitalists" had knowledge of them at the time. The simple fact remains: had a world

war not been in progress, there would never, under any
conceivable stretch of the imagination, have been an Allied
intervention in North Russia.

6 Collapse in the North

EARLIER I described how, at the time of the Brest-
Litovsk crisis, the Allied diplomatic missions in Petrograd
were obliged to leave that capital, which it was feared might
be seized by the Germans, and to repair to the provincial
town of Vologda, some three hundred miles to the east. Here,
in the course of time, they settled down in reasonable comfort; and Vologda now became a little diplomatic capital,
with a diplomatic corps but without a government. The unofficial envoys in Moscow tended to laugh at the Vologda diplomats—at their remoteness from the center of events and
their tendency to give credence to every anti-Soviet rumor
that came their way—and there was, indeed, something of
the absurd in their situation. But their presence in Vologda
had a serious purpose. They were reluctant to give the Germans the impression that the Entente had abandoned the
contest for the wartime orientation of Russia. And, remembering the manner in which both sides in World War I never
failed to exaggerate the intentions and activities of the Allied
envoys on Russian territory did worry the Germans a bit,
and did enter into their calculations as to the number of
armed men they could afford to remove from the eastern
front.

Actually, the diplomats did not remain in Vologda very
long. By the end of June the Soviet government began to
pick up evidences of the intentions of the British and French
to intervene forcefully in the Russian north, and also of secret
Allied contacts with the various opposition groups in Russia.
The Soviet leaders began, therefore, to view the Vologda diplomats and their activities with baleful anxiety, suspecting,
not without some justification, that certain of them were plot-

ting with the Russian Whites for a revolt against Bolshevik
authority in the entire Vologda area, and that this stood in
some connection with rumored landings in the north.

When, therefore, the German ambassador, Count Mirbach, was murdered in Moscow on July 4, and revolts by
the Left S-R's broke out in Moscow and in the city of
Yaroslav, between Moscow and Vologda, the Soviet leaders
became extremely apprehensive about the Vologda diplomats,
and began to urge them to move to Moscow. The reason
offered for these urgings was a concern for their safety;
and in this the Soviet leaders may have been partly sincere; they had, after all, been seriously embarrassed by Mirbach's murder. But the diplomats, recalling the recent fate of
the German, were not much impressed with the advantages
of Moscow from the standpoint of their personal protection.
They had good reason to suspect that a more compelling
motive in the minds of the Soviet leaders was the reflection
that if the diplomats could once be lured to Moscow, they
would serve as rather juicy hostages in the event of Allied
military intervention.

The exchanges that took place on this subject, by letter
and telegraph, between Foreign Commissar Chicherin and
Ambassador Francis, as dean of the diplomatic corps, make
delightful reading. Neither Francis nor Chicherin cared to
mention the thing uppermost in both their minds, which was
the probable imminence of an Allied intervention. For this
reason, their exchanges took on a disingenuousness extreme
even for the diplomatic profession. Here the deepest wiles of
Russian diplomacy were pitted against Mr. Francis's many
years of immersion in the intricacies of Missouri politics.
Chicherin painted in rosy colors the beauties and amenities
of life in the new Russian capital, and even murmured
things about Soviet enthusiasm for the views of Abraham
Lincoln. Mr. Francis dwelt on the friendliness by which he
felt himself surrounded among the inhabitants of Vologda,
pointed out that the danger most to be feared was that of
the German occupation of Moscow, and saw no reason for
a change of residence.

As these exchanges were taking place in mid-July, the
Vologda diplomats received a secret message from Major
General F. C. Poole, the commander of the North Russian
expedition, definitely confirming the British intention to
intervene in Archangel at the end of the month. Poole re-

quested the diplomats to try to get out of Soviet-held territory, through Archangel, before the expedition arrived. Their problem was first to induce the Soviet government to permit them to proceed to Archangel, and then to time their departure so as to arrive there not too long before the Allied attack, but under no circumstances after it.

On July 23, just after receiving a final urgent and dramatic appeal from Chicherin, the envoys asked for a locomotive for their special train, which had been standing in the Vologda station since March. Francis skillfully avoided saying in which direction they proposed to go. Some of the diplomats paced the station platform anxiously that night, contemplating with foreboding the possibility that the engine might be put at the wrong end of the train and that they would all wake up in Moscow instead of Archangel. But this ordeal, at least, they were spared. The engine was duly placed at the northern end of the train; and they proceeded to Archangel. Their arrival, as it turned out, was a bit premature. It anticipated the arrival of the Allied fleet by one week.

The presence of diplomats presented a real problem to the Bolshevik authorities in Archangel, who were now extremely nervous about everything the Allies did. They correctly suspected that their illustrious guests had arrived for no good purpose. They therefore loaded them onto a Russian vessel and dispatched them to the British-held port of Kandalaksha, across the White Sea.

A supreme touch of irony, and one which well illustrated the confusion in the Allied approach to Russia, occurred at the moment of the departure of the diplomats from Archangel, in the early dawn of July 29. Just as the ship was about to cast off, a train from the interior pulled into the dockside station and disgorged, among its other passengers, the members of a British commercial good-will mission, which some innocent official of the Board of Trade had chosen this moment to dispatch to Russia. These unfortunate people had actually got as far as Moscow before discovering that the situation in Russia was propitious neither to commerce not to good will, nor even to their own safety; and they had made a hasty escape to Archangel. They, too, boarded the diplomatic Argosy at the last second, enormously relieved to be seeing the last of Russia, and no longer especially concerned for the good will of its inhabitants.

In this way the Allied ambassadors escaped the unpleasantness that would probably have awaited them had they been on Soviet territory when the British force arrived. The numerous junior Allied military and consular staffs left in Moscow and Petrograd were not so fortunate. No one, of course, bothered to tell them of the Allied plans, or to give them a chance to get out in good time. Once the intervention had begun, hundreds of them were arrested and spent varying periods of incarceration in the hands of the Soviet secret police. The British naval attaché in Petrograd, Captain Francis N. A. Cromie, was brutally murdered by a mob on the staircase of the British embassy. Bruce Lockhart was obliged to endure weeks of confinement in the Kremlin as a prisoner of state, and only narrowly escaped with his life. The staffs were, however, finally released; and most of these people were out of Russia by the end of 1918.

The German embassy, meanwhile, had by this time also been withdrawn. It was, as I mentioned, on July 4, some four weeks before the beginning of the Allied intervention, that the German ambassador, Count Mirbach, was murdered. His successor, Helfferich, had arrived two or three weeks later, but spent only a few days in Moscow, during most of which time he prudently remained in the cellar of his embassy. He is said to have left the building only once during his entire stay. He was recalled early in August, and departed with a sense of relief no smaller than that of the English good-will envoys.

The result was that by the end of 1918 there was no longer any official representation of any of the major Western governments in Moscow. So far as the Allies were concerned, this was one of the prices paid for the dubious advantages of the intervention. How high a price this really was is something about which, of course, we can only speculate. In later years, it is true, Western diplomats would find that they could do little by their presence in Moscow to affect the outlook of the Soviet leaders or the course of the relations between their countries and the Soviet Union. It is possible, of course, that the results would have been no better even had the Allied governments contrived to retain some sort of representation there in 1918. But it is my own belief, with which some may not agree, that the Soviet leaders were at that time more impressionable, more accessible to outside stimuli, than they were later; that their attitude toward the United States in particular had not yet fully solidified; and that there were at that time certain slender possibilities for influencing them through personal contact, which obviously disappeared at a later date. I would be the first to admit, however, that nothing could have been accomplished in this way unless the Allied governments, as a corollary to leaving their official staffs in Russia, had refrained from the intervention.

But to return to North Russia. You will remember that Archangel was delivered, without bloodshed, into Allied hands by virtue of the fact that on the day before the arrival of the Allied fleet, a successful political *Putsch* was carried out against the Bolsheviki. This action was led by a Russian naval officer named Chaplin. He was, of course, in touch with the British command and appears, indeed, to have masqueraded in British naval uniform during the time he was preparing the overthrow. He and his associates in this action were, like most of the ex-officers, passionate conservatives, opponents not just of the second Revolution but of the first as well.

I described earlier the state of latent civil war that existed in the anti-Bolshevik camp between the conservative ex-officer element and the liberal S-R's. Let us now note how this worked itself out in North Russia.

No sooner had the landing been successfully carried out and a military front against the Communists established around the city, than the trouble began. The French, it seems, had also been negotiating with underground Russian groups, but this time with the S-R's. As a result of these French efforts, the S-R's were prepared to establish a government of sorts in Archangel in the wake of the liberation of the city from the Bolsheviki. The head of this government was to be a venerable figure of the Russian revolutionary movement, Nicholas Chaikovski—a socialist, a theorist, a man no doubt of purest motives and highest character, but wholly inexperienced in military matters and administration. He and some of his associates arrived in town just before the *Putsch;* and once the city had changed hands, they proceeded immediately, with Allied blessing, to set up their government.

Chaplin and his friends, glowing with pride over the success of their military uprising against the Bolsheviki, were amazed and indignant to discover that there was no place for them in the new regime. What followed was as tragic in its implications as it was ludicrous in detail. The sources of friction and confusion seemed to be without end. Within a matter of days after the landing, Chaplin and Chaikovski were at each other's throats. Sharp tension had also arisen between the new government and the British command, which tended to favor Chaplin. At this point the Allied ambassadors, having completed their peregrinations on the White Sea, arrived back in town and complicated things still further. They found themselves in agreement neither with each other nor with the British military command about the numerous political problems which at once arose.

From here on, the situation was little short of chaotic. Chaikovski and the ex-officers fought endlessly. They could not agree on how a military force was to be organized, who should command it, or even who should be responsible for law and order in the city. When Chaikovski suggested that Kerensky might be encouraged to come to Archangel, Chaplin announced that if he did so, he would have him arrested. With the British, Chaikovski fought over all sorts of things: over the measure of *his* powers as opposed to those of the British commander; over whether the red flag—still the flag of the liberal Russian Socialists as well as the Bolsheviki—should be flown from Russian buildings; over the establishment of a Russian military command; over censorship; over military courts; over just about everything. Both Russian groups intrigued frantically with the ambassadors, and labored, not unsuccessfully, to play them off against each other and against the British commander. All these quarrels served to disgust the working-class elements in the city, and to disillusion them both with the new government and with the Allies. The moral authority of the new regime rapidly waned. Its power was not openly challenged, in view of the presence of the Allied troops; but it was neither respected nor widely obeyed.

This ridiculous and basically dangerous situation came to a head, about one month after the landing, in a manner which was as revealing as it was appalling in its implications. On September 4, the American contingent, to the dispatch of which Wilson had so reluctantly and belatedly agreed, arrived in the port. You will recall that two of the three battalions were at once dispatched to the front, where things were not going well at all. The third was kept, for the moment, in the city; and it was arranged that on the sixth it should parade publicly before the British commanding officer, General Poole, and the Allied ambassadors. As the parade was nearing its close, General Poole casual-

ly observed to Ambassador Francis, who was standing next
to him in the reviewing stand, that there had been a revolution during the night and that the government had been arrested and sent to Solovetski Island, in the White Sea. To
this the dumfounded Francis could only reply: "The hell
you say." The general's statement turned out to be entirely
correct. The Tsarist ex-officers, bored with their exclusion
from public affairs and thirsting for some sort of excitement,
had kidnaped the government in the middle of the night,
placed them on a ship, exported them to Solovetski Island,
and usurped their powers.

The ambassadors were flabbergasted. They had been in
no way consulted. This development was politically disastrous.
Chaplin and his associates were anathema to the industrial
workers and to the rank-and-file members of the local garrison. With them in the seats of power, it would, plainly,
never be possible to recruit a Russian armed force locally;
yet to make this possible was, after all, the main purpose of
the Allied expedition.

Largely at the insistence of the American ambassador, the
government was brought back to Archangel and reinstalled.
Chaplin was exiled to a remote part of the province. The
British commander, General Poole, whom no one believed to
be wholly innocent of complicity in this episode, was soon
replaced by Major General W. E. Ironside,[36] who proved to
be a splendid person for the job. But the damage could not
be undone. The prestige of Chaikovski's government was now
wholly shattered. Within a few weeks it practically disintegrated, leaving the control of the area in effect to the British
commander and to such Russian military officers as he
could get to help him. This arrangement served to preserve
order so long as the Allied troops were there; but the lack
of any respected anti-Communist political authority in the
area, and of any sort of domestic-political appeal to the Russian people, was an insuperable barrier to the successful recruitment of a Russian armed force. In whose name were
the recruits supposed to be fighting, and for what? None
were particularly interested in serving foreigners for their
own sakes. The workers were hostile, the peasantry apathetic. The peasant could be induced to fight only for the
protection of his own village and his own property. He had
little interest in Russian politics on the national scale, and
still less in the complicated quarrels of the Allied missions
and the anti-Bolshevik Russian factions in Archangel. Such

Russian units as were eventually scraped together out of this skeptical and disaffected populace proved to be quite unreliable; many eventually revolted and went over to the Bolsheviki.

As a result of the complete political failure of the intervention, the military burden of defending the Archangel perimeter was now left almost exclusively to the tiny and wholly inadequate Allied contingent. All that this force could do was to dig in on a periphery some hundred miles from Archangel.

On November 11, only three months after the expedition had arrived, World War I came to an end. This placed in question the entire rationale of the undertaking. What were the Allied forces in Archangel supposed to be fighting for, now? To the Americans, in particular, to whom the expedition had always been portrayed as part of the war against Germany, this was a crucial question. Yet withdrawal was not immediately possible. The river and port were already rapidly freezing up. It was considered impossible to abandon abruptly the anti-Bolshevik Russians who had staked their lives and their political reputations on collaboration with the Allies. Besides, the Russian question was about to become the subject of discussion among the Allied statesmen at the Peace Conference. There was a general feeling that no decisions should be taken about the forces in Russia until the senior statesmen had a chance to meet and to decide what they wanted to do.

The forces therefore remained at their lonely outposts in the great northern forests. Very soon the terrible Arctic winter set in, with temperatures of fifty degrees below zero, and only two hours of daylight out of the twenty-four. For the Americans, this was a particularly excruciating ordeal. Homesick and bewildered, devoid of any plausible knowledge of why they were there, huddled in their snowed-in blockhouses, obliged constantly to be on the alert against Bolshevik raids against their exposed positions, lacking in any proper training or combat experience, devoid of any independent command of their own and in some instances very poorly officered by the British, these unfortunate men clung on through the seemingly endless winter.

It is no wonder, in these circumstances, that morale began to disintegrate. Disciplinary troubles, bordering in some instances on mutiny, occurred in a number of the Allied units. It was only with the greatest of difficulty that the troops could be kept in hand and induced to carry on.

Morale received a further blow when one of the forward American positions, which had been unwisely occupied and was particularly exposed, had to be abandoned and the force withdrawn, with great danger and hardship, under Bolshevik attack.

To understand the strain on these men it must be remembered that this was in the immediate post-hostilities period, following on a long and exhausting world war. Their comrades in all other theaters of operation were already being demobilized and returned to their homes. They alone had to endure this purgatory, and this for reasons never adequately explained to them.

By the time the statesmen in Paris got around to the discussion of the Russian problem, it was January 1919. The failure of the Archangel expedition to serve any useful purpose was already quite clear to Wilson and Lloyd George. The French and Italians wished to see the intervention continued; but neither was willing to put up troops for a reinforcement of the Allied contingent. Wilson never wavered in his determination that the American units should be withdrawn as soon as weather conditions permitted; and this was done. The Americans accordingly left in June and July 1919.

The timing and origins of the British decision to withdraw the remainder of the expedition are somewhat obscure. A decision to this effect seems to have been taken in London as early as the beginning of March 1919; but it was then decided to send a large fresh contingent to cover the withdrawal of the entire force. This relief contingent mounted a new and fairly successful offensive in midsummer, ostensibly to relieve the front before evacuation. Perhaps this *was* its only purpose. Yet one has the impression that, had the White forces in Siberia, under Admiral A. V. Kolchak, not then been in full retreat on the Urals front so that there was little possibility of linking up with them, it might not have been *too* difficult to prevail upon London to authorize the continuation of the action. Hope for a linking of the Siberian and northern interventions died hard in the British War Office. In any case, Kolchak *was* retreating; there seemed little prospect of linking up with him; and the British command in the north was bothered by mutinies among the Russian units associated with the expedition. There was, in these circumstances, little to be gained by pressing on. On September 27, a little over a year after the arrival of the expedition, the last of the British and other Allied forces left Archangel. A similar withdrawal was then promptly carried out at Murmansk. The intervention was over.

This final evacuation was, of course, an excruciatingly difficult step to take, in view of what it meant to all those Russians who had collaborated with the Allied expedition. The full burden fell on the last British commander, General Ironside, who bore it like a man and carried out the operation with composure and efficiency. General Ironside offered to evacuate as many as possible of those Russians who wanted to go. But the senior Russian military officer, General E. Miller, who had been brought in from western Europe to take this command and who was a man of superior character and intelligence (later to be kidnaped by the Soviet secret police in Paris), manfully refused the offer and declared his intention of carrying on.

Relieved of the stigma and the ambiguity of the association with the Allies, Miller did quite well for a time after their departure. But by January 1920, when the collapse of Kolchak in Siberia became generally known, Miller's force, too, began to disintegrate. The disintegration was so rapid that no complete evacuation was possible. Whole sections of the front just melted away, as they had in 1917 on the eastern front. Miller himself escaped at the last moment, traveling on an old American pleasure yacht which had been bought by the Russian government for a submarine chaser, and which was commanded, ironically enough, by the same Chaplin who had engineered the initial *Putsch* in the city, a year earlier.

On February 21, Red troops entered Archangel, to be greeted by the cautious citizens with a welcome no whit less enthusiastic than that which had originally greeted the arriving Allies. On or about the same time, Murmansk also was occupied by the Reds. Estimates of the number of Russians subsequently shot for collaborating with the Allies run from ten to thirty thousand.

The losses of the British forces in the Archangel intervention were 41 officers and 286 other ranks killed, and several hundred more casualties of other sorts. The Americans appear to have had 139 dead of injuries or accidents. This would have made for both British and Americans a total of less than 500 killed in the entire operation. If one compares these figures with the casualties suffered by the Allied forces on the western front, particularly the British, during the year 1918 alone, one will at once see how trivial in the military sense were these skirmishes in North Russia in relation to the major effort in which the Allied armies were then engaged.

7 The Siberian Intervention

ANYONE WHO sets out to give in brief compass an adequate picture of the origins of the Siberian intervention imposes on himself an almost impossible task. It would be utterly futile for me to attempt to give you anything like a chronological account of the maze of influences, misunderstandings, decisions, and coincidences that lay behind this most confused undertaking. All I can do is to attempt to describe some of the most important ingredients of this fantastic brew and to give in conclusion a rough idea of the manner in which they combined to produce it.

Let me remind you, first, of the geography. The main line of the Trans-Siberian Railway between Irkutsk and Vladivostok did not run, in 1918, entirely through Russian territory but passed through northern Manchuria. To be sure, an alternate route—the so-called Amur line—had been constructed shortly before the war on Russian territory, skirting the borders of Manchuria; but at the time of World War I the Amur line was still primitive and deficient in carrying capacity. The Chinese Eastern Railway, which was the Manchurian portion of the Trans-Siberian, was still the main route.

The Chinese Eastern was, in effect, owned and operated up to the time of the Revolution by the Russian government. Russian rights and privileges in the zone along the railway were such that the Russian government virtually controlled northern Manchuria. The Russian director of the

Chinese Eastern Railway was in the position of military governor of the entire region.

The exhaustion of Russia in the World War, and the final collapse of her power in the two Revolutions, naturally opened up for the Japanese—who controlled South Manchuria and were the leading rivals to the Russians in that area—a unique opportunity for extending their control to North Manchuria as well, and for gaining commercial domination of eastern Siberia. Formally, of course, the Japanese were allies of Russia. Until the Bolsheviki took Russia out of the war entirely, the Japanese were obliged, therefore, to exercise restraint and to proceed cautiously in their efforts to profit from the situation. But even in the Tsarist period, before the first Revolution, there had been much talk about a possible Japanese occupation of Siberia in the event that Russia should ever abandon the Entente and make a separate peace. The fear of this eventuality had become, in fact, something of an obsession to the people of Siberia. Now, with the Bolshevik Revolution and the departure of Russia from the war, this question and the question of the future of Manchuria at once became acute.

Of the two possibilities, it was the Manchurian one that most interested the Japanese. This also caused anxiety to the United States, in view of the traditional American interest in China and the Open Door. One must not forget that the Far Eastern intervention was a matter affecting not only Russia but also China.

So far as Siberia was concerned, Japanese policy in the months immediately following the November Revolution was governed by delicate compromises among a number of conflicting considerations. The Japanese wanted the dominant position in Siberia. They wanted military control of the Maritime Province. They did not want to make any direct annexation of Russian territory, but they wanted to be in the driver's seat there. They were frightened, however, of involving themselves in a costly military effort inside Siberia without the guarantee of American financial and political support. On the other hand, remembering unpleasant experiences they had had in their relations with the Western governments in the past, they were unhappy about the thought of trying to do anything in Siberia in conjunction with these governments. They were afraid this would hamper their freedom of action, and that they would be deprived of the fruits of their effort. If they had to collaborate with anyone in such a venture, they would have preferred that it be the weak government of northern China, which was dependent on them financially and militarily.

Naturally, these various considerations commended themselves in varying degree to different elements within the Japanese governmental structure, with the result that there was considerable internal disagreement, sometimes even contradiction and confusion, in the end-product of Japanese diplomacy.

So much for the Japanese. Now for the second background factor: the situation in Vladivostok.

In the port of Vladivostok there had accumulated, by the time of the November Revolution, a mass of war stores at least four times as great as the huge accumulation in Archangel. The Russian government, in its boundless inefficiency, had contrived to purchase war materials in America and elsewhere and to bring them to Vladivostok in quantities far exceeding the capacity of the Trans-Siberian Railway to remove them in any short space of time. When the November Revolution occurred, more than eight hundred thousand tons of these supplies were strewn, literally, all over the enormous port area of Vladivostok. Great quantities of them lay in the open air, exposed to all the vicissitudes of the weather, to pilferage and decay. This, again, was a source of indignation and constant anxiety to the Allies. The possibility of their seizure and removal by or for the Germans was, to be sure, greatly exaggerated in the Allied camp. But the stores did constitute an important factor in the Allied calculations.

As in the case of Archangel and Murmansk, the Bolshevik take-over did not occur immediately at Vladivostok. A number of factors—the greater cosmopolitanism of an oceanic port, the presence of foreign naval vessels, the extensive dependence on overseas contacts for supplies and the maintenance of economic activity—all these things delayed the process of Bolshevization. But here, as elsewhere, the Communists were tireless in their effort. The months following the November Revolution saw a steady growth of Communist influence in the port. With the advent of spring, Communist authority was predominant among the Russian garrisons there. And the attitude the Communists took towards the Western interests in the Far Eastern region was so contemptuous, so full of deliberate injury and insult, that it is no wonder the Western Allied representatives there

were turned into irate opponents of the Bolsheviki. They
were encouraged in this, of course, by many of the inhabitants, who begged for any sort of Allied occupation, other
than one by the Japanese alone, in order that they might
be spared the hardships of Communist rule.

Third, I must mention the attitudes of the British and
French governments.

I have already referred to the schemes entertained by the
Allied military planners at Versailles for the restoration of
an eastern front by combined action from Siberia and North
Russia. Some of the British also had dreams of extending
this action down the Volga and linking it up with anti-
Bolshevik forces in South Russia. This idea of the re-establishment of an eastern front by action through Siberia
arose in the first few weeks after the November Revolution.
Some of the British planners never lost their love for it,
nor abandoned their hope of its implementation, until long
after the war was over. In their efforts to bring it about,
they had the enthusiastic support of the French. The French
were at all times the ardent protagonists of an Allied intervention anywhere in Russia, and the more of it the better.
But in early 1918 they themselves were, of course, not in a
position to contribute any sizable military force to its accomplishment, in view of their commitments on the western front. The British were in the same position. This is
why, whereas all the enthusiasm for the intervention was
on the Anglo-French side, all the schemes for its implementation looked to the Americans and the Japanese to put up
the bulk of the forces.

Balfour and Lloyd George were personally never too keen
on these schemes. But they found it difficult to oppose in
wartime both their own military planners and the French.
They tended, therefore, to ease their position by saying
that if President Wilson could be persuaded, they would
go along. The result was to shift the military pressure to
the United States government. So intensive and high-powered was this pressure that throughout the first six months
of 1918 the Siberian question constituted Washington's leading problem of foreign affairs. More than any other question
of foreign policy, Siberia pre-empted the time and concern
of the senior American officials in this period. As the diplomatic battle over the subject proceeded, even the Foreign
Office in London gradually warmed to the cause. By June

1918 the British and French pressures on Washington had assumed the dimensions of a major campaign.

As in the case of North Russia, the leaders of the United States government, political and military, had no enthusiasm for any of these schemes. Time and time again they voiced to each other and to Allied representatives their skepticism as to what could be achieved by the entry of Allied forces into Siberia. They were most reluctant to encourage the Japanese to move troops into either Siberia or Manchuria; and they properly recognized that any move by any of the other Allies, or any encouragement given to the Japanese, would cause the Japanese to move at once. Wilson and the few associates with whom he discussed this matter were unanimous in the view—and it was an entirely correct one, as history would show—that even in the best of circumstances the Japanese could not be induced to move farther west than Irkutsk, which was still some three thousand miles east of the nearest German forces. For this reason the Americans simply doubted the feasibility of any effort to restore in this manner a front against the Germans. With the best of will, I am unable to find any flaw, even today, in this reasoning.

Wilson did, of course, eventually consent to send an American force. He did so for reasons which I shall attempt to explain shortly. But it was against his better judgment. Had it not been for the consistent British and French pressures in this direction, he would never have dreamed of doing it.

The fourth background factor we have to note is the presence of German and Austro-Hungarian war prisoners in Siberia.

At the time of the Russian departure from the war, there were in all of Russia about one million six hundred thousand war prisoners, of whom roughly half were in Siberia. These latter were not very closely guarded. A great many of them were working peacefully at regular jobs on farms or elsewhere. The overwhelming majority were the prisoners from the Austro-Hungarian Empire, and non-German-speaking. Germans made up something less than one tenth of the total.

As soon as the Communists seized Siberia, they busily set about trying to disaffect these men from their loyalty to their own governments, with a view to making thoroughgoing Communists of them and enlisting them in Communist armed units. In this they met with some small success. Many joined up in order to obtain better food and privileges. But only a small number of these proved to be reliable Communists, and not more than five to ten thousand at the most were ever armed by the Bolsheviki in all Siberia. Of these, scarcely any were Germans.

The German and Austrian governments strongly objected to this whole procedure. As soon as their prisoner-of-war missions appeared on the scene, after ratification of the Brest-Litovsk Treaty, recruitment of these men by the Communists was stopped, at German insistence. Thus the prisoners never at any time constituted a vehicle through which German military influence could have been exerted in Siberia.

But warring governments are not wholly rational; and for months on end the Allied chanceries were agitated by the specter of Siberia's being taken over by the Germans through the agency of these prisoners. The most fertile sources of scare-stories along this line seem to have been the French officials in Irkutsk, and Japanese officialdom generally. The French evidently hoped that the prospect of Siberia's being seized by the Germans in this way would stimulate American interest in an Allied military intervention. The Japanese were anxious to establish a respectable rationale for such unilateral action as they might wish, in future, to take. The Russian Whites, of course, also took great delight in encouraging the propagation of this particular myth which fitted so admirably with the myth of the Bolsheviki being German agents. Even the United States government, which was at first skeptical, was finally persuaded that the danger was a real one, and allowed itself to be importantly influenced by this conclusion.

I have spoken about the intensity of war hysteria on the Allied side at this period. In the readiness of the Allied chanceries to believe that Siberia was in danger of being seized by the German government through the agency of the war prisoners you have a good example of the damage this sort of hysteria can do.

The war prisoners were not the only body of men from the Austro-Hungarian Empire whose presence in Siberia at this crucial juncture must be mentioned. There was another, of even greater importance. This was the Czechoslovak Corps, sometimes known as the Czechoslovak Legion. I mentioned this body in connection with the northern

intervention. Composed partly of men from the Czech colonies in the former Russian Empire and partly of defectors
from the Austro-Hungarian army, this force, consisting in
all of some two divisions, was permitted by the Provisional
Government to become a part of the Russian army on the
eastern front in 1917. The Czechs were, of course, violently
anti-Hapsburg, and happy to fight on the Russian side, in
the belief that their country would gain at least its auton-
omy from an Allied victory. They were extensively used by
the Russians for reconnaissance work, and played a considerable part in the Galician campaign of the summer of
1917.

When the Russian army disintegrated, the Czech Corps
alone retained its discipline and combat capacity. For this
reason it was extensively used by the Russian command,
in the final stage of the breakdown, for guarding stores of
arms and ammunition. The Czechs, of course, took advantage of this, and occasionally helped themselves. By the
time the Brest-Litovsk Treaty was concluded, they were
excellently armed. When the disintegration of the Russian
army was complete, the Corps found itself, to its own astonishment, the strongest armed unit in Russia.

As the Germans moved into the Ukraine, which they began to do at the end of February in 1918, the Czech Corps
was obliged to evacuate the area and seek some new employment. Only by fighting a heavy rear guard action did
it succeed in avoiding encirclement and capture by the
Germans. As a result of arrangements made by the Czechoslovak National Committee in Paris, the Corps was now officially
classed as an Allied force, and was formally subordinated
to the French Supreme Command. It was the desire
of both the French government and the Czech leaders
that it be brought to the western front, for service there
against the Germans. Since there seemed at that time to be
no other suitable way of getting out of Russia, it was decided that the Corps should move across Siberia and be
evacuated through Vladivostok. In the month of March 1918,
accordingly, agreements were hastily concluded with the
Soviet government whereby the Czechs agreed to give up
all but a small portion of their arms, and the Soviet authorities agreed, in return, to give the Czechs free passage
across Siberia. By the end of March, the first trainloads of
these Czechs were already moving out in the direction of the
Urals and Siberia. By the middle of May, some fifteen thou-

sand of them had arrived in Vladivostok. The remainder were strung out along the Trans-Siberian in trainloads, all the way from a point west of the Volga in central Russia to Irkutsk—a distance of some three thousand miles. Their total number was in the neighborhood of forty thousand. Despite the agreement with the Soviet authorities, they had contrived to conceal stocks of arms in their trains, and were well equipped to take care of themselves.

By mid-May the passage of the Czech Corps through Siberia began to lead to considerable friction between the Czechs and the Soviet authorities. Both sides were at fault. Misunderstandings and poor discipline on both sides played a part. In the middle of May the situation was aggravated by a serious incident which took place at Chelyabinsk, in the Urals. A week or two later, fighting broke out between the Czechs and the Soviet authorities all along the road. The Czechs were at once enthusiastically joined by anti-Bolshevik Russian factions, who had been in the underground and who seized on the Czech uprising as a means of overthrowing the Communists and gaining power. There had, in fact, been some collusion. Within a few days after the uprising began, the Czechs seized, without great difficulty, most of this three thousand miles of railway from the Volga to the neighborhood of Irkutsk; and they took under control, together with their Russian White allies, a good deal of the neighboring territory. The Czech uprising led, in other words, to the immediate overthrow of Soviet authority throughout a major portion of western Siberia and the Urals.

Soviet propagandists have never ceased to charge the Allies with having instigated the Czech uprising. The charge is in fact false; but its political implications are not far short of the mark. The Allied governments could not have been more pleased than they were when they learned of the uprising. The French and British immediately seized on it as an opportunity for furthering their plans for the creation of a new eastern front. Many Allied officials, I have no doubt, regretted that they had not thought of such a possibility themselves; they would have been delighted to claim credit for it. But the fact is that they neither foresaw nor instigated it. It dropped into their lap like manna from heaven.

So much for the movements in the background. Now let me try to tell you briefly how it came about that the Allied

troops were sent to Siberia. Let us return to the beginning of 1918, and the diplomatic exchanges between the
Allied governments on this subject.

Since the Americans refused, initially, to consider participation in a joint Allied expedition to Siberia, the next move,
inspired by the British military planners at the Supreme War
Council, was to ask the United States to agree to invite
the Japanese to intervene alone, as mandatory for the
other Allies. At the height of the Brest-Litovsk crisis, in
February and early March of 1918, great pressure was
brought to bear on Wilson to accept this scheme. Again he
refused. When severely pressed, he said that he would not
object, if the others insisted on doing it, but he had no
confidence in the project, and would not give it his blessing.
The Japanese, on the other hand, refused to move without precisely this American blessing. They were reluctant
to get deeply involved in Siberia without a guarantee of
American financial and economic support for the enterprise.
By mid-March this scheme, too, was dead.

From mid-March to mid-May, exchanges on this subject
were dominated by the optimistic reports from Lockhart
about the possibility that the Bolsheviki might be brought to
request or accept an Allied intervention. New pleas were
addressed to Wilson: would he not approve a joint Allied
expedition if Bolshevik consent could be obtained? The
answer, in every case, was that he still could see no point
in it. He could not understand what military advantage was
to be derived. The Japanese would never go east of Irkutsk.
And he was not convinced that the Bolsheviki would ever
accept such a request. In this, too, he was entirely right.

The Allies now took a different tack. Having failed to
get the President's blessing as a prerequisite for Japanese
co-operation, they decided, in June 1918, to go after the
Japanese first and to extract from them, if possible, an assurance that they would be glad to participate in such an expedition if the President would agree to it. Had this maneuver been
successful, it would, of course, have left Wilson isolated, and
faced with a choice of yielding or obstructing the will of the
whole Allied community.

To Wilson's intense pleasure, the Japanese refused to be
caught on this hook. They replied in mid-June that they

... could not feel at liberty to express their decision before
a complete and satisfactory understanding on the question

was reached between the three Powers and the United States.[37]

The truth is that the Japanese military authorities, who were keen on a Japanese action in Siberia, had now had time to complete military preparations for an independent Japanese move, to be taken in conjunction with the helpless Chinese. Thus they were even more reluctant than before to get fouled up with the ulterior purposes of the Western Allies.

I have summarized all this very briefly. I cannot attempt to tell you how numerous and high-powered were the approaches made to the United States government in the course of the discussion of these various projects. In the first five months of 1918 alone, the United States government, in addition to affirming its position in innumerable diplomatic interviews, was obliged on six different occasions to make formal replies rejecting various Allied suggestions. Special Allied envoys were sent to Washington. Appeals were directed to Colonel House, as well as to the President.

These pleas and pressures rose in the month of June to a crescendo. There were several reasons for this. One was the crisis on the western front, where the Germans had broken through the French lines in their last successful offensive of the war. The sound of guns could now be heard in Paris. Preparations were under way for the evacuation of the city. Any expedient that might distract German attention from the western front, however desperate, was grasped at. A second reason was that news of the Czech uprising was now beginning to flow in, and the Allied capitals were becoming aware that large parts of Siberia were no longer in Bolshevik hands. There was a general belief, not only in the West but among Allied representatives in Russia as well, that the fall of the Soviet government was in any case imminent.

By the middle of June, Wilson, while still skeptical about the British and French plans, and in fact wearied and irritated by the endless appeals to which he had been subjected from this quarter, had finally come to the conclusion that the Siberian situation could no longer be simply left to look after itself. Something, he conceded, would have to be done. He let it be known to the Allies on June 18 that he was giving the entire matter fresh consideration, and would inform them shortly of his decision. This news,

of course, set the Allied chanceries aflame with gossip
and excitement. The pot of speculation and discussion proceeded to boil more furiously than ever.

The men around Wilson were all convinced that what
he had in mind was the dispatch to Siberia of a high-
powered American philanthropic and economic aid mission,
along the lines of the Hoover Commission that had functioned with such success in Belgium. But the President's
mind, as it turned out, was working along quite a different
tack. It was the plight of the Czech Corps that attracted his
attention and seemed to him to provide the handle by which
he could properly and effectively take hold of the perplex-
ing Siberian problem and disarm the pressures being
brought to bear on him from so many quarters.

Everything about the Czechs appealed to Wilson. He
liked little peoples, and disliked big ones. He liked Slavs
and disliked Germans. He admired Masaryk, who was now
in Washington, lobbying for the fortunes of his people. To
Wilson, the Czechs were innocent and idealistic, and in every
way eligible to be patronized.

To understand entirely how the American President's
mind was working, however, I must explain one more facet
of the situation of the Czech Corps, and tell of one more
development in that situation that occurred at the end of
June.

At the time of the Czech uprising there were, as I said
before, some fifteen thousand Czechs already in Vladivostok.
But there happened to be, at the time of the uprising, no
Czech trains on the two-thousand-mile stretch of railway
just east of Irkutsk, between that city and Vladivostok.
The Czechs could, of course, seize only those sections of
the railway where their trains happened to be. They thus
found themselves in possession of part of the railway west
of Irkutsk, but not of the eastern part. The Bolsheviki
dug in around the shores of Lake Baikal; and the Czechs
west of that point found themselves separated by two thousand miles of Communist-held railway from those of their
comrades who had already reached Vladivostok.

By the end of June, the Czechs who had reached Vladivostok had come to the decision that they must move back
to the rescue of their comrades farther west. But it was
impossible for them to use Vladivostok as a military base
against the Bolsheviki while the city was still in the hands of

the Soviet authorities. On June 29, therefore, they proceeded to seize Vladivostok; and they at once appealed to the Allies—as one Allied force to another—to support them in their effort to open up the Trans-Siberian Railway and to re-establish contact with their brethren in central Siberia and the Urals.

Curiously enough, the Czech seizure of Vladivostok occurred on almost exactly the same day as the break between the Murmansk Soviet and Moscow. Thus, by sheer coincidence, the two ports most prominently involved in the projects for Allied intervention fell at the same time into hands eager for such intervention and prepared to welcome it with open arms. It was also sheer coincidence that this should have occurred at precisely the moment when Wilson was on the verge of a decision as to what to do about the intervention in both areas.

During just the days when all this was happening, the Supreme War Council met again and issued the last and most high-powered of many appeals to President Wilson to agree to intervention in Siberia. A joint Allied expedition was again urged, and it was stated as the unanimous opinion of Marshal Foch and the Allied military representatives at the Council that the immediate dispatch of such an expedition was essential for the victory of the Allied armies in the war against Germany.

This appeal reached Washington and was handed to the President by the British ambassador on the afternoon of July 3. On the same day the President learned of the seizure of Vladivostok by the Czechs and of their appeal for aid.

All the following day, July 4, the Secretary of State, whom the President had taken into his confidence, interspersed his other duties with work on the formulation of the decision to which the President was now inclined. On the 5th, the President summoned the key members of his Cabinet and the Chief of Staff to the White House and read to them his decision. The elements of it were as follows:

The establishment of an eastern front via Siberia as suggested by the Supreme War Council was physically impossible and could not be considered. The situation of the Czechs, on the other hand, warranted an Allied effort (and I quote the President's words) "to aid those at Vladivostok in forming a junction with their compatriots in west-

ern Siberia."[38] Provided the Japanese government would
agree to co-operate, the United States government would,
the President said, be prepared to join in getting immediate
supplies of arms and ammunition to the Czechs at Vladivostok and in making available a military force to guard their
line of communication as they moved westward. A force of
seven thousand Americans and seven thousand Japanese was
suggested. The Japanese were to send troops at once, the
Americans as soon as they could get them there. Meanwhile marines, landed from the Allied naval vessels in
Vladivostok, would help the Czechs to hold the city and to
mount their offensive. Finally, it was to be publicly announced that the purpose of the landing was to aid the
Czechoslovaks against German and Austrian prisoners of
war.

This was the essence of Wilson's decision. It represented
a refusal to accede to the appeal of the Supreme War Council, and the selection of an independent course which had
practically no relation to the French and British request. It
was based on serious misinformation about the German-
Austrian prisoners of war, whom Wilson conceived as controlling those portions of the Trans-Siberian not in Czech
hands. It was also based on naïve and unsound assumptions
about Japanese policy and it reflected a somewhat sentimental and idealized view of the Czechs. But the idea that this
small proposed American force should attempt to overthrow the Soviet government and to inflict some other regime on the Russian people never entered the President's
mind at all.

8   The Allies in Siberia

AS I have shown, President Wilson based his decision on
the understanding that the passage of the western body
of Czechs to Vladivostok was being impeded by armed German and Austrian war prisoners. It was for this reason, he

thought, that the Vladivostok Czechs had now decided to move back westward, with a view to opening up communications with their brothers in western Siberia and making possible their continued movement to Vladivostok. The United States was at war with Germany and Austria; and it seemed to the President entirely proper that American soldiers should assist an Allied force, opposed by armed enemy nationals, to extract itself from a chaotic situation, in order to get to the western front.

Wilson's logic, in this case, was sound enough, but his facts were either partially out of date or incorrect. In the first place, it was of course not the war prisoners who were standing in the way of the union of the two bodies of Czechs: it was the Russian Communists. Secondly, Wilson believed that the Czechs were still serious in their intention to get out of Siberia and to proceed to the western front. Actually, the western group of Czechs had now become actively involved, under French and British encouragement, in the Russian civil war in the Urals area. Misled by initial successes, these Czechs were fighting side by side with the Whites against the Communists all through that region. Together with the Whites, they were pursuing the strategic plan, so favored in British military circles, of a junction with the Allied and White forces in the Archangel region. Of all this, Wilson knew nothing.

Before the American troops could reach Siberia, this situation had changed even further. Ironically, the junction between the Vladivostok Czechs and the ones farther west was effected just about two days before the American commander, General William S. Graves, reached Vladivostok with the bulk of the American forces. The main purpose these men had come to serve was thus actually achieved before they arrived. At the other end of the Trans-Siberian Railway, however, the new Red army, which Trotsky had been recruiting and training during the summer, was now beginning to attain real strength. The Czechs were beginning to find themselves seriously overextended and in a precarious military situation. President Wilson's expressed friendliness to their movement caused them to look to the United States for assistance. But Wilson had never dreamed of sending an American contingent deep into the interior of Russia for participation in what was really a Russian civil war. Such a thing was never considered at any time in Washington. Thus, the presence of the American forces in eastern Siberia, in addition to being no longer useful for the main purpose it was designed to serve, soon became a source of bitterness and anti-American feeling among the Czechs themselves, who were precisely the people it was supposed to aid.

But I have jumped ahead of the diplomatic side of my story. I was speaking about the decision the President announced to his inner cabinet on July 5, 1918. The problem at once arose of communicating this to the other Allies. Wilson had taken his decision, as was his habit, in complete loneliness and privacy. He was a man who was not given to consulting with anyone, and particularly anyone not under his own authority. The very idea that he could take a decision of this sort without prior consultation with the other governments involved was a revelation of Wilson's unfamiliarity with the manner in which diplomatic business has to be transacted.

In these circumstances, it is not surprising that the result of this step was not to bring order into the conflict in eastern Siberia and Manchuria but to throw that whole situation into the most appalling confusion.

The British and the French, who now realized that Wilson, after listening to their appeals, had simply taken unilateral action without even the courtesy of advising them in advance that he was going to do so, at once took similar action of their own. They dispatched small military forces and numbers of high officials to Siberia. This took place, of course, without any military or political agreement with the United States—a circumstance from which confusion could not fail to ensue.

The Japanese, while contriving to maintain the pretense of falling in with Wilson's proposal, actually used it simply as a pretext for an expedition of their own on many times the scale Wilson had envisaged. The situation in Manchuria, as a result partly of the Czech seizure of Vladivostok and partly of Wilson's decision, collapsed at once. It gave way to what was, in effect, a Japanese occupation of northern Manchuria and of the Chinese Eastern Railway, for which the Chinese were compelled to act as cover. By the time the Americans finally got there, the whole region of eastern Siberia and Manchuria was in a state of indescribable confusion, with power divided among the Czechs, the Bolsheviki, the Japanese, the Chinese, and two frightful Cossack generals supported by the Japanese, one at one end of the Chinese Eastern Railway and one at the other.

The attempt to achieve, through diplomatic correspondence, some sort of intimacy with the Japanese concerning policy in this region began two days after Wilson's decision, on July 7, when the matter was first taken up with the Japanese ambassador in Washington. It may be said to have been continued almost without interruption for several years to come—even after the departure of the American troops. It was never successful.

Embarrassed by the leaks which began to occur all over the world as soon as the matter had been mentioned to the Japanese, Wilson restated his decision in a long *aide mémoire*, which he typed himself, and which was delivered confidentially to the Allied governments on July 17. A few days later, the Japanese, without prior warning to Washington, announced their own decision to send an expedition, in terms that took scant heed of the President's views. Wilson, whose hand was now forced, at once made public large portions of his *aide mémoire*. This remained the only detailed and authoritative statement ever made of the American reasons for beginning the intervention. It was directly along the lines of the July 5 decision which I have already described. In addition to being based on incorrect information about the Czechs, it was almost wholly out of date within two months after it was written. Yet it was the only political instruction ever given to General Graves, who had to command the Siberian expedition. It was handed to him personally on the eve of his departure for Siberia by the Secretary of War. The only explanation the Secretary had time to give him on that occasion consisted of the following words:

This contains the policy of the United States in Russia which you are to follow. Watch your step; you will be walking on eggs loaded with dynamite. God bless you and good-by.[39]

The text of this American document, which as I say constituted General Graves's orders as well as the public announcement, made it abundantly clear that the American expedition was not conceived by Wilson as a form of military intervention against the Soviet government. Military intervention—the same document stated—

... would add to the present sad confusion in Russia rather than cure it, injure her rather than help her, and ... would be of no advantage in the prosecution of our main design, to win the war against Germany.

The United States government could neither take part in such an intervention nor sanction it in principle; the only legitimate objects for which American troops could be employed were "to help the Czecho-Slovaks ... to guard military stores ... and to render such aid as might be acceptable to the Russians ... "[40]

The American forces, numbering actually a little more than seven thousand men, reached Siberia in August and September 1918. During the year and a half they remained there, their service consisted mostly of guarding limited sections of the Trans-Siberian Railway. I have been able to establish only two occasions on which they participated in any military action against Soviet forces. The first was an incident which took place before General Graves arrived. A small American advance detachment, sent from the Philippines, was persuaded by the Japanese general in Vladivostok to take part in an action which, as the Americans were incorrectly assured, was against German and Austrian prisoners. The Americans did not in fact get into the front line, and I am unable to establish that they ever fired any shots in this engagement.

The other instance of American action against Communists was also a minor one. A detachment of Americans was put to guarding the Suchan coal mines, near Vladivostok, where fuel was obtained for the operations of sections of the Trans-Siberian Railway. At first, relations were good between this detachment and the local inhabitants. But the atrocities of Russian Cossack units in the vicinity—units nominally friendly to the Allies—alienated the population and led to the creation of a partisan movement. When these partisan bands fell under Communist influence, trouble began at the mines; and the Americans were obliged to take action to secure the surrounding territory. This action, too, was on a very minor scale, and involved only a handful of casualties. It was purely defensive, from the American standpoint.

The battle in which the advance American detachment was induced to participate, as I have just related, was one fought against a Communist force opposing the Czechs and the Japanese not far from Vladivostok. It occurred in August

1918, only a few days after the arrival of the first Allied forces in Siberia, and was entirely the result of Japanese initiative. The Communist force was routed and destroyed; and there turned out to be no further serious Bolshevik resistance all the way to Lake Baikal. Since the western group of Czechs had by this time broken through the strong Bolshevik positions on the southern shores of the lake, the road was thus freed of Bolshevik military influence all the way from Vladivostok to the Urals. This removed the necessity of any further action against Communist forces in the eastern part of Siberia, to which the American and Japanese interventions were confined. The nearest hostility on any serious scale between the Bolsheviki and the Whites, during the remainder of the time the Americans were in Siberia, was in the area between the Urals and Baikal, thousands of miles away.

General Graves's battles were therefore mostly of a diplomatic nature and were conducted primarily against the Japanese, the British, and the Cossack generals, all of whom he loathed to the bottom of his soldierly heart. There was, on one occasion, even a small military encounter between the Americans and the forces of one of these Cossack generals.

Within a few weeks after the Allied forces arrived, World War I came to an end. The question may well be asked: Why, in view of the fact that the Czech situation had changed and the war had ended, did the Americans remain in Siberia for another year and a half? Many Americans were asking themselves this question at the time, including Wilson's Secretary of War, Newton D. Baker. Two weeks after the end of the World War, in November 1918, he wrote to the President urging immediate and complete withdrawal. "Two reasons"—he observed—

. . . are assigned for our remaining in Siberia. One is that having entered we cannot withdraw and leave the Japanese. If there be any answer to this it lies in the fact that the longer we stay, the more Japanese there are and the more difficult it may be to induce Japan to withdraw her forces if we set the example. The second reason given is that we must have a military force to act as guardians and police for any civil relief effort we are able to direct toward Siberia. I frankly do not believe this, nor do I believe we have a right to use military force to compel the reception of our relief agencies.[41]

The President himself fully agreed with this view. If he had felt that the decision was his to make, he would have withdrawn the force immediately. But throughout the winter and spring of 1919 he was at the Paris Peace Conference, and he did not wish to take action independently until some general policy toward Russia had been thrashed out with the other Allies. When he returned to the United States in the summer of 1919, he was obliged to throw himself into his tragic and unsuccessful struggle for ratification of the Versailles Treaty and acceptance of the Covenant of the League of Nations. In the midst of this, as you will recall, he was stricken with paralysis; and the United States was for many months effectively without a Chief Executive. In these circumstances, action was postponed during the period of the Peace Conference, and subsequently became a matter for decision by the President's subordinates. Some of the latter, particularly people in the State Department, were strongly anti-Bolshevik and would have liked to see American support given to the anti-Bolshevik regime then established in western Siberia under Admiral A. V. Kolchak. Like the other Allies, they were misled by momentary military successes Kolchak had in the spring of 1919, and concluded that his general chances of success were much better than was actually the case. It was not until August and September 1919 that the American government satisfied itself that Kolchak was failing, and could not be effectively aided except by the direct intervention of foreign troops on a major scale. Any such assistance was regarded at all times in Washington as quite out of the question. By the winter of 1919, the Kolchak regime had collapsed.

In addition to the hopes placed momentarily on Kolchak, there were two other considerations that caused Wilson's subordinates to keep the troops in Siberia throughout the year 1919. The first was that the United States government had involved itself with the other Allies and White Russian elements in an elaborate scheme, called the Inter-Allied Railway Agreement, for operation of the Trans-Siberian and Chinese Eastern railways during such time as Allied troops might be in Siberia. The presence of the American force was needed to meet American commitments under this arrangement. Actually the operation of the scheme was wholly farcical: the Japanese and the others did precisely as they pleased on the sectors of the railway under their military control, letting the Americans foot the bills and supply technical assistance when and as it suited their purposes. But the impulses of a misplaced idealism died slowly in Washington; and the more that Americans saw of Japanese activity and purposes in Siberia, the less inclined they felt to quit the scene and to leave everything to the Japanese.

It was not until the end of 1919 that the policy makers in Washington were able to convince themselves that the American force could not do any more good by remaining in Siberia. It was now becoming clear, furthermore, that Kolchak's resistance to the Bolsheviki was collapsing. The American force, unless removed, would soon be thrust into a conflict with the Communists. The decision was therefore taken at the end of 1919 to remove the troops. The last of them were out by April 1920, just one and a half years after they had entered. When the last contingent left Vladivostok, the Japanese sent a military band to the docks which entertained the departing Americans to the tune of "Hard Times Come Again No More."[42] It had indeed been a turbulent and unhappy episode for everyone. General Graves had defended to the last ditch his orders not to get mixed up in Russian politics or internal affairs, with the result that the other Allies had denounced him as a Bolshevik—whereas the Soviet government, now, implies that he was the head of an imperialist force sent out to destroy the Soviet government. Probably the best epitaph on this expedition was an editorial observation of the *Literary Digest*, made during the final phases of the intervention. "Some"—the *Digest* remarked—

... might have liked us more if we had intervened less ... some might have disliked us less if we had intervened more, but ... having concluded that we intended to intervene no more nor no less than we actually did, nobody had any use for us at all.[43]

After the American troops departed in early 1920, the Japanese stayed on. For two and a half years longer the United States kept up a steady diplomatic drumfire on the Japanes government with a view to bringing the Japanese also to quit Siberia. This included raising the issue in a major way at the Washington Naval Disarmament Conference in 1922. When these efforts achieved a successful issue with the retirement of the Japanese from the Siberian mainland in the fall of 1922, the Far Eastern Republic, which was the Soviet puppet regional government for eastern Siberia, publicly conveyed to the United States government its thanks for the friendly interest shown in this question.

It would, of course, be argued on the Communist side: Ah, yes, but this merely reflected the jealousy of the American capitalists, who, being deprived of their prey, wished to see that the Japanese did not get it in their place. By way of answer, there is one other incident which we ought to note. When Maxim Litvinov came to Washington in 1933, to negotiate about the resumption of diplomatic relations between the United States and the Soviet Union, he came prepared to advance, over and against the claims which the United States had against the Soviet government, counterclaims for the damages allegedly caused by the United States in the Soviet Union through its participation in the intervention. In the course of the negotiations, Litvinov was shown some of the official American documentation relating to the Siberian intervention. Exactly what these documents were, I do not know; but when the negotiations were over, Litvinov provided the President, as part of the final settlement, with a public letter saying that following his examination of certain documents of the years 1918 to 1921 relating to the attitude of the American government toward the expedition into Siberia, the Soviet Union agreed to waive any and all claims of whatsoever character arising out of the activities of the military forces of the United States in Siberia.

So much for the Americans. How about the British role? The British, as I said before, immediately on learning of Wilson's decision, dispatched to Siberia a small armed force consisting of one battalion of the Middlesex Regiment, under the command of Colonel John Ward, which had been stationed at Hong Kong. In addition to this, the British sent a senior military representative in the person of Major General Alfred Knox, and a High Commissioner, Sir Charles Eliot.

The Middlesex battalion seems to have numbered approximately one thousand men. One detachment from this battalion fought in the initial engagement north of Vladivostok which cleared the rail line to Irkutsk. Its commander, like the Americans, was under the impression that the opponents were war prisoners rather than Russian Communists; but in his case the distinction was probably not important, since he regarded the Bolsheviki as German agents anyway and never for an instant doubted that the destruction of Communist power in Russia represented something in the nature of a sacred duty for the Allies. This commander, curiously enough, was a Labour M.P. from Stoke-on-Trent.

Almost immediately after this one decisive battle in eastern Siberia, Ward was instructed to take his little force to the Urals, where the real fighting against the Bolsheviki was going on. This he did, being obliged on several occasions to resort to rather forceful action against some of his own "allies" in order to protect his person and to assure the transit of his force. In Omsk, which was then the seat of the anti-Bolshevik Siberian government, he and his men remained over the winter.

The arrival of the British force at Omsk coincided almost precisely with a number of bewildering events—bewildering, that is, from the standpoint of their implications for the intervention. One was the end of the World War, which demolished the validity of the thesis that the intervention was directed against Germany. The second was the assumption by Admiral Kolchak of supreme power in the Omsk government, and the complete suppression of the S-R element on which that government had originally been founded.

This, in turn, had two important and, from the Allied standpoint, fateful effects. The S-R's were the friends of the Czechs; and with their suppression the Czechs lost all interest in the White cause and ceased to fight. From then on they were only a source of trouble and demoralization in the anti-Bolshevik camp; actually it was they who finally handed Admiral Kolchak over to the Bolsheviki to be tried and executed. Secondly, the elimination of the S-R's helped to estrange the Kolchak regime from the Siberian peasantry. The relatively advanced and independent peasantry of western Siberia was strongly S-R in its sympathies. Its estrangement was quite fatal to Kolchak's prospects. His greatest military difficulty consisted in the fact that he had masses of officers but very few men. Now, with the disaffection of the peasantry, he was unable to raise men by voluntary recruitment, and was forced to impress them by the cruel and outrageous methods which seemed natural to the officers through whom he had to work. The effect of this was to drive many peasants out of their villages into the woods and to create in this way a partisan movement which the Communists quickly penetrated and took under their con-

trol. Before Kolchak, under Allied urging, tried to recruit
an army in this manner with a view to pushing through to
Archangel, the Bolsheviki were so weak in western Siberia
that there can scarcely be said to have been a real Communist movement there. By the time Kolchak had finished
his tragic experiment, there was a vigorous and well-organized
Communist movement, stronger than any other Russian
political force in the region, and prepared to take Siberia
over for fair as soon as the Allies got out.

Ward and his men arrived at Omsk just as this change
was taking place and just as the Siberian winter was setting
in. They never went to the front. They remained at Omsk,
serving as a bodyguard for the large British military mission,
and sometimes for Admiral Kolchak himself. From the
moment of the end of World War I—which coincided, as I
say, with the arrival of this British force and with Kolchak's
assumption of supreme power—no Allied force took any
further part in actual hostilities against the Bolsheviki, with
one bizarre exception. An armored train, operated by naval
gunners from the H.M.S. *Suffolk*, which was lying at anchor
in Vladivostok, went all the way to the front on the European side of the Urals and took part in the hostilities
there until January 1919. The engagements conducted by
this unit, at a distance of approximately four thousand miles
inland from the supporting vessel, represent surely something
of a record in the application of naval gunfire against shore-
based defenses.

At some time during the winter, the Middlesex Battalion
was reinforced by the Ninth Hampshire Territorial Battalion,
which performed similar garrison duties. This battalion, which
also numbered about one thousand men, never saw combat
against the Bolsheviki. The presence in Siberia of this small
British force, which participated in only one extremely confused battle against the Bolsheviki some weeks before the
Armistice in the West, could scarcely be said to represent
an all-out military effort of the "British imperialists" to overthrow the Soviet government.

Much more serious in its implications was the economic
and military aid given to Kolchak by the British government.
This amounted, in monetary terms, to some 75 million
dollars, worth at that time two or three times what it
would be worth today. Kolchak's forces were largely
British-armed, and to some extent clothed in British uni-
forms. In the end, of course, the Communists got most of

these arms and this equipment, just as they did the American arms sent to China prior to 1948.

If, therefore, it is wholly inaccurate to charge, as does Mr. Khrushchev today, that the British launched an all-out military effort to overthrow the Soviet government, it is perfectly correct to say that they supported, to the best of their ability, from the summer of 1918 to the summer of 1919, the opponents of the Bolsheviki in the Russian civil war in Siberia. The main reason they did this was that they had involved themselves with these people prior to the Armistice, in the rather fatuous hope that a new eastern front could be created against the Germans through the agency of the Russian Whites. Having once got themselves into this involvement, and having learned that their White Russian associates were fatally disunited and helpless without foreign support, they hesitated to withdraw and to abandon their unhappy allies to the tender mercies of the Bolsheviki. This, more than any other single factor, delayed the withdrawal of the British troops from what almost everyone in London, beginning prominently with Lloyd George himself, recognized as a fruitless and most unfortunate involvement.

What I have just said about the British could be said roughly of the French, except that the French sent neither any sizable body of armed men nor any serious amount of actual military aid. The French contribution took the form, primarily, of several high-ranking military officers who, it was hoped in Paris, could somehow or other contrive to take command of the whole situation. This device operated mainly to compound the existing confusion, and to saddle the French government with the maximum moral responsibility for the Siberian intervention without its having made any appreciable physical contribution.

I shall not attempt to describe the other Allied expeditions that were sent to Russia in the years 1918-1920. There was a British expedition into Central Asia, under Major General Sir Wilfred Malleson. There was a British expedition into the Transcaucasus, under Major General L. C. Dunsterville. After the Armistice, British occupational forces remained for about a year in various parts of the Caucasus. There was a brief French intervention on the northern coast of the Black Sea, in the winter of 1918-1919; and about this, the less said the better. The British also strongly supported an effort by another Russian general, Nicholas Yudenich, to capture Petrograd in the later months of 1919. I shall not weary you with the accounts of these expeditions. You would find them depressingly similar to those I have already described, and the details would merely strain your memories. I shall therefore content myself with saying a few final words on the significance of the intervention as a whole.

These ventures, without exception, were serious mistakes. They reflected no credit on the governments that sent them. The impression they made in Russia was deplorable. Until I read the accounts of what transpired during these episodes, I never fully realized the reasons for the contempt and resentment borne by the early Bolsheviki toward the Western powers. Never, surely, have countries contrived to show themselves so much at their worst as did the Allies in Russia from 1917 to 1920. Among other things, their efforts served everywhere to compromise the enemies of the Bolsheviki and to strengthen the Communists themselves. So important was this factor that I think it may well be questioned whether Bolshevism would ever have prevailed throughout Russia had the Western governments not aided its progress to power by this ill-conceived interference.

All this suffices, I hope, to document the fact that I personally am no friend or apologist for the Allied intervention. But to jump from these appreciations to the assumption that the standard Soviet complaints about the intervention are justified is to jump much too far.

Soviet historiography portrays the intervention as a major deliberate military effort by the Western governments, mustering all the force they could, to overthrow the Soviet government. Nothing could be further from the truth. Wilson abhorred the very thought of intervention; so did his Secretary of State, and his Secretary of War. Lloyd George was on the whole completely skeptical as to its soundness. In authorizing the expeditions, both Wilson and Lloyd George deferred, reluctantly and unhappily, to the urgings of eager subordinates, who professed to know all about Russia, and whose advice it was difficult not to take.

Never did the intervention occupy anything like a central place in Allied purposes. Measured against the other preoccupations of the Western governments at this time, these expeditions were little sideshows of policy, complicated and obscure in origin, conducted absent-mindedly, and embrac-

ing in their motivation many considerations having nothing
to do with a desire to overthrow Soviet power for ideological
reasons.

It is alleged today in Russia that the expeditions were
"smashed" militarily by the Red army. This, incidentally, is
a latter-day discovery; Lenin never claimed anything like
this. The truth is that real fighting took place between Allied
and Bolshevik forces only in one theater, in the Russian
north, and here only on a small scale. Elsewhere, aside
from one or two skirmishes, the fighting was done by the
Russian Whites. In not one single instance that I can discover were Allied troops withdrawn because they had been,
or were being, defeated on the field of battle.

Soviet historiography alleges that the smashing of the intervention was greatly aided by the proletariat of the West and
by the Communist sympathies of the intervening troops. The
charge is exaggerated and distorted. Dissatisfaction was built
into all the expeditionary forces by the nature of the circumstances. It was not primarily Communist propaganda but
war-weariness, homesickness, and the spirit of demobilization which made it difficult for the Allies to keep troops in
Russia.

If the Bolsheviki had a real complaint against the Allied
governments, it was not on the score of the direct Allied
military interference, which was confused, halfhearted, and
pathetic, but rather on the score of the military aid, particularly in stores and munitions, given to the Russian Whites.
Here it was particularly the British government which had
the responsibility. It was officially stated in London that the
total contributions of this nature amounted to something
close to one hundred million pounds in the money of that
day. The Communists are right in charging that this huge
expenditure was incurred largely with a view to overthrowing
Soviet power; and they can, of course, take satisfaction from
the fact that this effort was unsuccessful.

If one were to have to sum up the whole story of the intervention, one might put it this way. For motives which
initially consisted primarily of a desire to restore resistance
to the Germans in the East, but which certainly also involved an active distaste for Soviet power and a strong desire to see it replaced by one more friendly to the Allied
cause, the Allied governments involved themselves, in 1918,
in a series of halfhearted efforts to give aid and support

to anti-Bolshevik factions in Russia. In entering on these ventures, the Allied governments seriously underestimated the divisions among the various elements in the anti-Bolshevik camp, and failed to see what harm could be done, and how grievously these divisions would be exacerbated, by an attempt to combine the inner political struggle of these groups with a revival of Russia's war effort against Germany. The confusion was increased by the termination of the World War just as the various expeditions were getting under way. As a result of these factors, the Allied efforts were unsuccessful and played, generally, into Communist hands.

We in the West may well search our consciences today to see what were the deficiencies of Allied statesmanship which led to such deplorable results. But of all the parties who might have a right to be aggrieved by these unhappy ventures, the Russian Communists, who were not without responsibility with regard to the circumstances of their origin and who profited from them handsomely in many ways, would not necessarily stand at the top of the list.

9 Russia and the Peace Conference (I)

WHEN THE senior statesmen of the Allied and Associated Powers met in Paris, at the end of 1918, to shape the peace that was supposed to justify all the slaughter and misery of the long war, it was expected that the result of their labors would be the creation, not just of a peace in Europe, but of something resembling a new world order. The vast amount of governmental authority they represented, the inordinate prestige of President Wilson at the moment, the sweeping, total nature of the Allied victory, and the extravagance of the promises the Allied statesmen had made to the peoples during the war as to what might be expected to flow from such a victory—all these factors had combined to give everyone a greatly exaggerated idea of what such a peace conference could and should produce.

So far as Germany was concerned, the conference was predicated on that unconditional surrender which had been the goal of all Allied policy in the final months of the war. The German people, it was agreed, should not even have a voice in the framing of the peace; they would take what they got. But how about the Russian people? In Russia, hostilities had not ceased. In Russia, on the Bolshevik side, there was still open hostility, scorn, recalcitrance, with regard to Allied purposes. Despite numerous Allied expressions of friendship for the Russian people, there was no Russian representative to take part in the proceedings of the conference. Germany, then, was absent from the discussions at Paris because the Allies wished her to be absent; Russia was absent because there was a virtual state of war between the Allied governments and the effective power in Russia.

I scarcely need to point out that the absence of these two powers, Germany and Russia, spelled right then and there the fatal inadequacy of the Versailles Conference as the foundation for a European settlement. To see the force of this observation, we have only to remember that World War II began with the conclusion of the Nonaggression Pact between Stalin and Hitler. A stable postwar arrangement, in other words, had been rendered impossible before the war ever came to an end: by the Russian Revolution and by the principle of unconditional surrender.

To Wilson, in particular, the absence of Russia at the conference was little short of tragic. It is worth digressing for a moment, here, to note Wilson's previous relation to the problem of Russia.

The figure of Woodrow Wilson, which in its time was the object of so much devotion, so much hatred, and so much scorn, is now becoming clearer and sharper under the light of contemporary scholarship; and a fascinating figure it is, with its tremendous contrasts of brilliant insight and appalling personal deficiencies. Wilson, you will recall, had been an outstandingly successful President up to the beginning of the World War. His efforts up to that time had related almost exclusively to domestic affairs. The reforms which he instituted in this field were sound and bold. Some of them have had a beneficial effect on American life down to this day. But his troubles began when the World War

broke out. This event was almost coincidental with the death
of his first wife, which was a heavy blow to him and which,
I cannot help but feel, cost him something of his personal
strength. At the same time he was suddenly propelled into
the tremendous problems of foreign affairs created for America
by the outbreak of the European war.

Despite his unfamiliarity with the European scene, Wilson's inital reaction to the war in Europe seems to me to
have been quite sound. He pleaded for what was in effect
a negotiated peace, as opposed to a punitive one. Like
Lenin, he sincerely wished for a peace without reparations
and without annexations. An imposed and punitive settlement would—he observed prophetically in January 1917—

... leave a sting, a resentment, a bitter memory upon which
the terms of peace would rest, not permanently, but only as
upon quicksand.[44]

Yet, before the war was over, he had changed his views
and was as strong as any of the others for what we, during
World War II, learned to call "unconditional surrender."
What was it that had caused this change of heart?

I believe it was the Russian question. This question seems
to have played a special part not only in the President's
intellectual calculations but in his emotional reactions
as well. His success at home had been founded largely on
his appeal to common people against what were then called
the "interests"—the reactionary forces, that is, of big business and worldly success. His image of himself as a statesman was built around his role as the defender of the helpless, the simple, the innocent, against the economic and
social mighty of this world. The most serious problem of
foreign policy he had had to face before the World War
was the troublesome Mexican situation of 1912-1915. Here
he had labored to appear as the unselfish friend of the
Mexican people, concerned only to do them service, not
to bring them harm. The fact that this approach had not
worked in Mexico had been for him a great disappointment;
but the dream was not shattered. On the contrary, the frustration in Mexico seems to have made him all the more
eager to vindicate the concept in some other framework of
circumstances.

When the Russian Revolution came, the whole focus of
this emotional-political complex in the President's mind was
brought to bear on Russia. He pictured the Russian people

as a race of frustrated idealists, who had never before had a friend or a mouthpiece, and who, now that their Tsarist oppressors were gone, would be sure to respond to his sympathetic and benevolent touch. He felt, I think, that they could be introduced into the world balance of power as his own allies against the arrogant and reactionary forces predominant in the European governments, with whose narrow and selfish war aims he was so disgusted. This is what he meant when he said, on hearing of the February Revolution, that "the great, generous Russian people" had "been added in all their naïve majesty and might"[45] to the forces that were fighting for freedom in the world, for justice, and for peace.

His hopes for the future support of the Russian people were a keystone in his plan for the postwar era. This is why he insisted in the final months of the war that the Russian problem could be solved only by the action of an enlightened Peace Conference, and not by military intervention into Russian affairs. This is why he built his Fourteen Points speech around the principle of liberal treatment of Russia in the postwar period. It was for this reason that when the Allies pressed him to agree to Japanese intervention in Siberia, he replied that one should leave the determination of all questions that might affect the permanent fortunes of Siberia to the Peace Conference. It was for this same reason that nothing, in the German and Austrian peace feelers of the last months of the war, infuriated him more than the suggestion that the Brest-Litovsk Treaty should be maintained in force as the price for a German accommodation with the West. It was, in fact, the draconic nature of the Brest-Litovsk settlement, as he saw it, and the fear that it might disturb his favored scheme, that finally swung him from his aversion to a dictated peace to an acceptance of the idea of total victory and unconditional surrender.

Wilson came to Paris, therefore, at the end of 1918, profoundly disturbed about the Russian problem and most anxious to see something done that would put an end to the Russian civil war and bring Russian representatives to the Peace Conference.

Lloyd George shared this view. As the opening of the conference approached, he became increasingly convinced, to use his own words, "that world peace was unattainable as long as that immense country [Russia] was left outside the

Covenant of Nations."[46] He would have gone far to bring about Russian representation at the conference.

Not so Clemenceau. He was firmly against Russian representation. The World War—France's conflict with Germany—was for him the only important issue. Russia, as he saw it, had betrayed France in the war. She had thereby excluded herself as a partner in the peace talks. The peace to be concluded did not concern her. His concern was not that Bolshevism should be fitted into the new world order; it was that Bolshevism should be destroyed or, if this was not possible, that a quarantine zone should be erected around it.

In the weeks just preceding the opening of the Peace Conference, the Soviet government repeatedly attempted to convey to the Allies its desire for an immediate and peaceful termination of the intervention and for the establishment of normal political and commercial relations with the Western countries. The Bolshevik leaders were now well aware that none of their Russian opponents would be able to hold out in the absence of Allied military support. They were therefore willing to make serious concessions in order to get the foreign troops out. The Sixth All-Russian Congress of Soviets, convening immediately after the Armistice, addressed to the Allied governments a formal appeal for peace, which was followed up by telegrams to the Allied governments and various proclamations of the same tenor. Shortly thereafter, Litvinov was sent out to Stockholm to try to establish contact with the Allied governments. He succeeded in speaking there with one or two subordinate British and American agents. This occurred just at the time the Paris Conference was convening. Litvinov assured these Allied representatives that the Soviet government was anxious for peace and was prepared to compromise on all important points, including the Russian state debt to the Allies, protection to foreign enterprises in Russia, and the granting of new concessions. It was against the background of these far-reaching assurances, together with the dismal prospects for the Allied intervention, that the Allied statesmen initiated their discussion of the Russian problem in Paris at the beginning of 1919.

Lloyd George described as follows the situation as it existed at the outset of the conference:

Personally I would have dealt with the Soviets as the *de*

facto Government of Russia. So would President Wilson. But we both agreed that we could not carry to that extent our colleagues at the Congress, nor the public opinion of our countries which was frightened by Bolshevik violence and feared its spread....[47]

Other expedients had therefore to be pursued. We can see today, with the advantage of hindsight, that the real possibilities open to the Allied statesmen for doing anything constructive about Russia at the conference were extremely limited. Nothing the Allies could have done would have served to overthrow the Bolsheviki or to make them anything else than what they were. The Allies could not stop the Russian civil war, nor could they assure the victory of those they regarded as their friends. They could not create a friendly, well-behaved Russia and bring its representatives to Paris. The best they could have done, at that moment, would have been to trade a withdrawal of the Allied forces from Russia for a promise on the part of the Russian Communist leaders to grant an amnesty to those Russians who had collaborated with those forces and thus offended the Soviet government. It is true that such an amnesty would not have had any very enduring effect: the amnestied Whites would certainly not have ceased to oppose Soviet power, and the Soviet authorities would soon have found ways of punishing them for doing so. But such an arrangement would at least have given the Allied governments a reasonably graceful means of exit from what was, in the best of circumstances, a most embarrassing and unprofitable involvement.

It will be useful for us to examine why not even this modest minimum could be achieved by the Allied representatives at the Paris Conference.

There were really five different attempts at the Paris Peace Conference to do something about the Russian problem. First there was an invitation to the warring factions in Russia to send representatives to a conference with Allied delegates on the Island of Prinkipo in the Sea of Marmara. Secondly, there was a brief and valiant personal effort by Mr. Winston Churchill to bring things to a head and to compel the Bolsheviki either to cease hostilities at once or to suffer a greatly increased Allied military effort against them. Thirdly, there was an attempt by the American and British governments to sound out the Soviet leaders by sending a secret diplomatic agent, Mr. William C. Bullitt, to Moscow to talk to them. Fourthly, there was a project, initiated by Herbert Hoover with the collaboration of the Norwegian explorer, Fridtjof Nansen, to get food to the hungering Russian population on terms that would force a clarification of the political situation. Finally, after all of these other starts had failed, there was an attempt to create a new rationale for supporting the anti-Bolshevik factions in Russia by pinning them down to a public statement of liberal and democratic purposes.

I should like to examine each of these initiatives in turn, as briefly as possible, and to attempt to identify the reasons for their failure. We will find these reasons instructive and revealing, I think, not just for the failures of Allied statesmanship at that moment but also for some of the later problems of the Western relationship to Soviet power.

First of all, the Prinkipo invitation.

It was Lloyd George who took the initiative, at the outset of the conference, in proposing that representatives of all the warring factions in Russia be invited to Paris to consult with the Peace Conference, on the condition that they first cease hostilities against one another. This suggestion was immediately snagged on Clemenceau's violent objection. He flatly refused to receive any Bolshevik delegates in Paris. He would resign, he said, rather than do it. This disposed of Lloyd George's proposal.

Wilson, who had favored the British proposal, then suggested that the Russian representatives be invited to meet with the Allied delegates at some other place than Paris. It was suggested that a suitable place would be the Island of Prinkipo in the Sea of Marmara. Travel to that place, it was argued, would not involve the transit of the Soviet delegates through any third country. Clemenceau disapproved of the whole idea, but said he would go along for the sake of solidarity. He suggested that Wilson should draw up an appropriate proclamation. This Wilson proceeded to do. His draft was accepted by the others, including Clemenceau, and was immediately published to the world.

The proclamation was a characteristically Wilsonian document, full of wholly sincere professions of disinterestedness and of a desire to serve the Russian people. Like the original British suggestion, it envisaged a truce in the Russian civil war as a prerequisite for the Prinkipo Conference: if the parties would not stop fighting, their representatives would not be received. February 15—a day only three weeks off—was named as the opening date for the conference.

This proposal was a naïve one. What the Bolsheviki and their Russian opponents were interested in was each other's total destruction. There was no room here for amicable discussion. Since the document stemmed from Wilson's pen, it would be easy to assume—and some have done so—that the proposal was only another reflection of the naïve American conviction that man is a reasonable animal, dominated by good will. Wilson was much laughed at for this step. But it was quite unjust to charge him with the authorship of it. It was in a meeting of the Imperial War Cabinet in London on the last day of December 1918 that the idea had its origin. The Americans, actually, were not particularly sanguine about it. Wilson's Secretary of State, Robert Lansing, wired privately to his deputy in the State Department that nothing was likely to come of the proposal; it had been adopted only because military intervention was a failure; the alternative would have been to remain silent and let things take their course. This, Lansing said sadly, would have satisfied no one.

Lansing's pessimism was wholly justified. The invitation was flatly rejected by the Russian Whites. Their representatives in Paris had been quietly encouraged by the French, behind Wilson's back, to decline the invitation. They appear, in fact, to have been assured by the French that they needn't worry—they would continue to have Allied support even if they turned down the invitation. This action on the part of the French did not remain concealed from the President; and it may be presumed to have been one of the things that did not particularly endear his Continental colleagues to him.

The Soviet reply, while not wholly negative, was evasive about the truce, and somewhat insulting in its language, after the fashion of early Soviet diplomatic communications to capitalist governments. This, together with the refusal of the anti-Bolshevik groups to sit down at a table with the Communists, was sufficient to kill the proposal.

The two replies—Communist and non-Communist—were delivered to the conference on February 12. President Wilson was scheduled to leave for the United States two days later, for an absence of several weeks. This combination of facts—the failure of the Prinkipo plan and the

President's imminent departure—caused considerable perturbation in the British government, particularly among those members of the Cabinet who did not share Lloyd George's skepticism about the usefulness of the intervention and who wanted to see some incisive action agreed upon at once. Plainly, if Wilson got away before any new decisions were taken, things would just drag on, and there would be many weeks more of uncertainty and inaction. Lloyd George was detained in London at that moment, by political difficulties at home. It appears to have been decided, in the light of this fact, that Mr. Churchill should go over to Paris, attend the last meeting of the Council of Ten on the day of Wilson's departure, and attempt to get the President's agreement to some definite and incisive course of military action in Russia, as an alternative to Prinkipo.

Just how and why it was that Mr. Churchill (who disagreed with Lloyd George thoroughly on everything having to do with the Russian question) should have been selected for this mission is unclear. Lloyd George said in his memoirs that "Mr. Churchill very adroitly seized the opportunity . . . to go over to Paris and urge his plans upon the consideration of [the others]."[48] The uninitiated American historian may be permitted to wonder whether Lloyd George himself did not adroitly seize the opportunity to let Mr. Churchill work off some of his steam against Wilson's glacial aversion to everything that had to do with military intervention, and against the complete unwillingness of any of the other Allies to put up money or forces for an expanded military effort in Russia.

In any case, Mr. Churchill did join the session on the day of Wilson's departure. It was, of course, a full and busy day. The senior statesmen were preoccupied with many other matters. It was not until about seven o'clock in the evening, when everyone was tired and the dinner hour was pressing, that the talk got around to Russia. In these circumstances, the discussion was unavoidably cursory and inconclusive.

We come up at this point, incidentally, against one of the basic reasons why the statesmen at Paris failed in their effort to deal with the Russian problem. I have in mind here the inherent defects of what we might call "summit diplomacy"—of the effort to transact important diplomatic business by direct meetings between senior statesmen. These defects are many. The multitude of ulterior problems that press up on a prime minister or a head of state is so great that no single subject, especially one not regarded as of primary importance, is apt to receive detailed and exhaustive attention. Nor can the senior statesmen stay with a problem for any great length of time. Their time is precious; other responsibilities take them away. In the present instance the very fact that both Wilson and Lloyd George were obliged to leave the conference at this juncture and, incidentally, that Clemenceau was seriously wounded by a would-be assassin four days later, shows clearly how the treatment of any important international subject is endangered when its negotiation is left to those who hold the supreme positions.

In any case, to return to our narrative: on the late afternoon of February 14, at the meeting of the Council of Ten, with Wilson fidgeting to get off to the railway station, Churchill brought up the Russian question and emphasized the need for clearing up at once the uncertainty resulting from the inconclusive outcome of the Prinkipo proposal. He pointed particularly to the deterioration of the military situation of the anti-Bolshevik forces in Russia and to the weakened morale of the Allied units there. To this Wilson responded by saying that the Allied troops were doing no good in Russia; they did not know for whom or for what they were fighting; the groups they were supporting showed no political promise; they ought to be withdrawn at once. As for Prinkipo: if Russian delegates could not be brought to the west, perhaps an effort could be made to get in touch with them through informal representatives.

Churchill stressed, in reply, the debt of loyalty the Allies owed to the anti-Bolshevik forces with whom they were associated. Wilson admitted that this was a dilemma, but pointed out, very truly, that the Allied forces would have to leave Russia someday: it was no good putting off the day of reckoning.

On this inconclusive note, the session of the fourteenth ended. For three days after Wilson's departure, Churchill continued to press, in the absence of both Lloyd George and Wilson, for issuance of a ten-day ultimatum to the Bolsheviki to stop the fighting, with the understanding that if it was not accepted, the Supreme War Council would see what could be done about overthrowing the Soviet government by force of arms. But the report of these suggestions, relayed to Lloyd George and Wilson, drew indignant protests from both of them. Neither would entertain the thought of anything like an intensified military effort in Russia. Mr. Churchill was obliged to retire in frustration. Immediately after Churchill's return to England, Clemenceau was shot. With that, all three of the top figures were out of action. Discussion of the Russian problem at the senior level stopped for several weeks. Intensified intervention, as a means of dealing with the Russian situation, had been proposed, and in effect rejected, by the conference.

Wilson, in the discussion on the day of his departure, had hinted at the desirability of getting in touch with the Soviet leaders through informal representatives. This was not an empty phrase. What he had in mind, unquestionably, was an idea which had been suggested to Colonel House by the well-known American journalist, Lincoln Steffens. Steffens had suggested the dispatch of a private exploratory mission direct to Moscow. The idea commended itself to House and evidently to Wilson. Mr. William C. Bullitt, an attaché of the American delegation at the Peace Conference, was selected for the task. Steffens was to go with him. Mr. Bullitt, you will recall, was destined fourteen years later to be the first American ambassador to the Soviet Union. He was, at the time of this first visit to Russia in 1919, twenty-eight years old, liberal in his views, brilliant, inexperienced, and greatly excited.

The British were informed of the project and evidently approved of it. At a later date Lloyd George and his private secretary, Mr. Philip Kerr (later Marquess of Lothian), denounced Bullitt's subsequent revelations about this mission as a tissue of lies; and Lloyd George conveyed the impression that he had had nothing to do with it. It is possible that Bullitt may have been unintentionally inaccurate in some of his statements. But he did produce, on this later occasion, the text of a private note handed to him by Mr. Kerr before his departure for Russia, to which was appended a list of the conditions upon which Kerr personally thought it would be possible for the Allied governments to resume normal relations with Russia. These included a general cessation of hostilities, an amnesty to Russians who had fought on the Allied side, and the eventual withdrawal of the Allied forces. It was, perhaps, improper for Bullitt to make public this note, as he subsequently did; but I am not aware that its authenticity has ever been denied. It was with this document in his pocket that Bullitt set off for Moscow. One can only regard his visit, therefore, as having British as well as American sanction.

The Americans said nothing to the French about Bullitt's mission. They were under the impression that the French had deliberately sabotaged the Prinkipo proposal behind the scenes, and they did not wish this second effort to be similarly frustrated.

Bullitt and Steffens arrived in Moscow in mid-March. They were well received. Bullitt had talks with Lenin and others of the Soviet leaders. Both men were favorably impressed by the evidences of discipline and singleness of purpose on the part of the Soviet government, and by the sincerity of the desire of the Soviet leaders to put an end to the civil war and the intervention. They obtained from Lenin, after some discussion, the draft of a document having the form of an Allied proposal to the Soviet government. Bullitt was assured that if this proposal were actually made by the Allied governments not later than April 10, it would be accepted by the Soviet leaders.

It was probably an unwise method of procedure, on Bullitt's part, to return with such a document. It left to the Allied governments no latitude of negotiation. By taking cognizance of the document, they would obviously place themselves in a position where they could only take it or leave it. Any alteration in its text at the Allied end would have given the Soviet government formal grounds for refusing to accept it. Nevertheless, it was in substance not an offer to be lightly rejected from the Allied standpoint. It did provide for a cessation of hostilities between the various existing governments and factions in Russia, for a raising of the Allied blockade, for the opening up of the channels of communication, for a withdrawal of Allied troops and a termination of Allied military support for any Russian groups. Most important of all, it promised a general amnesty for those who had supported the Allies.

The Allies, as subsequent events were to demonstrate, would have been well out of it on these terms. It is a pity they were not accepted. But this was not to be. Bullitt, having wired his findings from Helsinki, got back to Paris in the last days of March, bursting with the importance of what he had accomplished. To his astonishment and chagrin,

he found that the whole situation had changed. The senior
statesmen, now back in Paris, were locked in a series of Her-
culean disagreements on questions of the treatment of Germany. These days constituted, in fact, the first great crisis
of the conference. Bullitt seems to have reached the scene
just at the time when passions were at their peak and the
strain on everyone was the greatest.

Whether Wilson and Lloyd George ever gave serious attention to the proposals with which Bullitt had returned
does not appear from the records. Wilson, pleading a headache, refused to receive him and shunted him off to Colonel
House, saying to House that he himself had a single-track
mind and simply could not take on the Russian problem
in addition to what he was already thinking about. Bullitt
was profoundly offended by this brush-off, and sneered ever
afterwards about the President's headache. But here he
was probably unjust. The episode occurred within a day or
two of Wilson's nervous and physical collapse, at the beginning of April. He may well have had a headache on the
day in question.

Bullitt appeared before the other members of the American delegation at the conference, and spent a day talking
with them. The following morning, according to his own
statement, he had breakfast with Lloyd George, General
J. C. Smuts, Sir Maurice Hankey, and Kerr. He later cited
Lloyd George and Smuts as having been strongly in favor
of a solution along the lines embodied in the Soviet proposal, but Lloyd George, he said, was frightened by the
attacks being launched against him in England from the
Conservative side over the Russian question. Waving a copy
of the *Daily Mail*, Lloyd George said—still according to
Bullitt—"As long as the British press is doing this kind of
thing how can you expect me to be sensible about Russia?"[49] He expressed doubt that Bullitt's tale would be believed. He talked of sending some prominent Conservative
to Russia to find out for himself and to tell the public what
the Bolshevik attitude was.

From this point on the matter seems to have bogged
down completely. Colonel House passed Bullitt on to some
of his own subordinates who were actually averse to the
Bullitt proposals and had a wholly different idea as to what
ought to be done. The April 10 deadline proposed by the
Soviet government was allowed to pass without any Allied

reaction. This, of course, obviated the entire proposal; for, once the deadline was passed, the Soviet government was no longer committed. If anything were now to be done, the matter would have to be entirely re-negotiated.

In the ensuing days the Bullitt mission was the subject of insistent queries in the House of Commons on the part of alarmed Conservatives, partisans of the intervention, who had heard rumors of Bullitt's trip and of the proposals with which he had returned, and who feared that the British government might be on the point of accepting them. On April 16, Lloyd George, temporarily back in London, took the bull by the horns, appeared in the House of Commons, and made a major policy statement on the Russian question. He was then asked by one of the members whether he could make any statement on the approaches or representations alleged to have been made to his government by persons acting on behalf of such government as there was in central Russia. To this Lloyd George replied that they had had nothing authentic—no such approaches at all. But he did think he knew to what the Right Honorable Gentleman referred:

... There was some suggestion that a young American had come back from Russia with a communication. It is not for me to judge the value of this communication, but if the President of the United States had attached any value to it he would have brought it before the conference, and he certainly did not.[50]

Lincoln Steffens, who had accompanied Bullitt on his trip, heard somewhere that Lloyd George's reason for washing his hands of Bullitt in this way was to protect himself against the French, who, having learned of the Bullitt mission, were now accusing Lloyd George of having gone behind their back. This sounds quite plausible.

Bullitt, in any case, being unaccustomed to the cruelty of politics and perhaps to the personal amorality which is the concomitant of high political authority, was doubly stung by this public denial. His cup of bitterness overflowed. He was disillusioned anyway with the form the Peace Treaty was assuming under the hammering of the European Allies. He blamed Wilson for surrendering his ideals. A few weeks later he resigned, reproaching Wilson bitterly with having "so little faith in the millions of men, like myself, in every

nation who had faith in you."[51] When the journalists asked
him what he proposed to do, he said he was going to go
down to the Riviera and lie on the sands and watch the
world go to hell. Some months later he spilled his own story,
with passionate indiscretion, to a senatorial committee anxious to discredit the President in the fight over the League.
Neither Wilson nor his British friends ever forgave him
for doing so.

The reasons for the failure of the Bullitt mission lie to
some extent in the partiality of Colonel House's entourage
to another idea, which remains to be discussed. But I think
it worth noting, before we go on to that, the other factors
that led to Bullitt's failure. One of these was certainly the
general atmosphere of confusion that attends any large multilateral gathering of senior statesmen—in other words, the
characteristic inadequacy of summit statesmanship, which
I talked about earlier. Closely connected with this was the
great difficulty which is always involved in any attempt of
a coalition of sovereign governments to negotiate with a
single hostile political entity, particularly in a confused and
rapidly moving context of circumstance. This is something
that requires centralization of authority, complete privacy of
decision, and a highly disciplined mode of procedure. These
are not the marks of coalition diplomacy. Their absence is
something that has bedeviled the statesmanship of the Western democracies down to the present day.

An even more important cause of Bullitt's misfortune was
no doubt the domestic-political situation in England, which
did not permit Mr. Lloyd George to do what he thought
would have been sensible about the Russian problem. Here
you get into another of the characteristic disadvantages of
democratic diplomacy—the fact that a system of government
under which the executive power is sensitively attuned to the
waves of popular sentiment, and of parliamentary opinion, is
one which finds it difficult to adjust rapidly and incisively to
a complicated and fast-moving series of circumstances, especially when controversial domestic issues are involved. De
Tocqueville once observed that "a democracy can only with
great difficulty regulate the details of an important undertaking, persevere in a fixed design, and work out its execution
in spite of serious obstacles."[52] All this was doubly true of the
representatives of democratic governments who struggled with
the Russian problem at the Peace Conference in 1919.

10   Russia and the Peace Conference (II)

BUT THERE was another reason for the failure of the Bullitt mission. At the time of Bullitt's return to Paris a new proposal was being entertained in the entourage of Colonel House. House's leading subordinates were evidently influenced by the anti-Bolshevik feeling that predominated in the State Department and in the Allied social circles generally, and contrasted strongly with the realistic appreciation shown by Wilson and Lloyd George for the dangers of the intervention.

The scheme which, during Bullitt's absence in Russia, had begun to commend itself to these gentlemen was one which centered around the person and activities of the future American President, Herbert Hoover. Hoover was at that time Director of the Commission for Relief in Belgium, an American organization which had functioned with spectacular success during the war in getting food relief to the population of German-occupied Belgium. Hoover, a mining engineer by training, had been given complete control of this operation. He had plenty of money at his disposal. He had been able to draw on members of the executive staffs of American businesses all over Europe, now displaced by the war. He was a ruthless and effective administrator; and his organization, unencumbered with the usual burdens of governmental bureaucracy, was able to do an effective and impressive job.

As the war came to an end, Hoover's organization moved into other areas of Europe, bringing urgent food relief to the peoples, and particularly to children and other specially needy portions of the population. Hoover was, in fact, made Food Administrator for the Allies generally. This position gave him in many situations considerable political power; and he did not fail to make this influence felt in a number of instances, in the interests of the success of his program.

To people who were impressed with Hoover's operations, and the power that had gravitated into his hands, it was only a step to the assumption that if he could move into Russia with a food relief program, as he had done into various parts of central Europe, he would be able to extort an end of the civil war on terms favorable to Allied interests, as a price for the food relief. Whether this would involve the fall of the Soviet regime was, I think, not clear in the minds of most people who entertained the idea; but it was assumed that at least the Russian Communists could be confronted with the choice between moderating their behavior and their principles of conduct, or accepting the onus of denying the proffered food to a Russian population, large parts of which were already starving.

On March 28, 1919, just after Bullitt's return to Paris, President Wilson received a long letter from Hoover recommending the establishment of a relief commission for Russia along the lines of the Belgian one. The plan was not, I hasten to explain, the result of any friendly sentiments on Hoover's part toward the Soviet regime. Hoover, whose experience as a mining engineer had included service in Russia before the war, had no friendly feelings toward the Bolsheviki. It was his view that the Allies should insist, as part of the price for their support of such a scheme, that the Bolsheviki cease hostilities against their opponents in Russia and stop their propaganda abroad. Communist political activity was now beginning to make serious headway in other countries of Europe and to be a source of real worry to a great many upstanding people. Just one week before Hoover wrote his letter, the Communists had seized power in Hungary, where Hoover's Food Administration was attempting to organize a relief action. Hoover no doubt shared the horror which many people were now experiencing on their first contact with this new doctrine and their realization of what it might mean for Europe. Thus he took pains to specify that his plan did not involve any recognition of what he called "the Bolshevik murderers" any more than England, in supporting the Belgian relief program, had entered into a relationship with a hostile Germany. His idea was that a neutral figure should be placed in charge of the program; the latter should publicly ask for Allied support; the Allies should then state the conditions on which they would support the program. These conditions would be such as to place the Soviet government, as I have just suggested, before the choice of falling in with general Western desiderata or accepting the onus of denying the food to the Russian people.

The idea of using food as a weapon was one which had a very strong appeal to the American mind. It appealed to some of the most dangerous weaknesses in the American view of international affairs, and had, in my opinion, a most pernicious influence on American thinking. Since the money and the food would be donated by Americans, the action could always be portrayed to people at home as an altruistic and benevolent one, and made to contrast favorably with that evil and awful thing called "power politics" of which the European countries were presumed to be chronically guilty. No use of force was involved. No troops had to be kept on foreign soil as sanctions for this diplomacy. One was relieved of the sordid ordeal of political negotiations and compromise. One simply defined one's conditions and left it to the other fellow to take it or leave it. If he accepted, all right; if he declined, so much the worse for him.

It was, of course, true that anyone making such an offer had a perfect right to define the conditions of it. It is also only fair to recognize that the conditions laid down by Hoover's organization were moderate and reasonable, and usually essential to the successful operation of the program. In no instance were they ones that sought any territorial acquisitions or other illicit gains for the United States. A certain basic decency of the whole procedure was assured by the very mildness of the aspirations of an America still deeply rooted in the tradition of isolationism.

But the farther you got away from the orderly and liberal forms of society prevailing on Europe's Atlantic seaboard, and the closer you came to the more primitive political conditions of eastern Europe, the more difficult it became to define conditions for the distribution of food that were not simultaneously conditions for the adjustment of domestic political realities. To insist on the fair and impartial distribution of food was to insist on moderation and liberality of political behavior generally; but to insist on this, in terms of Russia and eastern Europe, could be the most violent and outrageous of interventions in the domain of domestic political affairs. People in that part of the world were inclined to ask: What was the use of having power if you could not deprive your enemies of food and channel it to your friends?

Wilson, very much preoccupied by the crisis over the German problem to which the Peace Conference itself had, by

April 1919, advanced, turned Hoover's letter over to Colonel House. Hoover, meanwhile, who was not the man to doubt that any recommendation of his would be instantly accepted, had proceeded to implement his idea by summoning Fridtjof Nansen to Paris, and asking him to accept the titular leadership of the proposed Relief Commission for Russia. Nansen, after agreeing to do this, was persuaded to support Hoover's letter with another letter of his own to the Big Four senior statesmen at the conference. The text of this letter, incidentally, had been drafted for him by Hoover. In this letter, Nansen formally proposed the relief action which Hoover had suggested, and asked on what conditions the Allied governments would approve it.

Nansen's letter was delivered to the members of the Council of Four on April 3. This was one of the darkest and most dramatic days of the Peace Conference. It was the day on which President Wilson, worn with strain and frustration, collapsed and took to his bed for a period of some days. On the previous day, April 2, the awkward questioning about the Bullitt mission had begun in the House of Commons. There was more of this questioning on the third; and the spokesman for the government felt obliged to assure the House that "the Allied Governments had received no proposals for an honorable understanding with the present rulers of Russia"[53]—a statement which might have been technically defensible but was certainly quibbling. We may be fairly sure that Lloyd George had by this time made it clear to Wilson and Colonel House that there could, in these circumstances, be no question of a follow-up on the Bullitt proposals. Wilson's illness precluded any discussion of them, anyway, at the top level.

House, encouraged by his subordinates, therefore seized on the letter from Hoover and Nansen as a means of evading Lenin's offer. Here was an alternative scheme which, if successful, appeared to spell less risk for the Allies, and could bring no embarrassment if it did not succeed. House charged his subordinates with the task of preparing a reply to Nansen. He disposed of Bullitt by suggesting to him that the Allied reply to Lenin could be embodied in the terms of the Nansen proposal, and suggested that he merge his efforts with those who were handling the Hoover-Nansen initiative.

House's subordinates at once produced, for Bullitt's edification, a draft which—unbeknownst, apparently, to Bullitt— also had proceeded from Hoover's pen.

Bullitt tried his best to work into the letter to Nansen something resembling a response to Lenin's proposal; but without success. The most he was permitted to do was to polish up Mr. Hoover's somewhat jerky prose. This edited version was duly laid before the Big Four, who signed it as a formal communication of the Peace Conference, and dispatched it to Dr. Nansen on April 17. It was at once released to the public, and was splashed over the headlines of the world press. In it, the Allied statesmen welcomed the Nansen proposal and went on to define the conditions on which they would be prepared to support it. A cessation of the hostilities in Russia was stipulated; but in contrast to Lenin's proposals, nothing was said about any withdrawal of the Allied forces. Distribution and transportation within Russia, it was said, would have to be under the supervision of the proposed Relief Commission; but, subject to this supervision, the distribution of the food in Russia was to be "solely under the control of the people of Russia themselves." The people in each locality—Dr. Nansen was told—

. . . should be given, as under the regime of the Belgian Relief Commission, the fullest opportunity to advise your Commission upon the methods and the personnel by which their community is to be relieved.[54]

Was there ever, one wonders, any greater nonsense than this curious document, bearing the signatures of Orlando, Lloyd George, Wilson, and Clemenceau? The provision for supervision of all Russian transportation by the Relief Commission meant simply taking one great and vital branch of economic and military administration out of the hands of the Russian government entirely. This the Soviet government could never have accepted without a disastrous collapse of its prestige. But beyond this, how could the people of any Russian locality act as a collective entity in such matters, even assuming that experience and tradition had fitted them to do so, unless they were in some way organized and represented for this purpose? This meant elections—elections of public bodies with real power. But the Russia of the spring of 1919 was, God knows, in no condition to conduct elections of any kind. It was ravaged by hunger and cold and confusion and a civil war which had now advanced to the utmost degree of bitterness and commitment on both sides.

Who was to organize such elections? Who was to stand guard over their impartiality? Who was to see and to count the ballots? Where was the Russian whose detachment toward the civil war was so great and so generally recognized that others would consent to place their lives and that of their families in his power by handing to him a secret ballot? The very suggestion of local community action of this sort reflected a terrifying naïveté as to what the Russia of that hour was really like.

Nansen took the letter from the Big Four and tried to transmit it by wire to Lenin. Despite the fact that Clemenceau had signed it, the French government's radio station refused to send it. Again, as in the case of the Prinkipo proposal, the French were sabotaging the very measures to which Clemenceau had agreed. Cap in hand, Nansen went from one of the Allied governments to the other, vainly trying to find one that would consent to transmit the note the Allied statesmen had themselves signed. He finally got it sent, apparently through German channels. It was not until May 4 that the Soviet government picked it up, as it had picked up the Prinkipo proposal, from the air waves.

What were the Soviet leaders to make of such a communication? A resignation of their powers over food distribution, over the transportation system, and over local government, coupled with the continued presence of the foreign troops in Russia, would plainly spell the end of their regime. The deadline for acceptance of the proposals they had handed to Bullitt had long since lapsed. They were now doing better in the civil war, both militarily and politically, than they had done in March. They needed the food, needed it badly, in fact; but they were in no mood to entertain Western schemes which concealed under the mask of a food relief program the destruction of their political system.

The reply which they sent was signed not by Lenin but by Chicherin. It was polite enough in its tone of address to Nansen personally; but it was unsparing in its denunciation of the Allied note. It was clear that the Soviet leaders smelled, in the provision for a cessation of hostilities, an Allied effort to trick them of the military victory in the civil war which they were quite confident would be theirs if there were no increase in the Allied military effort against them. To require a cessation of hostilities meant, Chicherin pointed out in the reply, to prevent the belligerent who had every reason to expect successes from obtaining those successes. This, he went on to say, was a purely political act. It had nothing to do with food relief. Nansen's humanitarian intentions were being obviously abused, he charged, by the Allied governments. The Soviet government had repeatedly offered to discuss a cessation of hostilities; it was still ready to do so, but only if there could be a discussion also of the true reasons why the war was being waged against it—and a discussion with its real adversaries, the Allied governments, not just with the puppets of those governments: the Russian Whites. The Bolsheviki were prepared to meet at any time with Nansen and his collaborators; but they could not accept the Allied conditions.

While all this was going on, the Big Four had begun to discuss the attitude they should adopt toward Kolchak. It was Wilson who raised the question on May 9, a few days before Chicherin's reply was received. The effort of the American troops to maintain a detached and neutral position vis-à-vis the warring Russian factions had by this time aroused the ire both of the Allied governments and of Kolchak and his followers and associates, who simply could not understand why the Americans should refuse to participate in the effort to overthrow the Bolsheviki. There was a growing danger of clashes between the American forces and the Russian Whites. Wilson brought this to the attention of the Peace Conference, and said that he thought the situation could not go on much longer. Either the American expeditionary force must be instructed to support Kolchak, or must be withdrawn at once. The American government had little confidence in Kolchak. Therefore he, Wilson, favored the withdrawal of the American contingent.

Lloyd George pleaded for a postponement of the decision. He was under the impression, as were the French, that Kolchak was doing very well indeed: that he had the Communists on the run, that if one only waited a little while the Bolsheviki would be finished. Kolchak would then be easy to deal with.

As we know today, this was not so at all. The high-water mark of Kolchak's spring offensive had really been passed some two to three weeks earlier. By the time this discussion took place in Paris, Kolchak was not only again on the defensive, but he had begun that retreat which was to lead, within the year, to his political and personal destruction. The reason why the statesmen in Paris did not know this was that they were making the same mistake the Americans were destined to make forty years later in the case of the Chinese civil war: they were drawing their information exclusively from the side which they wanted to see win. The Allies had no observers, at this point, on the Bolshevik side. They *had* had observers there some months earlier, but these had been lightheartedly sacrificed to the interests of the intervention itself. The Allied governments were now paying the penalty for this sacrifice, in the form of very poor and unreliable information about Russian conditions. It was a heavy price.

Wilson himself was not much impressed with these optimistic reports of Kolchak's progress. He continued to favor withdrawal of the American troops. But his spirit had by this time been broken in the battle over the Versailles Treaty. He yielded reluctantly, in the end, to Lloyd George's opinion, observing sadly that the British had more experience with intervening in remote countries than had the Americans. And as a result of Wilson's yielding on this point, the American forces remained in Siberia almost a year longer than would otherwise have been the case. Wilson did suggest, however—and the suggestion was favorably received—that an effort might at least be made to pin Kolchak down to some sort of public assurance that he would, in the event of his political and military success, introduce a liberal and democratic system of government in Russia.

It was this suggestion that the statesmen had on their minds when Chicherin's reply to the Nansen proposal was laid before them, on May 20. Nansen wanted to accept the Soviet offer. He proposed to send his own representatives to Stockholm for discussions with the Bolshevik delegates. Wilson thought there was merit to some of Chicherin's points, and would probably have wished to encourage Nansen. But Clemenceau, once more, refused to hear of it. It was clear, he said, that Bolshevik power was now on the decline. The Communists had rejected Nansen's offer— founded on pure humanitarianism. What could you do with such people?

No one had any very good answer to this; and the discussion degenerated into a desultory post-mortem over the manner in which they had all become involved in this miserable Russian situation in the first place. Lloyd George said the British objective in the intervention had been the restoration of the eastern front; but this had necessitated collaboration with the Russian Whites; one could not now leave them in the lurch. Wilson recalled that the Americans had gone into Siberia only in order to help the Czechs get out; but when they got there, the Czechs had refused to leave. His own sense of frustration, he indicated, was complete. For the first time, he said, he had ceased to experience any chagrin over the fact that they had never had a policy toward Russia; there was no policy that they could have had.

There is something very sad in this confession. For two long years, the Russian situation had lain close to Wilson's heart. Earnestly he had hoped to demonstrate, in his handling of Russian matters, the principles to which he was so profoundly attached. It was he who had said, after all, in the Fourteen Points speech, that the treatment of Russia by her sister nations would be the acid test of their good will, of their comprehension of her needs, of their own intelligent and unselfish sympathy. Now all these high hopes lay in the dust.

Actually, in this sad confession Wilson was close to the heart of the matter. The beginning of wisdom, in the Russian question of 1919, was the recognition that there was nothing more the Allied governments could accomplish by the retention of their forces in Russia.

But Wilson was in a lone and helpless minority. There was no further discussion of Chicherin's reply. Nansen was left, for the moment, to die on the vine. Instead of pursuing the Nansen project, the senior statesmen went on to order the drafting of the communication to Kolchak, asking him to clarify his democratic intentions. By May 26, the draft, prepared by Mr. Philip Kerr, was ready and approved. It was dispatched that very day and, again, was made public.

This document, representing the last action to be taken at the Peace Conference on the Russian question, opened with the extraordinary proposition that the time had come for the Allied and Associated Powers to make clear "once more" the policy they proposed to pursue in regard to Russia. (Unkind critics might well have asked on what previous occasion they had made this clear.) The note then went on to promise to the doomed Kolchak, whose power was already rapidly disintegrating, the assistance of the Allies in munitions, supplies, and food, to the end that he might install his regime as the government of all Russia. He was asked, however, to give assurances that he would, if successful, convene a constitutional convention; that he would permit free local elections; that he would not attempt to restore the old order; that he would make certain concessions in the nationalities problem; that he would bring Russia into the League of Nations; and that he would agree to assume the indebtedness of former Russian governments.

The principal purpose of this note was simply to provide a moral and political basis for the participation of the United States government in the supplying and provisioning of Kolchak. The British had already given all they could. The French and Italians had nothing to give.

The answering note represented, of course, an empty gesture. Paper promises were a dime a dozen during the Russian civil war. The issuance of the desired assurances cost Kolchak precisely nothing. The reply, actually, was largely drafted for him by the French and British representatives at his headquarters, who thought they knew what President Wilson wished to hear. Very soon after this reply was received in Paris, the decline of Kolchak's fortunes became too obvious to be longer ignored. Wilson, who had never been convinced that things were as they had been represented to him, sent his own representative to Siberia to find out the true facts. This representative, the American ambassador to Japan, Mr. Roland Morris, reported that, without direct reinforcement by an Allied contingent of at least fifty thousand men, Kolchak could not possibly maintain himself, and that further shipments of supplies and munitions would simply be wasted. This killed the whole project, so far as the United States government was concerned. Kolchak proceeded rapidly to his early and tragic demise.

With this, the last of the efforts of the Peace Conference to deal with the Russian problem passed into history, devoid, like all the earlier ones, of any positive result. And not only, let us note, had no positive goals been achieved, but the Allies had succeeded in forfeiting, in the course of their handling of this problem, the only favorable and useful possibility that did lie, briefly, before them: a deal with the Soviet government that would have permitted a relatively graceful and early withdrawal of the Allied forces from the Russian scene, by agreement with the Soviet government, on the basis of a stipulated amnesty for those Russians who had collaborated with the Allied forces.

If I have imposed on your patience by going over in such detail the efforts of the Peace Conference to do something about Russia, it has been because I thought these experiences instructive as examples of the manner in which governments—and particularly liberal democratic governments—actually work. This question of the "how" as distinct from the "what" of diplomacy is, I assure you, of tremendous importance; and of all the questions having to do with diplomatic undertakings, it is the one for which there is, in our Western countries, the least understanding. It can really be questioned whether the Allied governments, organized as they were organized, and working together as they were attempting to work together in the Russian question in 1919, could have hoped to implement successfully any policy toward Russia at all.

What do we see when we look back, from this standpoint, over this series of episodes in the record of the Peace Conference? We see, first of all, the shocking lack of any unity or intimacy of approach among the various Allied governments. They had never reconciled their various views of what the world was supposed to be like after victory over the Germans. They had been fighting for different things and pretending, in an endless flow of beautiful phrases, that what they were fighting for was the same thing. Their confrontation with the Russian problem tore the mask off a great deal of this equivocation and hypocrisy.

Second, one sees the almost insoluble technical problem that is inherent in coalition diplomacy as such. This is aside from the question of differences of outlook in themselves. It is the problem of how such differences are to be reconciled in such a manner as to permit a flexible, alert, and firm conduct of policy on behalf of the group as a whole. An occasional single decision is by no means enough. When one is dealing with situations as complicated as that of Russia in 1919, one needs decisions day by day. And one needs something more difficult to define—something I can describe only as a consistency of style and methodology. This is precisely what a coalition, operating on the basis of sporadic tortured compromises, finds it difficult to achieve.

One sees again the characteristic limitations of summit diplomacy about which I have already spoken. One sees the senior statesmen harried, pressed, groaning under the spotlight of publicity, under the limitations of physical and nervous strength, under the multitudinous pressures of high position, flitting from problem to problem like bees from one flower to another, touching each only briefly and sporadically, hoping always that some sort of pollination will spring from their magic touch. And one sees how inadequate this is for a task—namely, the task of diplomacy—which is really one of style, of perseverance, and of ceaseless vigilance.

On top of this we see the characteristic deficiencies of the democratic system of government from the standpoint of the conduct of foreign policy. I shall not dwell on these. Both Wilson and Lloyd George were more sensible and perceptive in their instincts as to how the Russian problem ought to be treated than was the public opinion by which they were faced at home, or the subordinates through whom they had to work. One comes away from the reading of their experiences at the Peace Conference with a question as to how much democracy was benefited by having men of such experience and—in the Russian question at least—of such good sense, since their impulses were so brutally negated by opinion at home and by lack of discipline within their own establishments.

Finally, there was the inadequacy of the information at the disposal of the Allied governments. This deficiency was compounded by their tendency to lean on the Russian Whites for most of the information they obtained. It is not to deny these people our sympathy to point out that they were not the most impartial of sources on the Russian civil war. Sometimes I think it might be made a maxim of democratic statesmanship in difficult situations to seek its information, however distasteful this might be, from the study of its enemies rather than from the consultation of its friends.

This inadequacy of information was not just one of knowledge but also one of understanding. It was not just a matter of day-by-day factual information; it was a matter of being able to envisage and apprehend the spirit of another society. In the inability of the Allied statesmen to picture to themselves the passions of the Russian civil war, as in their stubborn belief that the principles of liberal parliamentarianism ought to have some relevance to the situation in Russia, you had the reflections of what I fear we must call a certain parochialism of the Anglo-Saxon mind, and particularly the American mind, of the late nineteenth and early twentieth centuries. We represent, all of us, a society in which the manifestations of evil have been carefully buried and sublimated in the social behavior of people, as in their very consciousness. For this reason, probably, despite our widely traveled and outwardly cosmopolitan lives, the mainsprings of political behavior in such a country as Russia tend to remain concealed from our vision. The comprehension of these motives is something against which our conscious minds rebel, as against something uncongenial and dangerous to the sources of our own spiritual security. To this tendency even the statesmen of Paris in 1919 were not immune.

These were only some of the technical deficiencies of Allied statesmanship in its relation to the Russian question at the Peace Conference. But I think we should note that all of this operated against the background of a great and pervasive conceptual error, which was an inability to assess correctly the significance and the consequences of the war in which Europe had just been engaged. The meaning the Allied statesmen had insisted on reading into the war now blinded their judgment of the possibilities of the peace.

The fact is that Russia was already lost to the purposes of Western statesmanship long before the Peace Conference began. There had always been an element of artificiality in Russia's participation in World War I on the Allied side. The Tsar's government had had its own reasons for entering that war. Even these were reasons which had meant nothing to the great mass of the Russian people. How much less comprehensible to them must have been the motives and calculations of people in London and Paris! The mental and spiritual world of the Russian peasant was leagues and centuries removed from that of the people who manned the Western governments. France and Britain, in other words, had contrived to draw to their aid in an intra-European contest the resources of a people on the periphery of Europe who had no idea of what this was all about, no real interest in the outcome of the struggle, no commitment to the things the Allies were fighting for. The terrible military effort had proved too much for the system of government in that country, and had produced not only its breakdown, but a lasting embitterment of the people against the West. The moderate political elements, who had constituted a link to respectable Western thought, had been discarded. The Western governments were faced on the Russian scene with a group of fanatics profoundly and incurably hostile to Western ideals and traditions. These people drew their political strength from the measureless bitterness of a great people who had never known self-government and whose blood and substance had only recently been exploited by others, in tremendous quantities, for a struggle they did not understand. The effort of the Western Allies to have Russia's assistance in the war had proved too great a strain for the very governmental arrangements on which that assistance rested—the bond had snapped. The result was that Russia was finally estranged and lost to the purposes of the peace. The price of having Russia as an ally in the war for three years was the loss of Russia as a partner in the construction of the peace.

Had the Western governments perceived, in 1917, the folly of trying to keep Russia in the war, and had they moved at that time to terminate the struggle—not on Lenin's terms but on the basis that Lord Lansdowne so futilely recommended—something might still have been salvaged from the wreckage, and Russia might still have been able to make some positive contribution to the peace. The insistence on continuing the war for another year, and on trying to restore an eastern front regardless of its effect on Russian political life, destroyed even this possibility. The statesmen at Paris, who sought Russia's collaboration in the building of a new world order, never understood that it was already much too late. At the time of the Paris Conference Russia's potential usefulness to the postwar West already lay, like so many tens of thousands of Europe's youth, buried in the dust of the war—a casualty to the dictates of hatred, vindictiveness, self-righteousness, and revenge. It had been put there by the same statesmen who, in 1919, wrung their hands over Russia's absence as they set about, at Paris, to shape the peace.

11   Germany and the Founding of the Comintern

THUS FAR I have dealt only obliquely with that phase of Russia's relations with the West which was destined to have the greatest importance during the Twenties and Thirties: namely, the relations with Germany. I have told about the Brest-Litovsk Treaty of March 1918, and how it was followed by a German occupation of the Ukraine, not dissimilar to that which took place during World War II. And I have also mentioned the murder of the German ambassador, Count Mirbach, on July 4 of that year. Let me take the story up from there.

The German government was as a whole not too seriously annoyed with the Soviet government over Mirbach's murder, which they rightly attributed to the Left S-R's. But they were also not quite satisfied with the rather lame amends made by the Soviet government for it. This question dragged on as an issue between the two governments until the German collapse four months later. Mention has also been made of the fact that another ambassador was sent, but remained only for a few days. Upon his return to Berlin, in August 1918, the embassy staff was withdrawn to German-occupied territory, where it remained until the final German defeat in November.

The Soviet government, during the summer of 1918, had its own representative, Adolf Joffe, in Berlin. Joffe was, of course, a professional revolutionary. Hopes ran high at that time in Moscow for an early revolution in Germany. Joffe regarded it as his business rather to promote the German revolution than to maintain good relations with the Kaiser's government. He refused, on ideological grounds, to present his credentials to the Kaiser in person. He entertained close relations with a number of the left-wing Socialists, and supplied them as liberally as he could both with funds and with subversive literature. This was the first somewhat naïve example of the Soviet use of its diplomatic immunities for subversive purposes in another country.

The nature of Joffe's activities did not remain concealed from the German government. People in Berlin became increasingly fed up with the evidences of his abuses of his position. Less than a week before the German collapse and revolution of November 1918, the German Imperial authorities therefore staged an incident in which a Soviet diplomatic bag was said to have fallen and broken open at a railway station in Berlin, revealing large quantities of subversive literature inside. There is some evidence that the literature, in this instance, had actually been put there by the police themselves. But there is no question but that the Soviet embassy had been violating its privileges in a flagrant manner. Joffe and his numerous staff were promptly expelled and sent back to Russia.

This was, as I say, only a few days before the end of
the war and the overthrow of the Imperial German government. As the war ended, there was thus no diplomatic contact between Moscow and Berlin, the German embassy having
been withdrawn from Moscow, and the Soviet envoy having
just been expelled from Berlin.

The German Revolution of November 9 led, as you will
recall, to the Kaiser's abdication and to the establishment of
the German Republic, initially under Socialist leadership.
This at once gave an entirely different aspect to Soviet relations with Germany. From now on, Moscow's relations with
Germany would be very prominently determined by her relations to the European Socialists generally. For this reason,
it becomes necessary to have a glance at this point at
the development of the relations between the Russian Bolsheviki and the Socialist movement outside of Russia.

Prior to World War I, the Socialists of all European
countries had been united in the so-called Second International—an association of Socialist parties and groups from
a number of countries. The Second International was seriously split by the questions which the war posed for Socialists everywhere. The main split was between those who
favored supporting the war effort of their respective countries,
and those who felt that Socialists owed it to working-class
solidarity to take a negative attitude toward the conflict, as
an imperialist and unworthy war, and to deny support to
their respective governments in the effort to conduct it. The
Bolsheviki, of course, belonged to this latter group.

The representatives of the antiwar faction contrived to
meet twice during the war in Switzerland, once at Zimmerwald and once at Kienthal, for the purpose of thrashing out
some sort of common program. In these conferences even
this extreme group split once more, the minority faction
being made up of the Bolsheviki alone, with a tiny coterie of
supporters drawn, I believe, exclusively from minority segments of the German and Swedish Socialist parties. The issues
on which Lenin differed from the others at Zimmerwald and
Kienthal are so hairsplitting and involve such complicated
nuances and contradictions that I cannot go into them in
detail. Suffice it to say that Lenin, as the extremist which he
was, favored efforts at immediate revolution—efforts to turn
the "imperialist" war into a civil war—in all the warring
countries. His opponents accepted this as an ultimate goal but

would have been content, initially, to see international action that would stop the war, and let revolution come at a later stage.

At the time of the Russian Revolution, therefore, Lenin and his faction represented only a tiny and not very significant minority-within-a-minority of the European Socialist moment. His support outside of the Russian party was negligible.

Inside Germany, the Socialist movement had divided along lines similar to that of the Second International itself. A large, vigorous radical group, calling itself the "Independent Socialists," had split off the Social-Democratic Party. Within this Leftist faction, an even more radical minority group, called the Spartacist League (*Spartakusbund*) had crystallized at the end of the war. It was led by two striking and talented revolutionaries: Karl Liebknecht and Rosa Luxemburg. Liebknecht was a German, the son of a prominent German Socialist. He was a man steeped from childhood in the powerful German Socialist movement. Rosa Luxemburg was the most talented and prominent of a considerable number of left-wing Socialists in Germany whose origins had been in the Russian or Polish Socialist movements. These were, for the most part, people from the so-called Jewish Pale, which extended along the western border of the Russian Empire, and to which a large portion of the Russian Jewry was confined. It was in large measure the discrimination against Jews in the empire which had driven so many of them into the ranks of the revolutionary movement; and these Jewish revolutionaries included many remarkable and talented people. About half of the Russian Social-Democratic Party was drawn from this source; and of those who were able to leave the empire, many joined Socialist parties in other countries, notably Germany and Poland. Rosa Luxemburg was such a one.

Liebknecht and Luxemburg had spent long periods in German prisons during the war, but had been released just before the German breakdown. They had contrived to establish this separate group, the Spartacist League, within the family of the Independent Socialists. It was this group which then came to be regarded as the foundation of the German Communist Party.

Actually, it is important to remember that even the members of the Spartacist League were not entirely followers of Lenin. In those vital questions of organization which had so agitated the Russian revolutionary movement before the war, and which had led to the split of the Russian Communist Party into Bolsheviki and Mensheviki, the leaders of the Spartacist League, particularly Luxemburg, had sided with the Russian Mensheviki. This was a very important distinction, for it spelled the difference between the democratic and the dictatorial approaches to a future Socialist state. Rosa Luxemburg had not hesitated on many occasions to cross swords with Lenin over this issue in the course of the fierce ideological debates that had wracked the radical Socialist groups in the years before and during the war. The German Communist Party thus had its roots partly in Menshevism rather than Bolshevism—a situation which it would take Stalin many years, and the shedding of much blood, to alter.

As signs of the impending German collapse began to mount in the early autumn of 1918, the Russian Communists followed the German political situation with passionate intensity. You will remember that, at that time, they considered the retention of their power in Russia impossible unless their Revolution could be in some way extended to other countries. They looked to Germany, as I noted earlier, both as the most likely country for such a development and as the most important place where it could conceivably take place.

In the last year of World War I, following the Bolshevik seizure of power in Russia, Communist propaganda made considerable headway among the German troops still stationed on the eastern front. As the war drew to a close, there were signs of great social unrest throughout the German scene. It was no wonder that the Bolsheviki, then fighting for their lives in the Russian civil war, faced with staggering problems of economic reconstruction at home, despairing of help from the Allies, and convinced that their survival depended on the spread of revolution to other countries, placed all their hopes on Germany.

The Kaiser's abdication and the German surrender immediately produced a crisis in the ranks of the German Socialists. It suddenly became clear that the Socialists would now have to take power—a responsibility they had never before had to bear. The shock of this unexpected confrontation with responsibility was too great for the shaky unity of the Socialist camp. It split wide open. While the Majority

Socialist leader, Philipp Scheidemann, was proclaiming the establishment of the German Republic from the balcony of the parliament building, Liebknecht was proclaiming the establishment of a Soviet Germany from the balcony of the Imperial Palace a mile away. In these circumstances, the high command of the German army held, for the moment, a sort of balance of power. It offered its support to what it viewed as the lesser evil: the Majority Socialists. The latter, having no alternative other than civil war, accepted this support with some relief, and agreed to collaborate with the army in making possible an orderly demobilization of the troops and in preventing the immediate establishment of a Soviet dictatorship in Germany.

One can very well understand the alarm felt by Friedrich Ebert, the new first Socialist Chancellor in Germany, over the activities of the Socialist left wing. The example of the Russian Revolution, one year earlier, was in everybody's mind. Ebert recalled very well the fact that Kerensky had also been a moderate Socialist. He had no desire to see the German Revolution captured by the extreme left wing of German Socialism after the pattern of the November Revolution in Russia.

Despite the army's support, it was not possible for the Majority Socialists to establish their position securely at once. Extreme left-wing elements, including both the Spartacist League and the Revolutionary Shop Stewards of Berlin, had a considerable following in Berlin and elsewhere. For the first few weeks after the Revolution, conditions in the defeated Germany were chaotic. It was hard to tell what was happening. In Berlin, in particular, power was virtually divided between the two factions.

This being the case, it is not surprising that the Russian Communists, who found it hard to get information anyway, were bewildered by what they could learn about the German situation, and at a loss to know how to tackle it. Although they had been extremely sharp in their attacks on the moderate German Socialists, and never failed to denounce Ebert and Scheidemann as traitors, they seem to have assumed that the new regime would welcome good relations with them. Immediately after the Revolution, they instructed their ambassador, Joffe, to return to Berlin, assuming that he would of course be accepted. They also made a token offer of a shipment of grain to the German government. To their amazement, Ebert refused to receive

Joffe, and turned down the grain. The Russians at once realized where they stood. From this time on, their effort was directed undeviatingly to an attempt to tear down the power of the German Majority Socialists and to build up within Germany a radical faction subservient to their own influence, which could produce a second German revolution in the true Bolshevik tradition. This, they hoped, would provide for them the international support they still considered indispensable to their survival in Russia.

Let me add that they would, in my opinion, not have behaved much differently even had the new German Socialist government responded more favorably to their initial advances. But their tactics might then have been more cautious and more subtle. As it was, once it became clear that Ebert was having none of it, that he was in no sense amenable to their influence and could not be used by them for their own purposes, caution was no longer in order. It at once became an urgent need of Soviet policy to produce a formal split between the Spartacist League and the remainder of the Socialist movement, and then to penetrate the League and alter its character in such a way that it would be a fully useful and reliable follower of the Leninist line. To this end, Lenin dispatched several senior Bolshevik agents to attend the first legal congress of the Spartacist organization (previously it had been underground), due to take place in Berlin at the end of December of 1918.

Only one of these delegates got through to Berlin, the rest being successfully obstructed by the German military command. The one that got through was Karl Radek, the same man who had thrown the revolutionary pamphlets out of the train window to the German troops when the Soviet delegation pulled into Brest-Litovsk for the talks with the Germans. Radek, like Rosa Luxemburg, had been a member of the Polish Socialist Party, though personal relations between the two were actually very strained. Radek, who had been for some time in Germany, had a certain independent following among German left-wing Socialists, particularly in Bremen. He was thus able to exert influence on the development of the German Communist movement, not just as a representative of the Russian Communists but also as a figure in German socialism in his own right.

Under Radek's influence, the Spartacist League, at its first congress in the last days of 1918, broke entirely with the Independent Socialists and set itself up as a separate party under the name of the Communist Party of Germany. This event is usually regarded as the birth of the present German Communist Party.

A fortnight later, Liebknecht became involved in an effort led by the Revolutionary Shop Stewards in Berlin to seize power in the capital. The Shop Stewards, a curiously informal but violently radical group of people, were not identical with the Spartacist League, but only close to it in their extremist attitude. This effort at an imitation of Russia's November Revolution was suppressed by irregular, conservative voluntary units—the spiritual and organizational forerunners of the Nazis. In the course of the suppression of the uprising, both Liebknecht and Rosa Luxemburg were arrested. They were brutally executed the same evening, their bodies being thrown into the Landwehr canal in the fashionable West End of Berlin. The destruction of these two outstanding leaders of the radical socialist movement served momentarily to weaken the German Communists in their competition for power internally. But at the same time, it played very well into the hands of Moscow's desire to win dominant influence and control over the party; for the others were now more humble, more dependent, and more amenable to outside guidance.

While these things were going on, Lenin and his associates had been alarmed to note that the Second International was beginning to recoup its forces. Its leaders had called a new congress, to convene in February 1919. Lenin had always insisted that the war spelled the end of the Second International, and that its demise must be followed by the creation of a Third International to take its place. The effort at revival greatly disturbed him. He realized that it was dangerous to the prospects of revolution in Europe, as he wished to see it come about, to permit the moderate Socialists to monopolize once again the international organization of Socialist groups the world over. Now that there was a German Communist Party, it was particularly important to provide a new international framework in which both the German and Russian Communist Parties could be embraced, in order that the German Communists, and left-wing Socialists generally, might not drift back into the old, more moderate one. In January, therefore, just as the statesmen in Paris were beginning to discuss the Russian question, an invitation was issued from Moscow to a number of left-wing Socialist parties and organizations in other countries to send representatives to a gathering to be held in Moscow looking toward the foundation of a Third International.

This congress took place from March 2-6, 1919—a few days before Bullitt's arrival in the Russian capital. It was a rather pathetic affair, attended by only thirty-five persons, of whom all but a handful were at that time actually resident in Russia. Most of them had been hand-picked by the Russian Central Committee from the Communists among the international minority groups of the old Russian Empire, some of which had now gained nominal independence. Only five representatives, coming respectively from Germany, Austria, Norway, Sweden, and Holland, arrived from abroad. The German representative had been instructed by Rosa Luxemburg before her death to oppose the foundation of the new International; and it was only with great difficulty that he could be persuaded to abstain on the crucial vote rather than to record his opposition. The decision to set up a Third International was thus actually taken simply by the Russian Communists themselves, together with four delegates from minor European countries, whose credentials were not too firm. But Lenin's purpose was served: an organization was now in existence; a nucleus had been created around which could be grouped world-wide opposition to the Second International.

These same first months of 1919 saw great social ferment, accompanied by the outbreak of radical-socialist uprisings in many parts of Europe. All over Germany the two extreme wings of the political spectrum, radical-socialist workers and semi-fascist reactionary bands, feuded and fought over the heads of the coalition of moderate Socialists and moderate army officers which ran the country. Sometimes the workers succeeded in winning and holding power for a short time, in one part of Germany or another. When this happened, it was generally regarded as a Communist revolution and as the work of the long arm of Moscow. Respectable folk everywhere, having in mind the Russian Revolution, trembled for the future of the West.

Particular alarm was occasioned in western Europe by the temporary establishment at that time of Communist regimes in Hungary and Bavaria. The Hungarian Communist government, set up in March 1919, was a mixed Social-Democratic and Communist affair. The Allies, with their crushing territorial demands on Hungary in favor of the

Czechs and Rumanians, were themselves largely responsible for this turn in Hungarian political life. The trend to the Left was, for the Hungarians, largely one of desperation. The Communist regime, headed by Béla Kun, a returned war prisoner from Siberia, lasted for some four months before it was suppressed by the intervention (with Allied encouragement) of Rumanian forces—a form of liberation which the Hungarian people scarcely enjoyed and which did not endear the Allies to them.

The Bavarian uprising, followed immediately by the proclamation of a Bavarian Soviet Republic, was particularly confusing to people elsewhere. It took place in April 1919. It was led by two Russian Socialists, both named Levin— one of whom spelled his name Leviné, presumably so that they could be told apart. This fact, plus the familiar Soviet terminology by which the regime described itself, convinced everyone that the action was directly inspired by Moscow. The new regime was brutally suppressed by nationalist opponents only three or four weeks after its inception.

Actually, none of these events seems to have owed its origin to Moscow's direct instigation. In the case of most of the German episodes, not even the German Communists were originally behind them, though they often tried to climb on the bandwagon at a later stage. Levin and Leviné were, as it happened, not Bolsheviki at all, but S-R's in their Russian status, and apparently not even Communists in Germany. They acted entirely on their own. In Hungary, the initiative first came from the Hungarian Social-Democrats, who had been rendered desperate by Allied vindictiveness and naïvely hoped for Russian military support against the Allied terms. Only later was the development captured in large measure by Béla Kun, and even he was not in close touch at that time with Moscow. Throughout this whole period Moscow was, in fact, largely cut off from Europe. It had no organizational facilities for running such activities there.

Yet all these stirrings and uprisings were, in another sense, deeply influenced by the Russian Revolution and particularly by its second, Bolshevist phase. If Moscow was not directing events by instruction, it was usually inspiring them by example. All the European radical-socialist groups had been stirred and impressed by the fact that a radical-socialist revolution had, after all, taken place in Russia. There was none of these groups that did not have its dreams and

hopes to some degree inflated by this fact. At a later date
—very soon, in fact—Moscow *would* clamp its disciplinary
hold onto all that portion of European socialism that was
prepared to accept it. But in the year 1919, when the most
spectacular Communist revolutionary successes of the postwar period were being registered in Europe, it was only by
example, not yet by precept, that Moscow was influencing
the European radical-socialist movement.

That this was so was not generally understood at the time
in countries further afield. The reports of these uprisings
caused the Western Allies, in particular, much alarm. The
Hungarian Socialist government was proclaimed on March
21, 1919; the Bavarian one, two or three weeks later. You
may remember that this was just the time when Bullitt returned to Paris with Lenin's proposals to the Allies. That
the alarming news from Hungary and Bavaria had something to do with the negative reaction in Paris and London
to these proposals and the thought of any sort of deal
with the Bolsheviki at that time, seems unescapable. Thus
the international revolutionary attitude and policies of the
Soviet regime began to interfere at an early date with its
desire to regularize, on the overt level, its relations with the
Western Allies.

After the failure of the initial uprising in Berlin in January
1919, when Liebknecht and Luxemburg were killed, the German Communist Party was severely repressed by the
moderate-socialist government. It was forced, in fact, to go
partially underground again. In the action taken at that time
against the party, Radek was himself arrested. When the
government realized who he was—realized, that is, that he
was virtually a representative of the Soviet government—
it removed him from the regular prison regime and placed
him in a sort of honorable internment, in which state he
was kept throughout most of the year 1919. The German
government was now beginning to react to the full harshness of the Versailles peace terms, which gradually became
known throughout the spring of the year and were finally
published in full on May 7. It at once occurred to many
moderately socialistic and conservative Germans that Germany might be obliged, despite the general distaste for Lenin's regime, to turn to Russia—as the only great power not
committed to the Versailles settlement—in order to have
some flexibility of action and *some* alternative course, in the
face of the solid front of rejection and punitive demands

with which she felt herself faced on the Allied side. This feeling was accentuated by the food blockade which the Allies, against the protests of Hoover, insisted on continuing to impose upon a submissive and hungering Germany. Just what advantages one might be able to derive from future relations with Russia was at that time not at all clear. But in the light of the Allied attitude, there was a general feeling in Berlin that one did not wish, now, to spoil anything unnecessarily. It was felt unwise to prejudice the only favorable possibilities the future appeared to hold.

So Radek was detained in relative comfort. He was permitted to receive visitors and communications. From his place of detention he kept in touch with the struggling German Communist Party, which was much in need of guidance after the death of its two leaders; and he gave it such advice as he could. Occasionally he received visitors from the bourgeois and conservative camps, who had heard about this odd prisoner and were curious to see what he was like.

Subsequent writers have tended to read a somewhat sinister meaning into these few early meetings between Radek and members of the moderate and conservative classes in Germany—to see in them the beginnings of a conspiracy between the German generals and the Soviet regime. This was much exaggerated. Radek was at that time not even in touch with Moscow, which was then largely isolated and had no normal communications with Germany. The meetings reflected in the main only curiosity on the part of his visitors. But in the liberality with which he was treated there was indeed a harbinger of that relationship between Moscow and the German Right which was destined, after many vicissitudes, to constitute the decisive factor in the outbreak of the Second World War, twenty years later.

When Radek was released, at the end of 1919, this was a sign that Germany was prepared to make a beginning at the restoration of the lost relationship between Berlin and Moscow. And the reason for this was part of a political logic destined to manifest itself time after time in the next ten or fifteen years. Let me try to describe it.

During the latter phase of the war, the Allies, and even Woodrow Wilson, had insisted that there must be a revolution in Germany as the price of peace. They professed themselves unwilling to deal with the Kaiser and the German militarists, who were held responsible for the outbreak and

conduct of the war. But they repeatedly indicated that the
Allies bore no ill will toward the German people, and
that, if this unworthy leadership of the Kaiser's government
were shaken off and an honest, well-meaning, peace-loving
regime set up in its place, the German people had no reason to fear the future.

In what was done at the Peace Conference, this concept
seems to have been ignored. A revolution *had* occurred in
Germany—but the Allies acted as if it had not. The Germans were not admitted to the council table. Peace terms
were worked out which, if not mortally destructive from
the German standpoint, were humiliating, irritating, and onerous in many ways. Even more powerful, perhaps, in its
psychological effect, was the action of the French in insisting on the maintenance of a food blockade of Germany
for more than a year after the Armistice, out of no apparent
motive other than a desire to cause a type of suffering
which could only hit hardest the poorest and most helpless
elements of the civilian population, and particularly the
children—people who had had no responsibility for the
policies of the old Imperial regime.

I do not mean to argue about whether the Germans "deserved" this. I find this word "deserve," when applied to an
entire people, too vague to have historical usefulness. But
I would like to point out that this was a somewhat contradictory Allied policy. One could not have it both ways. If
the purpose was to make Germany suffer, then surely it
would have been better to leave the Kaiser and generals in
power, to bear the onus of this situation and to reap the
responsibility they had invited. If, on the other hand, men
of basic good will—and there can in my opinion be no
doubt that men like Ebert and Scheidemann answered to
this description—were to be asked to take over, then it was
illogical to saddle them with conditions of peace which
could only serve to produce disillusionment with the promises they had made to the German people and to discredit
them as factors in German political life. If it was to be a
punitive peace, then the old regime should have been forced
to bear it. If one was going to insist on a change of regime,
then a punitive peace made no sense at all.

If the peace *was* to be punitive and destructive, and if
one did *not* wish to leave the Kaiser's government in control to bear the political burden of enforcing it internally,
then surely it would have been better not to leave Germany

a united state at all, or at least not the only great united state in central Europe. It was Jacques Bainville, the Bourbon historian, who described the Versailles settlement as being too mild for the hardships it contained, and who accurately predicted that an aggrieved Germany, left as the only great state in central and eastern Europe, would not fail some day to dispose easily of the small new states by which it was surrounded. To break up the Austro-Hungarian Empire, to leave Germany united, and then to penalize a new German regime which had no part of the responsibility of the war, was to invite trouble.

The inconsistency and folly of this course was compounded by one more factor. This was the fact that Russia, too, was not associated with the Peace Conference. A frustrated, embittered Germany would have every reason to swallow its ideological distaste for a Soviet government which, like itself, had no obligation to the Versailles settlement, and to seek, in such collaboration as it could arrange with that government, escape from the strictures which that settlement envisaged.

In this way, the pattern of the events that led the Western world to new disaster in 1939 was laid down in its entirety by the Allied governments in 1918 and 1919. What we shall have to observe from here on in the relations between Russia, Germany, and the West follows a logic as inexorable as that of any Greek tragedy.

12   1920—The Year of Transition

THE YEAR 1920 was the connecting link, in Russia's relations with the West, between the wholly abnormal state of intervention and civil war with the absence of all official relations, which prevailed in 1919, and the general pattern of official relationships, which was established during the period 1921-1924. As such, it was an important transition; and it is with this in mind that I should like to describe its principal developments.

The collapse of the combination of forces, Russian and non-Russian, which constituted Bolshevism's opponent in the civil war, gave to Lenin and his associates for the first time the opportunity to fashion with some degree of deliberateness their policies toward the Western governments. At the beginning of 1920, none of these governments had as yet recognized Soviet Russia in any way. None entertained official relationships with it. But they were now terminating their hostile measures against it; the troops were being withdrawn. The blockade was lifted in January. The Supreme War Council, in February, even went so far as to advise the new states in the Baltic area, which had split off from the Russian Empire, to abandon their attitude of hostility toward the Soviet regime and to attempt to re-establish normal commercial and official relations with it.

In the face of these circumstances, Soviet policy throughout 1920 was an ambivalent and seemingly contradictory one. On the one hand, the Bolsheviki needed the help of the Western powers in their effort to restore economic life in Russia. Besides, they were still very conscious of their extreme weakness, and they actively feared anything in the nature of a union of the capitalist governments against them. They were anxious, therefore, to play the capitalist governments off against each other; and this was something which, as they saw it, could best be done by concluding outwardly normal relations with them and by exploiting the greed of Western capitalists for concessions of one sort or another in Russia. Ideology taught the Bolshevik leaders that a lust for profits on the part of its monopolists was the only serious motivation behind the policies of the capitalist state; and they hoped, by offering crumbs of economic favor to one capitalist group or another, to keep them bidding against each other and at odds with each other, and to prevent them from ganging up against Russia before such time as the world revolution could take place and draw their fangs. All this spoke for the re-establishment of outwardly normal official relations with the West.

At the same time, the Kremlin's belief in the imminence of a European revolution, and not only in its *imminence* but in its *essentiality to the preservation of Communist power in Russia,* continued throughout this entire year of 1920. Everything conceivable was done to promote revolutionary socialist tendencies in Europe. This, of course, was a policy bitterly hostile to the respective governments.

There was thus established, at this early date, that ambiguity and contradictoriness of Soviet policy which has endured to the present day: the combination of the doctrine of co-existence—the claim, that is, to the right to have normal outward relations with capitalist countries—with the most determined effort behind the scenes to destroy the Western governments and the social and political systems supporting them.

Before I proceed to talk about what occurred in 1920 in these two contradictory aims of Soviet policy, I must tell you of one complicating factor which did not fit into the general pattern of 1920 and therefore caused much confusion to everyone concerned. This was the Polish-Russian War of that year.

You will recall that the Versailles settlement included the establishment of an independent Poland out of lands which, for more than a century, had been divided among Russia, Austria, and Prussia. One of the great disadvantages of Russia's absence from the Peace Conference was that while the conference was able to establish, after a fashion, the western frontiers of this new Polish state, it had no means of establishing an agreed frontier between Poland and Russia. It endeavored to get the Poles to agree, for their part, to a line (subsequently known as the Curzon line) somewhat in the neighborhood of the one that has existed since 1945; but the Poles, led by Marshal Joseph Pilsudski, had at that moment dreams of grandeur which included the wildest ideas of expansion to the east, and even envisaged a considerable dismemberment of the old Russian state, to Poland's advantage.

In the early part of 1919, the Poles, taking advantage of Soviet weakness, occupied as much territory as they could eastwards, for the purpose of placing a *fait accompli* before the Supreme War Council and the Allied governments, and forcing them to acquiesce in the establishment of a greater Poland in the east. The Bolsheviki, absorbed in the civil war, could hardly resist at that moment. In the autumn of 1919, however, the Poles moderated these aggressive actions and even entered for a time into some rather desultory secret talks with Soviet representatives, designed to quiet things down and allay Soviet fears. They did this, curiously enough, because they were at that moment afraid that the Russian Whites, under General A. I. Denikin, who were pressing Moscow hard from the south, might actually succeed in unseating the Soviet government. The Poles, in contrast to their French patrons, did not want the Russian Whites to win, because they were correctly convinced that the Whites would be more averse than the Bolsheviki to the establishment of an independent Poland. They therefore restrained themselves throughout the autumn of 1919.

When it became evident at the turn of the year that the anti-Bolshevik cause in the Russian civil war was lost and that there was no danger of the Whites winning, the Poles immediately made plans for a full-fledged attack on the Soviet Union. On the face of it, this was madness. The Polish state had existed only a few months. Its governmental arrangements were confusion incarnate. The country was rampant with hardship and disease. It counted at that moment thirty-four thousand cases of typhus among its population; 1,315,000 Polish children were being fed at that time by the American Relief Administration. For a small country in this situation to launch an all-out military attack on Russia was a fantastic enterprise, and one which properly shocked and angered the Western governments, to whose somewhat sentimental benevolence the Poles owed the restoration of their national independence in the first place.

Nevertheless, Marshal Pilsudski persisted with his plans. Evading repeated Soviet pleas for settlement of differences by negotiation, he proceeded, in April 1920, to negotiate an agreement with the hard-pressed anti-Bolshevik regime which still survived in a portion of the Ukraine. Three days later, on the strength of this agreement, he launched an offensive which carried Polish forces in a fortnight all the way to the Dnepr River, and ended with the capture of Kiev on May 7.

The Red army, relieved of most of the pressure from its internal enemies, at once responded with a vigor which the Poles had not anticipated. It mounted in mid-May a two-pronged counteroffensive. General Mikhail Tukhachevski, who was later to be the leading victim of Stalin's purge of the Officers' Corps in the '30s, countered with an infantry attack on the northern section of the front and turned the Polish left flank. Meanwhile, the well-known cavalry general, S. Budenny, harassed Polish communications in the south with his calvary units. These tactics brought a decisive change in the tide of the war. In June the Poles were forced to evacuate Kiev. At the beginning of July a major Soviet offensive, launched in the north, carried Tukhachevski's army to the gates of Warsaw. Frantically, the Poles now appealed to the Allies for support. The Allies were torn between a desire, on the one hand, to say to the Poles "It serves you right" and alarm, on the other, at the advance of the Red army towards the heart of Europe, particularly the German frontier. They responded in characteristic fashion by sending, in addition to more shipments of munitions, a high-powered mission of distinguished citizens to supplement the numerous contingent of French military advisers already attached to the Polish army. Just as the members of the mission were arriving on the scene, Pilsudski himself mounted a desperate but boldly conceived counteroffensive. Taking advantage of the lack of coordination between Budenny and Tukhachevski, he pushed through between the two Russian forces, got at Tukhachevski's communications, and forced the Red army to withdraw as precipitately as it had advanced. By the end of August, the Reds had been pushed out of what was ethnically Polish territory, and both sides were sobered and tired of the exercise. Parleys began in September, which soon led to a cessation of hostilities and the negotiation of a border settlement. The new frontier, agreed upon at that time, endured until the Nazi-Soviet Nonaggression Pact of 1939. This was a line considerably to the east—that is, more favorable to Poland—than the Curzon line. In this respect it reflected the Polish successes in the final stages of the Russian-Polish War. But I wonder today whether, in the light of all that has happened since, the Poles were really well advised to extort it in this way.

So much for the Russian-Polish War. It was really only a delayed phase of the Russian intervention and civil war: delayed because the Poles did not want to be associated in any way with the White Russian opponents of the Bolsheviki, and preferred to tackle the Russian Communists themselves.

Now for the main features of Soviet policy toward the West in this period: world revolution on the one hand, and the revival of diplomatic contacts on the other. For the Soviet government of 1920, the hope for world revolution was still largely centered in Germany. Here, misfortune continued to dog the Soviet heels. Karl Radek got back to

Moscow at the end of January 1920, fresh from his odd combination of prison and diplomacy in Berlin. He tried to tell Lenin and the others that Germany was not ripe for revolution, that Communist plans there must be laid for the long term rather than the short term. This advice was not accepted. Instead, Moscow settled down, now that the Russian civil war was over, to a heightened effort to promote an immediate Communist revolution in Germany. The task was not an easy one. The existing German Communist Party, in addition to being not entirely amenable to Moscow's influence, represented still only a small fraction of the German working class. In elections held in June 1920, for example, the Independent Socialists, who were themselves only the more radical wing of the German socialist movement, polled nearly five million votes, whereas the Communists received only 450,000.

In March 1920, the German Communists suffered a severe reverse when they failed to take advantage of a situation which actually presented them with considerable opportunity. This was the so-called Kapp *Putsch*: a vigorous effort by extreme Nationalist freebooters to seize the capital and the government. Berlin was, in fact, momentarily occupied by these elements; but the Nationalist action was frustrated within a matter of days by a highly successful general strike mounted by the Social-Democrats and the trade-unions. The Communists, reluctant to associate themselves with anything that somebody else might get, or share, the credit for, committed the grievous political mistake of initially opposing the strike, and were later forced to reverse their position and to attempt to climb on the bandwagon themselves in the most ignominious fashion.

In view of the weakness of the German Communists, Lenin's policy throughout 1920 took relatively little account of them, but was directed primarily at producing a split within the large Independent Socialist Party, with a view to breaking off the left wing of that party and bringing it under Soviet influence.

In July 1920 the Second Congress of the Third International was held in Moscow. It was a much more impressive show than the one which had taken place the year before. In place of the paltry thirty-five delegates (most of them hand-picked by Lenin) who had attended the First Congress, there were now over two hundred present, and many of these really did represent groups of some importance in the outside world. The fact of Soviet success in clinging to power had spoken more eloquently than the rigid fanaticism of Lenin's ideological position.

The Second Congress was held just at that moment in July when the Red army was approaching the gates of Warsaw in the course of the war with Poland. A large war map was kept in the hall. Every day the red flags that marked the battle line were moved further westward, to the cheers of the excited delegates, who saw in this changing battle map the inexorable march of Communism into central and western Europe.

The Second Congress was used by Lenin to lay down a list of twenty-one conditions on which, and on which alone, Communist groups and factions would be admitted to the Third International. These conditions were deliberately drawn up in such a way as to be unacceptable to the moderate Socialist leaders abroad and to oblige the revolutionary wing of the Socialist movement to split off from the remainder. In the case of Germany, this tactic was afterwards reinforced by a visit of G. E. Zinoviev, the Russian head of the Third International, to the Congress of the German Independent Socialists which was held at Halle in October. The result was finally to produce, at the end of 1920, the desired rupture in the German Socialist movement. The left wing of the Independent Socialists split off and combined with the Communists, to form an expanded German Communist Party.

The new party had about 350,000 members, as compared with the mere 50,000 which the old party had had. It at once got busy, under Russian direction, to prepare a revolutionary action. This action was launched, finally, in the spring of 1921, just a year after the Kapp *Putsch.* It consisted largely of an attempt to use, again, but now under Communist direction, the instrumentality of the general strike which had been used to such good effect by the Social-Democrats the year before. But, this time, the effort proved completely unsuccessful. It was not supported by the German working class as a whole. Its failure brought home to Moscow, for the first time, in an inescapable manner, the futility of the effort to bring revolution to Germany at this juncture and in this way, and laid the groundwork for the acceptance by the Soviet government of the conclusion Radek had propounded more than a year earlier: namely, that Communist plans for Germany would have to be laid for the long term and not for the short term.

While these efforts were going on in Germany and while similar but less serious revolutionary efforts under Soviet inspiration were going on in many other countries, the effort to establish outwardly normal relations with these governments was also already in progress. It began with the newly formed Baltic countries. Little Estonia became, by virtue of a treaty signed on February 2, 1920, the first non-Communist state to have anything resembling normal relations with the Soviet Union. Later in the year, similar treaties were signed with the Latvians, the Lithuanians, and the Finns. It is ironic to reflect that these little countries, the first to establish normal relations with Moscow, should also have been, together with Poland, the first to be swallowed up again by Moscow in 1939, when Russia and Germany moved together to smash the European order established by Versailles.

In Britain, the question of relations with Russia was a hotly contested issue throughout the year—so much so that by October a commentator in the *Sunday Times* described Russia as being, next to finance, "the master question in our politics."[55] Lloyd George found himself caught here between the pressures from the Labour Party and the trade-unions, on the one side, pressures which were very violent indeed, and the feelings of Conservative circles, led by a member of his own Cabinet, Mr. Winston Churchill, on the other.

Lloyd George himself had always opposed the policy of intervention, and favored the restoration of some sort of relationship with Russia; and we may suppose that he was the leading spirit in bringing about the changes of Allied policy—the ending of the blockade and the moderate advice to the border states—which were announced during the winter. On February 10, on the occasion of the opening of Parliament, he publicly inaugurated the basic change in Britain's Russian policy by a speech in the Commons in which he urged that the intervention he superseded by the opening of commercial relations. "We have failed"—he said—

. . . to restore Russia to sanity by force. I believe we can save her by trade. Commerce has a sobering influence. . . . Trade, in my opinion, will bring an end to the ferocity, the rapine, and the crudity of Bolshevism surer than any other method.[56]

Whether Lloyd George really believed this, I do not know. The view was not a correct one. The Bolsheviki had no intention of permitting private individuals in Russia to trade freely with foreign countries. They were prepared to permit the central organs of the old producers' co-operatives, which had survived the Revolution, to act as a façade for the government's foreign trade monopoly, if this would make the Western governments any happier; but they meant to keep complete control of commercial operations in their own hands, at the Russian end; and the future would show that they were quite capable of conducting foreign trade, in their capacity as a government trade monopoly, without losing their Communist principles. My own feeling is that Lloyd George, who, to use the words of one of the British newspapers of that time, had intuitions if not principles, realized that the bait of trade was the best way to wean conservative circles in England from their horror of having any dealings at all with the Bolsheviki.

In any case, things now began to happen. A Labour M.P., acting on behalf of the British government, negotiated with Mr. Litvinov, at Copenhagen, an agreement about the repatriation of prisoners of war—a procedure which is a normal first step in the composing of differences between enemies tired of fighting each other. This task being successfully accomplished in the late winter, the Soviet government, acting through the cover of the co-operatives, which seemed more respectable in Western eyes, was permitted to appoint a trade delegation to proceed to London and begin discussions looking to the conclusion of a trade agreement. There was some difficulty about the composition of the delegation. One of its members, Mr. Litvinov, was still regarded by the British government as a particularly subversive person. But the delegation, minus Mr. Litvinov, did arrive, and on May 31, 1920, to the general horror of the Conservative press, its members were received at Number 10 Downing Street by the Prime Minister, Mr. Bonar Law, Lord Curzon, and one or two others.

The visit was described the next day by the *Manchester Guardian* in the following words:

The blow has fallen. A Bolshevist, a real live representative of Lenin, has spoken with the British Prime Minister face to face. A being, as Serjeant Buzfuz would say, erect upon two legs and bearing the outward form and semblance of a man was seen to approach 10, Downing Street, yesterday, to ring at the door and gain admission. . . . The Bolshevist pretends to go downstairs like any ordinary mortal, but without doubt in doing so he conceals some deep design. Probably if scrutinised his method of locomotion would be found to depend on some inhuman device. Meanwhile, Mr. Lloyd George has seen him and lives. Not only does he live, but, whether he walked down any steps or not, we are informed that he motored off afterwards to help to enthrone an archbishop. We trust that the archbishop will receive a double portion of archiepiscopal anointment to avert the evil influences. However, Mr. Lloyd George was not trusted with M. Krassin alone. He was duly chaperoned by Mr. Bonar Law, Lord Curzon, Sir Robert Horne, and Mr. Harmsworth, a combination which might make head against Lenin and all his works. Anyhow, the great contact is made, and the British Empire still stands.[57]

Actually the course on which the British government had embarked in attempting to establish normal commercial and *de facto* relations with Russia did not run smoothly. The French, who feared any such rapprochement between England and Russia, endeavored constantly to turn the bilateral talks into ones between the Russians and the Allies as a whole, and then to increase the severity of the Allied terms. The question of Communist propaganda, particulary in the Middle East, agitated the Conservative press and always constituted a troublesome bone of contention. A difficult legal problem arose out of the fact that the Soviet government was not a recognized government. But the greatest difficulty was presented by the Polish-Russian war.

On July 2, the head of the Soviet delegation, L. B. Krassin, left for Moscow, taking with him a set of terms laid down by the British government as a basis for the resumption of trade and *de facto* relations. These terms included an armistice, a settlement of private claims, and an agreement on noninterference in internal affairs. The Soviet government accepted these terms on July 9. But this was exactly the time that the Allied governments were considering the Polish appeal for aid in the face of the threatening Soviet advance toward Warsaw. The British government now countered the Soviet acceptance of the agreed terms by demanding that the Soviet government should, in addition, agree to cease hostilities against Poland and to send representatives to a general conference with the Allies, Poland, and the Baltic States. There was considerable bitterness in Moscow over this stepping-up of the British demands at a moment when the Soviet government had just agreed to what it understood to be the maximum British terms. All this somewhat delayed, but did not entirely stop, the process of negotiation.

Throughout the summer there was an angry tug of war between the Labour Party, which favored the Soviet side in the Polish-Soviet war, and the Conservatives, who favored the Poles—each trying to sway the policy of the government. The Labour Party and the trade-unions had sent delegations to Russia in the spring of the year. These returned with strong pro-Soviet, though not uncritical, reports which undoubtedly had a considerable influence on liberal and trade-union opinion. During the summer the dockers actually succeeded in preventing the departure of certain shiploads of munitions for Poland, an action which was matched by the refusal of the German dockers at Danzig to permit similar shipments to pass through that point, and the refusal of the German government to permit such shipments to pass through Germany.

After the conclusion of the Polish-Russian war, these alarms and excursions died down; negotiations for a commercial treaty continued through the autumn and the winter; and in the crucial month of March 1921 the Anglo-Soviet Trade Agreement was finally signed. Its commercial effects were not great, and there was destined to be many another hitch in the course of Anglo-Soviet relations; but *de facto* relations were finally established by this means, and the abnormal situation of 1920-1921 was partially overcome.

While these things were going on, a similar development, but one with quite different implications, was taking place in the relations between Russia and Germany. At the outset of 1920, the German government was anxious to resume relations with Russia, but feared to proceed in this direction faster than did the Allies, lest this have the effect of increasing the severity of Allied measures against Germany. As soon, therefore, as the British undertook prisoner-of-war negotiations with the Russians, the Germans did the same. An agreement on this subject was signed in April. It was followed by the exchange of what were ostensibly representatives for the work of repatriation of prisoners. The Germans sent to Moscow for this purpose Gustav Hilger, who was to play a prominent role in German-Russian relations in later years. The Russians sent to Berlin an experienced negotiator, Victor Kopp. In July, it was agreed that these representatives should have diplomatic privileges. Their exchange thus amounted, in effect, to the re-establishment of *de facto* relations.

Hilger has told in his recently published memoirs how he attended the somewhat primitive diplomatic dinner by which the Soviet government marked the third anniversary of the Revolution—the forerunner of the monumental forty-year anniversary ceremonies staged in Moscow in 1957—of how he found himself, to his horror, seated at the right of the Soviet Foreign Minister, as "the first and only representative of a great power from the West," and of how he was later reproached by the conservative German press for having

... sat down behind the same table, at the head of a horde of Asiatics, together with bloodstained murderers and hangmen, in order to discuss with them the prospects of world revolution, instead of caring about the fate of the tortured German prisoners of war in Russia.[58]

Hilger was not the first bourgeois representative in Russia to be faced with the charge at home that his efforts to settle practical problems with the Russians constituted a form of treason to his own society.

The course of the Polish-Soviet war naturally produced great excitement in Germany. No one knew what would happen if the Red army captured Warsaw and advanced to the new German frontier. Moderate and conservative German opinion was torn between a sneaking delight, on the one hand, at seeing a portion of the Versailles settlement thus ruthlessly smashed by someone other than themselves, and a lively apprehension, on the other hand, lest the approach of the Red army stampede the entire German working class into the acceptance of Communist rule. In the face of this situation, a cautious neutrality was observed, with a certain edge in favor of the Soviet side. By this time, General Hans von Seeckt had become the head of the new pocket army which the Germans were permitted to maintain by the Versailles settlement. (He was to be the guiding spirit in the later inauguration of secret military arrangements between Germany and Russia.) At this period he kept a very steady hand on German policy. Realizing that a Soviet incursion into Germany would force the Allies to recognize the stake they themselves had in the preservation of the integrity and influence of the German state, he refused to permit his military subordinates to make any plans to resist the Soviet advance. The most that was done was to request the Soviet government to permit a German staff officer to be attached to Tukhachevski's staff. This was refused; but the Soviet government did promise that its troops would not cross the German border.

As the year 1920 came to an end, it found both influential Germans and influential Russians more interested than ever in the possibilities for collaboration between the two countries. For reasons of prudence vis-à-vis the Allies, and in some instances even of a sincere surviving hope of the establishment of a fruitful and acceptable relationship between Germany and the West, the Germans were still refraining from going beyond the exchange of what were nominally representatives to effect the repatriation of prisoners of war. The clandestine contacts between the new German army, the so-called *Reichswehr*, and the Soviet government had not yet begun. But with the survival of the crisis of the Russian-Polish War, with von Seeckt's assumption of control over the *Reichswehr*, and with the beginning of the German effort to overcome the restrictions placed by the Versailles settlement on German rearmament, the road was now clear for a new development of Soviet-German relations.

By the spring of 1921, in short, both the Western countries and Russia had begun to learn, or seemed on the way to learning, a lesson basic to the problems of the world of the future: namely, that just because you have an enemy, and recognize him as such, it does not necessarily mean that you are obliged to destroy him or can afford the luxury of all-out attempts to do so. That this lesson should have flowed, and should have been dimly learned, from the events of 1917 to 1921 was not surprising. That it should be so little remembered by so many people three and a half decades later is something I have never been able fully to understand.

13 The Approach to Normal Relations

THE EVENTS of the winter and spring of 1921 brought home to the Soviet leaders in a number of ways the need and the possibilities for drastic change in the policies they had pursued up to that time.

We have already noted the failure of the effort of the German Communists to seize power, in March 1921, by means of a general strike. This demonstration that a Communist seizure of power was still not feasible in Germany— the most important and promising of the European countries from the revolutionary standpoint—made it clear that the general European revolution, on the occurrence of which Soviet policy had originally been staked, was not going to come about at any early date. The Third Congress of the Communist International, meeting in June and July, 1921, was obliged to recognize this fact. The war, it was noted in a resolution of the Congress, had not ended directly with a proletarian revolution; the "open revolutionary struggle of the proletariat for power" was "slackening and slowing down in many countries," and the bourgeoisie had some reason for regarding this as a major victory. This, the Comintern considered, did not mean that the prospects for world revolution had become hopeless. The line of the Comintern did not involve the fixing of any particular date for the proletarian revolution.[59] But it did mean that revolution might be long delayed. There had been a time in 1918 and 1919— Trotsky confessed in his speech to the Congress—when it had seemed

... that the assault would mount and move forward in higher and higher waves ... and that the working class would in a year or two achieve State power. It was a historical possibility, but it did not happen. ... History has given the bourgeoisie a fairly long breathing spell. ... The revolution is not so obedient, so tame, that it can be led on a leash, as we imagined.[60]

A delay, then, would ensue. How long this delay would be, no one could tell. In the intervening period of unknown duration, Communist tactics in the capitalist countries would have to be largely defensive and preparatory, designed to produce the basic preconditions for a revolutionary situation, and to train the various Communist parties as instruments for an eventual seizure of power, rather than to try to produce revolutions at home.

This frustration in what had been, after all, the central objective of Soviet foreign policy was matched, in early 1921, by bitter problems and frustrations in the domestic field. It is true that the Soviet government was now relieved—for the first time since it had come into power in 1917—of the necessity of waging war against external or internal "class enemies." But by this time Russia lay in a state of economic and organizational ruin which defies description. What six and a half years of foreign war, revolution, civil war, and foreign intervention had done to Russia is something most of us here, happily for us, are probably incapable of imagining. One of those situations had been achieved (they had been known during the Thirty Years' War, and were to appear again, here and there in Europe, during World War II) where civilization seemed largely to have broken down, where human life was one swamp of poverty, hunger, disease, filth, and apathy—where people took on the qualities of wolves, and man often became the enemy of man in the most intimate physical sense, as in a jungle.

On top of all this, there began, in the spring of 1921, a major famine in some of the principal grain-growing regions of Russia. The causes of this famine lay partly in the general state of economic breakdown, partly in the results of the doctrinaire experimentation with Russian agriculture in which the Soviet leaders had already indulged themselves. It was, you will not be surprised to learn, the United States which stepped in at this point, in a spirit of sweetness and light, to bring relief to the famine sufferers and, incidentally, to the Soviet government as well. This was done by the American Relief Administration, an organization which, as was mentioned earlier, was founded during the war by

Herbert Hoover, initially for the feeding of the Belgians, and which had taken over the distribution of food supplies throughout a good part of Europe as the war came to an end. By 1921 many of the other tasks of the A.R.A., as it was generally known, had been completed, and the organization was available for work in a new area.

Herbert Hoover, as we have already noted, had no particular liking for the Soviet regime, and no reason to wish to help it to retain power. His main motive in bringing aid to Russia in 1921 and 1922 was certainly to alleviate innocent human suffering, and the efforts of his organization were addressed strictly to this end. Something in the neighborhood of ten million Russians appear to have been saved by A.R.A.'s operations from death by hunger or disease. At least that number, in any case, received A.R.A.'s aid; and it is difficult to see how they could have remained alive without it. It is also difficult to see how the Soviet government could have overcome the food crisis, or even the threatened breakdown of its transportation system, without this contribution from A.R.A. The problem of getting seed grain into the ground in a famine-stricken countryside was almost insoluble; and it seems to have been, at one point, only A.R.A.'s willingness to make food available to railway personnel that kept the railways in operation. The Soviet government was, thus, importantly aided not just in its economic undertakings, but in its political prestige and capacity for survival, by A.R.A.'s benevolent intervention.

This political aid was desperately needed. The month of March 1921, witnessed, in addition to the beginning of the famine, a grievous political setback to the Communists in the form of the so-called Kronstadt mutiny: an uprising against the Soviet government by the sailors of the Kronstadt naval base, on the outskirts of Leningrad. This uprising was led in part by the very same sailors who had originally played so prominent a part in supporting the Bolshevik seizure of power in 1917. The uprising was suppressed, in fierce fighting, by regular Soviet military units. The fact that the Soviet leaders found it necessary to take up arms in this way against members of their own political constituency, who could not possibly be described as "class enemies," was both a severe blow to their domestic-political prestige, and a warning of the momentary bankruptcy of the policies they had been following.

The fact is that with the end of civil war and foreign

intervention, a significant change had entered into the feelings of the people: the sort of change which invariably occurs after the dramatic and heroic moments of history. The spirit of sacrifice was giving way to lassitude, weariness with causes and ideals, a yearning for return to the reassuring preoccupations of private life. Just as the human individual cannot maintain the heroic tone beyond a certain point in personal life, so a collective body of mankind has limits in its ability to live heroically. There comes a time when people want to eat and sleep and mend their clothes and think about their children.

It was in the face of all these developments—the frustration of world revolutionary effort abroad, the economic breakdown at home, the incipient famine, the Kronstadt mutiny, and the obvious signs of physical exhaustion and flagging enthusiasm among their own followers—that the Soviet leaders proceeded, in 1921, to a reappraisal of their policies, both domestic and foreign.

During the years of war and struggle, the need for a strict husbandry of available resources had compelled the Soviet government to take economic life extensively under its control and to keep it going by the crude exertion of governmental power. These measures were generally known by the term "war Communism." They had sufficed for the military needs of the moment, and they had given Russia, in those initial years of Soviet power, something of the appearance of a truly socialized state. But actually, they did not go deep. It was soon apparent that they would not be adequate for the needs of the reconstruction and development of a peacetime economy. The situation cried out, in particular, for investment capital; and this could not easily be created or provided by a continuation of the wartime methods. The only visible alternative was a policy of concessions to private initiative, in agriculture and in industry, designed to free resources then being concealed or withheld from the economy, and to enlist the initiative of the peasant and of the private investor in the process of economic reconstruction. Reluctantly, but manfully and with resolution, Lenin recognized the necessity of such a course, and sponsored it. He admitted that it involved a certain retreat from what appeared to be an advance towards the goal of socialism. This, he said, was a regrettable necessity—a single step backward, in order to make possible two steps forward at a later stage. But one had no choice but to take it.

This new course of domestic policy, which came to be known as the New Economic Policy—the NEP for short—was adopted in early 1921. Involving as it did a readiness to make use of private capital from *internal* sources in the interests of Russian reconstruction, the NEP set a precedent for the utilization of *foreign* private capital as well, if it could be got. If it was all right to tap the resources and initiative of the *domestic* bourgeoisie in the interests of socialist construction, then what was wrong in principle with tapping the resources and initiative of the *foreign* bourgeoisie as well? Since one could not overthrow the international bourgeoisie, might not one exploit *them* and enlist *their* help, too, in the rebuilding of Russian economy?

It was on the basis of such thoughts that the Soviet leaders turned, in 1921, to a more serious effort to order their relations with the major Western countries. This effort was, to be sure, not entirely new; I don't wish to overwork the spring of 1921 as a transitional point. Ever since early 1918, the Soviet government had been holding out to foreign capitalists the possibility of economic concessions of one sort or another in Russia, and particularly of the exchange of Russian raw materials for Western capital goods. But in the earlier years, these approaches to the Western powers had been conceived primarily as a political device: as a means of whetting capitalist appetites and playing the capitalists of different countries off against one another, with a view to averting or weakening efforts at military intervention. There was as yet no proper appreciation of the importance these proposed economic exchanges would eventually have for the Soviet regime.

It took the appalling economic breakdown of the winter of 1920-1921 to bring this realization to the Soviet leaders. With the intervention a matter of the past, with a major program of internal economic reconstruction pressing upon them, and with the recognition that the capitalist society of the West was there to stay for some time and that it possessed resources of capital which might be virtually essential to Russian recovery—with all of this, relations with the Western governments achieved a new seriousness in the eyes of the Soviet leaders; and they now allotted a high priority to their development.

What was it that Lenin and his associates most wanted as they approached the Western countries in 1921?

First and foremost they wanted credits: money and capital, provided of course this could be had on terms that would in no way limit their freedom of action as a revolutionary regime—their freedom, that is, to proceed with the realization of the goals of socialism at home, and to pursue their world revolutionary purpose abroad. They had very clear ideas as to what was vital to the safeguarding and development of their power at home and to the preservation of the ultimate possibilities for revolutionary activity abroad. None of this would they sacrifice. But to the extent foreign credits could be had without forfeiting these things, they would take them.

Second, they wanted trade. They wanted the ability to exchange what little they had to sell for things they desperately needed to import. They themselves had established a governmental monopoly of foreign trade. They considered this monopoly vital to their retention of power within Russia. They would not permit private parties in Russia to trade. But they wished desperately to trade themselves. They wished to be permitted to trade freely, as would a private concern, on the world markets. In 1921 this was still possible only in most limited degree. Soviet trade was hampered in many places by boycotts, by juridical difficulties, by lack of credit, by political attitudes. These they wished to overcome.

Finally, they wanted diplomatic recognition—full-fledged, *de jure* recognition from the major capitalist governments. Why? Partly because they thought it would facilitate the extension of credits abroad and the development of their foreign trade; partly because it would give added protection against any renewal of military intervention; and partly because they had already become aware of the political value, and the subjective satisfactions, of prestige—even in the community of non-Communist states.

It was, when you stop to think of it, an amazing demand which the Bolsheviki, with their initial bid for credits, trade, and recognition, were placing on the Western governments in 1921. It was without precedent in the history of the modern national state. If we were to attempt to combine in one formula the various elements of this demand, putting them, that is, together into a single imaginary statement of the Soviet leaders to the Western governments, it would run something like this. The Soviet leaders would say:

"We despise you. We consider that you should be swept from the earth as governments and physically destroyed as individuals. We reserve the right, in our private if not in our official capacities, to do what we can to bring this about: to revile you publicly, to do everything within our power to detach your own people from their loyalty to you and their confidence in you, to subvert your armed forces, and to work for your downfall in favor of a Communist dictatorship. But since we are not strong enough to destroy you today—since an interval must unfortunately elapse before we can give you the *coup de grace*—we want you during this interval to trade with us; we want you to finance us; we want you to give us the advantages of full-fledged diplomatic recognition, just as you accord these advantages to one another.

"An outrageous demand? Perhaps. But you will accept it nevertheless. You will accept it because you are not free agents, because you are slaves to your own capitalistic appetites, because when profit is involved, you have no pride, no principles, no honor. In the blindness that characterizes declining and perishing classes, you will wink at our efforts to destroy you, you will compete with one another for our favor. Driven by this competition, which you cannot escape, you will do what we want you to do until such time as we are ready to make an end of you. It is, in fact, *you* who will, through your own cupidity, give *us* the means wherewith to destroy you."

I give you this condensation of the Soviet approach with some hesitation, because I fear that it may sound extreme and overdrawn. I can only assure you that this formulation is not one whit sharper or more uncompromising than the language consistently employed by the Soviet leaders at that time. I do not believe that it embraces a single thought which did not then figure prominently in their utterances.

Let me just recall, by way of illustration, that the governmental leaders of the Western countries were rarely referred to in Soviet official utterances, at that time, otherwise than as "imperialists," "plunderers," "pillagers," "oppressors," or "criminals." The seriousness of the Soviet revolutionary purpose vis-à-vis Western society was reiterated endlessly. It was the constant theme of all Communist utterance. The following passage from a Comintern resolution in 1922 is typical of thousands of others:

> The Executive Committee ... declares that the ... Comintern will not let its freedom be hampered by any obligations whatever. We are the deadly enemies of bourgeois society. Every honest Communist will fight against bourgeois society to his last breath, in word and in deed and if necessary with arms in hand. Yes, the propaganda of the Communist International will be pernicious for you, the imperialists. It is the historical mission of the Communist International to be the gravedigger of bourgeois society. . . . [61]

There were those in the English-speaking countries who argued that the Comintern statements didn't really count: that the Comintern was an organization peripheral to the Soviet government. This view was not well-founded. The Russian members on the body which issued the statement just quoted included Lenin, Trotsky, Bukharin, Radek—a group whose authority in the Soviet government was absolutely decisive.

I know of no political fiction more flimsy and absurd than that of the lack of responsibility of the Soviet authorities for the world revolutionary activities then centered in the Comintern. It was Chicherin, the Soviet foreign minister, who issued the invitations to the first Comintern Congress in 1919, to which he was also a delegate. The next two years in the life of the organization were marked by the successful effort to bring all its branches under the most intimate and sweeping control of the Russian Communist Party; and so absolute was the priority given to this effort that Lenin insisted the left-wing socialist elements abroad be forced to divide on this issue, at the cost of greatly reducing the number who retained their Comintern connection. He preferred here, on the international scene, as he had always done within the Russian Social-Democratic Party, to have a smaller following abjectly subordinate to his own authority than to have a larger one which might conceivably manifest a will of its own.

There are others who, while recognizing the responsibility of the Soviet leaders for Comintern utterances, have chosen to interpret these utterances as "just propaganda," the exaggerated expression of pious aspirations for social change elsewhere, gestures of sympathy for the woes of the working class abroad, not to be taken literally or seriously. I can only say that whoever indulges himself in this illusion will never understand the nature of the issues that divided the Soviet world from the West in those early years. The Comintern was a highly disciplined and extremely serious organization, partly political, partly military, the purpose of which was the promotion of revolution abroad. It meant business; and it meant it in as serious and ruthless a way as any conspiratorial organization has ever done. It played for mortal stakes. It resorted, without compunction, to the taking of human life wherever it considered that its interests so demanded and the dictates of prudence permitted. There can be no question but that such victories as it sought in western Europe would have been, if the Soviet leaders had had their way, of the bloodiest—and not just in the course of the struggle but in the retribution exacted afterward. Foreign Communists were specifically instructed—in a Moscow Comintern directive of 1921—

... to keep alive in the minds of the proletariat the idea that at the time of insurrection it must not itself be deluded by the enemy's appeals to its clemency. It will set up people's courts, and with proletarian justice settle accounts with the torturers of the proletariat.[62]

We know from the Soviet and Hungarian examples (not just from the Hungarian example of 1956, but also from that of 1919) what that meant.

The basic opportunism of the Soviet bid for credits and recognition, as well as the contempt for the integrity of bourgeois purpose which underlay it, were equally well documented. Time after time it was stressed to the faithful that the capitalists would eventually acquiesce in Soviet demands for trade and credits, not because they wanted to but because they would have no choice. "We are convinced," said L. B. Kamenev in March 1921—on the day before the signing of the Anglo-Soviet Trade Agreement—

... that the foreign capitalists, who will be obliged to work on the terms we offer them, will dig their own grave.... Foreign capital will fulfill the role Marx predicted for it. ... With every additional shovel of coal, with every additional load of oil that we in Russia obtain through the help of foreign technique, capital will be digging its own grave.[63]

A year later, Lenin was saying:

Do not forget that in recent years the most urgent, daily, practical and obvious interests of all the capitalistic powers have demanded the development, consolidation and expansion of trade with Russia. And since such interests exist, we can argue, quarrel, break off relations on some issues . . . in the end, basic economic necessity will force its way. We cannot be sure of the exact time . . . but we can confidently predict that progress will be made.[64]

Radek, with his gift for coarse polemic, put it even more sharply:

Capitalism is capable of adapting itself to [varied] conditions; if conditions in Russia are impregnable and if at the same time the capitalists are guaranteed some profit, they will toe the line.[65]

So much, then, for the illustrations of the attitude with which the Soviet leaders approached the Western powers in 1921. It boils down to the fact that you had here a regime, the attitude of which towards Western governments, psychologically and politically, was equivalent to that which would prevail toward an enemy in time of war. This regime was indeed waging, on every front except the overt military one, every form of warfare it knew how to wage, and with the most deadly intent. Not being at that moment in a position to pursue open military warfare with any prospect of success, it attempted to make a virtue of this relative helplessness, and demanded simultaneously all the advantages of normal political and commercial intercourse.

This was, of course, a mockery of the entire Western theory of international relationships, as it had evolved in the period from the seventeenth to the nineteenth centuries. It is true that the institutions of diplomacy originated—in the Orient, in Rome, in Byzantium—among potentates whose pretensions to power were, like those of the Soviet government, universal and messianistic, who were also reluctant to admit the full equality of any other ruler, and whose aim in having any dealings at all with foreign rulers was generally either to lull them into a false sense of security or to induce them in some way or other to accept a position of subordination and inferiority. The origins of modern diplomatic institutions, in other words, lay in the relations between enemies, not between friends. The old Russian state—the Grand Duchy of Muscovy—carried this tradition down to the seventeenth century, and never did entirely free itself from it.

But in Europe, it seems to me, this concept lost its validity with the religious wars and the decay of the Holy Roman Empire. The national state of modern Europe, bitterly as it might feud with its neighbors over questions of *relative* advantage, was distinguished from the older forms of state power by its abandonment of universalistic and messianic pretensions, by its general readiness to recognize the equality of existence of other sovereign authorities, to accept their legitimacy and independence, and to concede the principle of live and let live as a basic rule in the determination of international relationships. This did not, I reiterate, eliminate wars and struggles over limited objectives; but it did mean as a general rule that once another state had been recognized as a sovereign entity, one did not attempt to extinguish it entirely, or to deny to it the basic right to order its own internal affairs in accordance with its own traditions and ideas.

It was this theory that the Bolsheviki challenged on their assumption of power in Russia. They challenged it by the universality of their own ideological pretensions—by the claim, that is, to an unlimited universal validity of their own ideas as to how society ought to be socially and politically organized. They challenged it by their insistence that the laws governing the operation of human society demanded the violent overthrow everywhere of governments which did not accept the ideological tenets of Russian Communism, and the replacement of these governments by ones that did. The Soviet leaders, let us remember, professed it their duty and that of all right-minded followers to exert themselves to the utmost to bring about these political changes. And they reserved to themselves by implication the right to determine just what persons and groups might properly be regarded as legitimate successors to the regimes that were to be overthrown. It was not even enough by any means that people should be Socialists, or even that they should profess themselves specifically to be adherents of the ideas of Marx and Engels, for them to be regarded as eligible to govern. Soviet denunciations of those groups and individuals within the Socialist camp that were closest to themselves ideologically, but resistant to Moscow's authority, were, if anything, even more bitter and uncompromising than those directed to the most wealthy and aristocratic re-actionaries. A Socialist was not, in their view, a proper Socialist nor qualified for support until he had received the seal of approval in Moscow. But this meant, in effect, that Moscow established itself as the arbiter as to which foreign factions, in power or out of it, were deserving of popular support—which foreign governments might be tolerated, and which should be opposed and overthrown. It was this which was irreconcilable with the theory of international relations that had grown up within the Western community of states.

The significance of this situation has been somewhat obscured by those Western historians and commentators who have been unable to perceive any difference in principle between the attitude of the Soviet Union toward the Western countries and that of the Western countries toward the Soviet Union. After all, they have said, were not the Western governments equally hostile to Russia? Did they not attempt to overthrow the Soviet regime by their intervention in 1918-1919? Could the challenge to existing concepts of international relations properly be laid only at the Soviet door? Was not the Western rejection of socialism as a conceivable governmental system just as important in the breakdown of the established theory of international life as the Soviet rejection of capitalism?

It is my belief that the answer to these questions is "No." Any unclarity on this point can lead to a grievous misunderstanding of some of the basic elements of Soviet-Western relations. There were, in those initial years of Soviet power, some very significant differences between anti-Sovietism in the West and the hostility which the Soviet leaders entertained for the Western powers. This hostility from the Communist side was preconceived, ideological, deductive. In the minds of the Soviet leaders, it long predated the Communist seizure of power in Russia. Anti-Sovietism in the West, on the other hand, was largely a confused, astonished, and indignant reaction to the first acts of the Soviet regime. Many people in the Western governments came to hate the Soviet leaders for what they *did*. The Communists, on the other hand, hated the Western governments for what they *were*, regardless of what they did. They entertained this feeling long before there was even any socialistic state for the capitalists to do anything to. Their hatred did not vary according to the complexion or policies or actions of the individual non-Communist governments. It never has. The government of Hitler was not more wicked or more repugnant in Moscow's eyes than that of Great Britain. The British Labour governments were in no respect superior, as seen from Moscow, to those of the Conservatives. The Swedish and Norwegian governments have realized general socialist aims to a very high degree; yet no greater merit could be conceded to them from the Soviet standpoint than, let us say, to the government of General Franco. The Baltic governments were not given any credit in Moscow for being the first to order their relations with the Soviet Union; they were, on the contrary, the first to be swallowed up by Moscow as a consequence of the agreement with Hitler in 1939.

What better proof could there be that it was not the manifestations of the *behavior* of the non-Communist states to which Moscow took exception, but their very nature, as Moscow saw it? In Moscow's view, non-Communist statesmen were regarded as incapable of doing good intentionally. If by chance they did something that was in Moscow's interest, it was because circumstances and their own short-sightedness forced them into it. In thirty years' experience with Soviet official literature, I cannot recall an instance of a non-Communist government being credited with a single generous or worthy impulse. All actions of such governments favorable to Soviet interests or even responsive to Soviet desiderata are invariably attributed to motives less than creditable: as a bowing to necessity, a belated yielding to the demands of outraged opinion, or the accidental subsidiary product of some sinister ulterior motive. Even during the common struggle of World War II the Soviet government meticulously refrained from endorsing the wartime motives and purposes of its Western allies. Since the war came to an end it has not hesitated to portray these motives and purposes to its own people as sinister and reprehensible in the extreme, not markedly superior, in fact, to those of Hitler.

It should be clear from this that we are dealing here with no mere reaction to Western behavior. Moscow's attitude towards the Western powers does not really flow, as Soviet apologists have so often alleged and as even Khrushchev sometimes suggests, from the fact that Soviet feelings were injured by the Allied intervention in 1918. The intervention increased Soviet contempt for the Western adversary; it did not increase the hatred and rejection that stamped him as an adversary from the very day of the Revolution.

Surely, this approach cannot be equated with that of the pragmatic West, where for forty years the argument over the attitude to be taken toward Soviet power has revolved around the questions of interpretation of the behavior of the Soviet regime. There have undoubtedly been individuals here and there in the Western countries whose hatred of what they understood to be socialism has been so great that they have felt it should be rooted out with fire and sword, on straight ideological grounds, wherever it raised its head. But such people, surely, have been few; and I do not think that their views have ever been dominant in any of the major Western governments. I recall no suggestions in the Western chanceries that the initial government of the Weimar Republic, for example, ought to be overthrown on grounds of its socialist complexion. I have yet to know an American who thinks it our duty to overthrow the governments of Sweden and Norway for ideological reasons. Had the Soviet leaders contented themselves from the outset with saying that they felt that they knew what was good for Russia, and refrained from taking positions on what was good for other countries, Western hostility to the Soviet Union would never have been what it has been. The issue has never been, and is not today, the right of the Russian people to have a socialistic ordering of society if they so wish; the issue is how a government which happens to be socialistic is going to behave in relation to its world environment.

Second (and I am reverting again particularly to those early years) Soviet hostility to the West was highly organized, and equipped with a permanent political weapon and program in the form of the Comintern. Nothing of this sort could be said concerning Western policies toward the Soviet Union. Hostility to the Soviet government in the Western countries was sporadic, diffused, and disorganized. It flowed from many different sources. It was never fused into a single organized effort. Such actions as the Western governments took against Soviet purposes were almost never coordinated among them and, even within those governments, such measures generally sprang from a confused pattern of hesitations and inner conflicts. If action hostile to

Soviet interests did occasionally flow from the turgid processes of Western democracy, this was the momentary and
coincidental outcome of the encounter between many conflicting forces. Action hostile to the Western governments,
on the other hand, flowed from Moscow in a single unin-
terrupted stream over the course of decades. And this was
not the result of any manifestations of popular opinion within Russia; it reflected the deliberate will of a regime which
kept its own counsel, which did not consult popular opinion, and the word of which was law within the area to
which its power extended.

The world of Western capitalism and liberalism, which
the Bolsheviki challenged at the moment of its maximum exhaustion and overwroughtness in the closing phases of the
First World War, was certainly capable, on occasions, of
some very ugly and unpleasant, sometimes brutal, sometimes
stupid reactions, when it felt itself challenged and threatened
by an outside force. It is characteristic of those who think
of themselves as nice people (and to this category we
Anglo-Saxons outstandingly belong) that they are slow to
react to provocation but once they feel their interests or
their security to be seriously jeopardized, they respond with
a peculiar violence and vindictiveness and with a notable
lack of political discrimination. In the initial Western response to the phenomenon of Soviet power there were many
things which it was easy for Soviet propagandists to depict
as the products of blind prejudice—as fear of the loss of
inherited privilege or hatred of the very idea of giving a
break to the underdog.

But to equate these isolated manifestations of Western behavior with the Bolshevist approach to Western capitalism is
to ignore the whole great intellectual and spiritual turmoil of
Western society between the two wars, to ignore the role of
public opinion and the constant interaction of conflicting
forces that was the determinant of governmental conduct
everywhere in the West, to ignore the glaring contradictions
that were constantly in evidence in Western policies toward
Russia, and to join the Communists in the effort to clothe
with the semblance of reality one of the most monstrous of
Leninist fictions: the image of a conscious, clearly delimited
international social force, known as "the bourgeoisie," enjoying a unity of ideological outlook, equipped with an executive high command and a genuine discipline of political
action, shaping the moves of the Western governments as the

fingers shape the movements of the glove in which they lie. Unless we assume this to be true—and surely there could be no greater travesty of Western democratic society than this —the equation of the attitude of the two sides breaks down.

14 Western Reaction to the Soviet Bid

WHAT WAS the reaction to the triple bid with which, as we have seen, the Soviet leaders approached the Western powers in 1921: trade, credits, recognition?

The demand for trade presented no great difficulty, so long as credits were not involved. The Western countries suffered, in the aftermath of World War I, from a general crisis of overproduction, and there was sharp competition for export markets. Why this should have been so much more the case after the First World War than after the second—why the powers of absorption in the domestic markets were so much smaller in the Twenties than in the late Forties—is something for which I have yet to hear a convincing explanation. But it *was* this way. Any opportunity to export was regarded, in those years, as golden; and the prospect of reopening and developing the great Russian "market," as it was still called, exerted a powerful fascination on many Western minds.

In the prewar days, Russia had been a moderately great trading nation. Her average imports in the years 1909 to 1913 had run to something like one and a half to two billion dollars. This was a respectable sum, but small compared with the size of the country. For certain individual Western countries, however, particularly Germany and England, trade with Russia was of greater significance than these figures would suggest. And when the war was over there was keen interest in both these countries in developing once more their export trade to Russia as well as in obtaining Russian raw materials. England's traditional im-

ports of timber and flax from North Russia were of particular importance.

On the other hand, it was misleading to speak in 1921,
as many people still did, of the "Russian market." The word
"market" implied a place where you could buy and sell in
accordance with the laws of normal commercial inter-
change: on the basis, that is, of supply and demand and
price. None of this applied in the case of the new revolutionary Russia. The government had monopolized foreign
trade; the only purchaser in the whole great Russian territory was the Soviet government itself. And even this government made its purchases in foreign countries. It had no
choice but to do so. It had abolished commercial law as
such within Russia; it had rendered the Soviet currency
worthless for international trading purposes; by abandoning
the principle of impartial justice and making the courts into
administrative agencies of the central political power, it had
destroyed the legal basis for international commercial transactions on Soviet territory. When, therefore, it wished to
buy or sell, it was obliged to make the transactions abroad,
using foreign currencies, foreign credit facilities, and the
protection of foreign courts.

We should also note that in deciding what things to buy
and what things to sell, the Soviet government was not
governed by normal commercial considerations. It regarded
trade with the capitalist world as a regrettable temporary
expedient, necessary in order to enable Soviet Russia to
achieve within the shortest possible time a state of economic and military self-sufficiency. For this, an infusion of capital goods from the West was recognized as necessary; and
Moscow was prepared, since it had initially no credit, to
pay for this, as much as possible, by exports of raw
materials. But the aim of this limited exchange, I repeat,
was the eventual achievement of military-industrial autarchy.
Soviet trade was thus, in Soviet eyes, a "trade to end
trade." And the Soviet trade monopoly, in deciding what to
buy and where, was motivated primarily not by questions
of price but by the demands of this program of self-
sufficiency. It is true that, having once made up their minds
that they wanted to buy something abroad, Soviet trade representatives would naturally look around to see where it
could be had on the best terms. This was *one* of the factors
that entered into their calculations. Western manufacturers
and exporters thus had a limited possibility of competing

for those orders which the Soviet government had already decided to place abroad. But they had no means of affecting the initial decision. Trade with Russia in the Soviet period was consequently a far different thing than the entry into the Russian "market," as people remembered it from pre-war days; and the possibilities for the Western exporter were severely circumscribed.

Since a fundamental aim of Soviet industrialization was the achievement of military strength, and since Soviet intentions towards the governments and social systems of the Western countries were—as we have seen—actively hostile, it was sometimes argued then, as it has been more recently by many people in the United States, that one ought not to strengthen a self-declared enemy by trading with him. This question, the perennial issue of what is called today "East-West trade," was actually one which long predated even the establishment of Soviet power. It was a serious problem as early as the days of the Grand Duchy of Muscovy. In the sixteenth century, when Elizabethan England was sending considerable quantities of goods to the trading point of the Russian foreign trade monopoly of that day, at the mouth of the Narva River on the Gulf of Finland, the Poles tried to warn the British government against the dangers of this trade. The terms they used in these warnings were ones which, but for a certain archaic quality, might well have issued from the lips of American cold war enthusiasts of recent years: "We know and feele of a surety" —a Polish note of that time read—

... that the Muscovite, enemy to all liberty under the heavens, is daily growing mighty by the increase of such things as he brought to the Narve ... , by means whereof he maketh himself strong to vanquish all others. ... We do foresee, except other princes take this admonition, the Muscovite, puffed up in pride with those things that be brought to the Narve, and made more perfect in warlike affairs, with engines of warre and shippes, will make assault this way on Christendom, to slay or make bound all that shall withstand him, which God defend![66]

This was a reasonable argument in 1568; and it was a reasonable argument in 1921. But the fact is that self-denial of this sort in matters of trade has never been within the self-disciplinary power of the Western capitalist community except in time of war. The great obstacle to any attempt to inhibit trade with Soviet Russia has always been the lack of adequate international solidarity—the fact that there was always someone who placed the hope of profit higher than the need for uniformity of policy among the respective countries—the fact, in other words, that if *you* did not supply Russia with the things she wanted, somebody else would. It is a revealing fact that the signing of the Anglo-Russian Trade Agreement of 1921 is said to have been rushed through on the British side at the last moment, after months of hesitation, because word had just reached London that the Russians were placing an order for several hundred locomotives in Germany. Moscow, to tell the truth, was not entirely wrong in the confidence it placed in Western economic rivalry as the one factor which, more than any other, would render the capitalist world exploitable in the interests of its own undoing.

Moscow's demand for trade thus met, all in all, with a ready response in the West. It was not even made conditional on diplomatic recognition. Soviet trade with the United States, for example, developed rapidly in the Twenties despite the fact that there were no official relations between the two countries at all.

Trading operations by the Soviet foreign trade monopoly began on a serious scale in 1922, and developed rapidly and steadily, until they reached a peak in the years 1930 to 1932. Soviet trade never quite achieved, during the period between the two wars, the dimensions of prewar Russian trade. It remained at all times small in comparison with Russia's size and population and general economic strength. In the period between the two wars her share of world imports was at its highest in 1931, and it was then only 2.7 per cent. The comparable figure for exports was 2.3 per cent, achieved in 1932. This was approximately the same as that of countries like Sweden and Switzerland, which had something like one-twentieth of the Soviet population.

In general, then, we may say that the Western countries made no difficulties about the Soviet demand for trade, so long as it did not include a demand for credits. But when it came to the question of credits and recognition, the Western powers were inclined to make difficulties. It will be worth our while to examine why they did so.

Two main arguments were adduced. The first, which bore more closely on the question of recognition, had reference to the ambiguous and contradictory attitude of the Soviet regime toward the non-Communist world, as we have noted it in these lectures. But it is important to note that the objection was not usually formulated in this way. It generally assumed the form of the charge that the Soviet leaders were conducting subversive "propaganda" abroad. This charge figured repeatedly in Western diplomatic protests to Moscow; it popped up frequently in the negotiations about credits and recognition; it led to the incorporation in a number of treaties and agreements between the Soviet government and Western countries of clauses in which the contracting parties agreed not to conduct propaganda against each other.

I have always been struck with the shallowness of understanding which this formula revealed. Surely the Western governments had a stronger case than this. The "propaganda" was only one facet of something much deeper and more important. This was the hostility itself, the principled rejection of the legitimacy of the Western governments and social systems, and the militant action taken in the name of these attitudes. The Soviet leaders were not just making propaganda for their views. They were not just exhorting people to adopt a different outlook on the ordering of society. They were endeavoring to manipulate in a systematic way the political process within other countries. They were organizing groups of followers within those countries, indoctrinating them with an attitude of disloyalty to their own governments, whipping them into disciplined conspiratorial bodies, training them in the arts of revolutionary action, teaching them how to overthrow governments and how to seize dictatorial power, and finally, as a deliberate and cynical policy, encouraging them to incriminate themselves under the laws of their own governments to a point where any withdrawal into normal life would become hazardous and unpromising. This, surely, was more than mere propaganda. It was one thing to urge your theoretical views, it was another thing to give them organizational effect in the form of clandestine operations in foreign countries. In restricting their protests to the propaganda theme, as they generally did, the Western governments were revealing how poorly they understood the nature of the force that was being brought to bear against them, how little they had analyzed it, and how inadequately prepared they were to deal with its methods and tactics.

In addition to this, such protests as they did make on the score of propaganda were often halfhearted and unconvincing. The Soviet government could not fail to notice, in the case of England, that the protests were much sharper when it came to Soviet propaganda in southern Asia—in Persia, Afghanistan, and India—than when it came to England. From this they must have concluded, and I think rightly, that London was protesting against this propaganda not on principle, but simply because the Middle East was the area where propaganda hurt. The British protests must have seemed to them the best possible proof that they had found the vulnerable point in England's armor—that their efforts were having important effect. The Western governments, in other words, were too little interested in the theory of diplomatic intercourse to protest against propaganda on the point of principle; they protested only when they felt themselves really stung in some tangible political way.

Finally, there was the fact that the Western governments, when it came right down to signing agreements with the Soviet government which seemed to hold promise of promoting trade with Russia, generally contented themselves with clauses about propaganda which were obviously perfunctory and useless. These clauses, as a rule, bound the Soviet government not to conduct propaganda, but said nothing about the Communist Party or the Comintern. This was an obvious subterfuge. Such clauses never restrained in any appreciable degree the freedom of action of the Soviet leaders in the matters at hand. They must, again, have been regarded by Moscow as a particularly odious bit of Western cynicism and hypocrisy: as efforts to pull the wool over the eyes of the Western public in the hope of getting a greater cut of Soviet trade.

The second and more important factor which caused the Western governments to resist Soviet demands for credits and recognition was the matter of debts and claims: the fact that the Soviet government had disclaimed responsibility for paying the foreign debts of its predecessors, the Tsar's government and the Provisional Government of 1917. This was the subject of an enormous volume of discussion and correspondence among the various governments in the first decade after World War I.

At the time of the outbreak of the war, Russia had had the greatest foreign indebtedness of any country in the world. This indebtedness was greatly increased during the war by virtue of credits granted by the Western Allies to the Russian governments for wartime purchases. In 1914, the foreign debt of the Tsar's government had amounted to something over four billion gold rubles. This represented some two billion dollars in the money of that day, more nearly equivalent to five billion dollars, I should suppose, in our present currency. By 1917 this indebtedness had grown to twelve billion rubles. In addition to this the Soviet government, on its assumption of power, nationalized foreign property, or property in which foreigners had an interest, in such quantities as to lead to claims against it by foreign owners in the amount of a further two billion rubles. The total claims against the Soviet government by the Western parties amounted, therefore, to something in the order of fourteen billion rubles—something like twenty billion dollars, I would suppose, in today's currency.

Of the prewar Russian state debt, amounting to 3.8 billion rubles, eighty per cent was owed to France, much of it to small private investors who had purchased Tsarist treasury bonds. In point of nationalized property, too, France stood in first place, followed closely by Britain, Germany, and Belgium. (A number of the public utilities in Russia were Belgian-owned.) The United States hardly came into the picture, so far as the prewar debt was concerned; and only 6 per cent of the claims for nationalized property were American. But America did figure prominently in the war debt, on account of the credits which Washington had extended to the Provisional Government in 1917.

These claims against the Soviet government were only a part of the whole complex of international monetary claims that dominated relations among the great powers in the wake of World War I. The Western European Allies were trying to collect vast sums from Germany under the head of reparations. The United States was trying to collect from the Western European Allies similar vast sums, which it had made available to them in the form of credits during the war. And here, now, were the Western Allies and the United States both advancing similar demands on Soviet Russia.

To my mind this whole great chain of effort, beginning with the endeavor of the United States government to collect its war debts from the former European Allies, was misconceived, shortsighted, and deleterious in highest degree to the development of postwar relationships. I don't know with whom I have less sympathy: with the Allies, in their effort to collect these staggering sums from Germany and Russia, or with the United States, in its effort to make equally absurd exactions from the Allies. None of these sums could conceivably have been transferred without producing grievous maladjustments in the world economy. This alone should have been a warning. But this was only a part of the case against the effort to collect them.

Behind all these undertakings there lay the failure of the statesmen to realize that World War I and the Russian Revolution that attended it had worked a basic change in the situation of the Western world—a change so profound that it was idle to attempt to found the reconstruction of Europe on prewar relationships of any kind, on any calculations of guilt or prior obligation, or indeed on anything other than the situation one had before one's eyes when hostilities ended. The war, which Allied statesmen still insisted on viewing as a contest supposed to yield to the victor all the just fruits of virtue triumphant, had been really a shocking, irreparable act of self-destruction on the part of Europe as a whole, a debauch of violence so destructive and so injurous to all concerned that no hopeful approach to a repair of the damage could be founded on allegations about who had owed what to whom at one stage or another before or during the calamity. You couldn't draw blood from a turnip. Amid the general economic wreckage and prostration of postwar Europe it was idle to suppose that there could be, on top of the general work of reconstruction, great one-sided transfers of national wealth.

The task of rebuilding Europe could have been undertaken with some prospect of success only if one had started with a general attitude of humility and mutual helpfulness, humility before the memory of the many millions of young men who had been killed or maimed in this ghastly encounter, and mutual helpfulness as it is normally practiced in the wake of any great natural catastrophe: a flood or a fire or an earthquake—without question, without discrimination, with promptness, with dedication. In the face of the immeasurable, irreparable sufferings and sacrifices of that First World War, beside which even the miseries of the second look pale so far as western Europe is concerned, I

cannot see how there could have been room, at its conclusion, for any feelings other than ones of shame and remorse, that all of this had transpired by man's decision
and man's hand. To go scratching around, instead, to find
out who had owed what to whom at some earlier date—
or, as in the case of reparations, what was the proper price,
in monetary terms, of a calculated greater guilt—this was the
reaction, surely, of shocked and confused people, unable
still to realize the extent and significance of the tragedy, too
overwhelmed even to make any proper start at clearing
of moral wreckage. I cannot help recalling, in this respect,
the prophetic words of Lord Lansdowne, in his letter to
the *Daily Telegraph* on November 29, 1917, one year before
the end of the war. "We are not going to lose this War"—
Lansdowne wrote—

... but its prolongation will spell ruin for the civilised world,
and an infinite addition to the load of human suffering which
already weighs upon it. Security will be invaluable to a world
which has the vitality to profit by it, but what will be the
value of the blessings of peace to nations so exhausted that
they can scarcely stretch out a hand with which to grasp
them?[67]

The indignation with which this letter was received at the
time in the Western countries was a part of the same
confusion of the spirit that caused people still to believe,
in the immediate postwar period, that the building of a new
life could best be founded on stupendous exactions by one
nation on another.

As one reads back today into the records of the numerous postwar conferences (I believe there were twenty-
three of them in the space of three or four years) and into
the other diplomatic correspondence of the time, there is
something infinitely dreary and sterile about these intermin-
able wranglings over debts and reparations. They were
only an excuse for real statesmanship. Nothing of consequence ever came of them. The hairsplittings, the bickerings,
the legalisms, the tortured compromises over tables of sums
in the millions and billions that had no existence in material
reality—they all seem scarcely worth studying, today. Staggering investments of the time of experts and statesmen
were expended on them, and to no avail. Even while they

were in progress, real life was moving on—the mysterious life of the feelings and attitudes of men, which is all that really counts in politics—was moving on in ways that were unfortunately not under anyone's control, in ways that were in no one's interest, in ways that began to point already to the new tragedies of the Thirties and Forties. Yet people could not see this movement of events—it was obscured from them by the great columns of unreal figures by which they allowed themselves to be bemused.

The Soviet government countered the claim for repayment of war debts by submitting a colossal bill for damages allegedly done by the Western powers during the intervention. Nobody took this counterclaim too seriously. But it was, after all, mostly the Americans and British who had an interest in the war debts; and no one, as we all know, ever feels sorry for *them*. The French, in particular, who were the prime movers in the whole international effort to collect money from the Soviet government in the postwar years, were not greatly interested in this item, and did not press it strongly. There was thus a general tendency among the Western powers to go along with the Russians on this point, to acquiesce in the cancellation of the war debts in compensation for the alleged damages of the intervention, and to reserve the really heavy diplomatic pressures for the prewar state debt and the confiscated property.

In the matter of the prewar state debt, the Russians professed themselves ready to pay *something*—not as a matter of right but as a practical concession, and then only on condition that new credits would be extended to them on a considerable scale. Their position, in essence, was that if large-scale credits were made available to them now, in the postwar era, they would consent to pay a moderate quota of extra interest, perhaps 2 or 3 per cent, on these credits, with the understanding that this extra interest might be applied to the settlement of the old claims. At the same time, they insisted that the old claims would have to be greatly scaled down.

It is possible that agreement might have been reached on some arrangement of this nature, had it been a question of the old state debt alone. But it was over the question of the nationalized property that the negotiations finally foundered. The French and Belgian governments, both heavily interested in this item, held out for complete

physical restitution of the confiscated properties to their
former foreign owners. This the Soviet government, for
rather obvious reasons, flatly refused to accept. It would
have been plainly incompatible with a Socialist system of
economy to turn hundreds of industrial establishments over
to unlimited exploitation by foreign private owners. Moscow
was willing to grant some preference to former owners in
the leasing out of properties, on concession, to foreign en-
trepreneurs for limited periods of time, as part of the New
Economic Policy. It even murmured things from time to
time about paying some compensation in individual instances if, again, additional credits were granted by the
old owners to offset these payments. Beyond this, it would
not go.

On this point, the negotiations broke down, in 1922; and
the breakdown ruined what chances there might have been
for the extension of long-term commercial credit by
Western financial circles. The Soviet government eventually
got around this by inducing the German, Italian, and Austrian governments to guarantee, to the tune of some hundreds
of millions of dollars, short-term commercial credit for
deals concluded with the Soviet trading agencies. This did
not give Moscow the cheap long-term credit which it
wanted; but it did help. And, within a year and a half of
the breakdown of negotiations between the Western governments and the Soviet Union over debts and claims, diplomatic recognition, as we shall see, was accorded anyway
by both the British and French governments, regardless of
Russia's continued unwillingness to meet old obligations on
terms acceptable to them.

What it boiled down to, then, was that Russia, after
starting out by demanding trade, credits, and recognition,
got trade and recognition from the Western Allied governments without making any concessions at all on the subject
of debts and claims. She did not get the long-term credits
she wanted; but she covered this need in part by arrangements with the German and Italian governments for government guarantees of short-term commercial credit: an
arrangement which both cheapened the credit and greatly
increased its availability.

The lesson of this Western attitude was not lost on
Moscow. The Western governments had shown themselves
vacillating and compromising in the matter of "propaganda,"

where questions of principle were involved, but sticky on
the subject of debts and claims, where hard cash was what
was being talked about. They had proved more sticky,
furthermore, about the private property claims than about
the question of the prewar state debts. Why was this? The
Soviet leaders, with their Marxist-trained minds, could not
help reflecting that in the case of the private property
claims, the interests of a few big owners, some of them great
corporations like the Royal Dutch Shell, were at stake;
whereas in the case of the Russian state debt, it was, after
all, only the Western common taxpayer or, in the case of
France, the small bondholder, whose interests were affected. What better set of circumstances could there have
been to confirm them in their suspicion that parliamentary
democracy in the Western countries was a sham and that
the governments were really no more than the spokesmen
for the great capitalist interests and monopolies that operated
behind the scenes?

The only government that may be said to have held, in
that early period, to a position towards Russia based
squarely on principle was the Democratic administration of
Woodrow Wilson, in Washington. In August 1920, at a
time when Wilson himself was lying helplessly ill in the
White House, his Secretary of State, Bainbridge Colby,
wrote as follows to the Italian government, which had in-
quired about America's policy toward Soviet Russia:

It is not possible for the Government of the United States
to recognize the present rulers of Russia as a government
with which the relations common to friendly governments
can be maintained. This conviction has nothing to do with
any particular political or social structure which the Russian
people themselves may see fit to embrace. It rests upon a
wholly different set of facts. These facts, which none dispute,
have convinced the Government of the United States, against
its will, that the existing regime in Russia is based upon
the negation of every principle of honor and good faith, and
every usage and convention, underlying the whole structure of international law; the negation, in short, of every
principle upon which it is possible to base harmonious and
trustful relations, whether of nations or of individuals. . . .
Indeed, upon numerous occasions the responsible spokesmen
of this Power . . . have declared that it is their understanding
that the very existence of Bolshevism in Russia, the maintenance of their own rule, depends, and must continue to

depend, upon the occurrence of revolutions in all other great civilized nations, including the United States, which will overthrow and destroy their governments and set up Bolshevist rule in their stead. . . .

. . . there cannot be any common ground upon which [the United States] can stand with a Power whose conceptions of international relations are so entirely alien to its own, so utterly repugnant to its moral sense. There can be no mutual confidence or trust, no respect even. . . . We cannot recognize, hold official relations with, or give friendly reception to the agents of a government which is determined and bound to conspire against our institutions . . .[68]

This was a harsh position, and a negative one. But it was one based squarely on principle. It did not, as you will note, say one word about debts and claims. As such, I believe that the Soviet leaders understood it and respected it more than any other. On this ground, I think, one might have fought it out diplomatically with the Soviet government, and perhaps eventually some franker and more solid understanding would have come of it. But this position was overtaken, soon after its enunciation, by the fall of the Wilson administration and the assumption of power in Washington by the administration of Warren Gamaliel Harding, an administration noted neither for its interest in principle nor for its resistance to pressures from wealthy private interests.

The Harding administration lost no time in supplementing Colby's clear position with a resounding demand for satisfaction in the matter of debts and claims. On this now corrupted and dubious foundation, the United States policy of nonrecognition continued to rest throughout the Republican era, down to the inauguration of Franklin D. Roosevelt, in 1933.

F.D.R., of course, was a bird of a different feather. He had as little interest in collecting debts from Russia as he did in Soviet propaganda or in the theory of the Soviet outlook on international affairs. He therefore promptly yielded the United States position on both issues, the valid one and the dubious one alike, and conceded to Moscow the recognition it sought without obtaining satisfaction on either count.

This, then, was the general shape of the Western response to the initial Soviet bid for trade, credits, and recognition.

Russia got the trade. She got the recognition. Down to World War II, she never got the long-term credits. But she got short-term ones, and eventually she got some much better, in the form of American Lend-Lease.

15   Rapallo

I HAVE already commented on the theoretical folly of an Allied policy that attempted to impose a punitive peace on Germany by means of an instrument, namely the Treaty of Versailles, to which one of Germany's great neighbors remained uncommitted and, like Germany, unfavorably inclined. To do this was to invite Germany to seek in the development of her relations with this one uncommitted neighbor a path of escape from the strictures of the treaty. And this, in turn, meant the forfeiture by the Western community of the possibility of a united front in the face of Russian Communism. It presented the Bolsheviki with precisely that advantage on which they themselves believed their political fortunes outstandingly to depend: the ability to divide their capitalist adversaries, to deal with them separately, to play them off against each other.

The logic of this situation found no more vivid illustration than in the circumstances attending the conclusion of the Treaty of Rapallo between Germany and Soviet Russia on Easter Sunday, 1922.

The name Rapallo—actually that of the Italian seaside town where the treaty was signed—has come down through subsequent decades as a symbol of sorts, but a symbol of different things to different people. To Western liberals it has been the symbol of sinister German-Soviet conspiracy against the freedoms of the West. To unhappy Germans it has symbolized an independent German foreign policy—a policy which exploits the possibility of maneuver between East and West as a means of escape from the shackles of military defeat, as the alternative to hopelessness and passivity.

To Soviet ideologists it has appeared as the example of a useful and desirable agreement between the Soviet government and a bourgeois state, an agreement which affords to Moscow all the advantages of normal diplomatic and commercial intercourse without inhibiting its freedom to attack the political system of the bourgeois country in question. Even in recent years it has continued to be hailed by Soviet and East German ideologists as the example of the basis on which Soviet-German relations ought properly to rest.

Let us see what reality there was behind these various interpretations.

As the Soviet leaders turned to the task of the revival of trade with the West, their attention centered on Germany. Germany was the leading industrial power of the Continent. She was excellently placed to provide the things Russia needed. Beyond this, less difficulty was to be expected, in Germany's case, on the subject of debts and claims. Germany scarcely figured in the prewar debt, and in the war debt, of course, not at all. She did have property claims, but they were not as serious as those of some of the Allied powers. And she was now so humbled, so ruined, so desperate, so without alternatives, that she could be expected to be less sticky about such problems and more interested in getting trade started at once, without formalities or preconditions.

Taking advantage of these circumstances, the Russians pressed the German government, in 1921, to go ahead and establish regular diplomatic relations with the Soviet government, without waiting for similar action by the Western Allies. This, the German government was unwilling to do. The German president, Friedrich Ebert, being sincerely desirous of following a policy of accommodation with the West, continued to insist that Germany should not move faster than the Western governments in the re-establishment of formal relations with Moscow. In general, the foreign ministers and other cabinet members tended to agree with the president. But at lower levels in the German government, there was difference of opinion. In the Foreign Office, in particular, there was a group of able people headed by Baron Ago von Maltzan (later to be ambassador in Washington), who strongly favored an independent policy towards Russia, designed to give Germany an alternative, and thus to enhance her bargaining power towards the West. These people came to be referred to, in German government circles, as the "Easterners." They had important allies in military and business circles. With each diplomatic rebuff which Germany received in Paris and London, the hands of this faction were strengthened. They were able to say to the others, on such occasions: "You see, now, what you get for relying on Western generosity. You will make no progress that way. Our only hope lies in proving to the Western governments, by developing an independent relationship with Moscow, that we are not completely at their mercy, that we do have an alternative, that the West stands to lose if it pushes us too far."

The year 1921 saw two striking instances of the manner in which Allied policies played into the hands of the "Easterners" in Berlin. The first occurred in May, when the French and British finally presented to the Germans the reparations bill which it had taken them three years to agree on between themselves. It was a bill for 132 billion gold marks. This was a sum which could not have been raised by any democratic German government. It could not have been transferred, even if raised, without utterly disrupting international exchanges. The second instance, occurring in the fall of the year, concerned the League of Nations decision on the future of the disputed territory of Upper Silesia. Acting under heavy French pressure, the League Council issued a decision which deprived Germany of the important Silesian industrial district, previously a part of Germany. The Germans considered this decision to be not only unjust but in conflict with the results of a plebiscite only recently held in Silesia under the auspices of the League itself. In particular, they felt that if they were to be asked to pay staggering reparations, they should not be deprived of their second most important industrial region. Both of these developments strengthened the hands of the "Easterners," and made it difficult for others to resist their arguments.

By the beginning of 1922, even the German chancellor of the day, Dr. Joseph Wirth, was inclined toward an Eastern orientation of German foreign policy. But the fort of loyalty to the West continued, for the moment, to be tenuously held by President Ebert and by the new Foreign Minister, Walter Rathenau. Rathenau, a prominent German industrialist, was a man strongly pro-Western in his political and cultural orientation, and one who believed deeply in the necessity for a general accommodation with the West.

Such was the situation at the beginning of 1922. But there is one more thing that I ought to clarify before I get into the episode of the Genoa Conference. It was just at this time, in 1921 and 1922, that there began to be secret arrangements for collaboration between the German and Soviet military establishments about which so much has been written, and which are often associated with the name of Rapallo. Actually this military collaboration had entirely independent origins, and had little bearing on the political problems I have been speaking about. It was entered into by the respective military authorities of the two countries for reasons of the purest and coolest expediency: by the Germans, because it enabled them to evade some of the restrictions imposed by Versailles on their rearmament; by the Russians, because it permitted them to get German help in rebuilding a military industry and in training the new Red army. On the German side, these arrangements were held as a very closely guarded secret within the military establishment. It was not until the fall of 1921 that any of the civilian cabinet members were made privy to what was going on; and then the secret was divulged only to two of them. Their knowledge of this had nothing to do, so far as I can ascertain, with the origins of the Rapallo Treaty.

So much for the background.

In the fall of 1921 and the winter of 1922, the idea arose in Europe of convening a great international conference with a view to the reconstruction of the European economy. The situation was not dissimilar to that which preceded the launching of the Marshall Plan in 1947. The European countries were seemingly unable to recover, by their own individual efforts, from the economic effects of the war. To many, it appeared that there would have to be some great collaborative effort, on an international scale, if recovery was to be achieved. Lloyd George, the British Prime Minister, whose domestic-political position was slipping and who felt the need for a foreign-political triumph to redress the balance, made himself a principal sponsor of this suggestion. The result was a decision to call a general European conference, at Genoa, in April 1922. Here, for the first time since Versailles, both the Russians and the Germans—the two bad boys of the European family—were to be invited. Russian participation was regarded as particularly important, because it was widely believed that

Europe's recovery would not be possible without the recovery of Russia as well and without the reintegration of the Russian economy into that of the Continent as a whole.

It was initially envisaged that the two main subjects of discussion at Genoa would be the inclusion of Russia in the process of European reconstruction and the problem of German reparations and war debts. But Poincaré, who came into power in France just as preparations for the conference were getting under way, resolutely refused to permit the question of reparations to be placed on the agenda. The Germans, he insisted, were not to have the opportunity of bringing their grievances on this score before a European forum. This left nothing for the conference to talk about but the problem of Russia.

The Soviet leaders viewed all this with mixed feelings. To the extent that it presented a possibility of Russia's getting economic aid from the West, they welcomed it. They themselves, in fact, had independently suggested something of this nature. They decided, therefore, that it was better, on balance, to accept the invitation, and did. But they were worried over the prospect—which became more and more of a certainty as the day of the conference drew near— that the Western governments would start out by raising the question of debts and claims, and would make satisfaction on this score a precondition for any re-establishment of commercial relations with Russia. They were especially fearful of the prospect of being faced, at Genoa, with a united front of their capitalist creditors.

For this reason, they redoubled their pressure on Berlin to conclude with them, in advance of the conference, a special bilateral treaty which would provide for the resumption of full diplomatic relations and a mutual cancellation of claims. And here, they had in their hands a most effective instrument of pressure on the Germans—an instrument with which the Allied governments had themselves obligingly provided them. I must explain what this was, because it lay at the heart of the whole Rapallo development.

At the Versailles Conference, in 1919, the French, having in mind the fact that Russia was not represented there but believing that the Soviet government would soon be overthrown, had arranged for the insertion in the Peace Treaty of an article—No. 116 to be exact—which specifically reserved to Russia (it didn't say to *what* Russia) the right to obtain restitution and reparations from Germany, on the strength of the treaty, if at any time a Russian government should wish to avail itself of this privilege. What the French had in mind, in inserting this paragraph, was this: Private individuals in France had, as we have already noted, invested heavily before the war in bonds of the Tsarist Russian government. These bondholders were clamoring for their money; and this clamor was embarrassing to the French government. French statesmen therefore hit on the following idea. A new, friendly, non-Communist Russian government would satisfy the claims of these French investors, and would reimburse itself for this expenditure by taking another chunk out of the flesh of the Germans, who were regarded as good for any amount of this sort of exploitation. Hence, Article 116, providing that Russia should, whenever she wanted, be cut in on German reparations.

The Soviet government had, so far as I know, never at any time considered availing itself of Article 116—its position had, in fact, always been flatly against reparations in general. Lenin had come into power in 1917, after all, on a platform of "no annexations, no indemnities." But the Germans were not sure what the Soviet attitude would be if the Allies began to put pressure on Moscow to pay the Tsarist debts and to reimburse themselves at German expense. And for this reason, Article 116 hung over the German head in 1921 like the sword of Damocles. If nothing were done to change the situation, the Genoa Conference threatened to bring this sword down.

The Russians, in their effort to split the Germans off from the rest of the Western community even before the conference convened, made very good use of this instrument. They carefully spread the word around that France was offering to Russia economic aid, credits, and a large war indemnity, to be paid not by France but by Germany, on the strength of Article 116.

Up to the time of the conference, the Germans had resisted these pressures manfully. But they were seriously worried. For them, the refusal of the French to permit reparations to be discussed at Genoa came as a great blow. They had hoped that a general discussion of the problems of European recovery would serve to convince others of the economic folly of the attempt to collect reparations from Germany on the contemplated scale. The French attitude seemed to cut off the last chance of relief from the reparations burden. What was worse: there was now a possibility that new reparations might even be added to the old ones, through the operation of Article 116.

In this situation, there was considerable force behind the Russian pressure on the German government to establish diplomatic relations with Moscow in advance of the conference, in return for an assurance that Article 116 would not be invoked. Rathenau, hard pressed in this direction, did go so far as to permit junior Foreign Office officials to sit down with their opposite numbers from the Soviet side and to work out some of the language of a possible bilateral German-Soviet agreement along these lines. But he refused to sign anything of this sort in advance of the Genoa Conference. He still desperately hoped that Germany's policies, both vis-à-vis Russia and with regard to European reconstruction generally, could somehow be merged with those of the Western community on the basis of agreement to be reached at Genoa, and that Germany would thus be spared the necessity of a bilateral deal of this sort with Moscow.

These, then, were the circumstances in which the Genoa Conference convened on April 10, 1922. Aside from the Paris Peace Conference, it was the first great summit conference of this century. In some ways it was much like the ones of our own day. Hundreds of wholly useless junior officials were dragged along, and there was a fearful overcoverage by the world press, whose representatives crawled over Genoa in a ratio of several superfluous reporters to each superfluous diplomat. The weather, in this instance, was not propitious. It was cold and rainy. A chilly wind blew down out of the mountains and tore at the palm trees. Everybody froze in the hotel rooms. It was not exactly a happy conference.

Lloyd George, with an eye to his political fortunes at home, chose to head the British delegation in person. For the same reason, I suppose, he deliberately dispensed with any senior Foreign Office advice. The Foreign Secretary, Lord Curzon, was a man who, though violently anti-Russian, was admirably fitted by talent and experience to handle negotiations with the Soviet government. Nevertheless, he was left behind. Out of a total British delegation of 120 persons, only three—and these, people of very junior rank and limited experience—were drawn from the Foreign Office. As his major adviser, Lloyd George selected a gentleman by the name of E. F. Wise, a section chief in the Board of Foreign Trade, who had visited Russia briefly in earlier years but was scarcely experienced in international political matters.

The feelings with which Lord Curzon viewed this markedly nonprofessional excursion into diplomacy may be judged by the prophetic words of a note which he wrote to a friend while the Genoa Conference was in progress:

When I reflect that the P.M. is alone at Genoa with no F.O. to guide him, and with that arch-Bolshevik, Wise, running to and fro between the Soviets and himself, and when I recall the whole trend of his policy for the past three years—I can feel no certainty that we may not find ourselves committed to something pregnant with political disaster here.[69]

The Russian delegation was headed by the Soviet Foreign Minister, Georgi Chicherin. I find it impossible to give you an idea of the atmosphere of the conference without saying a word about him. A nobleman by birth, connected by family with the old Tsarist foreign office and even at one time himself employed there as a research scholar; well educated; a scholarly person; not really a Bolshevik by background but an idealistic, intellectual socialist who had thrown in his lot with the Soviet cause at the time of the Revolution and now passionately believed in it; a man who had sat in an English jail during the war for his views; a man who never spared himself, who was without personal life, who worked twenty hours out of every twenty-four; who wrote every diplomatic note personally; whose office was the scene of a monumental scholar's disorder with books and papers and Foreign Office files lying in heaps all over the place; a man who worked by preference at night and detested daylight, and whose eyes, consequently, were red and blinking, like those of a ferret, when you took him out into the light of day; a hypochondriac; a stooped peering figure of a man, devoid of personal vanity, whose carelessness of dress equaled the disorder of his office—but, withal, a man who lived in his work, who believed in it passionately, who pursued it with a seriousness, a dedication, a self-denial, and an eloquence that put every bourgeois statesman of his day to shame: this was Chicherin; and a more appealing character from the ranks of the Russian revolutionaries I do not know. He believed—as I see it—in many of the wrong things; but he believed in them for the purest of motives. And when I try, as a historian, to follow the progress of the political cause he represented, my sympathies are often with him, even when they are not with it.

Chicherin's statement at the opening plenary session in Genoa was a sensation. It was, remember, the first time that a Soviet representative had appeared at a major international gathering. The great crowd of diplomats and journalists was full of an amused and slightly contemptuous curiosity. Chicherin did not disappoint them. Faced with a situation in which there seemed to be little to be gained for international communism by any conceivable agreement with those who dominated the meeting, he did what Soviet statesmen have always done in such circumstances: he talked, figuratively speaking, out the window, to the crowd outside, to the workers of the world, appealing to them to put pressure on their governments. Speaking in his shrill, passionate voice, in terms which contrasted incongruously with the suave platitudes of the speakers who had preceded him, he started with a classic definition of peaceful co-existence—one which Khrushchev could buy today.

"Whilst maintaining the standpoint of their Communist principles"—he said—

...the Russian delegation recognize that in the present period of history, which permits the parallel existence of the old social order and of the new order now being born, economic collaboration between the States representing these two systems of property is imperatively necessary for the general economic reconstruction.[70]

Then he went on to throw the book at his listeners. He demanded the general limitation of armaments, and the complete abolition of the weapons of mass destruction. He called for a world economic conference, at which would be represented not only all the governments but also all the labor unions of the world. He demanded a redistribution of world gold stocks, and an internationalization of all the great waterways.

However, all this was of course only the opening gun. After this first general session, the conference broke up into subcommittees, and the real diplomacy began. Here it was to be demonstrated that ideological passion on the part of the Soviet delegation was not at all incompatible with extremely shrewd and hard-boiled diplomacy. The basic Soviet purpose, let us remember, was the splitting off of the Germans from the others, and the achievement of a separate German-Russian agreement.

In the main political subcommittee, the British opened the discussion by introducing a memorandum which went into the whole subject of Russian debts and private property claims against the Soviet government and suggested a series of arrangements by which these should be met. This memorandum had been prepared, in advance of the conference, by French and British experts. At several points, it made mention of Article 116. It was, therefore, admirably designed to frighten both Russians and Germans. Neither of these two delegations had seen the memorandum before its introduction. To give them a chance to study it, the subcommittee was adjourned for forty-eight hours.

The French had tried, initially, to have the Germans excluded from this subcommittee. The others had been unwilling to do this. Now the French, to achieve this purpose in another way, insisted that the work of the subcommittee should be suspended for some days and that private and secret discussions should be conducted in the interval between the British and French and the Russians, from which the Germans would be excluded. This proposal was accepted; and for two days, the second of which was Good Friday, such discussions proceeded, in Lloyd George's residence, the Villa Alberti, while the Germans were left to sit on their hands and to wonder what sort of deviltry was being cooked up against them.

One must remember that German representatives were subjected, in those years, to an extensive social ostracism at the hands of Allied diplomats everywhere. I seem to recall from personal experience that as late as 1927 the thought of a German appearing on the Geneva golf links still threw consternation into the hearts of ex-Allied officials serving at the League of Nations. In 1922, these feelings were very much in evidence; and it was difficult for the Germans to maintain anything resembling normal diplomatic contact with the Allied delegations at Genoa. Three times, in that first week of the conference, Rathenau asked for an appointment with Lloyd George. The German Chancellor made the

same request. None of these requests was granted—a fact
which in itself was a signal discourtesy.

On Friday evening, after the first day of the discussions
at the Villa Alberti, there appeared in the headquarters of
the German delegation the secretary of the Italian Foreign
Minister, Giannini. Professing to speak in the name of the
French and British, Giannini told the unhappy Germans that
the talks in the Villa Alberti were proceeding very well,
and that it was expected that agreement would shortly be
reached on the basis of the Anglo-French memorandum.
Rathenau replied that in this case the Germans would
have to take whatever independent action they could to protect their interests. This warning was repeated the following
day by Maltzan to Lloyd George's adviser, Mr. Wise.

What lay behind Giannini's visit I have never been
able to ascertain. The information he gave was quite
erroneous. No agreement had been reached, was being
reached, or would be reached, in the discussions between
the Russians and the others at the Villa Alberti. The talks
there got snarled up at once on the question of debts and
claims; and at no time was there the remotest danger of
an agreement involving the implementation of Article 116.
But the Germans couldn't know this; and the Russians
took good care not to tell them what the real score was.

On Saturday, the rumors multiplied around Genoa of an
imminent agreement between the Russians and the French
and British. Bear in mind that up to this time, the Germans
had been given no opportunity to state their views on any
of the subjects under discussion. They now saw their worst
fears materializing before they had even had an opportunity
to state their case. They spent Saturday evening sitting
gloomily around in the lobby of their hotel, and finally went
to bed in a state of great worry and depression.

At 1:15 in the morning, the telephone rang in Maltzan's
hotel room. It was one of the Soviet delegates, speaking
from the Soviet headquarters at the nearby seashore resort
of Rapallo. There was nothing wrong with the Russian timing.
Would the Germans, it was asked, like to come out later
that day and discuss the question of a separate German-
Soviet agreement? Maltzan said he would call back. The
members of the German delegation assembled in Maltzan's
room, in their pajamas, and debated the issue through the
dark hours of this early Easter morning. The session was al-

ways afterwards referred to, in the German Foreign Office, as "the pajama party."

It was Rathenau who held out longest. The idea of a general international settlement, both with Russia and with the West, had been quite particularly his dream. As an industrialist—one of the heads of the German General Electric Company—he was a great believer in the economic integration of Europe. (In this, he was forty years ahead of his time. The European Coal and Steel Community would have been his dish.) Of all the Germans present he, least of all, wanted to cut loose from the West in the relationship to Russia.

But the danger now seemed undeniable. If he did not act, the last chink of hope, the last chance for an active and hopeful German foreign policy, would presumably disappear. Russia would be added to the circle of Germany's creditors. The last escape hatch would be barred.

At five o'clock in the morning, therefore, word was sent to the Russians that the Germans were willing to talk. Two attempts were made, in the early morning hours, to get in touch with Mr. Wise and to let the British know of the German decision. On the first occasion, the word came back that Mr. Wise was asleep and could not be disturbed. The second time, a chilly voice answered that the gentlemen had gone out of town for the day, and could not be reached.

The Russian and German delegations therefore met later in the morning, as scheduled, at Rapallo. The talks proceeded favorably. The Russians were careful not to disabuse the Germans of the misimpression under which they were laboring. By late afternoon, complete agreement had been reached. The text of the bilateral German-Soviet Treaty lay on the table, ready for signature. It contained a sweeping mutual renunciation of all financial claims of every sort, thus relieving the Germans of the nightmare of Article 116, and giving the Russians assurance that the Germans would not someday appear in the ranks of their foreign creditors.

Word was sent to Rathenau, who had been waiting in a nearby hotel during the final preparation of the text, that the time had come for signature. Just as he was about to get into his automobile, to go to the Soviet headquarters, he received word that Lloyd George was trying to reach him by phone, to arrange an interview. In greatest agony of spirit, he paused for a moment; but the way back seemed too long and tortuous and uncertain to be contemplated.

He was heard to mutter twice to himself, in French: *"Le vin est tiré; il faut le boire."* With that he got in the car, drove over to the Soviet headquarters, and signed.

One feels—at least, I do—intensely sorry for this unhappy man at this difficult moment. He was a deeply cultivated person, a real European, a member of that remarkable circle of Jewish intellectuals, grouped around the artist Max Lieberman, who formed so distinguished a part of the genteel society of prewar Berlin. As Germany's first Jewish Foreign Minister, he was already the butt of much criticism at home and the recipient of a flood of abusive anonymous communications. Less than two months later he was to die at the hands of a Nazi assassin. He had had premonitions of this disaster when he left for Genoa, and undertook the journey in great heaviness of spirit. "This period, which you describe as the supreme one of my life," he wrote to a friend on the eve of departure, "is the most difficult; it is nothing else than a farewell to everything. I know that what I am undertaking will mean the break-up of my life, whether I wish it or not." I cannot help but see in the plight of this man at this moment the embodiment of the profligate carelessness with which the Western democracies treated the moderate and well-meaning elements in the German Weimar Republic, of the needless way in which they forfeited the collaboration of these people in the preservation of the interests of the West, of the iron logic with which an emotional and vindictive anti-Germanism in the Western countries played into the hands of Soviet policy makers.

I need scarcely recall to your memories the utter stupefaction and the crescendo of indignation with which the news of the conclusion of the Rapallo Treaty was received in London and Paris. The French delegates at Genoa began ostentatiously packing their suitcases. In Paris there was talk of a call to the colors. For days the French and British papers boiled with indignation. This "unholy alliance," the *Times* said, was a bombshell, "an open defiance and studied insult to the Entente Powers." Action was demanded "to teach Germans and Bolshevists alike that the Allies are not to be defied or flouted with impunity." Even in later years, neither of Lloyd George's official biographers would be able to describe the incident otherwise than as an example of the most cold-blooded German treachery. Thus can history be misunderstood, on the strength of subjective prejudice.

I must add one last bit of irony. When the signature of the treaty became known, the leaders of the German delegation were summoned peremptorily before Lloyd George, who had hitherto refused to receive them. He demanded angrily to know why they had not approached him before signing with the Russians. It was pointed out that he had declined four separate requests for just such an interview. Why, then, he said, did you not get in touch with my subordinates? The Germans replied that they had described their entire situation twice to Mr. Wise in the two days preceding the event, and had tried in vain to reach him again on Sunday before leaving for the Russian headquarters. Lloyd George's reply to this argument stands as a classic example of the political art: "Who," he asked with ruffled brow, "is Mr. Wise?"

This, I think, is substantially the story of Rapallo. I need no longer labor the moral of the tale. The treaty concluded was innocuous. It did not represent anything in the nature of an alliance. It contained no secret clauses. The German military had no foreknowledge of its signature and nothing to do with the final event. The document provided merely for the resumption of full diplomatic relations between the two powers, for the mutual cancellation of claims, and for most-favored-nation treatment. It was not the result of a prearranged plot. The news of its conclusion came as no less of a surprise to the government in Berlin than to the governments in London and Paris. Official sentiment in Berlin was by no means enthusiastic. The German President, in particular, was furious. Above all, the treaty was in no sense a precedent for the Nazi-Soviet Non-aggression Pact of 1939—an agreement which went much further and embraced elements which the German statesmen of 1922 would never have dreamed of accepting.

For the Western Allies, Rapallo meant the forfeiture of the collaboration of Germany as a possible partner in a united Western approach to the problem of Russian Communism. But it also meant, though Western statesmen did not realize it at the moment, that their own policy of coupling debts and claims with recognition had been decisively undermined.

Rapallo could justly be described as the first great victory for Soviet diplomacy. It successfully split the Western community in its relation to Russia. It drove an entering wedge, on terms favorable to Moscow, into the problem of diplomatic recognition and the resumption of trade relations between Russia and the West. That Chicherin and his associates deserve much credit for this, on the basis of their skillful exploitation of the circumstances that arose at Genoa, cannot be denied. But it seems clear to me that the most important determining factor in this development was the weakness of the diplomacy of the Western democracies: its smugness, its superficiality, its national-emotional bias, its dilettantism of execution, its state of enslavement to the vagaries of domestic politics in the democratic setting. To these shortcomings, must be added, lest we Americans become too complacent, the inexcusable denial of America's presence and interest at this crucial moment. The United States refused flatly to take any part at all in the Genoa Conference.

I would like, then, in conclusion, to ask you to note— on the example of this episode—the standard components for a rousing Soviet diplomatic success: one part Soviet resourcefulness and singlemindedness of purpose; two parts amateurism, complacency, and disunity on the part of the West. It is not the last time, in examining the history of Soviet foreign policy, that we shall see this recipe play a part, as the Soviet government advances from the initial weakness of 1921 to the pinnacle of power and success it occupies in the wake of World War II.

16　Britain, the Soviet Target

IN THE early Twenties, Britain still appeared to the Soviet leaders as the greatest of the world powers. The United States at that time figured only remotely in the Soviet scheme of things. If it was to Germany that Soviet attention turned particularly in the initial period, in both the revolutionary and the diplomatic contexts, this was only because the chances for immediate success seemed best there, not because Germany was necessarily the most important of bourgeois countries. Given the strength of the German socialist movement and the prevailing unrest there in the aftermath of military defeat, it was natural that Soviet hopes should have gone in that direction. But beyond Germany loomed England. Germany was an exhausted, ruined country, which presented revolutionary opportunities. But Britian was still, in the Soviet view, the ultimate enemy. Here was the great proud bastion of world capitalism: the place where all the threads of imperialist power came together—the innermost temple of international finance—the place from which, generally, the peoples of the non-European world were ruled and exploited. It was here, in the London City, that the great abhorrent spider of monopoly capital was believed to have his hidden lair. It was from here that he spun his invisible webs of economic bondage, which only the genius of Marx had been able to perceive and to expose. It was from here that he flung these webs out over the distant continents; to snare the helpless peoples, to enslave them in the silken strait jacket of financial dependence. Finally, it was here, in the great country houses of England, that he consumed, in arrogant luxury, the stolen products of other people's toil.

The fact that whatever reality this image might once have possessed had been extensively undermined by World War I seems to have been as little apparent, initially, to Moscow as it was to many people in England itself. This is how the Soviet leaders saw the Britain of that day. And the problem it presented for Soviet foreign policy, from the revolutionary standpoint, was a long-term one. The chances for early revolution in England itself were not good. Of course, there were these discontented dockers, these restless ex-service men, these parvenus-intellectuals embittered by their poverty and by the lower- or middle-class accents which barred them forever from admission to the fraternity of the upper class. With such people something could perhaps someday be done. One should at least not ignore them. They would come in handy when the disintegration of Britain's imperialist power finally set in; out of their ranks might be built the Communist movement of the future. But these were long-term prospects. This old mother-

oak of Britain, fed by its overseas roots, was too strong
to be successfully assailed at the center. It was its widespread
root system beyond the oceans that had to be attacked.
The cultivation of the national-liberation movement among
the underdeveloped and dependent peoples provided the most
promising point of departure.

But, for the moment, Britain was important to Soviet Russia in another way. It was to England that Russia's exports
of food and raw materials had traditionally gone. In these
exports of timber, of flax, of grain, and of oil, the old
Russia had found a major source of foreign exchange.
Perhaps this trade could be revived. If it was primarily in
Germany and the United States that Moscow wanted to
buy, it was to England that Moscow wanted to sell. Beyond that, London was still viewed as the greatest single
source of financial capital. And Russia's position, in 1921,
was such that her recovery depended, or seemed to depend,
on the ability to procure capital far in excess of the possible
proceeds of her export capacity of that day. Besides, what
the British did still stood, in those days, as the precedent
which others would follow.

For all these reasons, Britain took first place as a target
for the Soviet effort to win diplomatic recognition and to
establish normal trade relations with the West. The pact
with the Germans had been important as a means of frustrating any attempt by the capitalist powers to form a united
front in their commercial and diplomatic dealings with Russia. It had improved Moscow's bargaining power vis-à-vis
the West. But Britain remained the key target.

To the English society of the 1920's, Soviet Russia had
not one but many connotations; and these were sharply
divisive in their effect. To Conservative opinion in Britain,
everything about the new Russia was abhorrent. The philosophy which the Soviet leaders put forward as the justification for their internal policies and for their provocative
external behavior was, to the conservative Englishman, simply disgusting and offensive. Its sweeping denial of the value
of the private virtues; its contempt for individual initiative
and thrift and hard work; its utter absence of respect for
honestly earned property and savings; its provocative secu-
larism; its ridicule of religion and persecution of the Church;
its scorn for subjective ethical standards; its belief that the
ends justified the means; its denial of the uses of an inde-

pendent judiciary; its cynical identification of justice with the interests of the state; its contempt for tradition and for the voice of experience; its dangerous dependence on abstract theory, and on a theory only sixty years old at that (a dependence bound to be particularly suspicious to a pragmatic people like the British); above all, the absolute, revelatory value it ascribed to this theory, as though all the generations that had gone before had been empty fools, as though the remainder of the whole great storehouse of history and experience had nothing to offer, as though Marx had discovered it all and for the first time—how could such things be other than shocking beyond utterance in a society where the afterglow of Victorian capitalism was still strong, where the Puritan virtues of thrift and industry and individual ethical obligation were still regarded as the true foundations of modern civilization? How could English people be expected to react otherwise than with a sort of breathless indignation, as though you had suddenly struck them in the face, at the suggestion that such principles ought properly to prevail in preference to their own, and to prevail in England as well as in Russia? What could be the effect, on people who respected and loved their own royal family, of the descriptions of that ghastly scene that had been enacted on a July night in 1918 in the cellar of the Ipatyev house in Ekaterinburg, in the Urals, when the imperial family of Russia—the Tsarina, the daughters, the family retainers, and the Tsar himself, the cousin of the English king, bearing his young sick son in his arms—had stood there in their helplessness, guilty primarily only of the accident of birth, to be mowed down with automatic rifles from a distance of six feet—and their bodies then to be dragged out into the forest on peasant carts and burned in an evil yellow conflagration that illuminated the whole night sky. Beyond this was the erroneous but widespread belief that the Bolsheviki had been German agents—a belief particularly prevalent in conservative circles in both Russia and England. Then there was the world-revolutionary side of the Bolshevik personality: the impudent claim to know what was good for England as well as what was good for Russia— the activities of the Comintern—the revolutionary propaganda to the Moslem world and the colonies. Add to this the malicious misinformation about Soviet conditions which was constantly reaching high society in the West—the stories of the nationalization of women and other distortions culti-

vated by the White Russian émigrés who frequented the
salons of Paris and London—and you will see that it was
hardly to be expected of conservative Englishmen that they
should react sympathetically and tolerantly to the demand of
Moscow for admission on equal terms to the privileges of
membership in the international community.

With the Labourites, the picture was quite different. To
them, the Russian Revolution and its consequences both
attracted and repelled. The Bolshevik experiment represented
for them the first application in practice of socialist principles which they themselves had been able to pursue only
as dreams for a distant future. They were both horrified
and excited by what they saw in this mirror of their own
principles. Many of the elements of the Russian Communist outlook which were shocking to English conservatives were not particularly shocking to the Labourites.
Property, while not the wholly abhorrent thing it was to
their Russian comrades, was for them at any rate not something semi-sacred, as it was to many conservatives; religion
was no fetish; their feelings about the British royal family
were ambivalent. They tended, to be sure, to dislike the
over-intellectuality, the extreme theoreticalness, the obvious
remoteness from the experience of work at the bench or
lathe, which they observed in the Russian socialists. They
were often surprised and estranged by things they heard
about the harshness and cruelty of Soviet methods. And
yet most of them could never free themselves entirely from
the emotional magnetism of the Russian Revolution. Here,
after all, crude as it might have been, was the first great
political triumph of socialism. Even when the personalities
of leading Russian Communists were not particularly attractive to the Labourite taste, those of the main opponents
of Russian Communism were always hideous. If it was not
exactly the right people in Russia who had triumphed, at
least the wrong ones had been confounded. The Russian
Revolution had been right in what it was against, if not
in what it was for.

Such views were, of course, a far cry from those of the
Conservatives; and this divergence was quite sufficient to
create resounding and enduring differences of opinion on
questions of policy towards Russia.

In postwar England the prospect of possible trade with
Russia was not a negligible consideration. There was

severe unemployment, and no small measure of economic distress. The Labourites saw in trade with Russia a means of helping to overcome unemployment. This was one of the main reasons they gave for favoring diplomatic recognition of Soviet Russia. One might have thought that British industrialists would have taken a similar view, and that this would have affected Conservative opinion. To some extent, this was so. But in those echelons of the City whose influence was strongest, there seems to have been greater interest in collecting past debts than in developing new trade relations which might provide a source of profit in the future.

Lloyd George, a Liberal and an opportunist, halfway between the Tories and the Labourites in many respects, had sided with Labour on the subject of economic relations with Russia. At his initiative, a provisional trade agreement had been concluded between the two countries in 1921. This agreement had provided for the exchange of *de facto* representatives—official representatives, that is, who lacked the full status of regular ambassadors. It was Lloyd George who, as we saw, sparked the abortive Genoa Conference. After the conclusion of the Rapallo Treaty, the sticky subject of "debts and claims" continued to be discussed with the Russians by the British and French in the further months of 1922, first at Genoa and then at The Hague; but no agreement could be reached.

In the autumn of 1922, Lloyd George fell from office; but his Foreign Secretary, Lord Curzon, was retained in the new Conservative cabinet of Bonar Law. Here, in this elegant and aristocratic martinet of the Foreign Office, you had the embodiment of that Conservative distaste of Soviet Russia which I mentioned earlier, coupled with the ultimate of what the British upper class could muster in personal arrogance and self-assurance. I cannot say whether it is true, as the famous story runs, that Curzon, on observing a group of English Tommies bathing in a canal in France during the war, exclaimed in astonishment that he never knew the lower classes had such white skins. I believe he used to tell the story on himself. True or apocryphal, it gives you an idea of the sort of person he was. Nevertheless, he was an extremely able man: the only one of the Western statesmen of that day who was fully a match, in industry and intellectual brilliance, for Chicherin. He proved this when the two met head-on at the Lausanne

Conference, in the winter of 1922-1923. Both Chicherin
and Curzon were old-fashioned persons; both had had their
diplomatic schooling in earlier years. Curzon's dislike of
Russia and Chicherin's dislike of Britain were thus both
founded in the Anglo-Russian rivalries of the pre-revolutionary
period. In each of these contending noblemen, traditional suspicions and resentments served to reinforce a genuine and
profound dislike for the social system the other represented.

Curzon's anti-Soviet policy was of such sharpness that in
the spring of 1923 he very nearly brought to a complete
rupture the existing *de facto* relations with Moscow. He
dispatched to the Soviet government at that time a very
sharply worded note—the celebrated "Curzon ultimatum"
—giving Moscow ten days to settle a number of British
grievances. Somehow or other, the affair was patched up,
and did not lead to a complete break. But it did aggravate
the political argument that was then going on between the
Tories and the Labourites as to how Russia ought to be
treated; and I suspect that it pushed the Labour Party
farther than it might otherwise have wished to go in
committing itself to a position in favor of immediate diplomatic recognition.

In any case, when, at the end of 1923, the Conservative
government fell and was replaced by Britain's first Labour
government, under Ramsay MacDonald, one of the first
things MacDonald did was to extend full diplomatic recognition to Moscow. This action, taken in late January 1924,
was matched at once by the Italians (there is, in fact, some
doubt as to which action came first). The example was soon
followed by a number of other governments, for whom
London's attitude was the decisive precedent. In this way
what we might call the log-jam of resistance to the formal
acceptance of Soviet Russia as a member of the international community was broken. It had taken six years, from
the time of the Revolution, for this point to be attained.
Another decade would have to ensue before the United
States would follow suit. Certain of the smaller countries,
notably Switzerland, Yugoslavia, and Holland, also still held
out. But it is not too much to say that MacDonald's action
spelled the formal recognition of Russia by a major portion of the capitalist world.

Before we go on with the story of MacDonald's effort
to regularize England's relationship with Russia I think

we should take note of another event that occurred in January 1924, only a few days before the act of diplomatic recognition was performed in London. This was the death of Lenin, which occurred on January 21. In view of this close coincidence in time, it may properly be said that the Lenin era was coterminous with the extreme diplomatic isolation which Russia experienced during the first years after the Revolution.

I should like to digress for a moment to have a brief glance at the role of individual personalities in Soviet policy in this early period, and to see what Lenin's death did, and did not, signify.

At no time prior to Molotov's assumption of the position of Foreign Minister in 1939 was the Commissariat—or, as it was later called, the Ministry—for Foreign Affairs the center for the formulation of Soviet foreign policy. We must remember, first of all, that this was a policy which embraced, in curious dialectical apposition, two quite contradictory elements: the desire to destroy bourgeois governments, on the one hand, and the desire to enjoy the advantages of normal intercourse with them on the other, so long as they continued to resist destruction. For the first of these objectives, the Comintern served as the executive agency; for the second, the Commissariat for Foreign Affairs. In each case, the actual formulation of policy, in major questions, took place somewhere else: in the higher echelons of the Party apparatus, notably the Central Committee and, above all, the Politbureau. It was here that the contradictions were reconciled, or at least dealt with. Comintern and Foreign Affairs Commissariat were only the administrative media through which the decisions of the Party were implemented.

In the process of policy formulation at the higher levels of the Party, Chicherin played only a very minor part. Until January 1918, he had not even been a member of the Bolshevik wing of the old Russian Social-Democratic Party. It was 1925 before he was admitted to the Central Committee. Admission to the Politbureau was something of which he never even dreamed. Lenin valued him, sometimes consulted him as an expert, occasionally even worked with him on the drafting of diplomatic documents. But he never viewed him as one who shared in the major decisions of the Party. When, on one occasion in 1922, Chicherin was rash enough to suggest that, in order to please the

American Relief Administration, nonproletarian elements of the population might be allowed to have representation in local soviets, Lenin was annoyed at this presumption, and said that Chicherin ought to be sent to a sanitarium.

With Stalin, Chicherin had no intimacy at all. On the contrary, the two men disliked each other. On at least one occasion, Chicherin attacked Stalin's views publicly in the *Pravda*, a form of challenge which the sensitive Stalin never forgot or forgave in anyone. If Chicherin was close to anyone in the Politbureau, it was probably Bukharin. But it was only after Lenin's death that Bukharin had, for a time, strong influence on policy. During Lenin's life-time, and during the periods in which he enjoyed good health, no one ever rivaled him or challenged his position of unique authority in the determination of *all* the policies of the Party, including Soviet foreign policy. In all such periods it was, primarily, *Lenin's* policy which Chicherin was obliged to execute.

There were, however, considerable periods, in those first years of Soviet power, when Lenin was unable to exert this authority. On August 30, 1918, he was shot and severely wounded by a fanatical member of the Left Socialist-Revolutionaries—Dora Kaplan. While he staged a rapid recovery and was back at his desk in a matter of weeks, it is hard to believe that this did not have some effect on his general physical condition. Three years later, in the autumn of 1921, his health began to weaken. He was obliged to spend much of the winter of 1921-1922 in the country, to avoid the pressures of his office; and in May 1922, while the Genoa Conference was still in progress, he was taken with the first of the three paralytic strokes that finally led to his death. After this first stroke, although he returned to his desk for a time in the autumn of 1922, his contribution to the formulation of Party policy was never again what it had been. For most of the time from the beginning of his illness in early 1922 to his death, two years later in 1924, he was plainly out of commission.

Major policy decisions were made, during this time, and again for some years after his death, by his colleagues, acting collectively as members of the Politbureau. Their decisions had, at all times, unchallengeable authority for Chicherin and his colleagues at the Foreign Affairs Ministry. However, their relative lack of unity and firmness, and their extensive preoccupation with problems of internal policy as well as with their own competition for power, meant that through the years of the mid-Twenties Chicherin was allowed—and sometimes even forced by circumstances to assume—a wider latitude of initiative and independent decision than Lenin's active presence would have permitted. In any case, since manner of execution is always a factor in diplomacy of no less importance than concept, much depended at all times on the style and tenor of Chicherin's diplomacy; and the mark of his vivid personality can be noted at many points in the record of Soviet foreign relations throughout those years.

How much the substance of Soviet foreign policy was affected by this is difficult to say. Chicherin's strong anti-British feelings were revealed in the sharpness of his various exchanges with Lord Curzon. They probably had some effect on the line of Soviet policy at both the Genoa Conference and the Lausanne Conference (on the problems of Turkey and the Straits) which followed shortly thereafter. On the other hand, the failure to reach agreement with the Western powers over debts and claims cannot be attributed to Chicherin. The rejection of the last possibilities for agreement in these matters reflected a decision taken by Lenin personally, during his brief return to official duties in the fall of 1922. The most that may be said is that Chicherin's aristocratic background and personality gave to Soviet diplomacy, in the years of his greatest activity as Foreign Commissar, a polish, a flexibility, and an approachability which it was never to enjoy during the Stalin era. While Chicherin had his own difficulties with the Soviet secret police, and was forced to assume that his own office was duly wired by these zealous guardians of ideological virtue, this did not inhibit his willingness to discuss problems freely and independently with foreign representatives. So long as his personality was dominant in the Foreign Office, there was a channel, albeit indirect, through which ideas could be exchanged with the Soviet regime by a foreign representative. In later years, even this could hardly be said to be the case. This was not the fault of Chicherin's successor, Maxim Litvinov. It reflected the wishes of Stalin, in whose scheme of things such normal diplomatic contact had no place.

But now—back to MacDonald and his action in extending diplomatic recognition to the Soviet regime. The novelty of his policy consisted in the fact that he consented

to take this step without insisting on a prior settlement of
the question of debts and claims. It was his hope that
this problem would prove easier to settle once relations had
been resumed.

But the question of debts and claims was not to be
thus easily disposed of. Moscow wanted, as a *quid pro quo*
for any settlement of debts and claims, a large financial
loan. But international loans, in those days, were usually
handled by private bankers. The bankers also had an interest in the debt settlement. No settlement which did not
receive reasonable support in the City was apt to be acceptable to Parliament; and certainly no loan would be forthcoming before such a settlement was made. MacDonald,
therefore, whose parliamentary position was weak, did
not even dare appoint an ambassador to Moscow before
making an attempt to solve this tangled problem. Instead,
he asked the Russians to send to London a delegation to
negotiate with the British government a so-called general
treaty in which not only the question of the debts and
claims but all other outstanding problems between the
two governments would be settled. After that, it was understood, ambassadors would be exchanged, and the way
would be open for arrangement of a loan.

The Soviet delegation arrived in London in the spring of
1924. Negotiations wore on into the summer. The good old
issue of debts and claims proved, once again, to be in-
tractable. In despair, MacDonald finally arranged to have
included in the draft treaty a clause which simply deferred
the whole question to later treatment. This, of course, also
deferred the question of the loan as well. In this form, in
September 1924, the treaty was submitted to Parliament for
ratification. But while the treaty was "lying on the table," as
the parliamentary saying goes, awaiting action on its ratification, the MacDonald government lost its support in the House
of Commons and was obliged to ask for general elections.
This was in October 1924. It was at this point that the
bizarre episode of the Zinoviev letter occurred.

No sooner had the date of the new elections been fixed
than the Foreign Office and certain London editors received, from clandestine and obscure sources, a copy of a
letter purporting to have been written in Moscow by the
head of the Communist International, G. E. Zinoviev, to a
man named McManus, who was one of the leaders of the
British Communist Party. It was a letter giving instructions

for the conduct of subversive work in England. Plainly, if such a directive were to become known to the public at that time, in the midst of the election campaign, it would be highly embarrassing to the Labour government, which had staked its policy on a friendly Soviet reaction to the act of recognition.

Actually, poor MacDonald was not guilty of any great naïveté about the doings of the Comintern. He had never denied the impropriety of some of its activity. If he was in any way naïve, it was about the possibility of inducing the Soviet leaders, by the mere act of recognition, to moderate this activity. "The Russian Government"—he had written before assuming office in 1923—

... did harbour for a long time a belief in a world revolution on Bolshevist lines; it spent money in foreign countries—my own included—promoting such a revolution; it used diplomatic privileges to carry on conspiracy and propaganda; it claimed for its agents ... the right to overthrow the governments to which they were accredited. ...

So long as the Third International lasted, he wrote, "we shall never be free from danger." But the worst defense against this, he thought, was

... the boycott of the Moscow Government, the wild whirl of forgery, of ignorance, of fake which has been nine tenths of the anti-Bolshevist propaganda in both Great Britain and America.[71]

It was for this reason that he had dared to take upon himself the onus of unconditional recognition.

This was, altogether, not an implausible position. But MacDonald, however sound as a statesman, was deplorably untalented as an executive. At the time when the copy of the so-called Zinoviev letter was received in the Foreign Office, he was off in Wales, campaigning for re-election. Certain of the Foreign Office officials, after examining the document, sat down and drafted a note of protest to the Soviet diplomatic mission; they sent this draft note, together with the offending document, off to the Prime Minister for his approval. MacDonald was at that moment terribly tired. He had his mind on other things. On receiving the file, he failed to realize what dynamite the document contained. He did not initial the draft note, which would have been the normal indication of approval; but he made some corrections on it, and sent the whole file back to the Foreign Office, in the trusting assumption that someone would investigate the authenticity of the document before proceeding further. These papers reached the Foreign Office on October 24, five days before the election. That same day, it was learned in the Foreign Office that the editor of the *Daily Mail* had a copy of the Zinoviev document and was planning to publish it the next day. To one of the senior officials of the Foreign Office, it occurred that if this happened, and the document had not yet been released by the government, MacDonald would be placed in a difficult position. He would be charged with having tried to suppress the letter and to conceal it from the voters. It was therefore decided in the Foreign Office to release the whole matter to the press. The head of the Northern Section signed personally the note of protest MacDonald had corrected, and sent it off to the Soviet diplomatic mission. Copies of both documents, the alleged Moscow directive and the British note of protest, were at once released to the press.

The effect was spectacular, and utterly disastrous. The press played up both items as a tremendous sensation. The Tories triumphantly pointed to the document as proof of the folly of MacDonald's Russian policy, and charged anyway that he had initially tried to suppress it. He had released it, they shouted, only when his hand was forced by its imminent appearance in the press. The left-wing Labour press, on the other hand, with the support of the Soviet mission, promptly declared the document to be a forgery. This made MacDonald, who had ostensibly released it, look like an even greater fool.

What could MacDonald do? Never, I think, has a man been placed in a more impossible position by his well-meaning subordinates. He could not know, off there in Wales amid the confusion of an election campaign—with the bands playing, with local political leaders running in and out, with people clamoring for his presence on speaking platforms—whether the document was genuine or not. Actually, it was wholly fraudulent: concocted, in all probability, by a group of White Russian and Polish forgers in Berlin. But MacDonald had no means of knowing this. If, now, he denied responsibility for its release, if he claimed, that is, that the Foreign Office had acted without his instructions, this would be cited as further proof that he feared the implications of the document and had meant to suppress it. If, on the other hand, he supported the Foreign Office, and thereby personally sponsored the authenticity of the document, it would be asked why it had taken him so long to wake up to an obvious state of affairs, and how all this jibed with his trusting Russian policy and the provisions of the treaty that lay on the parliamentary table—a document in which the Russians had promised, once again, to refrain from subversive propaganda. Even had he known the document was spurious, it would have done him no good to say so. He would merely invite the question as to what business his government had, anyway, foisting fraudulent documents on the public. Whichever way he moved, he was lost.

Four days later, the elections occurred. Labour was thrown out of office. This result was widely attributed to the effects of the publication of the Zinoviev letter. The more careful research of later historians has thrown considerable doubt on this conclusion. But at the time, it looked as though the Labour government had indeed fallen victim to a very successful election maneuver.

I ask you to note this incident as an example of the fantastic confusion which can sometimes occur in political life, and the difficulty the historian often has in trying to draw general conclusions from individual episodes. What could be concluded from these circumstances? Did the episode prove that the Soviet government was guilty of improper interference in Britian's internal affairs? No, for the document was a forgery. Did it prove that the Soviet government was innocent? No, for there was nothing very implausible about the document, in substance; other documents scarcely less incriminating were constantly being drawn up in Moscow; and at a later date the British government would bring some of them to public notice. Did it prove that reactionary officials in the Foreign Office simply deliberately tripped up MacDonald? No, the motives at least of the senior official who authorized the action were known to be of the purest. Could it be said, then, that *all* Foreign Office officials were innocent of ulterior motives in this matter? Not exactly. The man who signed the note, the head of the Northern Section, was indeed a very anti-Soviet person and one who, from the distance of nearly forty years, does make a rather odd impression. He was shortly thereafter to be dismissed for speculation in French francs; the high point of this financial involvement appears to have been at just the time of the Zinoviev incident; and there is some evidence which suggests that his part in the whole affair was more than meets the eye. What does it then prove? Only, so far as I can see, that one should be careful of protesting documents the authenticity of which one has not verified; and also that it is a bad thing for a prime minister to try to run for re-election and handle Foreign Office matters at the same time.

Well, this, in any case, was the end of the Labour government. The Conservatives returned to power as a result of the election. They promptly withdrew the proposed treaty from the table of Parliament. Ambassadors were not exchanged. The negotiations over debts and claims were not renewed. Relations with Russia continued to string along in the most abysmally bad state for another two years. On May 12, 1927, the British government instituted a raid on the premises of the Soviet Trade Delegation in London (the so-called Arcos raid); citing as justification evidence of subversive activity brought to light by this raid, it broke off relations altogether. They were not resumed until 1930. In short, the Zinoviev letter episode set back the normalization of Anglo-Soviet diplomatic exchanges for just about five years.

When regular diplomatic contact was resumed, in 1930, MacDonald was again Prime Minister. Now, for the first time, full ambassadors were exchanged. King George V still objected strenuously to receiving and being obliged to shake hands with the representative of the murderers of his cousin; but his objectives were overridden. Kings, like everybody else, have to make their compromises.

On this second occasion, nobody bothered any more about the issue of debts and claims. The economic crisis had now finally thrust this unhappy issue into the background. No preliminary conditions at all were attached, this time, to the exchange of ambassadors. Lenin, in refusing to make a settlement on debts and claims in 1922, had been vindicated by the passage of time. It is often true in international affairs that all things come to those who wait.

So much for the story of the way in which diplomatic relations were re-established between England and Russia.

Now just a word or two of comment on the question of principle which was here at stake.

There were, as you see, three solutions of the problem of relations with Russia that commended themselves, at one time or another, to various Englishmen. MacDonald would have ignored the ideological disparity entirely and would have extended—indeed, eventually did extend—full *de jure* diplomatic recognition to Moscow in the belief that even if the behavior of the Soviet government was improper, the absence of diplomatic relations was not the best way to counteract it. Lord Curzon and the Tories, on the other hand, long saw no need for any diplomatic relations whatsoever. Moscow, so far as they were concerned, could well be ignored. In a sense, this view persisted among the Tories even after recognition had become a fact. Lloyd George adopted a middle view, and took a middle course: that of *de facto* relations. He didn't do this, of course, on principle (Lloyd George rarely did anything on principle); but still, this was one solution.

The issue involved here—the issue of how you deal with a power which openly avows its total enmity towards you but professes an intention to carry it forward not on the plane of direct military warfare but on the plane of limited political and economic competition—still remains. It confronts us today particularly in the case of Communist China. As we have seen, MacDonald's solution—the establishment of *de jure* rather than *de facto* relations—was the one which eventually established itself and became the standard practice of the international community, so far as Russia was concerned. I am still not sure, in retrospect, that it was the right one. That you could not fully ignore Russia, as the Tories wished to do, I entirely understand. Even in personal life, we do not have the luxury of being able to ignore evil entirely. We all have to make our compromises with the Devil, and to have our dealings with him. But personally, I have always liked to think of my own relations with the Devil as being of a *de facto*, rather than a *de jure*, nature. However that may be—and I must admit that the distinction has worn thin on occasions—deal with the Devil we must, and come to some sort of terms with him we must—as individuals and as collective bodies of citizens—if only for the reason that we are simply not *that* superior, for the reason that each of us, be it an individual or a nation, has a little of the

Devil in himself. Whether the answer is *de facto* or *de jure* relations is arguable; perhaps the distinction ought to be abolished. The answer is, in any case, not the absence of any relations at all.

17   Stalin as a Statesman

THE DISCUSSION of Anglo-Soviet relations in the Twenties has taken us beyond the time of Lenin's death and into the period when Stalin's influence began to make itself increasingly felt in Soviet diplomacy. It might be well, therefore, before we go on with the story of Russia's foreign relations, to have a look at the personality, human and political, of Stalin himself.

It is hard to approach this subject without speaking first about the great ethical conflict which wracked the Russian revolutionary movement of the nineteenth century. It was the conflict between the utopian humanitarianism of the ends and the harshness of the means. On the one hand, you had the unquestionable purity of the ideals by which these revolutionaries were driven; on the other, you had a terrible suspicion, growing gradually on the part of many of them into a belief, that the only path to the early realization of these ideals led through the perpetration of great cruelty against others. They came to feel that in the unwillingness of many social idealists in the past to practice cruelty and to shed blood deliberately had lain the source of their political failure—that only through a ruthless callousness toward *individual* human life could the way be found to the elimination of such things as ruthlessness and callousness in their relation to *people in the mass*—that there was even a certain superior virtue and self-sacrifice involved in the employment of evil means for worthy ends: it meant that a few accepted the burden of guilt and unpleasantness in order that others might have the privilege of remaining guiltless. This was, in short, the classic Dostoyevskian dilemma.

I sometimes think the entire trend and fate of the Russian revolutionary movement can be explained in terms of the inability of the Russian intellectual class of the nineteenth century to cope with this dilemma. The S-R's, in particular, got carried by it into a belief in the propriety and efficacy of personal terrorism. In deference to this belief, they assassinated literally thousands of people—over seven hundred in the year 1907 alone. That many of their incidental victims were quite innocent (they included, after all, such people as children and casual bystanders) the terrorists would not for an instant have denied. It was their belief that not only guilty blood but innocent blood as well had to be shed in order that the good of the greater number could be served; and this even added, in their eyes, to their own heroism; for it was harder, after all, to kill a child than to kill a police agent.

The Bolsheviki did not share this belief in personal terrorism. They rejected assassination as a normal means of political struggle. They rejected it not because they thought it was morally wrong but because they considered it was, as Lenin himself said, "inopportune and inexpedient."[72] But their rejection of individual terrorism did not in any sense signify a repudiation of violence. Lenin, scarred no doubt by his brother's death on a Tsarist gallows, wholly accepted the need for violence in the overthrow of the power of the propertied classes. He believed, to be sure, in using violence only to the extent that it was absolutely necessary in order to promote one's political ends. He had no particular liking for it, I think. There was no sadism in his personality. He simply viewed violence as a regrettable necessity. You are probably all familiar with the sad observation he once made to the effect that one would like to stroke and caress human beings; but one dared not do so, because they bite.

One of the first points at which Lenin had occasion to authorize the resort to violence for Party purposes was in the use of brutal and criminal methods as a means of procuring funds for the support of Party activity. It is revealing and symbolic that it should have been precisely at this point, and in this connection, that Stalin came in.

Prior to the abortive revolution of 1905, the Party had done rather well in getting contributions from respectable upper-class sources—well-meaning people who perhaps salved pangs of conscience over their wealthy condition by these donations to the struggling revolutionary movement, never suspecting that they might be on the list of its prospective victims.

When the disorders of the 1905 revolution made more evident what the Russian revolutionary parties were really up to, these benevolent sources of financial support began to dry up. In the period between 1906 and 1914 the Russian Social-Democratic Party suffered not only from loss of support and from grievous disunity, as between its Bol-shevik and Menshevik wings, but also from severe financial difficulty. There were those in the Party who wished to meet the financial deficits by resorting to methods which, while they were called by more polite names within the Party, we would most easily recognize as those of black-mail, extortion, and banditry. This was particularly true in the Caucasus, where the combination of corruption, racial rivalries, and rapid economic development (particularly the opening up of the Baku oil fields) had already produced an underworld of fantastic color and dimensions. The revolu-tionary movement found itself in intimate contact with this underworld when it, too, was caught up in a struggle with the police.

The leadership of the Social-Democratic Party, in the period before the final split, officially opposed methods of violence as fund-raising devices; and this attitude became binding for the large Menshevik contingent which made up the majority of the Party in the Transcaucasus. But Lenin, while outwardly accepting the Party's position, had no ob-jection in practice to seeing the coffers of his own faction replenished by these dubious devices, wherever this could be quietly and inconspicuously done. There is no question but that he tolerated and encouraged actions of this sort, particularly on the part of the Caucasian comrades, during the difficult years from 1906 to 1912. And all signs indicate that it was in this dim realm where revolutionary politics merged with common criminality—in this world of fierce racial and personal hatreds, of intrigues and plots, daggers and murders, of fantastic vows and equally fantastic be-trayals—that Stalin had his origins as a revolutionist.

Let us recall to mind, at this point, the duality that marked the Bolshevik faction as a whole. The Bolsheviki, as a political entity, embraced two quite disparate wings.

Abroad, in the emigration, there was what I might call—if I may use a sort of Freudian and sociological term—the cosmopolitan-legitimate wing of the party: *cosmopolitan,* because it was composed of people who were citizens, not exactly of the world, but at least of the world socialist movement: international socialists, at home in a number of languages and countries, and trained to view the cause of socialism as an international one, in which Russia took by no means the first place of importance; and *legitimate,* in the sense that these people felt themselves to be a part of something which had a great and deep sort of legitimacy, which was founded in the very respectability of Marxism as a science. These people lived and moved in the world of European intellectual socialism. They acquired its manners and affectations. In its approval they sought the rewards of their effort. They acknowledged a respect, if not for the opinions of all mankind, then at least for those of a considerable segment of it. They professed to hate the "bourgeoisie" as a class; but in their habits and personal outlooks there was a good deal of bourgeois propriety and self-respect—sometimes even pretension.

Opposed to this wing of the Party was that which remained in Russia and functioned, perforce, in the underground. This wing I should like to call the criminal-defiant one: *criminal,* because an outstanding feature of its psychology was the fact that it was outside the law in relation to its own environment; *defiant,* because it had the typical psychology of the hardened and committed outlaw, of the person who has burned his bridges, who regards his breach with society as final and irreparable, who has accepted society as an enemy whether or not society has accepted him in the same way, and who seeks vindication for his rebellion in the very glamour of his struggle against society, in the danger he undergoes, in the valor he exhibits in thus exposing himself to this danger, in the fear and respect he engenders in his own criminal circle by the extremity of his despair, his resolve, and his lack of scruple. These underground Bolsheviki were the original bad boys—unregenerate and incorrigible. And nowhere, let us note, were these qualities more pronounced, nowhere do they provide more of a contrast to the mild intellectual sincerity of the exiled wing of the Party, than in the seething, savage underworld of the Transcaucasus.

I need not tell you in detail about Stalin's early youth. You know that he was born in Gori, Georgia, in 1879, in a humble family. He is said to have been cruelly treated by his father. He attended in Tiflis a seminary for the training of priests of the Christian Church of the Eastern Orthodox rite. He was expelled from this seminary shortly before graduation, apparently for having belonged, while in it, to a secret Marxist discussion group.

Thirteen years were to elapse between the time of Stalin's expulsion from the seminary and his recruitment, in 1912, into the senior echelons of the Bolshevik Party, for work outside his native Caucasus. The record of his activities and movements during these thirteen years is extremely unsatisfactory. The vagueness, the omissions, the contradictions, the inconsistencies, the many fluctuations in the treatment of this subject by official Soviet historians at different periods: all this suggests that the real record must contain many items which neither Stalin himself, nor for some reason, his successors, have wished to see exposed to the scrutiny of historical scholarship.

Three hypotheses have been advanced to explain this state of affairs. One is that Stalin was concerned to conceal his obscurity in the Party at that time. Another is that he was so closely connected with certain of the criminal fund-raising activities of the Party that an exposure of his doings in those years would not fit well with the carefully cultivated image of the later great statesman. The third hypothesis is that he was an ordinary police informer, or at least that his relations with the police were such that they would be difficult to explain. My own feeling is that all three of these hypotheses may have had some truth in them.

There was brought to light some years ago a document purporting to come from the Tsarist police archives in Siberia which, if genuine, would prove beyond question that Stalin was, in the period between 1906 and 1912, a police informer.[73] With one or two exceptions, the surviving old hands of the Russian Communist movement now in exile in the West have expressed their belief that this document itself is not genuine. To be sure, I have found none of them who does not readily affirm that Stalin would have been quite capable of denouncing individual Party comrades to the police for reasons of personal jealousy and revenge; but they doubt that he would have done it just for money or out of political conviction. To them this appears a more significant distinction than it would to many of us.

I have devoted some time to the study of the document and its background. All I can say is that if it is *not* genuine—and it is true that certain aspects of it make a somewhat odd impression—there is still a great deal to be explained as to how and where it could have come into existence at all. Paper and ink preclude the possibility of its being a recent forgery. Yet the early mills for the fabrication of anti-Bolshevik documents—the ones that operated just after the revolution and in the '20s—were run, without exception, by reactionary White Guard elements. These people had a poor knowledge of the history of the revolutionary movement, and this ignorance was generally visible in their work. Whoever wrote this particular document, however, had an intimate knowledge of the affairs both of the revolutionists and of the police. If, then, the authenticity of the document has not yet been demonstrated beyond challenge, nobody has yet offered a plausible theory as to by whom, when, and why it should have been concocted as a forgery.

However this may be, it is clear that Stalin moved, throughout these thirteen obscure years, in Bolshevik revolutionary circles in the Caucasus or in their political neighborhood. He probably joined the Party in 1904. It is likely that he was expelled in 1907, by the local Menshevik majority, in connection with his participation in acts of banditry and blackmail. He was exiled three or four times from the Caucasus by the police, but always, up to 1912, under strangely mild and lenient conditions. He attended three Party gatherings outside the Caucasus: one in Finland, one in Stockholm, one in London. On the second of these occasions, in 1907, his credentials were sharply questioned by the Mensheviki; and Lenin, who supported Stalin's admission to the Congress despite the weakness of his credentials, was forced to confess—or at least to claim—on the floor of the conference that he had no idea who this man was.

There is a considerable body of evidence, quite aside from the document just mentioned, which suggests that Stalin even in those early years was known to his comrades in the Caucasus as a troublemaker—a person with a fondness for stirring up resentments and suspicions among others, for provoking others into quarrels and acts of violence, and in this way getting his revenge on people who had in some way offended him or stood in his path.

In 1912, for reasons as yet unclarified, Stalin was suddenly lifted out of his obscurity and made a member of the Central Committee of what was now the Bolshevik Party, the split with the Mensheviki having by this time been completed. If, in the past, his relationship to the Party had been unclear, from this time on it appears to have been quite straight and normal. It is suggested in the controversial document that at this point he ceased to give information to the police. However that may be, with this turning point in his career, which marked his first acceptance by the Party in a position of honor and responsibility, the leniency of treatment which he had theretofore enjoyed at the hands of the police abruptly ceased. In the following year, 1913, he was exiled seriously and for fair, to eastern Siberia, where he remained for four years, until the outbreak of the Revolution in 1917.

When in 1917—having been liberated by the first Russian Revolution—Stalin returned to Petrograd and resumed activity as a senior official of the Party, he had still had relatively little contact with that brilliant cosmopolitan-legitimate wing of the party to which I referred a few moments ago. His previous experience in the central offices of the Party outside the Caucasus had been very brief, and related to a period already four or five years in the past. To the people around him—the Trotskys, the Zinovievs, the Kamenevs, the Bukharins—Stalin was at that time almost an unknown quantity. N. N. Sukhanov, the Boswell of the Revolution, referred to him in his memoirs as constituting in 1917 only a sort of a "gray blur" in the background of events—a quip, incidentally, for which Sukhanov was later to pay with his life in one of Stalin's concentration camps. These intellectuals, who made up the great majority of Lenin's entourage, were men far better educated than Stalin, more literate, more eloquent, more prominent in the revolutionary movement. They were the great dramatic figures of the Revolution. Stalin was only a colorless drone in the Party's administrative offices. He didn't even speak proper Russian—at least he didn't speak it with a proper accent—to say nothing of the foreign tongues in which so many of the others were proficient. He was without originality in the intellectual and literary sense. He had no personal charm, no oratorical gifts.

Compare these facts, now, with what we know today to have been Stalin's personal nature. This was a man dominated, as his whole subsequent record of thirty years in the public eye demonstrates, by an insatiable vanity and love of power, coupled with the keenest sort of sense of his own inferiority and a burning jealousy for qualities in others which he did not possess. He had certain well-known characteristics of the Caucasian mountain race to which his father is said to have belonged—an inordinate touchiness, an endless vindictiveness, an inability ever to forget an insult or a slight, but great patience and power of dissimulation in selecting and preparing the moment to settle the score. He is said once to have observed that there was nothing sweeter in life than to bide the proper moment for revenge, to insert the knife, to turn it around, and to go home for a good night's sleep. At the same time, let us note, he was a man with the most extraordinary talent for political tactics and intrigue, a consummate actor, a dissimulator of genius, a master not only of timing but of what Boris Nikolayevsky has called the art of "dosage"—of doing things gradually, of measuring out what the traffic would bear on any given occasion. He was a master, in particular, of the art of playing people and forces off against each other, for his own benefit. It was not he, actually, who inserted the knife; he had ways of getting others to do it for him. He merely looked on with benign detachment, sometimes even with grief and indignation.

If we picture to ourselves a man of this temperament, and then bear in mind the situation in which, as we have just seen, he found himself placed, in the initial period following the Revolution, it will not be difficult to see why he should have reacted in ways that were bound to affect his conduct as the head of the Soviet state. He was, first of all, extremely sensitive to the loneliness of his position vis-à-vis other leaders of the Party. He had not shared their background and their attainments. This world of international socialism, of which the center was not Russia but Germany—a world populated primarily by German-speaking people: Germans, Austrians, or, in predominant majority, members of the brilliant Jewish-socialist movement of Poland, who were at home in all of these countries of central and eastern Europe—this was a world to which Stalin did not belong, and knew he did not belong. Its values were not his values. Of its own inclination, it would, he knew, never respect or support him. He could win leadership in this world only by outwitting it, by intimidating it, by exploiting its inner contradictions, and by enlisting against it the forces of the Communist underground movement in Russia and of the young recruits who flowed into the Party after the Revolution on the flood tide of its political success. These latter elements, like himself, had no intimacy with the older Party intellectuals. To all of them, the myths and memories surrounding the Party's former life in exile—the struggles, the feuds, the arguments, and the intrigues of Geneva and Vienna and Krakow—were remote and unreal, already passing into history. Stalin, in short, exploited against the previously exiled wing of the Party both that portion of the old Party which had served in Russia and the many postrevolutionary fair-weather adherents to whom the heroic days of the struggle in exile would never be more than a legend.

In those years immediately after the Revolution the former exiles still constituted, in effect, the political and ideological leadership of the Party. Stalin had to exercise the utmost prudence in opposing them. If he attacked them prematurely or rashly they would muster against him not only their great following within the Party in Russia but also their many followers and admirers abroad. They would isolate him. They would alienate from him the whole great European socialist movement, to which they had personal access and over which they had influence—the movement of which Russian Communism originally conceived itself a part, in which it aspired to leadership, from the umbilical cord of which it was still too weak to be severed, and without which the Revolution in Russia made no ideological sense.

Stalin was well aware of this danger. It made a profound impression on him. He could never forget it, in later years. Even after his ascendancy in Russia had become virtually unchallenged, the pretense had always to be maintained that at least a large portion—the virtuous and correct portion—of the European socialist movement was enthusiastically in accord with his regime in Russia, and looked to it with admiration and fidelity. This pretense was the revelation of his greatest anxiety. There was hardly a time, from Lenin's death in 1924 to his own death in 1953, when Stalin did not have the whip hand over his rivals, internally, by virtue of his control over the professional apparatus of the Party and the police. Yet he seems never to have lost the fear that if his rivals ever succeeded in enlisting against him the moral force of socialist opinion *outside* Russia, his rule could be shaken and he could be lost.

Out of this nightmare flowed some of the well-known aspects of his motivation as a statesman. From this, there came his aversion to really spontaneous and successful revolutions by any of the foreign communist parties. He recognized clearly that so long as these parties remained struggling opposition groups, caught in the network of their own semi-criminal defiance of established authority within *their* respective countries, they would have a dependence on Soviet support—a dependence which he, as head of the Soviet state, could exploit in order to keep them under control. Their condition would be similar to his previous condition in the Caucasus; he would know how to deal with them. If on the other hand they were actually to come into power and to achieve the ability to dispose, as he was now able to dispose, over the resources of a great country, this dependence would be lost. From this came his insistence on rigid disciplinary control of the foreign communist parties, even at the expense of their morale, of their popular appeal, and of their prospects for coming into power. So long as he could control in this way at least a portion of the foreign communist and socialist movements, he could be sure of preventing the growth, within that portion, of that defiant and hostile untiy, and particularly of that alliance between it and his rivals at home, which remained to his dying day the greatest of his fears.

It was, of course, not only the world of foreign socialism and communism which Stalin feared and with which he had to contend. There was also the bourgeois world—the so-called "capitalist encirclement." This, too, could be a mortal danger to him, if its hostility ever again took the form—as it had in 1917 and 1918—of war and military intervention.

Now, it is important to note that during the decades of Stalin's rule this danger of military hostility against the Soviet Union by capitalist countries was sometimes real and sometimes not real. There were times when Russia was indeed threatened—primarily by the Germans and the Japanese—and there were times when she was not threatened at all. Yet these fluctuations in the degree of external danger found no reflection in the interpretation of world realities which Stalin put forward for internal consumption. He generally portrayed Russia to his followers as threatened, whether this was true at the moment, or whether it was untrue. Not only this, but he took pains to confuse as far as possible in the public mind the two dangers here involved —the danger of opposition to himself by foreign socialists and communists, and the danger of capitalist intervention.

Why did he do this? He did it because the one fear was respectable, the other was not. One concerned the fortunes of the movement and the country; the other concerned his personal position. He wanted to hide his fear of foreign socialism and communism, and to disguise the measures he took to defend himself against this danger, behind an apparent concern for the security of the Soviet Union. It was to this end that he constantly and systematically exaggerated the possibility of hostile military intervention against the Soviet state. It was to this end that he labored so assiduously to identify communist and socialist rivals with hostile bourgeois forces—calling the German Social-Democrats "Social-Fascists," confusing Trotsky with Hitler in the nightmarish inventions of the purge trials, forcing his communist victims with monotonous regularity, over the years, to confess to being the agents of foreign interventionists, as a last act of expiration and self-humiliation before being shot.

But do not be deceived as to which of these apprehensions—the admitted one or the concealed one, the apprehension of danger to his personal position or that of danger to the Soviet state—was the greatest. Trotsky, and all that Trotsky represented, was Stalin's real fear; Hitler was largely his excuse for fear. This is why his measures of defense against Hitler were singularly unreal and ineffective. He was prepared for the pretense, the artificial bugbear, of capitalist intervention, but not for its reality. On the one occasion, after Lenin's death, when this specter took on flesh and blood and became a reality—when the German troops, that is, stormed into Russia in 1941—this man, who had cried "Wolf" so long and insistently, became for the first time quite paralyzed and helpless, lost his nerve, and had to be bailed out by the men around him.

To say these things is not to imply that Stalin had no real policy towards the bourgeois world or no real interest in Russia's relations with it. He was a man of extraordinarily wide and sensitive understanding of political issues and events, even on the world scale. He rarely missed a trick. He recognized perfectly clearly the forces of the non-Communist world. He accepted them, in the traditional Soviet Communist manner, as hostile forces, viewed them without sympathy or pity, and dealt with them no less coldbloodedly than he did with the component forces of the world communist movement.

But here, too, his fundamental motive was the protection of his own personal position. Sometimes the interests of his personal position were identical with those of the Soviet state in its rivalry with the bourgeois world. Sometimes, as we shall see, they were not. But whether this identity was present or was not present in a given instance made no difference. It was the protection of his personal position that came first; and this was the key to his diplomacy.

The policies to which this preoccupation led were, in essence, very simple. From the bourgeois world, as from his political entourage in the world of communism, Stalin wanted only one thing: weakness. This was not at all identical with revolution. Unless other states were very small, and contiguous to Russia's borders, so that there were good prospects for controlling them by the same concealed police methods he employed in Russia, Stalin did not want other states to be communist. He was concerned only that they should be weak, or that they should at least expend their strength not against him and his regime but against each other. For this reason his favored strategy was a simple one. It could be summed up in the single phrase "divide and rule." It consisted in the instinctive effort—the same to which he was so addicted in personal life—to divide his opponents, to provoke them to hostile action against each other, to cause them to waste *their* strength in this way, while he conserved *his*.

This strategy was applied, without distinction, towards all external forces: communist, socialist, and capitalist alike. It was applied both within national boundaries and on the international plane. It was applied to social as well as to political entities. It was a policy of universal disintegration of opposing force, only rarely restrained, and then only for short periods, in deference to specific tactical considerations. Otherwise, it knew no bounds and no inhibitions. Communist was played off against communist; but communist was also played off against capitalist. Country was played off against country, poor against rich, liberal against conservative, labor against capital, but also labor against labor, colored against white, developed against underdeveloped, inferiority against superiority, weakness against strength.

Little effort was ever made on Stalin's part to create new issues. He was content to make the most of those apples of discord with which Nature had so liberally endowed the human community. His agents were taught to search for these existing differences and to exploit them to the limit. It was largely a matter of indifference to Stalin *what* others fought with each other about; the main thing was that they should fight. He was no doctrinaire ideologist. He knew that theoretical ideas meant things to other people; no one, in fact, was more sensitive than he to the understanding of *what* it was that they meant, or more skillful in exploiting the political-emotional impulses to which ideas gave rise. But he did not share these impulses. He only understood them. To him, ideas meant nothing in their own right. They had meaning only as the determinants of action—as the symbols and rationalizations of political attitudes. He could therefore be—and was—quite catholic in his use of divisive and disruptive tactics. Whatever was not *his* could, on principle, well be weakened. The only thing you had to watch was that the weakening of one side did not proceed so fast that the other had a bloodless triumph. No force must be annihilated before it had done its own work of destruction.

And these principles went for domestic as well as for foreign policy. Stalin, in fact, did not really recognize a difference. To him, the border between foreign and domestic affairs was an artifical one. He was, in his own eyes, the enemy of all the world. The Russian people and the Russian Communist Party were as much his adversaries as were the German Trotskyites or the Yugoslav renegades or the world of capitalism. Just as the Party itself remained, down to World War II, officially and formally a conspiratorial organization within Russia, working within and against the very popular masses which it was supposed to represent, so Stalin's personal secretariat remained a conspiracy within and against the Party as a whole.

But there was a difference. Outside Russia, Stalin's physical power was extremely limited. He could of course occasionally arrange to have a kidnaping or an assassination carried out under the noses of the capitalist police; but this was expensive, complicated, and hazardous. In Russia, these inhibitions did not exist. And it was here that his whole unconscionable ambition and ruthlessness found their expression. We know pretty well today what at one time we could only suspect: that this was a man of incredible criminality, of a criminality effectively without limits; a man apparently foreign to the very experience of love, without pity or mercy; a man in whose entourage no one was ever safe; a man whose hand was set against all that could not be useful to him at the moment; a man who was most dangerous of all to those who were his closest collaborators in crime, because he liked to be the sole custodian of his own secrets, and disliked to share his memories or his responsibility with others who, being still alive, had tongues and consciences and might be susceptible to the human weaknesses of remorse or indiscretion.

As the outlines of Stalin's personal actions begin to emerge, through the fog of confusion and irrelevance with which he loved to surround them during his lifetime, we are confronted with a record beside which the wildest murder mystery seems banal. I cannot attempt to list the man's crimes. Trotsky seriously charged that Stalin poisoned Lenin. He certainly wished to give him poison. He evidently either killed his young wife in 1932, or drove her to suicide in his presence. There is every probability, in the light of evidence now available, that it was Stalin himself who inspired the murder of his Number Two in the Party, S. M. Kirov, in 1934. How many others there were among the senior members of Stalin's intimate entourage who, while ostensibly in good standing, died as a result of Stalin's malignant ministrations, we can only guess. There are at least half a dozen—including the writer Maxim Gorky and such close Party comrades as Sergo Ordzhonokidze and A. A. Zhdanov—of whom this seems probable. That the man who split Trotsky's skull with an ax in Mexico City in 1940 did so at Stalin's instigation is beyond question. By way of response, apparently, to what seems to have been some opposition to his purposes on the part of the seventeenth Party Congress in 1934, Stalin killed, in the ensuing purges of 1936 to 1938, 1108 out of a total of 1966 of the members of the Congress. Of the Central Committee elected at that Congress and still officially in office, he killed 98 out of 139—a clear majority, that is, of the body from which ostensibly he drew his authority. These deaths were only a fraction, numerically, of those which resulted from the purges of those years. Most of the victims were high officials of the Party, the army, or the Soviet government apparatus.

All this is aside from the stupendous brutalities which Stalin perpetrated against the common people: notably in the process of collectivization, and also in some of his war-time measures. The number of victims here—the number, that is, of those who actually lost their lives—runs into the millions. But this is not to mention the broken homes, the twisted childhoods, and the millions of people who were half-killed: who survived these ordeals only to linger on in misery, with broken health and broken hearts.

Plainly, such excesses reached far beyond what was required for the protection of one man's personal position. In part, they seem to have been the product of real mental disturbance. But even to the extent they represented rational action from the standpoint of Stalin's personal interests, they coincided only in a limited area with the real needs, external and internal, of the country at the head of which he stood. Much of what Stalin did was irrelevant to the needs of Russia. Another part was clearly in conflict with those needs. In some ways, certainly, Russia benefited from Stalin's indisputable qualities of greatness. But in other respects there was a price to be paid for his leadership, externally as well as internally—a price which is still being paid, not just by Russia but by the world at large.

It is probably too early, today, to draw the balance. One of the reasons for the sort of inquiry these lectures represent is the need for disentangling these various components of the historical record and for ascertaining how much of Stalin's activity as a statesman was directed to his own interests and how much to Russia's. And even within this latter area, where the national interests of Russia were at stake, it is necessary to ask to what extent the problems to which Stalin was addressing himself were real external problems, having their origins in the nature of Russia's external world environment, and to what extent they were problems created initially by the nature of Soviet diplomacy itself. To what extent, in other words, was Stalin fighting an inevitable competition of international life and to what extent was he fighting himself? This is one of those historical questions to which there will never be a precise, objective answer; and yet seek for an answer we must, for unless we bear this distinction in mind, and form—at least for our own individual purposes—some rough idea of the relative weight of the two components, we cannot arrive at any critical appraisal of Stalin's diplomacy at all.

It remains only to mention the contrast between Stalin, as a statesman, and the man he succeeded in the position of supreme power in Russia. The differences are not easy ones to identify, for in many instances they were only ones of degree and of motive. Lenin, too, was a master of internal Party intrigue. He, too, was capable of ruthless cruelty. He, too, could be unpitying in the elimination of people who seriously disagreed with him or seemed to him to stand in the path of the best interests of the Party. No less than Stalin, Lenin adopted an attitude of implacable hostility toward the Western world; and so long as the Western powers were stronger than Russia, which was the case throughout his lifetime, he, too, based his policies on the hope of dividing them one from another and playing them off against one another.

But behind all this there were very significant differences. Lenin was a man with no sense of inferiority. Well-born, well-educated, endowed with a mind of formidable power and brilliance, he was devoid of the angularities of the social parvenu, and he felt himself a match for any man intellectually. He was spared that whole great burden of personal insecurity which rested so heavily on Stalin. He never had to doubt his hold on the respect and admiration of his colleagues. He could rule them through the love they bore him, whereas Stalin was obliged to rule them through their fears. This enabled Lenin to run the movement square-ly on the basis of what he conceived to be *its* needs, without bothering about his own. And since the intellectual inventory of the Party was largely of his own creation, he was relieved of that ignominious need which Stalin constantly experienced for buttressing his political views by references to someone else's gospel. Having fashioned Leninism to his own heart's desire out of the raw materials of Marx's legacy, Lenin had no fear of adapting it and adjusting it as the situation required. For this reason, his mind remained open throughout his life—open, at least, to argument and suggestion from those who shared his belief in the basic justification of the second Russian Revolution of 1917. These people could come to him and talk to him, and could find their thoughts not

only accepted in the spirit they were offered but responded
to by a critical intelligence second to none in the history of
the socialist movement. They did not have to feel, as they
later did under Stalin, that deep, dangerous, ulterior meanings
might be read into anything they said, and that an innocent
suggestion might prove their personal undoing.

This had, of course, a profound effect on the human climate that prevailed throughout the Soviet regime in Lenin's
time. Endowed with this temperament, Lenin was able to
communicate to his associates an atmosphere of militant optimism, of good cheer and steadfastness and comradely loyalty,
which made him the object of their deepest admiration
and affection and permitted them to apply their entire
energy to the work at hand, confident that if this work was
well done they would not lack for support and appreciation at
the top of the Party. In these circumstances, while Lenin's
ultimate authority remained unquestioned, it was possible to
spread initiative and responsibility much further than was
ever the case in the heyday of Stalin's power. This explains
why Soviet diplomacy was so much more variegated and
colorful in Lenin's time than in the subsequent Stalin era.
In the change from Lenin to Stalin, the foreign policy of a
movement became the foreign policy of a single man.

All this rendered even more difficult the problem which
Soviet power in Russia presented for the outside world.
In Lenin's day the differences were deep, and seemingly
irreconcilable; but it was possible, if one had the wit
and the brutality to fall in with the tone of Soviet discussion, to talk about them with the Soviet leaders, and
to obtain at least some clarification as to where things
stood. In Stalin's day, this was no longer possible. He
had no taste for even that brutal, sardonic, uncompromising frankness with which Lenin faced the representative of
the class enemy. His addiction to the arts of deception was
too profound to be separable from his intellectual calculations. Unlike Lenin, who could view objective reality as
something apart from himself, Stalin was able to see the
world only through the prism of his own ambitions and
his own fears. The foreigner who talked to Stalin could never
be sure just what he was dealing with—whether it was the
interests of the movement or the interests of Stalin which
stood in his path. Against this background, even the nature of the antagonism between the two worlds tended

to become blurred and ambiguous. Not until the personality of Khrushchev replaced that of Stalin at the pinnacle of authority in the Soviet regime did it again become possible, as it had been in Lenin's time, to have at least a clear-cut dialogue about the differences that divided the Russian Communist world from its non-Communist environment.

To many, this distinction will not seem important. "An enemy," they will say, "is an enemy. An antagonism is an antagonism. What difference does it make if one can discuss it?" This is the absolutist view.

But it is not the only view one can take. One can remember that *some degree* of conflict and antagonism is present in every international relationship; *some* measure of compromise is necessary everywhere, if political societies are to live together on the same planet. Those who bear this in mind will be inclined to doubt whether there is such a thing as total antagonism, any more than there is such a thing as total identity of interests. Whoever sees it this way will realize that the illusion of total antagonism can be created only by a complete absence of effective communication; and for this reason he will be inclined to doubt, as I myself must confess to doing, whether an enemy with whom one can communicate is really entirely an enemy, after all.

18   Stalin and China

IT HAS been my hope that each of these discussions would yield one or two broad, general reflections which would help us to understand what it was that happened in the relations between Soviet Russia and the outside world, and how all this operated to produce the enormous disharmony of the present day which we refer to as "the cold war."

Nowhere, I must say, do I find it harder to do this, harder to bring any sort of order out of the chaos, than in the case of Russia's relations with the Orient. In Europe, you dealt with relatively well-defined and permanent political entities. In East Asia, this was true only of Japan proper. In China, everything was in a state of endless flux: there was a kaleidoscopic flow of names and faces; regimes came and went; power coagulated and power dissolved; nothing that seemed true one day was quite true the next. In Europe, similarly, the words we use had at least an approximate relevance to real conditions. In East Asia, this was scarcely the case. The entire vocabulary of Western politics and historiography is inadequate as a means of understanding and describing the political realities of the Orient. For both these reasons, it becomes terribly difficult to discover, in the record of Far Eastern diplomacy, that which was really significant and permanent and to isolate it from that which was not. Sometimes one is moved to suspect, in despair, that nothing was either one or the other; but this, too, I am sure, would be an exaggeration. The fact is, quite simply, that we are dealing here with a wholly different world not only geographically but also in thought and feeling, perhaps even in the nature of political reality.

It might be asked why, if these discussions are directed primarily to Russia's relations with the *West*, it is necessary to talk about East Asia at all. The answer is that East Asia represents one of the theaters in which the conflict of interest between Russia and the West has proceeded. Not only that, but Moscow's policies towards Europe were often importantly influenced by the experience she was having in her relations with the East.

The one element of Russia's policy in Asia which stands out with reasonable definiteness and clarity in the historical record is the sheer geopolitical necessity of protecting from foreign penetration and domination those areas of Asia— Manchuria, Outer Mongolia, and Sinkiang—which lie adjacent to the Russian borders. For decades, the Tsar's government was absorbed in this task. Before the building of railways and the opening up of China and Korea to penetration by the great powers, this question was less urgent for Russia. But by the end of the nineteenth century, the development of modern techniques of transportation and communication had facilitated the extension of great-power influence into hitherto untouched, or little touched, areas.

With these developments, and with the simultaneous settlement of Siberia, Russia's Asian border became a problem
to her as it had never been before.

Please do not misunderstand me. I do not mean to say
that Russia's interest in these regions was only a reaction
to the imperialism of others. You could just as well put
it the other way around. The building of the Trans-Siberian
Railway by the Tsar's government, and particularly its extension across Manchuria, was itself a stimulus to the activity of the other powers. They feared Russia's expansion
into China as much as she feared theirs.

The fact is (and it is a fact we tend to ignore in these
days when we are all such good anti-imperialists) that the
process of nineteenth-century imperialism took place everywhere in a highly competitive atmosphere; so that to refrain from being imperialistic yourself did not generally
mean to spare the area in question from becoming the victim of imperialism. The alternative to the establishment of
American power in the Philippines, for example, was not a
nice, free, progressive Philippine Republic: it was Spanish,
German, or Japanese domination. Abstention on our part
from the taking of the Philippines could have been argued,
and was, from the standpoint of *our* interests; it could
scarcely have been argued from the interests of the Filipinos
themselves. And so it was in the great underdeveloped,
politically unorganized spaces that lay between Russia and
China.

In the period immediately following the Revolution, the
Soviet leaders made a great point of condemning the former
Tsarist-Russian hegemony in these border areas as imperialistic, and of promising the Chinese people that never,
never would Soviet Russia move along this path. In 1919
and 1920, fulsome proclamations were issued in Moscow
denouncing the unequal treaties by which Russia and China
had previously been bound, renouncing all the privileges and
rights flowing from these treaties, promising henceforth to
live with China on a basis of complete equality. Initially,
these promises even included the transfer to China of the
Chinese Eastern Railway, which before the war had been the
property of the Russian state. But this promise was made
during the extremity of the Russian civil war in 1919, at a
moment when it was of vital importance to keep the Chinese from giving aid and comfort to Kolchak. As soon
as Kolchak was defeated, the Soviet leaders had second

thoughts. The Chinese authorities in North China and Manchuria were at that time, in the Soviet view, Japanese puppets. Did one really want to turn the railway over in effect to the Japanese? The answer obviously was no. So Moscow reneged on this offer by the simple device of denying that the offending passage had ever been included in the original proclamation, and struck out on a line of policy which kept this railway in Soviet hands for another fifteen years—until 1935, that is, when the Japanese, not the Chinese, forced them to sell it.

This is a good point at which to remind ourselves that throughout the period between the two wars, the greatest problem for Soviet foreign policy in the Far East was the Japanese penetration in Manchuria—a phenomenon which had been stimulated by Russia's extreme weakness around the time of the Revolution. There was no more ardent desire on the part of Soviet policy makers than to see Japanese influence removed from the Manchurian area. But throughout the Twenties and the Thirties, Russia remained too weak to take anything more than a defensive attitude in this question. Her main concern—and the best she could hope—was to prevent the Japanese from advancing still farther and encroaching on Soviet territory itself.

In Outer Mongolia, a different situation prevailed. This great region, which in the years just before the Revolution had been a Russian protectorate, was formally part of China. As good anti-imperialists, the Russian Communists should, of course, have been content to leave it to the Chinese. But the Chinese lacked the power to administer and protect the region. And when the anti-Bolshevik forces lost out and were expelled from Siberia in the Russian civil war, some of their least attractive leaders—the Cossack officer, Grigori M. Semenov, and the Baltic baron, Roman N. von Ungern-Sternberg—took refuge in Outer Mongolia, terrorized its inhabitants with their bands of bloodthirsty followers, and made use of the territory as a basis for anti-Bolshevik military activity.

All this held considerable danger for the men in Moscow. Their only link with the Soviet Far East was the slender five-thousand-mile line of the Trans-Siberian Railway. Outer Mongolia lay close to the vulnerable part of this line that bends to the south around Lake Baikal. Semenov and Ungern-Sternberg were generally believed to be supported by the Japanese; and Semenov, at any rate, definitely was. To remain inactive would have been to invite penetration and domination of the area by the Japanese, acting in association with anti-Bolshevik Russian forces. This was particularly dangerous, because the part of Siberia just west of Baikal contained, itself, a large Mongolian population. If the Mongols to the south remained under Japanese and White Russian influence, this could become a source of disaffection for the Mongols within Siberia proper.

Faced with this problem, the Russian Communists acted in the best Asian tradition. They arranged the establishment of a puppet government in Outer Mongolia, got it to request their military assistance, intervened militarily, and restored, in effect, the old Tsarist protectorate—an arrangement which has endured to the present day.

All this had nothing to do, of course, with democracy. This was one of those situations (Americans sometimes find it hard to believe that they exist) where democracy was neither here nor there. The motives that prompted Soviet action in this case were exactly the same as those that had moved the Tsar's government to intervene in these areas in the first place. I have gone into these details in order to show how compelling, how inexorable, were the geopolitical considerations that governed Russian policy here, both before and after the Revolution. But let us note that at the basis of this geopolitical necessity there lay, invariably, the weakness of China. It was this weakness that brought the whole complex into play. The existence of a strong China clearly undermines the rationale for such a policy. The fact that today the control of the Chinese Eastern Railway and Northern Manchuria lies with China is a reflection of this fact. It will be interesting to see how long Russia will be able to retain her hegemony in Outer Mongolia, now that the alternative to it is not Japanese power but the power of China herself.

So much for the purely defensive part of Soviet policy in the Far East—the part that related to the border areas. But the question also arose: what should Soviet policy be towards the Orient farther afield—towards China proper and the other countries of the Asian mainland? In Europe, the answer had been at least reasonably clear. First, it was the incitement to revolution; then, after 1921, it was that (somewhat less hopefully), plus the tapping of the economic re-

sources of the great European powers in the interests of the
physical strengthening of the Soviet state. But what should
be the objective with respect to a great backward country
such as China—a country devoid of the classic prerequisites
for revolution in the Marxist sense, and so weak economically that its resources could contribute very little to Russia's economic development?

In the approach to this problem, Soviet policy makers
were bedeviled by a question to which, down to the present
day, they have found no adequate answer. It is the conflict
between the goals of social revolution and of national liberation. Let me attempt to define it for you.

You have, in the Marxist view, an individual who owns
none of the means of production and who works for someone else who does own them. He is the worker. He is exploited. Because he possesses no property, he is socially and
politically pure—capable only of worthy and constructive
impulses. You are for him; you are against the capitalist
who exploits him. So far, so good.

But it is not only capitalism that figures in the Marxist
scheme of things: there is also imperialism. Country A is
rich and highly industrialized. Country B is weak and underdeveloped. Country A dominates Country B economically:
drains it of its raw materials, builds industries on its territory,
profits from its cheap labor—in short, exploits it. That is
imperialism; and you are, of course, as a good Marxist,
against *that*. You are for Country B and against Country A.

But wait a minute. Country B, which you are for, does
not, as it happens, consist exclusively of downtrodden workers, languishing in the sweatshops operated by the capitalists
of Country A. Such workers make up, in fact, only a
negligible portion of its population—far too few to constitute
anything even like a mass movement. Despite the general
state of underdevelopment, the bulk of the population has a
social breakdown not wholly dissimilar to that of some of
the imperialist powers. Some people own property; some
work for others. If you look at this place through the
Marxist lens, you can, in fact, see what appear to be all
the familiar features of the Marxist landscape: poor peasant,
rich peasant, landowner, bourgeoisie, worker, capitalist, toiling intelligentsia, nontoiling intelligentsia, feudal reactionary
—what you will. A variegated society, in other words.

Now, are you sure, when you say you are *for* this

country in the name of anti-imperialism, that you are really for *all* of it? Even for its bourgeoisie, for its capitalists and lackeys of capitalism, for its nontoiling intelligentsia, for its reactionary military cliques? Can you reconcile this with Marxist doctrine, especially when it becomes evident that the exploitation perpetrated by these people upon their fellow citizens is no less oppressive—and sometimes more oppressive—than the exploitation conducted by the foreign capitalist? And what do you do, in particular, when it becomes apparent that it is precisely some of these people—some of the local exploiters—who are the heart and soul of the anti-imperialist movement, the movement for national liberation? Do you *support* them in the name of the struggle against imperialism, or do you *fight* them in the name of the struggle against capitalism?

This was the conflict with which Soviet policy wrestled in China throughout the period between the two wars, particularly in the years from 1923 to 1927. It is also, incidentally, the problem with which Soviet policy is contending today in Egypt and Iraq—perhaps tomorrow in Cuba.

In the case of China, the Russians never found any really satisfactory answer to this question, though endless variations were suggested and attempted. Both of the two objectives, the defeat of international imperialism and the defeat of indigenous capitalism, were too close to the Communist heart for either to be wholly rejected. It was clear to everyone in Moscow, therefore, that one tried, despite the conflict between the two, to do both. There was a difference, though. One's concern for the workers was permanent; they were to win in the end. The anti-imperialist bourgeois forces, on the other hand, were of course to be supported only temporarily, until they had done their work, after which they were to be destroyed or, to use Stalin's phrase, to be flung aside like worn-out jades. On this all were agreed. Lenin himself had said, after all, that the workers in such countries should enter into temporary alliance or agreements with the bourgeois national-liberation movements, for the purpose of defeating imperialism; but he had stipulated that they were not to merge with these movements entirely, that they were not to lose their own organizational identity; they were to retain their independent existence in order to undermine the political strength of their bourgeois allies. They were first to use the bourgeoisie as an instrument against the foreign imperialist; then they were, at the proper moment, to destroy it. Beyond this, Lenin himself did not go. His successors were left with the difficult task of putting this vague and contradictory injunction into practice.

There were, in the early Twenties, many centers of power in China. The relations between them were invariably ones of rivalry and struggle—struggle modified from time to time by temporary and highly unstable alliances which were marked, in turn, by a maximum of expediency and a minimum of good faith.

Of these various centers of power in the China of the early Twenties, two stood out in importance from Moscow's standpoint. One was Peking, where there still functioned, by tolerance of and arrangement with the local war lords, an authority terming itself the government of China and recognized as such by the powers. The other was Canton, in the south, where there was centered (also by arrangement with the local war lords) the Kuominating movement, headed by Sun Yat-sen. The Soviet leaders, with their general fondness for having two strings to their bow, played with both. From 1921 to 1925 Moscow labored to attain recognition from, and to establish normal relations with, Peking. This was not easy. The Chinese were, as always, reluctant to give up on paper even that which they had long since ceased to possess in fact. They were therefore sticky about the Chinese Eastern Railway and Outer Mongolia. But the precedent set by Britain's recognition of the Soviet government in 1924 was helpful. Formal diplomatic relations were established between Moscow and Peking later that year, on a basis calculated to save Chinese face while giving the Russians real control in both instances.

Diplomatic relations with Peking were moderately valuable to Moscow so long as they lasted. They contributed to Moscow's prestige. They gave the Soviet government a regular observation post in China, and a chance to have its voice in the problems of China's foreign relations. But the Chinese elements who stood behind the Peking government were regarded by Moscow largely as reactionary collaborators and allies of Western imperialism, and therefore of little use to the anti-imperialist cause. Sun Yat-sen's movement, being strongly nationalistic and at the same time socially progressive, was much more interesting as a possible vehicle of Soviet influence. The result was that in 1923 a high-powered Soviet adviser, Michael Borodin, was sent to reside, so to speak, at Sun Yat-sen's court. Under Borodin's direction, the loose political movement called the Kuomin-tang was whipped into a fairly tight militant organization, patterned structurally on the Russian Communist Party but having, as Moscow clearly recognized, a different ideological inspiration and political significance.

In addition to the non-Communist political forces of Peking and Canton there were, of course, also the Chinese Com-munists. The Chinese Communist Party had been founded only in 1920, by a motley band of intellectuals. By the mid-Twenties, it had achieved a certain degree of ideological unity, but it remained weak and without mass support. Its members accepted Moscow's leadership and submitted to Comintern discipline. For this reason, Moscow could not ab-solve itself of responsibility for the Party's political fortunes. But Stalin, for the temperamental reasons of which I have spoken, was much more interested in achieving the ex-pulsion of the imperialists from China than he was in pur-suing the will-o'-the-wisp of an early Communist revolution within that country. He viewed the Chinese Communists primarily from the standpoint of their potential usefulness to the anti-imperialist cause, and in view of their lack of mass support and their military helplessness, he did not rate this usefulness very highly. The result was that the Chinese Communists were instructed by Moscow, even before Borodin's arrival in Canton, to enter the ranks of the Kuo-mintang, to merge with it ostensibly, though retaining clandestinely their own organizational structure, their own discipline, their own bonds of subservience to the Comintern. From this delicate and ambivalent position within the Kuo-mintang, it was to be the task of the Chinese Communists to strengthen the Kuomintang in its anti-imperialist efforts, but yet at the same time to penetrate its organizational structure, to win domination over it from within, and thus to place themselves in a position where they could eventually take it over and use it as an instrument for the Communist con-quest of power within China itself. In this way, Moscow hoped to kill with one stone—at least, to appear to be killing with one stone—the two birds of international im-perialism and Chinese capitalism. It was over this impossibly delicate and contradictory undertaking that Borodin was sup-posed to preside.

To tell the Chinese Communists to merge with the Kuomintang was, of course, a violation of Lenin's injunction that Communist parties, while aiding the national-liberation

movements, were to retain their own political identity. But
this was rationalized on the grounds that Lenin had at one
time contradicted that injunction himself by urging the British Communists to merge with the Labour Party for the
purpose of distintegrating and destroying it. In this rationalization—ignoring national differences and invoking a precedent for a situation to which it was really quite irrelevant—
you had a good illustration both of the sacred, revelatory
quality attached to Lenin's words and of the schematic,
undiscriminating manner in which his successors attempted
to apply his recorded utterances to the situations of a later
day.

Sun Yat-sen died in 1925, a year after Lenin. His death,
leaving as it did a serious vacuum in the leadership of the
movement, served to enhance the importance of the Russian advisers. From this time on, the burden of shaping
Kuomintang policies, and of guiding the relationship between the Kuomintang and the Chinese Communists, fell
increasingly to Lenin's successors in Moscow, and particularly
to Stalin, whose authority, while still not unchallenged by
others in his entourage (especially in the field of foreign
policy) already exceeded that of any other single figure in
the Party. Stalin seems to have been particularly apprehensive, at just this time, about British policy in China, and
about the possibility of further British penetration there. It
was of course always difficult to judge how much of Stalin's
professed anxiety, in cases such as this, was genuine and how
much feigned. In the years 1926 and 1927, a relatively high
component of Stalin's professed fear of British intervention
in China appears to have been genuine. Certainly, his calculations must have been affected by the reverses suffered
in Russia's own relations with England in the mid-Twenties:
the fall of the MacDonald government amid the excitement
of the episode of the Zinoviev letter, the consequent failure
of the Anglo-Soviet treaties to be ratified, the return to office of the anti-Soviet Tories, and finally, in May 1927, the
Arcos raid and the rupture of Anglo-Soviet relations. On top
of this, there was the strain placed on the Rapallo relationship with Germany by the rapprochement of the mid-
Twenties between Germany and the Western powers—a
subject that will be treated further in the next of these
discussions. All this was enough to suggest to Stalin's suspicious
mind that the bogeyman of the Soviet imagination—an anti-
Soviet coalition of the Western powers, including Germany,

under British leadership—was beginning to take concrete shape.

It was presumably considerations of this nature that caused Stalin to attach such great importance to the anti-imperialist potentialities of the Kuomintang, as compared with the domestic-political potentialities of the Chinese Communists, and to insist on the subordination of the latter to the former. The same considerations explained the emphasis laid by Moscow on the creation by the Kuomintang of a regular armed force. In pressing the Kuomintang to establish such a force, Moscow showed little concern for the social origins of the corps of officers selected and trained for this purpose; it was more interested for the moment in their military competence and in their possibility for effectiveness against the imperialists. Here Stalin was no doubt misled by the success of Trotsky, during the Russian civil war, in making effective use of men from the officers' corps of the old Tsarist army, even where these men were far from having any sympathy with the principles of Communism. The appeal had been made successfully to these Russian officers on a straight patriotic basis. Why, Stalin must have asked, could not the same be done in the case of China? One of the results of this line of reasoning was that a promising young Chinese officer by the name of Chiang Kai-shek was brought to Moscow for training and then sent back to Canton to found there, and to head, a new military school to be known as the Whampoa Military Academy.

This, I suspect, laid the foundation for the catastrophe. No sooner had the Kuomintang armed force become a serious reality than Chiang Kai-shek made himself, by a series of brutal and questionable devices, not only its effective commander but also the dominant figure in the movement as a whole. And no sooner had he achieved this status than he began to take measures with regard to the Communists which made increasingly evident that a continued subordination to the Kuomintang might be not only their personal but also their political undoing. Anxious warnings that Chiang was taking an unfriendly and menacing attitude toward the Communists went forward repeatedly to Moscow, with pleas that the Communists be at once released from their bond of subordination to the Kuomintang and permitted to remove themselves from the danger area before it was too late. In Moscow, the question quickly developed into an acrid issue of Comintern policy. But Stalin, stubborn and on the defensive, stuck by his guns. Repeatedly, the answer went back to China that the Communists must continue to try to collaborate with the Kuomintang. It was made clear— if we may use a contemporary expression—that there was to be no "treason to Chiang Kai-shek."

In late 1926, despite the growing evidences of tension and disunity within the Kuomintang camp, the decision was taken to launch a military expedition northwards to the Yangtze, in order to enlarge the area of Kuomintang power. The expedition was successfully conducted in the military sense; but it led, as military success so often does, to open political disunity. The movement split. One faction, led by Chiang himself, headed for Shanghai and the treaty ports, with a view to getting control of their great financial and material wealth. A second faction, composed of what was regarded as the Kuomintang's liberal wing, established itself at the Wuhan ports, farther up the river, but fell increasingly under the influence of its own non-Communist and anti-Communist generals.

On the approach of Chiang to Shanghai, the Communist supporters in that city, still putting their trust in the Kuomintang as Moscow had ordered, rose up in a manner strikingly similar to the later uprising of the Polish patriots in Warsaw against the Germans at the approach of the Red army in 1944. Chiang behaved, on this occasion, so much like the Stalin of 1944 that one wonders whether the unoriginal and imitative Stalin did not take his cue from this example. What Chiang did was to pause at the gates of Shanghai and to wait for the Communists to fight it out with the anti-Kuomintang authorities in that city. Not until this fracas had ended with a Communist victory, and the anti-Kuomintang forces had been effectively destroyed, did Chiang enter the city, on Communist invitation, with his fresh forces. He then fell upon his exhausted Communist allies, slaughtered them off unmercifully, and thus emerged the undisputed master of the situation.

This was, of course, a dreadful reversal for Stalin's China policy, and a heavy blow to Moscow's prestige. It led naturally to bitter recriminations and heart-searchings in the Comintern and in the Central Committee of the Party in Moscow. From the time the news of the Shanghai events was received, it was finally recognized in Moscow that Chiang himself must be regarded as a traitor and an enemy. Stalin went along with this view, although, with his usual tactical skill, he contrived to evade personal responsibility for the disaster. But he was still reluctant to give up his belief that the Kuomintang could be employed as a useful instrument of Soviet policy. He insisted, therefore, that the Chinese Communists now adopt the same sort of semi-subservience to the more liberal wing of the Kuomintang, centered in the Wuhan ports, that they had previously been required to adopt toward Chiang. This, too, ended in a woeful set-back. The Wuhan Kuomintang, also under the domination of its military leaders, likewise proceeded, somewhat less dramatically but scarcely less effectively than had been the case with Chiang, to make short shrift of its Communist allies.

This completed the disaster. The Chinese Communist Party was decimated and forced to go underground. Moscow, with its remoteness and its lack of "feel" for the situation on the spot, had simply pushed it into the dragon's mouth. To save Stalin's face, the Party's leader, Chen Tu-hsiu, had to be expelled and denounced, without a shadow of grounds, as a Trotskyite. It was Mao Tse-tung who rescued some of the underground remnants of the Party and took them away to the hills to lead for many years the life of outlaws, in company with criminals and desperadoes, until, in the mid-Thirties, they could effect their long march around the periphery of China to the north and there, on the border between Chinese and Soviet power, lay the foundations of the new Chinese Communist movement.

What all this amounted to, of course, was that by the end of 1927 the effort of the Kremlin to build up and exploit a national-liberationist Chinese movement with a view to the expulsion of overseas imperialist power from China had ended in an irreparable fiasco. The movement, as soon as it acquired military strength, had got quite out of Moscow's control. Then it had turned, with contemptuous ruthlessness, to bite the hand that fed it. Not only this, but to the interests of this unhappy venture there had been sacrificed the incipient and not wholly unpromising Communist movement of China of that day—sacrificed to a point where remnants of it could survive for a decade into the future only as individual underground conspirators in the Chinese cities and villages or as a tiny band of outlaws in the remote fastnesses of the western mountains.

Why had all this occurred? What had gone wrong? What was the lesson of this catastrophe?

Stalin's political opponents—notably the Trotskyites—laid it to his willful departure from Lenin's principles, and charged him with having persisted in grave tactical errors.

This argument need not, I think, detain us long. We have no need to assume, as Stalin's Marxist critics felt obliged to do, that Lenin was infallible. And if Stalin did stretch Lenin's principle that Communist parties were not to merge with national-liberation movements, he didn't stretch it very far. These broad ideological propositions in which Russian Communists have always loved to clothe their actions have seldom corresponded entirely to the actual situations with which people were faced. For this reason, they have constantly been stretched for reasons of expedience. Lenin himself stretched them, with a cheerful lack of inhibition, whenever he found it useful to do so. This is how Communist doctrine soon acquired, after the Revolution, that rubbery consistency which it has today, and which permits it to be used as an infinitely flexible rationalization for anything whatsoever that the regime finds it advantageous to do.

It is true, of course, that Stalin persisted far too long in a line of policy which was jeopardizing the very existence of the Chinese Communist Party. The reason for this, apparently, was the fact that the matter became a prestige issue between him and his rivals in Russia. He was a man who hated to admit himself wrong; and it would not be the last time that he would sacrifice the interests of foreign Communists rather than confess himself to be in error and thereby yield a point to his opponents at home.

Beyond this, one sees at every hand, in the complicated record of this episode, the confusion occasioned by the fact that for people in Moscow—not to the same extent perhaps as for people in Washington, but also not in negligible degree—China was a different world, and not readily intelligible. The ground of China, as Mr. Conrad Brandt said in his excellent book on this subject,[74] was treacherous for this type of long-distance control. Here, again, the semantic confusion was appalling; and it was compounded by the insistence of the Russian Communists on attempting to describe in doctrinal terms things that would have been much better understood if presented in more traditional expressions. One has the impression, in going through this story of Stalin's difficulties in China, that the happenings there seldom were

what they appeared to be or what Moscow took them to be,
that the whole semantic baggage of revolutionary Marxism
was simply exploited in many instances by the supple Chinese to disguise impulses, necessities, plans, intrigues, and
possibilities of the various Chinese factions which in reality
had nothing to do with ideology at all. Moscow, in other
words, understood very poorly what it was doing. What occurred at that time in China was simply the painful demonstration of a truth which is deeply repugnant to Russian
Communism but with which Moscow is being more and
more forcefully confronted in our own time: namely, that
this is a multiple, complex world, not a simple one; that
truth is not unitary but multiple. The differences that divided
Russia—a Christianized country which had drawn its cultural influences from Byzantium and later from the Protestant
West—and the Oriental world of China were simply too
great to be fully bridged even by the attractive stereotypes
of Marxism.

In his preoccupation with the anti-imperialist cause in
China—in his desire to see British and Japanese and Americans expelled from that country and all the elements of their
special privilege and power there destroyed—Stalin was, of
course, as the British might say, on a hopeful wicket. This
was indeed the pattern of the future. The revolt of non-
Europe against Europe was indeed destined to be the dominant political reality of the middle decades of the present
century. And Stalin had some reason to feel that he ought,
by rights, to be the proprietor of this process. It was something with which the Russian Revolution was intimately connected. The Russian Revolution had been, in fact, the first
great phase of this movement—the inspiration and encouragement to millions of people farther afield who also wanted
to shake off European influence or hegemony.

Two decades later, the goal which Stalin pursued in
1927 in China would actually be entirely achieved: the imperialists would be utterly expelled—to the last man, to the
last pound sterling, to the last dollar, to the last missionary
—but not under Stalin's leadership. It would not be Stalin
who would realize for China the twin ideals of national
liberation and social revolution. It would be someone else.

Why was this? Why did Mao Tse-tung succeed where
Stalin failed?

The first reason was that Stalin's effort was premature. It

was, remember, not the force of Marxist ideas or even Communist political activity that finally destroyed the positions of the European powers in Asia in our own mid-century: it was the combined effect of the two great European wars. The first war weakened these positions and undermined them; but it took the second to complete their destruction. It was not—by the same analogy—Communist efforts which destroyed the old order in Europe itself in the Thirties and Forties, and eventually delivered the eastern half of the Continent into Communist hands; it was Hitler who did this. It was he who destroyed the powers of resistance of the peoples of eastern Europe and left them vulnerable to Communist pressures. And similarly in East Asia, it was not Moscow—and least of all Washington—which really delivered China into the hands of the Communists; it was the Japanese, whose occupation of large parts of the country destroyed the natural powers of resistance in the population, and whose final removal at the end of the war created vacuums into which the Communists were prepared to flow, whereas Chiang was not. Without World War II, it is hard to believe that Mao's triumph could ever have occurred.

Had Stalin waited another twenty years, his chances for success would have been better. But even then, I think it doubtful that he could have succeeded. If time was against him in 1927, so was space. He faced the fact that he was five thousand miles from the scene of action, and a foreigner, whereas Chiang and Mao were Chinese, and were right there.

Many Americans seem unable to recognize the technical difficulties involved in the operation of far-flung lines of power—the difficulty of trying to exert power from any given national center, over areas greatly remote from that center. There are, believe me, limits to the effective radius of political power from any center in the world. It is vitally important to remember this, particularly in the face of the fears one hears constantly expressed today that the Russians want universal power and will be likely to take over the world if we fail to do this or that.

There is no magic by which great nations are brought to obey for any length of time the will of people very far away who understand their problems poorly and with whom they feel no intimacy of origin or understanding. This has to be done by bayonets, or it is not done at all. This is the reason why, despite all that is said about Soviet expansion, the power of the Kremlin extends precisely to those areas which it is able to dominate with its own armed forces, without involving impossible lines of communication, and no farther. There are geographic limits to the possibilities of military occupation; and such colonial regimes as can occasionally be successfully established at points remote from the ostensible center soon develop, as has been demonstrated time and time again since the days of the Byzantine Empire, a will and identity of their own and become increasingly ineffective as instruments. In this way, the exercise of centralized power is gradually reduced, once more, to something like its natural limits.

What I am asserting is that universal world dominion is a technical impossibility, and that the effectiveness of the power radiated from any one national center decreases in proportion to the distance involved, and to the degree of cultural disparity. It was this reality that Stalin, in a very incipient way, was up against in his encounter with Chinese Communism and the Kuomintang in 1927. His lines of political authority were simply overextended. For that reason they were ineffective, and dangerous to all concerned. The result was the occurrence, then and there, in the relationship between Moscow and the Chinese Communists, of something the nature of which still puzzles many people today. It was not an overt break. Throughout his years in the wilderness, and even later, Mao continued to do lip service to his political affinity with Moscow and to pay to Moscow that tribute of outward deference which is required of all foreign communist parties. But I cannot believe that things were ever the same after 1927.

From this time on, Moscow had, in Mao—though this had at times to be concealed—an ally, but not a satellite. Chiang's massacre of the Shanghai workers in 1927 had demonstrated that Chinese Communism could survive and prosper only as an independent force, making its own decisions in the light of its own understanding of Chinese realities, not as a puppet of far-off Moscow. With this event, something snapped in the chain of authority and influence which Stalin had tried to fling to the shores of the Pacific.

A hundred and twenty years ago a brilliant French visitor at the Court of the Tsar in St. Petersburg, the Marquis de Custine, felt compelled to speculate in his letters home on the ultimate destiny of a tyranny so vast and so ponderous as that which he saw before him in the empire of Nicolas I. To him it seemed, he wrote, that a tyranny of such grandeur could have only one destiny: which was to take over the West and to teach us decadent Westerners, as he put it in his moment of despair and bitterness, how we could and should be ruled. But the old Russian hands in the Petersburg diplomatic corps had, he added, a different view. The destiny of Russian tyranny, they thought, was to expand into Asia—and eventually to break in two, there, upon its own conquests.

Today there are those who think this will never happen. There are also those who think it is about to happen. It is my own view, and one which the reflections I have put before you may have helped to illustrate, that in the case of Soviet Russia a little bit of this happened as much as thirty-three years ago.

19   The Rise of Hitler

I HAVE described two signal reverses of foreign policy that befell Moscow in the years from 1924 to 1926. One was the failure of Ramsay MacDonald's effort to regularize Anglo-Soviet relations in 1924 and the series of events which flowed from that failure: the political triumph of the Tories, the deterioration of the existing *de facto* relationship, and, finally, the Arcos raid and the complete rupture of relations in early 1927. The other was Stalin's failure in China. To these should be added something which I have mentioned only briefly: the partial cooling of the Rapallo relationship between Germany and Russia, which occurred in just these same years. This change was the reflection of Germany's rapprochement with the Western powers, conducted by the brilliant German Foreign Minister of ·that period, Gustav Stresemann. The fiasco of the Genoa Conference of 1922 had been followed by the disastrous episode of the French occupation of the Ruhr. Taking over in the aftermath of this low point in the fortunes of postwar Germany, Stresemann, with British help and by skillful diplomacy, succeeded in repairing the damage and in bringing Germany, once more, into an acceptable relationship with the Western powers. The problem of reparations was at least temporarily taken care of by the Dawes Plan, which went into effect in 1924. At the end of the following year, after many months of negotiations, there were concluded the Locarno Treaties, guaranteeing Germany's western frontiers. Although Germany's entry into the League of Nations presented greater complications, this, too, finally became a reality in the summer of 1926.

The Soviet government viewed this trend of German policy with deepest displeasure, and opposed it with every means at its disposal, but could not halt it. Stresemann was careful never to break off the Rapallo relationship entirely; he needed it as a bargaining counter with the Western powers; and he exploited it effectively for this purpose. One could say, in fact, that in this sense Rathenau's work, in concluding the Rapallo Treaty, lived after him and bore posthumous fruits he never dreamed of. But to Moscow, the value of Rapallo had lain in the possibility it presented of keeping Germany at odds with the French and British. Stresemann's refusal to accept this meaning of the treaty—his insistence on maintaining a balance in Germany's relationship with East and West—all this combined with the troubles in relations with Britain and China to give Stalin a sense of frustration about the development of Soviet relations with the capitalist environment. It encouraged him to withdraw from the effort to conduct an active foreign policy and to devote himself in the ensuing years to the economic strengthening of the Soviet Union, to the developing of Soviet military power, and to the consolidation of his own regime internally. The five years following 1927 might be called, in fact, a period of isolationism in Soviet foreign policy—a period of withdrawal from external affairs during which great internal changes were undertaken. I will not go into all the motives for these changes—they embraced both the necessities of Stalin's struggle against the Party opposition and certain domestic difficulties of the regime as a whole. Suffice it to recall that the year 1929, which witnessed the beginning of the great depression in the West, was marked in Russia by the launching of both those great internal programs which changed the face of Soviet life: the

First Five-Year Plan, and the forced collectivization of the peasantry. The Five-Year Plan was designed as the first step in a drastic program of industrialization, in which the accent was very much on military industry, a program which was never really terminated and which is still in process of implementation today. The forcing of the peasants into collective farms was probably conceived by Stalin, who was personally responsible for the whole undertaking, as a means of limiting the economic independence and bargaining power of the peasantry during the period of economic stress and strain which the industrialization process was bound to bring, and of giving the regime a firm and reliable control over the distribution of the grain supplies, in order that it could be sure at all times of being able to feed the cities, the industrial workers, and the army. Both these programs—industrialization and collectivization—were tackled in so brutal and reckless a way that they did great short-term damage to the economy and the morale of the country. By 1932 there was again, as in 1922, a full-fledged famine in many parts of the countryside—this time, entirely man-made.

Stalin could not escape all blame for this situation. When the programs began, he appeared to have coped successfully with his internal political opponents: Trotsky had been exiled; the leaders of both Left and Right oppositions had been forced into an apparently helpless passivity. But in the face of the dislocations produced by the two great internal programs, opposition again became vocal. Many people wondered what the country was coming to. Thinking that Stalin might really be destroying the basis for his own regime, some of the older oppositionists began, in fumbling, furtive efforts, to regain touch with each other, to sound out each other's thoughts, and to try to establish, in a tentative way, some organizational cohesion among their followers. Particularly the Right opposition, which had opposed harsh policies towards the peasantry, felt vindicated in its views and strengthened in its moral authority. Each of the main opposition factions, remembering how in 1917 the Bolsheviki had triumphed so largely because of their high state of organizational preparedness, feared to be caught napping if again, as in 1917, the regime drove things to the point of popular despair and chaos.

Stalin, aware of all this, was frightened and infuriated. At the end of September 1932, a bitter crisis boiled up within the Central Committee. Stalin demanded the death penalty against some of the oppositionists. His comrades successfully opposed it. He fell into an ugly mood. Difficulties developed between him and his' young wife. These difficulties were partly political. Her mother, who lived initially in the Stalin household, was by origin a peasant. She served as a channel for complaints to Stalin about the sufferings of the peasantry. Stalin insisted on her removal from the household. In early November there was an angry public scene between Stalin and his wife, at a social gathering. The wife left in tears. The next day her death was announced. Perhaps she killed herself; perhaps he shot her in a moment of passion. That he drove her to her death seems inescapable. He showed, afterwards, signs of remorse and sadness; gave her a curiously Christian sort of burial; followed the hearse on foot through the streets of Moscow; loved to talk about her with those who had known her well. There is no doubt that this tragic happening marked an acute crisis, both personal and political, in Stalin's life.

These details about internal conditions in the Soviet Union in the years 1929 to 1932 are necessary in order to show how preoccupied Stalin was at this time with internal developments. Note particularly the dates involved: the beginning of the Five-Year Plan in October 1928; the beginning of forced collectivization in 1929; the achievement of the high point of the economic dislocation in the year 1932; the resulting tension and the political and personal crises experienced by Stalin in the autumn of 1932. We shall have occasion to return to these dates in connection with the disintegration of the Weimar Republic in Germany.

Preoccupied with these internal problems, still smarting from his foreign-policy reverses of earlier years, Stalin's attitude towards relations with the capitalist world seems at this time to have been one of cynicism, skepticism, and angry contempt. Everywhere, in his eyes, the bourgeoisie—or moderate labor elements allied with the bourgeoisie—were in control. These regimes, he considered, had no future. The economic crisis would eventually ruin them. But this would take time. And when the final breakup came, it would present initially a problem of great danger and delicacy for Russia, because communist parties abroad were even greater problems for the Kremlin when they got near to the seizure of power than they were when they were struggling little opposition groups. Besides, it was not to be expected that world capitalism would go down to final defeat without some attempt to lash out at the center of world socialism by which it was threatened. Let the economic crisis, then, do its work. He would sit back and strengthen Russia, strengthen his own regime, against the day of the final showdown.

The only things Stalin wanted from the bourgeois world, in these years, were imports of machine tools and capital goods with which to overcome the crisis of the Five-Year Plan and to get Russia's industrialization fairly under way. Despite the absence of good political relations between Russia and any of the Western countries, it was not too difficult to get these things. Western firms, hard pressed by the economic depression, were in no position to turn down attractive orders from any quarter. The Western governments, struggling with the problem of mass unemployment, were in no position to discourage any sort of trade, even East-West trade, if it would help to keep people at work. Thus the years of 1928 to 1932 were a time of great upsurge in Russia's foreign trade. Imports of capital goods, machine tools in particular, from Germany achieved very sizable dimensions. They were supported by commercial credit, guaranteed by the German government on a considerable scale. The completion of this program of imports was of vital importance to Stalin as a means of overcoming the crisis to which the bungling of the Five-Year Plan had led.

Because he himself valued his political relations with the West so little, and because he reckoned that the Western governments were now in no position to cut off the trade even if political relations deteriorated, Stalin did not hesitate during those years to abuse Russia's relations with the Western countries for his own domestic purposes. To deflect some of the blame he was receiving for the deplorable situation in Russia, he proceeded to hold a series of mock trials and other demonstrations designed to persuade the Soviet people that the Western capitalist governments were attempting to sabotage the industrialization program, and that the hardships being suffered in Russia were the result not of bungling on the part of the Soviet regime but rather of sinister interference on the part of outside powers. Three times, in the course of the years 1928 to 1933, great propaganda trials, involving in each case foreign specialists as well as Russian engineers and technicians, were staged for the purpose of lending verisimilitude to this thesis. In taking these steps, Stalin appears to have been not in the least worried about the fact that the falseness of these cynical travesties were perfectly plain to foreign representatives and journalists; it was the less sophisticated Russian public, always sensitive to the idea of foreign espionage and interference, at which the spectacles were aimed. It also appears not to have bothered him particularly that the misuse of foreign citizens in this manner constituted an abuse of Russia's relations with the countries to which these victims belonged, led to great indignation and complaint in the respective capitals, and drew down bitter protests on the head of the Commissariat for Foreign Affairs. (The third of the three trials even led the British to establish, for a time, a partial embargo on imports from Russia.) Stalin's indifference to these repercussions was the measure of his cynicism about Russia's relations with the capitalist countries generally.

Not even Germany was spared in this abuse of Russia's external relations by Stalin in the interests of his domestic-political position. The first of the three trials—the so-called Shakhty Trial of 1928—involved the arrest of several German citizens, engineers, and technicians, and the public trial of three of them on obviously trumped-up charges. The fact is that the Rapallo relationship was at this time coming under heavy strain, generally. Under the impact of the economic depression the last of the restrictions of the Treaty of Versailles were crumbling away. The years 1929 and 1930 saw first the reduction, and finally the virtual termination, of Germany's reparations payments to the West. They also saw the end of the Allied occupation of the Rhineland and the withdrawal of the last Allied military control officials from Germany. At Geneva one seemed, for a time in 1932, to be close to a general disarmament agreement which would place Germany, for the first time, on an equal plane with the Western powers in military matters. It looked, in other words, as though Germany were finally to be readmitted on equal terms into the European community.

Stalin naturally watched all this with a jaundiced eye. He felt he had nothing to gain from the adjustment of Germany's relations with the West. To the degree the Germans succeeded in freeing themselves from the restrictive provisions of the Versailles Treaty, their relations with the Western powers would be unburdened, and they would become more independent in their relations with Moscow. Stalin's resulting irritation may have had something to do with his lack of hesitation in antagonizing the German government and public with the show trials. Not only this, but it had the effect of working a slight change in Russia's relations with the former Allies. If the Germans were going to flirt with the Western democratic powers, they would be shown that two could play at this game. The result was that from 1930 to 1933 there was a tendency on Moscow's part to get away from the one-sided relationship with Germany and to achieve a greater flexibility of policy by normalizing relations with France and Poland as well.

So much, then, for Russia. Let us turn to what was happening, meanwhile, in Germany.

The year 1928 represented the high point of the Weimar Republic: the point of its maximum stability, its maximum success, its maximum hope. It is rather sad to recall this, today. There was much that was unstable in the Weimar Germany; but there was also much that was enormously hopeful and exciting—much, in fact, which the remainder of Europe needed in the way of example and inspiration but did not know that it needed. I lived in Germany at that time; and I know of no more pathetic and tragic episode in the history of this past half-century than this first relatively brief and ill-fated German experiment in democratic government—an experiment which was the object of so much misunderstanding and indifference abroad, and which rested on so fragile a basis at home.

In any case, 1928 was its high point. The strength of the extreme parties of Right and Left had declined. The Social-Democrats and the Catholic Peoples' Party provided the active basis of German political life. The approaching accommodation with the West held out hope that the Republic would soon be carried over its last great foreign political hurdle.

Into this favorable situation the world economic crisis struck with devastating effect. Neither the Socialists nor the conservative business elements were prepared, ideologically, to cope with the strain which this development placed on German political life. In the light of their obligations to their worker constituents, the Social-Democrats found themselves simply incapable of solving the problem of retrenchment in the field of social security. They yielded, in March 1930, to what amounted to a government of economic experts under Heinrich Brüning—who was an honorable, moderate, well-meaning man. Because he had only minority support in the German parliament—the *Reichstag*—he was obliged to govern by emergency decree. Pursuing a rigid deflationary policy—unnecessarily rigid, as we know today— he finally succeeded by 1932 in licking the heavy financial problem which the depression had spelled for the German government, and was just getting set to tackle, against the background of a balanced budget, the problem of unemployment. But he had waited too long. This problem had now grown over his head. It had in fact assumed horrendous dimensions. As early as 1930 two out of ten labor union members in Germany were unemployed; in 1931 it was three out of ten, and in 1932, four. By mid-1932, in fact, only three out of ten union members actually had full-time employment.

The political effects of this trend were simply disastrous. At the Right and Left extremes of the political spectrum stood two parties—the Nazis and the Communists—which took a wholly negative attitude toward the Republic itself, which were determined to tear to pieces at the earliest possible moment the whole structure of republican government, and which were utterly unscrupulous in their methods. Both of these parties stood to gain by the growing despair of the unemployed and the other elements affected by the crisis. In the general elections of 1928, the Nazis received only 800,000 votes. In the similar elections of 1930, they received 6,400,000. By July 1932 the figure had grown to nearly fourteen million. Communist strength also increased during these five years, but not nearly so much: from approximately three million to approximately five million. Moderate-Socialist strength remained about stable.

In May 1932, Brüning was dismissed by the German President, Paul von Hindenburg, who had only recently been re-elected for a second term. This monumental old general, with his upturned mustaches, whom Wheeler-Bennett referred to as the "wooden Titan," had been a reasonably good president during his first term. He had at least showed a consistent loyalty to the constitution of the Republic. After his re-election, this began to change. He showed signs of senility. (I remember the witticism that went around Berlin at that time to the effect that Hindenburg was really dead but didn't know it because Franz von Papen had forgotten to tell him.) In any case, the conservative right-wing nationalists, restless under the effects of Brüning's economic measures, and probably worried by the fact that they were now being politically outflanked to the Right by the stormy growth of the Nazi movement, took advantage of Hindenburg's condition and of their social ties with him, and persuaded the old general to dismiss Brüning just when the latter appeared to be on the verge of important successes in domestic and foreign policy.

This was the beginning of the final crisis that led, within eight months, to the installation of Adolf Hitler in the position of Chancellor of the German Reich and thus to the fall of the Weimar Republic. I shall not attempt to describe the dramatic and complicated happenings of those eight months. Suffice it first to remember that Hitler came into power initially in a legal way, without violation of the provisions of the constitution. Secondly, let us note that even at this late date the Socialists and the Communists still had, together with the Catholic party, sufficient voting strength to overbalance the Nazis. Had they been united among themselves in the determination to preserve the Republic, they probably could have succeeded in doing so. For the explanation of the fact that they were not so united, we must turn now to the attitude, throughout this period, of the German Communists.

At the Sixth Congress of the Communist International, which convened in Moscow in 1928, just before the economic crisis began, the line was laid down that the spearhead of Communist political activity in Germany was to be directed squarely against the Social-Democrats. The latter were, in fact, to be called for agitational purposes "Social-Fascists"—with a view to obliterating in the minds of the German electors all real distinction between the Social-Democratic leadership and that of the extreme right-wing groups. That this involved a grotesque distortion and injustice, that it could only sow confusion, that it was bound to deepen the divisions among the parties of the German Left, and that it could not even constitute a really hopeful basis for political progress by the Communists themselves— all this was a matter of indifference to Stalin. He feared and disliked the moderate Socialists in Germany. He regarded them as pro-Western and anti-Rapallo. He feared, particularly, their influence on political trends within the Russian Communist Party, and specifically with relation to the Right opposition whose views inclined toward those of moderate socialism. He had no particular desire that the German Communists should prosper, and particularly not that they should prosper to the point where they themselves could take power in Germany; he knew that they would then be uncontrollable. He was content for all these reasons to exploit them as a weapon with which to weaken the Social-Democrats, to damage Germany's relationships with the West, and in general to disrupt the strength of the Weimar Republic, and to restore Germany's waning dependence on Moscow.

This, as I say, was the line laid down at the Comintern Congress in 1928. Throughout the ensuing years, down to and even after the Nazi take-over, it was never altered. No change of any sort was introduced into it to take account of the economic crisis, of the tremendous internal changes in Germany in those years, and particularly of the menacing rise in Nazi strength. Throughout this period, as the shadow of Nazi brutality and intimidation fell deeper and deeper over German political life, the attitude of the Communists toward the moderate opponents of Hitler remained undeviatingly hostile and destructive. It was clear that this aided the Nazis; but to this situation Stalin remained, to all appearances, frigidly indifferent.

Here, once more, the Russian Communists were partly the victims of their own doctrinaire preconceptions. Their ideology told them that a revolution could be conducted only by a class. A class, however, was something which could be determined only by the relationships of production. All the parties to the Right of the Social-Democrats were, in Moscow's eyes, bourgeois parties. The Social-Democrats themselves were charged, for reasons of political expediency, with being corrupted by the bourgeoisie and allied with it—indistinguishable from it, in fact. This meant that the bourgeoisie, in Moscow's view, was already in power in the final years of the Weimar Republic. There could be no revolution against it by the Nazis because it could not revolt against itself. Whether it was Brüning or Papen or Schleicher or Hitler who was Reichschancellor was of no importance to Stalin. All were members of the bourgeoisie; all served the same masters. Just as Soviet propaganda maintained that the moderate Socialists were no better than fascists, so it was obliged to maintain that fascists were no worse than, and no different from, any other kind of bourgeoisie. Stalin, in fact, appears to have derived comfort from the

growth of Nazi power. He believed that this would finally
bring about that destruction of moderate socialism in
Germany which the German Communists had alone been
unable to encompass, but which, once accomplished, would
finally open the way to easy Communist success. This was
a fantastically and fatefully erroneous view of German political realities; yet it was one which flowed logically from
the rigid limitations of Communist doctrine and one which,
as it happened, excellently suited the internal political
preoccupations of Joseph Stalin in his long and devious
struggle against his rivals in the Russian Communist Party.

You will have no difficulty, I think, in picturing to yourselves the political behavior of the German Communists,
under the discipline of this political line, in the crucial
years of Hitler's rise to power. At every point their role
was negative and destructive. It was the denial of their
support to Brüning which forced him to rule by emergency
decree instead of by a parliamentary majority and created
precedents which were later to be most unfortunately exploited by Hitler himself. It was their use of violence—their
incessant brawling on the streets with both Socialists and
Nazis—which provided much of the excuse for the eventual
monopolization of the police power by right-wing elements
and its use against the liberties of the Republic—indeed, for
Nazi violence of all sorts. When, in April 1931, right-wing
elements tried to break, by a popular referendum, the Social-
Democratic control of the Prussian government, which was
the real center of the forces of democracy in Germany, the
Communists joined them in this effort and added more than
two and a half million Communist votes to the anti-democratic total. It was, again, Communist violence in the streets
which Papen cited as justification for the final dismissal
of the moderate Prussian government in July 1932. And
when, on November 6, 1932, new general elections were
held in which there was a marked and surprising decline
of Nazi voting strength—which fact might have given
the Republic one last and vital chance—how did the Communists react? They took it as a sign that the Nazi menace
had passed. Elated by their own relative success in this election, they intensified their attack on the Social-Democrats.
At this time, less than three months before Hitler's take-
over, the Social-Democrats, in their despair, even appealed
repeatedly to the Soviet embassy in Berlin to induce the
German Communists to give them help against the Nazis.

The answer was consistently negative. Less than a fortnight before Hitler's assumption of the chancellorship, the
blunt answer was given by a secretary of the Soviet embassy: Moscow was convinced the road to a Soviet Germany
lay through Hitler.

How important was all this? Did it assure Hitler's triumph? No one can say for sure. It is true that the rise
of Nazi voting strength in those crucial years did not take
place at the expense of the Social-Democrats. The new
adherents to Nazism were either unemployed people who
had no place in the Social-Democratic movement, so closely
connected with the trade-unions, or new voters of all sorts
emerging to political activity out of the ranks of those who
had previously been apathetic. It is not possible, therefore,
to say that Hitler won just because the Communists weakened
the Socialists. The fact is that German patience was not
quite great enough. The final hump which the Weimar
Republic was about to surmount when Brüning was dismissed
in 1932 was not sufficiently visible to the mass of the
people to make possible a successful surviving of the political crisis. Large parts of the German public, and particularly the youth, fed up with the long years of economic
distress and hopelessness, were ready for some great emotional enthusiasm; and the Nazis gave it to them. I call
attention once more to the absence of the steadying influence of the fathers' generation: of those fathers who
weren't there because they were buried in the military ceme-
teries of the western front. These were the true sources of
Germany's inability to withstand the infection of Nazi totalitarianism; and it can be argued that the Communist
attitude did not decisively influence these trends—that the
Communist attacks on the moderate Socialists, in particular,
had little effect, because it was not at the expense of the
moderate Socialists that Hitler made his gains.

But in a wider sense I think the Communist responsibility
cannot be denied. The hostile attitude of the Communists
toward the Republic was not just a phenomenon of these
years of crisis. It was something which had been a burden
on German political life from the very creation of the Republic in 1918. Here was a brave experiment in democratic
and republican government in a country which had never
known anything of this sort before. All the odds were against
it. The Weimar Republic had to combat the effects of the
bitterness of defeat, the wartime losses, the biological dis-

balance, the economic disruption, the inflation, the social upheaval, the great spiritual bewilderment, as well as the vindictiveness and indifference of the Western Allies, the anti-republican prejudice of the army officers' corps, the general lack of any real democratic tradition, not to mention certain institutional weaknesses flowing from deficiencies in the Weimar constitution itself. The Republic represented a desperate sort of bet on the faith and the enlightenment and the responsibility of the average man in Germany. It represented an experiment which would have tested to the utmost the resources of the German people even had all segments of German political life been united in the desire to see it succeed.

But for the moderate German leadership of the 1920's and the early 1930's to have to bear, in addition to all the handicaps I have listed, the hostile pressure of a whole section of German political life, namely, the Communist Party, commanding anywhere between two and five million adherents, violently oriented against the whole success of the experiment and utterly unscrupulous in its determination to wreck it at any cost: this represented an added burden of no small dimensions. At the very outset, in 1918, it was the unrestrained use of violence by the Communist Left which more than any other factor forced the moderate Socialist leaders to accept the services of the German army for the preservation of order in the Republic, and to pay an appropriate price in catering to the interests and prejudices of the anti-republican officers' corps. We can see right there, in the record of the first days of the Republic, how greatly the presence of this unmanageable Communist Left increased the difficulties of moderate Socialist leadership. What the Communists did to democratic government in Germany was similar to what they did to Kerensky in the summer of 1917 in Russia: they put him, you will recall, in an impossible position between the Scylla of an anti-democratic army officers' corps and the Charybdis of destruction at the hands of his own left-wing extremists.

History has, of course, no proper answers to the questions of what might have been. I can only say that it seems to me obvious that the strength of the republican forces in Germany, throughout the period of the Twenties and the first two years of the Thirties, would have been of a different order had the political potential of these two million to five million Communists been added to the cause of democracy instead of being subtracted from it and mobilized against it. The fact that it was so subtracted and so mobilized was largely Moscow's doing. The fact that no change was made in this situation even in the years when the star of Nazi power was rising on the German political sky, and visible for everyone to see, was also the clearest possible expression of the Soviet political will. There may be, as Franz Borkenau pointed out in the excellent discussion of this subject in his book *European Communism*,[75] no reason to suppose that Stalin himself strongly desired the triumph of Hitler in Germany. But it is wholly evident, as Borkenau also points out, that he made no move whatsoever to prevent it.

In the light of these circumstances, no one can deny, I think, Stalin's responsibility for the failure of the Weimar Republic at what was probably the darkest hour of the night, just before the dawn—for its failure to get over the last barrier to what could well have been stability and permanence—for the degeneration of Germany into the horrors of totalitarianism, with the inevitable consequence of a second world war.

Do Stalin's successors regret all this today, when they look back on these events? Would they do it differently if they had it to do over again? The answer is by no means certain. The consequences of Hitler's accession to power were not entirely disagreeable to the long-term purposes of the Russian Communist movement. Hitler's triumph in 1933 put an end, after all, for more than a decade to come, to the possibilities for genuine rapprochement between the German people and the remainder of the West. It produced precisely that aggravation of the contradictions within the Western world on which both Lenin and Stalin had staked their diplomacy. It produced another world war, constituting the second great drain in a century on the spiritual and physical energies of the Western peoples and ending with the delivery of half of Europe into Soviet hands.

To be sure, Russia herself became inadvertently—despite Stalin's best efforts—involved in this war, lost some twenty millions of her people, and had her economic progress set back by roughly a decade. But what are people, in the philosophy of those who do not recognize the existence of the soul? And what is a decade, in the view of a movement which feels that it has discovered the secret of utopia which had unaccountably eluded countless previous generations?

In the mathematics of a materialistic ideology, there is no suffering, however vast, which would not be justified if the historical equation of which it was a part ended with the slightest demonstrable balance to the advantage of the dictatorship by which—and by which alone—such an ideology finds its political expression.

20 The Struggle Against Hitler, and the Purges

DURING THE six years of Hitler's peacetime regime in Germany, from 1933 to 1939, Soviet policy, as seen from the Western angle, had certain strange and inscrutable aspects. After first ignoring Hitler, Stalin turned around in 1934 and adopted what appeared to be a policy of alliance with the West against him. Russia joined the League of Nations. The Soviet Foreign Commissar, Maxim Litvinov, became the strongest protagonist at Geneva of a policy of collective resistance, within the League, to the aggressive tendencies of Nazi Germany. The Soviet government entered into negotiations with the French and Czechoslovak governments, and concluded with them treaties of alliance directed against Hitler. At the Seventh Congress of the Communist International, in 1935, Stalin reversed the pernicious line of exclusive hostility towards the moderate Socialists which had so facilitated Hitler's rise to power, and finally told the foreign communist parties in effect to merge their efforts with those of their moderate-socialist comrades in a united front against the march of European fascism. To be sure, it was now two years too late to save the great German Socialist and Communist parties, whose members were by this time dying in the torture cells of the Gestapo or rotting in the Nazi concentration camps. But the change nevertheless brought high hopes to many people on the liberal and left-wing side in the West. They saw in it the end of the long, destructive feud between Socialists and Communists the world over, the reconciliation of the two Internationals, the rise of a new proletarian unity in the face of the menace of fascism. This impression was confirmed at the outbreak of the civil war in Spain in 1936, when the Soviet government, in contrast to the British and French governments, came out squarely for the Spanish Republic and, for a short time, gave military aid on a major scale to the Republican cause. On top of all this, there were observable, at this time, certain hopeful innovations on the surface of political life within Russia: a new recognition by the regime of the validity of Russian national feeling—talk about patriotism and the "motherland"—a new constitution, ostensibly more liberal, prepared and proclaimed with great fanfares of official publicity. All this gave grounds for hope—and this hope did indeed become widespread in Western liberal circles— that the evil face of Hitlerism had at last awakened the conscience of the Kremlin to a realization of its duty to humanity as a whole; that the old asperities of the Bolshevik movement—its edginess, it suspiciousness, the devious secretiveness of its methods, its jealous aversion to any sort of collaboration with others—were at last beginning to melt before the burning danger of Hitlerism; that the Soviet regime, in other words, was finally growing up, attaining maturity, beginning to act like a normal government. To those Western liberals in particular who, despite all the discouragements, had never entirely lost faith in the Russian Revolution, who were still convinced that there must be *some* way, at *some* time, to find a common language with those who had inherited Lenin's mantle, it did indeed look this way. And yet . . .

Somehow or other, the dream never materialized. From the summer of 1936 on, Stalin unaccountably appeared to turn his back on the struggle against Hitler. Aside from Russia's brief involvement in the Spanish civil war, he appeared, from that time on, to address himself primarily to the destruction of his own apparatus of power. He launched a series of fantastic show trials and purges. He contrived in the course of some two years to conduct a veritable revolution from above, and an extremely destructive one at that, killing people by the thousands, destroying the greater part of the existing leadership of the country in Party, government administration, police, armed forces, and even in the Communist International, throwing the whole structure of power into a state of babbling terror and hysteria, cast

tremendous cloud of bewilderment and despair over all that
was left of educated Soviet society.

What had all this to do with the needs of the struggle
against Hitler? It weakened the Red army. It emboldened
Hitler on his path of aggression. It undermined Russia's bargaining power. It brought discouragement to her friends. It
weakened, and eventually disrupted, the new united front
of Socialists and Communists in Europe. And it was
accompanied, as we shall see, by signs of a growing disinterestedness, and increasingly bitter sort of detachment, towards the whole effort of collective resistance to Hitler—a
detachment which was finally to grow into the tragic cynicism of the Nazi-Soviet Nonaggression Pact of 1939.

What had happened to produce this change? Many Western liberals thought they knew. The Western governments,
they concluded, were at fault. They had, by their hesitations
and their timidity, disillusioned the men in the Kremlin—
disillusioned them in their new-found attachment to the cause
of democracy—caused them to lose confidence in the whole
undertaking of collective security.

Was this true? Was this the whole story? Let us go back
over this period, in a little greater detail, and see whether
we can find the answer.

I have pointed out the internal difficulties which had accumulated for Stalin by the year 1932, and have told you
about the political crisis of the late summer of that year:
about the frustration Stalin suffered in the effort to get his
associates to sanction extreme measures of punishment
against certain of the leaders of the opposition, and about the
emotional shock of his wife's death. The political discontent
with which he was faced at that time, within the ranks of the
Party and the governmental and cultural elite generally,
was widespread. It related not only to the hardships which
had been brought on the country by the industrialization
and collectivization programs: it related to Stalin's methods
generally. The material difficulties began to be overcome,
actually, in 1933. The harvest was better. Some of the
mistakes of the collectivization were corrected. The food
crisis was survived. In the material sense, life began to
pi   again. But all these difficulties had left a bad taste
       mouths. There was a growing sense of the need
       e in the character of the regime. There were
       the dictatorship be softened; that the system

become more human; that the basis of rule be widened so as to include not just the Party fanatics but wide circles of the new non-Party technical intelligentsia as well. A purely political leadership, composed of fanatical revolutionaries, was no longer adequate, people felt, for a country becoming rapidly industrialized. The regime must be liberalized, more closely connected with the mass of the people.

Pressures along these lines began to penetrate into the highest circles of the regime. They became extensively associated in many minds with the person of S. M. Kirov, the young and popular Party chief in Leningrad. He seemed to understand these demands and to sympathize with them. It was he who is said to have most strongly opposed the shooting of the old oppositionists. It was he who evidently pleaded for new blood in the Party—for a better treatment of the peasantry.

The year 1933 passed relatively uneventfully. Hitler's assumption of power seems not initially to have worried Stalin particularly. The same reasons that had made him blind to the danger of Hitler's rise to power in the first place now continued to obscure from his eyes the meaning of the final establishment of Nazi rule. He was still unable to recognize the revolutionary nature of the Nazi movement. Because it had no clear class basis, distinguishable from that of the other bourgeois parties, he could not see its triumph as a revolutionary development. The slaughter of the German Communists by the Gestapo left him apparently unmoved. Repeatedly, he caused Hitler to be assured that this constituted no reason why good relations should not prevail between the two countries.

Actually, Stalin's eyes were not on Germany only, at this time. He was much worried by the Japanese seizure of Manchuria: he recognized in that act an immediate threat to the Soviet Far Eastern borders. He was now busy trying to protect himself from this threat by selling the Chinese Eastern Railway to the Japanese puppet regime in Manchuria.

In view of the Japanese threat, a major objective of Stalin's policy throughout most of 1933 was the attainment of diplomatic recognition by the United States government. This was finally achieved with Litvinov's trip to Washington in November 1933, with the agreement concluded by F.D.R., and with the arrival in Moscow shortly thereafter of the first American ambassador to the Soviet Union, Mr. William C. Bullitt.

It might be worth our while to pause at this point and to have a closer glance at Soviet-American relations in these years of the Thirties.

Throughout the period of the Republican administrations, from 1921 to 1933, the Soviet Union continued to press behind the scenes for American diplomatic recognition; but the United States government clung to the differences over "propaganda" and "debts and claims" as reasons for its unwillingness to contemplate any such change. Meanwhile, despite the absence of regular relations, trade between the two countries developed favorably. American exports to the U.S.S.R. reached a peak of about 115 million dollars in 1930. After that, they declined. The decline was probably partly the reflection of the most favorable credit terms available to the Soviet government in other countries, particularly Germany and England; but after 1931 it was only part of a sharp decline in Soviet imports generally, occasioned by the fact that the Soviet government had overstrained its resources of gold and foreign currencies, and now found its current revenues adversely affected by the world economic depression. Soviet spokesmen contrived, nevertheless, to portray the decline in American exports to the U.S.S.R. as the result of the absence of diplomatic relations. A vast increase of these exports—a prospect especially attractive in the midst of the depression—was predicted in the event that relations should be regularized. This propaganda, supported by some large American firms interested in trade with Russia, was not without effect.

These ideas were supported by the effects of the Japanese seizure of Manchuria, which aroused in the American public mind the strong attachment this country had come to feel for the political and territorial integrity of China. This uneasiness, again, was ably exploited by Soviet representatives, who spread the thesis that Japan's aggressive policies in Manchuria were only the reflection of the absence of regular relations between the Soviet Union and the United States. Japan, it was suggested, was exploiting the fact that there could be no unity of policy between the two great opponents of her expansion onto the Chinese mainland.

These pressures failed to affect the Hoover administration, but they found their mark with the new administration of Franklin D. Roosevelt, which came into office in March 1933. Their force had no doubt been increased by Hitler's accession to power in the weeks just prior to inauguration day.

The result was that, after a period of feeling out the ground, F.D.R. invited the Soviet Foreign Commissar, Maxim Litvinov, to come to Washington to discuss the resumption of relations. When Litvinov arrived, some sharp negotiations ensued over the terms on which these relations should be resumed. No workable agreement could be reached on debts and claims, but a formula was found which sufficed to give to the public the impression that there was an agreement in principle. (Needless to say, the Soviet position on this item stiffened, once recognition was in the bag, and no final agreement was ever arrived at. MacDonald's experience, one might have thought, could have taught the United States government that this would be the case.)

F.D.R. did insist, however, that Litvinov sign a number of other "assurances" dealing with subjects on which, it was assumed, Americans might have particular anxiety in connection with the resumption of relations: propaganda, the legal protection of Americans in Russia, the right of such Americans to have religious liberty on Russian soil, and their right to seek information on economic conditions in Russia. These assurances were very curious documents. No one who knew anything about the Soviet Union could have imagined for a moment that they would restrain or modify the established behavior of the Soviet government in any way. Two of them—those dealing with economic espionage and with the legal protection of Americans in Russia—were ones the Soviet government had already signed in dealings with the Germans. It was, as it happened, I myself who had drawn the attention of the United States government to these clauses—as examples of valueless undertakings on the part of the Soviet government which had failed to inhibit in any way that government's behavior in practice. F.D.R. nevertheless recognized that these clauses had all the outward aspects of carefully worked-out technical-legal documents, and he correctly calculated that, in a country where foreign affairs were customarily the province of lawyers, people would be impressed and reassured by them. He was interested only in their momentary psychological effect on the American public, not on their effectiveness in practice. He was only following, here, the precedent established by John Hay, who had not hesitated to serve up to the other powers, in the first Open Door note, a document actually drafted by someone in the Chinese Customs Service, of the real meaning of which, in its relevance to Chinese conditions, he could have had very little idea, but which, again, looked formidably legal and technical, and gave the American public the impression that someone in the United States government had done a lot of hard work. It is significant that—despite the subsequent bland refusal of the Soviet government to pay any attention to most of these undertakings in practice (the one on propaganda was openly flouted two years later when the Seventh Comintern Congress was held in Moscow; the one on legal protection of Americans was defied many times, most recently in connection with the surviving flyers of the RB-47 plane)—I cannot recall that F.D.R. was ever seriously criticized in American opinion for accepting such assurances. Trade, too, failed to increase after recognition, and never even achieved, prior to World War II, the level it had reached in 1930, when there were no relations at all. But none of this seems to have occasioned any painful post-mortems comparable to those concerning our China policy of the mid-Forties.

F.D.R. was right in his recognition that the resumption of diplomatic relations between the two countries was something that had to come. It would have come, anyway, sooner or later. It is unnatural and abnormal for two countries of this size and importance to have no regular channels for communication. It might have been better if it had come with less exalted hopes and calculations as to its effects. But it was perhaps inevitable that a country which had so long exaggerated the effects of withholding recognition should exaggerate the significance of granting it.

Let us now return to Stalin and the problem presented to him, in early 1934, by the continued fact of Hitler's power in Germany. By this time, it was becoming increasingly difficult for Stalin to ignore the danger which the Nazi regime spelled for Russia. There had already been incidents. There had been rash Nazi talk about the Ukraine, as a future living space for the German people. On January 26, 1934, only shortly after the resumption of relations between Russia and the United States, Hitler concluded a ten-year nonaggression pact with Poland. This seems to have come as a blow to Stalin. It suddenly brought home to him how completely the Germans had cut loose from the old Rapallo concept. It suggested that Hitler was aiming at a deal with the Poles whereby he would obtain a revision of the Polish-German frontier in the north—an abolition, that is, of the Polish Corridor—and Poland would be recompensed by territory to be taken away from the Soviet Union in the region of the Ukraine. It was this, together with the growing evidences generally of Hitler's implacable ambition and undependability, that presumably moved Stalin finally to give over, to recognize the seriousness of the Nazi danger, and to sanction the various projects for collaboration with the West: the joining of the League, the pact with the French, and the change in the policy of the Comintern, which I mentioned earlier. All three of these major projects appear to have been launched during the year 1934. The diplomatic side of these efforts was conducted with great skill by Litvinov, as Foreign Commissar—himself a Jew, a sincere anti-Nazi, a Westerner by temperament, and a very able man.

But at the same time, quite concealed from the scrutiny of the outside world, disturbing things were occurring on the Soviet internal front. The internal tensions, outward appearances to the contrary, were not declining. The Seventeenth Party Congress was held in January 1934, just in the days when Hitler concluded his pact with the Poles. There is considerable evidence to suggest that Stalin was in some way crossed by this Congress. Its members did not outwardly challenge his position in the Party, but it looks as though they elected a Central Committee not entirely of his choice, and not entirely amenable to his wishes. There appears, in particular, to have been a successful insistence, somewhere along the line, that Kirov be brought down from Leningrad to Moscow, for work in the Secretariat of the Party—the hope being, only too obviously, that his influence should serve to counteract that of Stalin and to give support to the new and more humane line of policy which everyone was urging.

Please note, then, that just at the time when Stalin was being obliged to make, under the pressure of circumstances, a major foreign policy change which he had long been resisting, he found himself similarly pressed to make internal changes which he did not want to make. In these circumstances, his mind moved along a pattern very familiar to anyone who has ever studied his life. Stalin was not an original man. He was not apt to have profound and original

ideas for changes in policy. Such suggestions were more
apt to come from others. But when they did, and especially
if they became bruited about publicly before a decision had
been taken in the inner circle, this was something Stalin tended to regard as a manifestation of opposition to himself,
never to be forgiven or forgotten. Yet he was wise enough
to realize that these suggestions were, in themselves, more
often sound than unsound, and that they ought in the interests of the regime—even in his own interests—to be adopted.
His tactic, then, was invariably first to purge and discredit
the authors of the suggestion and then, when they had been
successfully forced into a situation where they would take
no credit for it, to make the change and to take the credit
upon himself.

This, in 1934, he set out to do with respect to the widespread demands both for a liberalization and humanization
of the regime, and for the admission of new blood into
the administration of the country. Work was put in hand on
the drafting of a new and ostensibly more liberal constitution. Other hopeful changes were made. But at the same time,
sinister things began to happen behind the scenes: in the
activities of the police, in the Party administration, in the
treatment of the old oppositionists, for whom Stalin, through
the secret police, was only too clearly plotting some kind
of elaborate revenge.

Maxim Gorky, the writer, was one of Stalin's few in-
timates. Gorky understood Stalin well, and clearly valued
him for his great talents. Gorky was himself one of the
strongest protagonists of a softening and humanization of
the regime. He evidently saw the signs of sinister measures
ripening in Stalin's mind. He is said to have worked hard
on Stalin, in 1934, to induce him to institute the new reforms *without* a purge of the oppositionists. Desperately, he is
said to have tried to persuade Stalin that there was no
conspiracy against him—that this was a fiction of his imagination—that it was quite unnecessary to institute a blood
bath.

But this was a losing battle. Stalin was not really a normal
man. Like Ivan the Terrible, he was the captive of a personal devil within his own soul; and since his wife's death, this
devil had begun to take over.

It was just at this time that Hitler shocked the world
by instituting among some of his own intimate followers the
so-called Blood Purge of June 30, 1934. This exhibition

of ruthless brutality against party comrades evidently made a profound impression upon Stalin. Alone among his leading associates he is said to have insisted that this act would strengthen, not weaken, the Nazi regime. He was, I am sure, filled with admiration. From now on, there was no stopping him.

The old head of the GPU, V. R. Menzhinski, had just died. Stalin now replaced him with a man, G. G. Yagoda, whom he thought he could easily handle, and whom he proceeded to surround with his own spies and agents. He made the secret police, in effect, a direct agency of his own personal power. Throughout most of the year 1934, furthermore, he resisted Kirov's move to Moscow, stalling it off on one pretext after another. Towards the end of the year, these pretexts began to wear thin. In early November, a decision seems finally to have been taken, presumably contrary to Stalin's wishes, that Kirov was to make the move in early December. On December 4, Kirov was assassinated in Leningrad.

We know today that the murder of Kirov was almost certainly a product of some sort of police intrigue with which Stalin himself was connected, or of which he at least had knowledge. This did not prevent him, as I said before, from putting on a great show of sadness and indignation, even to the point of publicly kissing the corpse. The event led, of course, to masses of new arrests and investigations, conducted by a secret police now very much under Stalin's personal control. In this way, he apparently learned new things which further inflamed his suspicions. It didn't take much, actually, to do this. As the new year 1935 got under way, things began to happen in rapid succession. A full-fledged administrative purge of the Party ranks was instituted. L. B. Kamenev and G. E. Zinoviev, who were in prison, were subjected to a secret trial. The secrecy of this procedure led to protests from the Society of Old Bolsheviks —the Old Guard within the Party. This still further infuriated Stalin. Steps were taken to suppress the Society, to purge and liquidate many of its members. V. V. Kuibyshev, reputedly Kirov's strongest supporter in the Politbureau, died, conveniently and somewhat mysteriously, in January 1935. Stalin broke off personal relations with Gorky, and warned him to cease his own agitation for reform. New powers were given to the GPU. A law was passed authorizing in effect reprisals against the children and families of political offenders. In the careful, patient, secretive way that was so characteristic of him, Stalin was making preparations for the real blood bath he was shortly to launch.

Meanwhile, in this year of 1935, things were not going too well on the foreign political scene. It proved practically impossible to stir up any effective resistance to Hitler in the League of Nations. The Italian attack on Ethiopia provided a striking example of the inefficacy of the League as an answer to the problem of fascist aggression. In France, where Pierre Laval had taken over in place of the strongly antifascist Louis Barthou, difficulties developed in the negotiation of the Franco-Soviet Pact. The language of the document was watered down almost to the point of meaninglessness. The French parliament delayed ratification for nearly a year, and then took the step only with so many hesitations and misgivings that it weakened the political effect of the action. Stalin had not hoped for very much from the pact; his main hope had probably been merely that the gesture of its conclusion would have a restraining effect on Hitler. By the time it was ratified, even this value as a gesture had been greatly reduced.

As for the collaboration between Socialists and Communists in Europe, the so-called United Front: this was working well in some ways—but not entirely satisfactorily from Stalin's standpoint. It did, seemingly, stop the advance of domestic fascism within France. But it had no effect on Hitler. And the extensive association it involved of European Communists with sensible, reasonable people in the moderate ranks of European socialism was already threatening to erode the sharp, suspicious militancy which was the basis of discipline throughout the Communist movement.

Such was the situation, then, at the outset of the fateful year of 1936. On March 7 of that year—only a few days after ratification of the Franco-Soviet Pact in the French Chamber of Deputies, and a few days before its ratification in the Senate—Hitler, in defiance of Germany's treaty obligations, and naming the Franco-Soviet Pact as his excuse, boldly reoccupied the Rhineland with German troops, and got away with it. The French wished to resist this move by military action. They certainly had at that time the power to do so. The British dissuaded them.

For Stalin, the German reoccupation of the Rhineland was

a heavy blow. It destroyed what little hope he may have placed in the effectiveness of Litvinov's efforts to stiffen the Western powers in their resistance to Hitler. Stalin must have seen quite clearly that Hitler's move represented a gesture of supreme contempt for the Franco-Soviet Pact. How silly he, Stalin, now looked: having struggled two years to get this mutual assistance agreement with the hesitant French, only to have Hitler march contemptuously into the Rhineland at the very moment of its ratification, and seize the territory with impunity from under the French nose. Such lessons were not lost on Stalin. He was too much of a realist not to see that here was a case where legalisms and paper promises had counted for nothing, but where bold, brutal action had been very successful. And he was obliged to note that this reoccupation of the Rhineland represented the satisfaction of Hitler's last major demand against the West. All of his remaining objectives—and particularly the territorial ones—lay to the East, in the direction of the Soviet frontiers. If the French and British had failed to stand up to Hitler when the aggression was in their own back yard, could they be expected to react with greater incisiveness when the blow went in the other direction?

From the moment of the German entry into the Rhineland, Stalin must have reckoned that it was only a matter of time before he must either fight Hitler or make some sort of deal with him. He could not, of course, hope by means of such a deal to purchase permanent immunity from the aggressive designs of a man like Hitler; but it was possible that he might by this means gain time for maneuver and for further military preparations. It was also possible that he might deflect the blow into a different direction. In either case, whether he tried to resist or tried to make a deal, he saw that he would be exposed to severe criticism among his comrades at home. If Hitler attacked—if Russia found herself involved, that is, in a major war—Stalin would be doubly reproached for his initial indifference to Hitler's take-over; and his leadership of the Russian Communist movement would be challenged by people who could claim that they, in contrast to him, had seen the danger promptly and had been against Hitler from the start. If, on the other hand, he succeeded in making a deal, he would be criticized (as indeed he later was) for abandoning the antifascist cause, for allying himself with the executioners of European communism. The only way out, as he saw it, was the physical elimination of anyone else who had ever had any aspiration to leadership within Russia—anyone who had ever opposed him in any way—anyone on whom popular confidence could conceivably fasten—anyone who could possibly profit from the inevitable political embarrassment which Stalin now saw looming up for himself. It would, perhaps, be too much to say that these considerations alone accounted for the purges. It is certainly reasonable to suppose that these considerations contributed to the complex of motives from which the purges flowed.

Within a few days after the German entry into the Rhineland, Stalin gave orders, secretly, for the preparation of the first of the three great purge trials which punctuated and marked the main phases of the hideous process. It was at this time that one finds the first recorded instances of people noticing that his reactions and behavior showed signs of genuine abnormality. Ironically enough, it was just after this—just as the purges were really getting under way—that the draft of the new constitution, on which a commission had been at work for several months, was published. It was, you see, an integral part of Stalin's concept of the purges that these reprisals against the governing elite should be balanced off by efforts to play up to the non-Party masses—efforts which, incidentally, were not entirely unsuccessful. The common people of Russia by this time had the iron in their souls; and they were not sorry to see the great and mighty of the Soviet regime destroying each other in this way.

There is a tragic irony, too, in the circumstances of Gorky's death, which occurred just at this time. In June 1936, while the first of the purge trials was being prepared, Gorky lay dying. By this time, he presumably had a pretty fair idea of what Stalin was up to. There is some evidence to suggest that his condition, too, was partly the result of Stalin's sly malevolence. (There are, incidentally, several others among Stalin's intimate associates who died in circumstances which invite similar suspicions.) It was during this mortal illness that Gorky read the draft, published in the papers, of the new constitution which he himself had urged on Stalin. The irony was not lost on him. "In our country," he was heard to remark on this occasion, "even the stones sing." Only the regime itself has never been willing to recognize the bitterness of this remark and to admit that the stone Gorky had in mind was in truth the heart of Stalin.

Not long after Gorky's death, in August 1936, the public trial of Kamenev and Zinoviev, along with a number of other unfortunates, took place. It was the subject of great bitterness and consternation throughout the higher echelons of the Party—not bitterness against the victims of the trial (everyone knew they were innocent, though they were not popular figures in the Party), but bitterness against Stalin for his shocking humiliation and degradation of old Party comrades, friends and associates of Lenin. And it was clear to everyone that Stalin meant this trial to be only the beginning. He had already given orders for the preparation of new trials: against the former Trotskyites, against the members of the former Right opposition. The great and widely beloved figure of N. I. Bukharin seemed to be particularly threatened. Aware of the discontent around him, and unwilling to face it directly, Stalin left Moscow before this first trial began, went to the Caucasus and sulked, leaving the onus of the imposition of the death sentences to be formally incurred by the members of the court, who dared not defy what they knew to be his wishes.

During Stalin's absence, at the beginning of September, there took place a plenary session of the Central Committee at which, once again, Stalin's will appears to have been defied by his associates. Bukharin was evidently supported; the investigation directed against him was, in any case, temporarily halted. Yagoda, the head of the secret police, who had once been close to Bukharin, appears to have come out on this issue against Stalin. The reaction was not long in coming. A telegram arrived from Stalin on September 25, insisting on the removal of Yagoda, demanding the appointment in his place of one of Stalin's most sinister henchmen, N. I. Yezhov, and calling for the most merciless purging of all traitors and unreliable elements within the Party ranks. The police, Stalin said in this telegram, should now do the things they ought to have done and failed to do four years earlier. What was "four years earlier"? It was the fall of 1932—the time of Stalin's first demands for the imposition of the death penalty against his political opponents, the time of his wife's death. This time in 1936, Stalin—a master political tactician—contrived to get the support he needed. Yagoda was dropped; Yezhov was appointed. From that moment on, the purges took that fantastic course which defies the powers of description and nearly defies the imagination. Heads rolled by the thousands, the tens of thousands, probably even the hundreds of thousands. A process of terror and panic, mutual denunciation and mutual extermination, was set in motion which is probably without parallel in modern history. In a vast conflagration of mock justice, torture, and brutality, at least two thirds of the governing class of Russia literally devoured and destroyed itself. The jailors and judges of one day were the prisoners and the victims of the next. And over this whole macabre procedure Stalin presided, with diabolic, cynical composure, with his customary self-deprecating manner of having nothing to do with it all—but presumably enjoying every minute of it, relishing every new exhibition of the misery and degradation and helplessness of his former aides and associates. For two years he let the conflagration proceed. Then, when the turn-over had gone far enough, with consummate skill —like one who thrusts rods into an atomic pile—he slowed down the process of destruction and brought it, relatively speaking, to a halt. One of the last to be shot was the Grand Inquisitor himself—Yezhov. He belonged to that final category of those referred to in Russia as "the witnesses," those who had to be killed because they had seen too much and knew too much.

But while all this was going on, something else of great importance had occurred on the international scene. This was the beginning of the Spanish civil war. The conflict broke out suddenly, as you may recall, in mid-July 1936, only a month before the opening of the first purge trial and Stalin's departure for the Caucasus. It began with a military attack by a group of generals, together with a few troops loyal to them, against the newly elected liberal-Republican government of Spain. At the beginning of August, the French, anxious to keep the conflict from growing into a major international one, proposed to the various interested powers, including the Soviet Union, a general agreement on nonintervention. This proposal was made in the light of the fact that the Germans and Italians were already giving aid on a considerable scale to the Spanish insurgents.

The Soviet government on August 23 accepted this obligation of nonintervention, albeit with strong warnings that the agreement would have to be lived up to by the Germans and Italians as well if the Soviet acceptance was to be binding. It did so, apparently, in the faint hope that this might serve to reduce the measure of German and Italian aid to the insurgents and thus enable the Republic to survive. Moscow had had nothing to do with the origins of the civil war in Spain. It had been, in fact, poorly informed on what was going on there. But it was clear that a fascist victory in Spain could very well lead to a fascist take-over in France as well and to the complete collapse of the entire antifascist cause in Continental Europe. This is turn would greatly hasten the dreaded day when Hitler, unhampered by opposition in the west, could turn to the east and proceed to realize his dreams of expansion in the Baltic and on the fertile plains of the Ukraine. Stalin, therefore, had powerful reason to fear an insurgent victory in Spain, particularly a quick and dramatic one. He obviously hoped, in initially accepting the nonintervention agreement, that this might serve to give the Republic something like a chance.

Nevertheless, two or three weeks later, a sudden and drastic change occurred in Soviet policy. At some time in the first half of September, the decision appears to have been taken in Moscow to intervene in Spain, clandestinely and informally, to be sure, but in a major way. Whether this was primarily Stalin's decision, or was taken on his initiative, I have been unable to determine. It appears to have been taken during his absence in the Caucasus, probably at the same session of the Central Committee which infuriated him by supporting Bukharin. However that may be, he must certainly have acquiesced at the moment.

The decision to aid the Spanish Republic having been taken, the operation was put in hand with unbelievable speed and energy. Within little over two months, hundreds of Soviet advisers had arrived in Spain; Soviet tanks and aircraft had been sent, and were in operation; Soviet officers were in effective charge of military operations on the Madrid front. In the face of the weakness and helplessness of the Republican government, Moscow simply took control over whole great areas of the governmental power: particularly military affairs, and everything to do with internal security. Within a short time, such key governmental functions as counterintelligence, censorship, and cryptographic communications were largely in Soviet hands. The Soviet government had its own tank and air units, which it operated entirely independently.

So far as one can see, this effort of military aid was initially conducted in perfectly good faith, with no other purpose, at the time, than to save Madrid and to assure the victory of the Republic. It did, unquestionably, save Madrid at that stage of the war. No attempt was made to encourage the Spanish Communists to exploit Soviet influence as a means of seizing power, though this party of course benefited politically from the Russian intervention. On the contrary, the Spanish Communists were required by Moscow to pursue a strict United Front line, and to support the moderate Spanish regime in its social policies as well as in its military struggle.

But this intensive phase of Soviet military intervention lasted only a very short time. By early February of 1937, the Soviet military effort began to taper off, and to give place to a policy of limited economic aid. Why was this? It may have been simply because Moscow realized that in view of the failure of the British and French to give serious aid, the Republican cause could not be won without a Russian commitment so extensive as to involve danger of a full-fledged military embroilment of Russia with Germany and Italy. But one also notices that this change in Russian policy occurred in January or February 1937, after Stalin's return to Moscow, at a time when he had just overcome the resistance of his colleagues to the arrest of Bukharin and the continuation of the purges. One notices, too, that in the course of the next two years the purges seem to have been addressed with particular savagery to Soviet officials who served in Spain. If elsewhere in the bureaucracy something like 60 to 80 per cent fell in the purges, the proportion among those who served in Spain—and including particularly those who served with greatest devotion and effectiveness—seems to have been closer to 100 per cent.

What was the explanation for this? It was, in my opinion, probably Stalin's fear of the great liberal idealism which attached itself, as an international phenomenon, to the Republican cause in the Spanish civil war. You must remember that this war, more than any event in modern history, became the repository of the hopes and enthusiasms of the entire socialist and liberal world of the West. People read into this Spanish struggle the epitomization of all the liberal hopes and dreams which the early part of this century had fostered—dreams which had suffered one major frustration in the economic crisis, and were now suffering another in the march of European facism. I have always personally doubted the soundness of this tendency to identify the issues of the Spanish civil war with Western liberal ideals. It has seemed to me that many other factors, irrelevant to political issues outside of Spain, were also involved. To my mind, the unfortunate Weimar Republic actually represented in a much less ambiguous way the things people thought they were fighting for in Spain. Be that as it may, Spain did become the great shrine of this sort of idealism. The Republican cause was marked by a general atmosphere of heroism and enthusiasm without parallel in the history of this century. This was infectious. The Russians in Spain felt this, could not help but feel it, along with others; and many of them yielded to it all the more readily because it contrasted so sharply with the terror and unhappiness of what was then happening in Russia. They were glad, thinking of the purges at home, to have at least something clear and great and inspiring to die for, instead of perishing obscurely in the dungeons of the NKVD on the issue of their own false confessions. They secretly hoped that somehow or other, in her association with the Spanish civil war, Russia would recapture her own soul, Soviet society would be regenerated. They hoped that the idealism of the Russian Revolution of 1917—now drowning in the nightmare of Stalin's purges—would be recaptured in Spain's revolution of the mid-Thirties.

Stalin knew all this. He never forgave them. This accounts, I think, for the savagery with which they were subsequently purged and exterminated. It accounts for the fact that as the Spanish struggle ran its course, Soviet attention turned less and less to the defeat of Franco and more and more to obscure, bitter, underground feuds with those elements in the Spanish Left Wing which were resistant to Soviet influence and domination. It helps to account for the suddenness of the withdrawal of Soviet interest in a real Republican victory—for the fact that Soviet policy so quickly and obviously settled down, after the winter of 1937, to a mere effort to prolong the conflict in order to engage German and Italian energies there as long as possible. There was nothing wrong with Stalin's instincts. He feared an insurgent military victory in Spain—yes. But he also feared the moral victory of those forces of decency and idealism which had rallied to the Republican cause. He knew that these forces, more than any other power, threatened to disintegrate the sort of regime on which he based his rule in Russia.

To summarize, then: Russia's brief participation in the Spanish civil war represented the last bizarre phase of Moscow's effort to strengthen the antifascist cause in western Europe. Like the other attempts, it foundered—partly on the timidity and vacillation of the French and British, whose behavior was indeed not such as to encourage any successful collaboration in resistance to Hitler, but partly, too, on Stalin's extreme fear of any extensive intimacy with the liberal and socialist world of the West—of any intimacy which could expose his own apparatus of power to Western influence and give sustenance to the opposition currents against him at home.

In this series of events, certain deeper realities seem to emerge. From the beginning of 1934—from the time when Stalin first became seriously aware of the dangers of Hitlerism —the great question was whether there was a real possibility of an effective coalition embracing both Russia and the major powers of western Europe, for the purpose of frustrating Hitler's aggressive ambitions and preventing the catastrophe of a second world war. Many Western liberals thought then that there was such a possibility, and many have continued to believe down to this day that there was. They blame primarily the French and British governments for the fact that this dream was never realized. They charge that these governments, by their timid, vacillating policies of appeasement, left the Soviet government no choice but to go its own way. Certainly, the French and British governments were vulnerable to such criticism. And the role of our government, too, which kept aloof from the whole affair, was not particularly glorious.

But actually this is not all of the answer. The fact is that Stalin's Russia was never a fit partner for the West in the cause of resistance to fascism. Russia herself was, throughout these years, the scene of the most nightmarish, Orwellian orgies of modern totalitarianism. These were not provoked by Hitler's rise. They originated, as we saw, in 1932, at a time when Stalin did not yet have any proper understanding of the Nazi danger. This internal weakness of the Soviet regime (for what else but the most extreme weakness can it be when a man sees himself unable to govern except by methods such as these?)—this weakness lay in Stalin's own character. It was this that caused him to fear an intimacy with Hitler's opponents no less than he feared the military enmity of Hitler himself. To the moral cause of

an antifascist coalition, the Soviet government of 1934 to
1937 could have added little but hesitant, halfway measures,
and a nauseating hypocrisy.

Anyone who looks deeply at the history of these years
cannot, I think, avoid the conclusion that Russia was never
really available, in the sense that Western liberals thought
she was, as a possible partner of the West in the combatting
of Nazism. Her purposes were not the purposes of Western democracy. Her possibilities were not the possibilities
open to democratic states. The damage that had been done
with the triumph of Bolshevism in Russia went deeper than
people in the West supposed. By the mid-Thirties the Western democracies, whether they realized it or not, were on
their own. There was no salvation for them from the East.
In those initial years of Hitler's power, they would have
done well to place greater reliance on their own beliefs and
their own strength. At that time, this strength, if resolutely
mobilized, would still have been enough. Two years later,
it would not be. Hitler's rearmament of Germany was moving too fast. Two years later they would be unable to defeat Hitler without accepting the aid of Russia; and for that
aid there would then be a price—a bitter price—the full
bitterness of which we of this generation are now being
compelled to taste.

21   The Nonaggression Pact

I HAVE tried to go beyond the straight narrative of events
to explain not just *what* happened but *why* it happened.
We have seen the great mistakes that were made on the
Western side in the years leading up to 1937: the Allied
policy of unconditional surrender in World War I, the un-
feeling treatment of the Weimar Republic, and the lack of
will in London and Paris that permitted Hitler to reoccupy
the Rhineland with impunity. We have seen the effects
of all this on the possibilities for an anti-Hitlerian coalition,

and the discouragement which this weakness brought to those people in Moscow who, like Litvinov, sincerely desired to see such a coalition come into being. But we saw also how little Stalin's Russia was itself really fitted to be a partner in such a coalition—how sick a man Stalin really was; how he feared the effects on his own regime of just such an association with the West; how he tore the governing structure of his own country to pieces in the purges; and how this, again, affected adversely both his qualifications as an ally for the West and the ability of Russia, independently, to stand up to Hitler's power.

If you let your mind run over this list of determining factors, you will see that by 1937 all the ingredients of high tragedy, all the complications of the drama, were already present. The Western democracies had contrived to get themselves confronted, at one and the same time, with two powerful adversaries—one centered in Berlin, the other in Moscow. One of these adversaries was now driving rapidly towards a showdown. The West had allowed itself to become so weak that it was not strong enough to defeat either one of these adversaries without the help of the other. It is important to remember this. It meant that as early as the late 1930's, no clean, moral victory for the West was any longer in the cards—no victory in the name of principles and ideals. Only the very strong, or those so weak that they do not choose to compete in terms of power, can enjoy the luxury of acting purely in the name of ideals; the others have to make their compromises. By 1937, an effort had, to be sure, been made to come to terms with one of these enemies, namely Russia, with a view to the instituting of a common opposition to the other. But this effort had been pursued without enthusiasm; there had been no mutual confidence; the undertaking plainly had no future.

Such were the elements of the tragedy. What followed— the last act—flowed with a terrible, fascinating, inexorable logic from what had gone before. The hour was now too late for anything essential to be altered. The rest was denouement.

Stalin was by 1937 deeply disillusioned with the prospects for inducing the French and British to put up any effective opposition to Hitler. Hitler's next moves, it was clear, would be towards the east, and it was not to be expected that the Western powers would do anything serious to oppose him. Plainly, this posed for Stalin the alternative of attempting to resist the German advance alone, by force of arms, or of coming to some sort of accommodation with Hitler. The weight of evidence suggests that it was the second course which most appealed to Stalin, and on which he began, in 1937, to stake his expectations and his policies.

The purges were at this moment just getting into high gear. Had Stalin at this time envisaged military resistance as the preferred course, then the first thing he should have done would be to halt the purges, to launch out on a policy of national unity (as indeed he later did when the war was really on), and to begin at once to build up both the strength and the morale of the Red army. If the prospect was resistance, the continuation of the purges made no sense.

If, on the other hand, Stalin was going to seek his safety in a deal with Hitler, then it was best that he should first settle his scores with his Party rivals—that he should get all these people out of the way who might make trouble for him in the implementation of such a policy, who might introduce irrelevant ideological arguments, who might attempt to mobilize against him—as he thought they were already secretly trying to do in Spain—the aroused liberal idealism of the Western world. In contemplating a deal with Hitler, Stalin must surely have had in mind the precedent of the Brest-Litovsk Treaty, by which Lenin had traded space for time and had kept the Germans at arms' length in 1918. He must have remembered that Lenin, on that occasion, had been faced with most bitter opposition on the part of certain Party comrades—opposition so bitter, in fact, that it had brought him to the verge of resignation from his position as leading secretary of the Party. All this could happen again.

If, then, it was a deal with Hitler towards which Stalin was steering his course, the purges made some sense, though even then only to a very abnormal mind. And it was along this line that Stalin's policy proceeded. Throughout 1937 and the first month of 1938 the purges were at their high point. Not only did Stalin decimate the ranking civilian echelons of the bureaucracy but he proceeded in midsummer, 1937, to slaughter off the major military leaders as well, and to follow this up with purges that destroyed or removed a very high percentage of the senior officers' corps of the armed services generally. There is no evidence

to suggest that these purged officers were the least com-
petent ones militarily, or that, even if they had been, *these*
violent means would have been the best way to achieve
their elimination. There are other ways of doing things. This
reckless attack on the armed services was not the work of
a man intending to improve military efficiency or of one
preparing a serious effort of military resistance. It was
the work of a pathologically suspicious and fearful person,
who saw himself being pressed into a situation where he
would probably have to make cynical and shabby compromises with a terrible adversary, and who feared that
certain of his political and military associates, if left alive,
would attempt to profit from his embarrassment.

The year 1937 was a year of watchful waiting in Soviet
foreign policy. Very delicately, I think, behind the scenes,
Stalin was already beginning to detach himself from any
one-sided commitment to the policy of collective security
against Hitler. For example, the Soviet ambassador in
Berlin, Jacob Suritz, who was a Jew and therefore scarcely
suitable as a possible vehicle for new political contacts
with the anti-Semitic Nazis, was cautiously replaced by a
non-Jew. But Stalin was too wise a bird to force the pace;
and the Nazis, for their part, continued to exhibit nothing
but the wildest and most flamboyant hostility to Russian
Communism.

Litvinov was permitted, therefore, to continue to plug publicly the collective security line. It was, after all, an anchor
to windward. He was also permitted to continue to prod
the reluctant French and British into putting up greater resistance to the German and Italian intervention in Spain.
So long as the Germans remained engaged there, Stalin
felt that he had some respite and could take time to complete the purges. But even here, time was running out. Stalin
knew very well, from the beginning of 1937, that the Spanish Republic would be defeated in the end. We may be
sure that he watched with the most anxious intensity for any
slackening off of the German activity in Spain, because he
knew full well that this would probably be the signal for
the dreaded switch of German policy towards the east.

He did not have long to wait. On November 5, 1937,
Hitler, as is now known, called his generals and his foreign
minister together for a secret strategy conference. He pointed out to them that German rearmament had progressed
to a point which permitted Germany to pursue actively not

only the smashing of the remaining strictures of Versailles, but also the objective he had himself staked out: of bringing into the German Reich all the German-speaking peoples of central and eastern Europe. The French and British, he continued, were still weak; they had not strengthened their armed forces proportionately to meet the German rearmament. How long this favorable situation would last, however, was uncertain. There was growing pressure for increased rearmament in France and England. In another two or three years, it might be too late: these countries might be too strong. One had to strike while the iron was hot. He proposed, therefore, to proceed at once to the realization of his major objectives in the east: the absorption of Austria into the Reich, the liberation of the Sudeten Germans from domination by the Czechs (which meant, in effect, the destruction of the Czechoslovak state), and finally the rectification of the territorial sacrifices which Germany had been obliged by the Versailles settlement to make to the benefit of Poland and Lithuania. This rectification would include the reincorporation of the ports of Memel and Danzig into the Reich, the destruction of the Polish Corridor, and certain adjustments of the German-Polish frontier further south, particularly in Silesia. It was these various objectives which Hitler, in the conference of November 5, 1937, declared his intention of achieving within the period of German military superiority now looming ahead.

Incidentally, it is of interest to note that when Hitler had outlined this program, Göering at once pointed out that in this case the German involvement in Spain would have to be liquidated. There was good reason, therefore, why Stalin should have regarded a German disengagement in Spain as the beginning of the period of high danger for the countries of eastern Europe.

In Hitler's case, there was no gap between the word and the deed. The decision having been taken, action followed promptly, boldly, and without backward glances. The liquidation of the Spanish involvement began at once. In the east, Austria was first on the agenda. Within a matter of weeks after the November conference, the heat was turned on the Austrian government. The aggressive Nazi faction in that country began to stir up every conceivable sort of trouble for the Conservative-Catholic government of Chancellor Kurt von Schuschnigg. Disorders of all sorts were provoked. Rumors were spread. Everything was done to un-

dermine public confidence and to give people the impression
that the days of Austria's independence were coming to an
end.

On February 4, 1938, one of Hitler's most violent Nazi
supporters, Joachim von Ribbentrop, was made German
Foreign Minister, replacing the relatively moderate career
diplomat, Baron ·Konstantin von Neurath—who, it was
no doubt felt, would hardly have been suitable for the
things that were now to be done. One week later, Schuschnigg
was summoned to Hitler's mountain residence at Berchtesgaden, near the Austrian border.

Poor Schuschnigg! Not suspecting what he was up against,
he came to the Berchtesgaden prepared to protest to Hitler
against the activities of the Austrian Nazis. To his horror
Hitler, without even asking him to sit down, burst forth at him
with veritable tirades of fury over various alleged misdeeds
of the Austrian government, demanded concessions which
presaged the early extinction of Austria's independence, and
reinforced these demands by repeatedly calling into the
room one or another of the German military leaders to
confirm Germany's ability to enforce these demands, if
necessary, by armed action. Shaken and desperate, Schuschnigg spent the ensuing days, back in Vienna, trying to
organize a plebiscite among the Austrian people on their
national future, hoping in this way to deprive the Germans
of any excuse for annexation. But this effort was rudely
terminated, on March 11, by a renewed Nazi ultimatum.
This time the Nazis demanded abandonment of the plebiscite and Schuschnigg's own resignation. On the following
day, German troops poured over the frontier and proceeded,
amid tumultuous excitement and delirious demonstrations
on the part of the Nazis, to occupy the country. The incorporation of Austria into the Reich occurred at once.

For those who did not experience these years, I wish I
could describe the excitement and drama of these events.
It is hard to visualize the tremendous head of emotional and
political steam which the Nazis had by this time developed.
Here was a great political movement on the march. We
must not let our distaste for Hitler's methods blind us to
the fact that this man was one of the greatest demagogues
of whom history bears record, and in many ways an able
statesman in the bargain. He was backed up by a party
which had fantastic powers of organization and was inspired by a fanatical, stormy determination to let nothing

stand in its path. It was not easy for people in those days
to know how far this political force was going to carry.
Many people in Germany and Austria who were at first
skeptical or even hostile were finally overwhelmed both by
the emotional impetus of the movement and by the success
Hitler had in achieving, by relatively bloodless means, objectives which the Weimar Republic had not been able to
achieve in many years of restrained effort. The overcoming of the economic crisis, the program for employment and
public works, the rectifications of many of the restrictions
imposed on Germany by the Versailles settlement: all these
things, which had proved beyond the power of the Weimar
Republic, Hitler accomplished, without war, in the space of
a few years. To understand what this seizure of Austria
meant, you must picture to yourself the sense of wild uncertainty and excitement by which central Europe was then
seized—the mixed feelings of dread and anticipation everyone in that part of the world was experiencing at the realization that, after all the long unhappy years of frustration
and economic suffering, things were once again on the
move. The ice was at last breaking; the old *status quo* of
Versailles was disintegrating; for better or worse, a new
Europe was in the making. So impressive were these results
that even Germans who had detested everything Hitler stood
for vacillated and asked themselves whether this man was
not indeed, behind all the demagoguery, a genius.

In the days of the Weimar Republic, the French and
British had sternly forbidden the so-called *Anschluss*—the
union of Austria and Germany. As late as 1932, when a
friendly gesture to Chancellor Brüning might have helped
him to avert the Nazi take-over, they had sternly reproved
his foreign minister, Dr. Julius Curtius, for merely suggesting
an economic union between Germany and Austria as a
means of alleviating the economic crisis. Now, when Hitler
seized Austria in a spirit of complete defiance, they remained inactive. This was partly the result, no doubt, of
their dislike for the conservative, semifascist, but still moderate government of Schuschnigg. Like Stalin, the Western
statesmen of that day found it hard to distinguish between
traditional conservatives and Nazis. This was again a hang-
over from World War I, when people in London and
Paris had felt that their main enemies were the conservatives of Germany and Austria. For this reason Czechoslovakia, not Austria, was their darling. Czechoslovakia was a

new republic, established by sincere protagonists of political
democracy, created by process of liberation from the Austro-
Hungarian monarchy. All this seemed virtuous and com-
mendable. But over the little rump-state of Austria there
still hovered, for Western eyes, something of the stigma of
the old Hapsburg court: too much charm, too much skepticism and despair, too little righteousness, too great a tolerance of human weakness. For these same reasons, perhaps,
Western liberals have subsequently tended to pass over
Austria's downfall and to identify the demise of Czechoslovakia, six months later, as the great turning point in European affairs generally, and in Soviet policy in particular.

I cannot quite see it this way. To Stalin's sensitive and
suspicious mind Austria's fall must have represented, I think,
a development of crucial significance. He must have drawn
from it, right then and there, practically all the conclusions
he was later believed to have drawn from the fall of
Czechoslovakia.

It was, at any rate, immediately after the seizure of
Austria, in March 1938, that the signs began to multiply of
a readiness on the Soviet side for a rapprochement with
Berlin. Repeated warnings were given—the first of them in
a statement made by Litvinov by way of reaction to Austria's fall—that time was running out on the Western powers
if they still expected to have Russia's help against Hitler.

Stalin's desire to avoid trouble with Hitler was unquestionably greatly heightened in midsummer, 1938, by the outbreak of serious hostilities between the Russians and the
Japanese in the area of the junction of the Soviet, Korean,
and Manchurian borders. There was no official declaration
of war, but there was some severe fighting. Stalin was at
all times keenly aware of the danger of becoming simultaneously embroiled with the Germans and the Japanese,
and the fact that he was involved in hostilities with one of
these parties must have increased his determination to keep
himself at peace with the other. Hitler, too, in mid-1938,
with the delicate task of cracking the Czechoslovak nut
looming immediately before him, appears finally to have felt
the need for doing what he could to keep the Russians
quiet through the coming crisis. For these reasons, both
sides were inclined to a relaxation of the tension between
them; and the signs of this were clearly apparent as the
summer advanced.

Throughout that summer of 1938, the Nazi buildup against Czechoslovakia proceeded apace; and in September there occurred the celebrated Munich crisis which rocked Europe to its foundations. With the details of this crisis—Chamberlain's meeting with Hitler at Bad Godesberg, his later dramatic flight to Munich, his concession that Hitler should have the Sudeten areas of Czechoslovakia, the Czech capitulation, the fall and flight of the Czech government, the occupation by the Germans of a large part of Bohemia and Moravia, and the reduction of what was left of the Czechoslovak Republic to the condition of a defenseless dependency of Germany—with all this, we are familiar. European history knows no more tragic day than that of Munich. I remember it well; for I was in Prague at the time, and I shall never forget the sight of the people weeping in the streets as the news of what had occurred came in over the loud-speakers.

The Munich agreement was a tragically misconceived and desperate act of appeasement at the cost of the Czechoslovak state, performed by Chamberlain and the French premier, Daladier, in the vain hope that it would satisfy Hitler's stormy ambition, and thus secure for Europe a peaceful future. We know today that it was unnecessary—unnecessary because the Czech defenses were very strong, and had the Czechs decided to fight they could have put up considerable resistance; even more unnecessary because the German generals, conscious of Germany's relative weakness at that moment, were actually prepared to attempt the removal of Hitler then and there, had he persisted in driving things to the point of war. It was the fact that the Western powers and the Czechoslovak government did yield at the last moment, and that Hitler once again achieved a bloodless triumph, which deprived the generals of any excuse for such a move. One sees again, as so often in the record of history, that it sometimes pays to stand up manfully to one's problems, even when no certain victory is in sight.

The great issue at stake in the Munich crisis was, of course, the validity of Czechoslovakia's treaties of alliance with France and with Soviet Russia. The Soviet treaty with Czechoslovakia provided that Russia was obliged to come to Czechoslovakia's assistance *only if France did the same.* As the crisis developed just before Munich, the Soviet government reiterated, with impeccable correctness, its readiness to meet its treaty obligations to Czechoslovakia, if

France would do likewise. This confirmed many people in the West in the belief that only Russia had remained true to her engagements at that crucial moment—that Russia had been prepared to assume the full burden of a war with Hitler over the issue of Czechoslovakia, had the Western powers only played their part.

This was substantially accurate in the juridical sense; but things were not exactly this way in practice.. You must remember a basic geographic reality which underlay the entire chapter of Soviet participation in the policy of collective security, and particularly the pacts with the French and the Czechs. This was the fact that whereas the Western powers had, in effect, a common border with Germany, the Soviet Union did not; it was separated from Germany and from Czechoslovakia by two countries, Poland and Rumania, both of which feared any movement of Russian troops onto their territory as much as they feared a similar movement of the troops of Hitler, and neither of which was at any time willing to say that it would permit Soviet troops to cross its territory in the implementation of Russia's obligations to Czechoslovakia or to France. This meant that no military planning for a passage of Russian troops across these countries was possible; and in the event of a war with Germany in which all three countries—France, Czechoslovakia, and Russia—might have been involved, the Western powers and Czechoslovakia could expect to become immediately engaged, whereas any Russian action would still have to await clarification of the Soviet right of passage across these intervening countries. In the reluctance of the Polish and Rumanian governments to permit transit of Soviet troops, the Soviet government had a ready-made excuse for delay in meeting its obligations of mutual assistance. This impediment was apparent at the time of Munich: the Rumanian government, in particular, was heavily pressed by the Czechs and the Western powers to declare its readiness to permit Soviet troops to pass; but I cannot find that it ever clearly did so. In any case, I myself had it from no less an authority than the German military attaché in Prague, whose task it had been to study this problem for the German High Command, that the physical characteristics of the Rumanian railroad network were such that, even had the Rumanians permitted the passage, it would have taken the Soviet command approximately three months to move a division into Slovakia over this primitive and indirect route. The implications of this state of affairs are obvious. The Russian expression of readiness to assist Czechoslovakia if France did likewise was a gesture that cost Moscow very little. It is fair to say that had the Czechs decided to resist, there was, for various reasons, a good chance that they might have been saved. It is hardly fair to say that they would have been saved by the troops of the Soviet Union.

After Munich, events took a rapid and dramatic course. Hitler, instead of being directed onto the paths of peace, was irritated and disturbed by the reaction to Munich in the West, particularly by the signs of a growing realization on the part of the Western governments that it was high time they rearmed. He had no intention whatsoever of forgoing the remainder of his program: the demands on Poland, Memel, and Danzig. Yet the sharp reaction to Munich in the West implied the danger that London and Paris might not be prepared to take any more of this lying down. The beginnings of the French and British rearmament effort meant that time was running out on him. This presented him with a difficult problem of policy.

For some weeks at the outset of 1939 Hitler appears to have toyed with the possibility of inducing the Poles to agree to the peaceful incorporation of Danzig into the Reich, and to the cutting of the Polish Corridor by a new German corridor across it. But the Poles, in a series of conversations conducted in January 1939, resisted these approaches. Furious at this recalcitrance, which cut off his easiest and most favorable prospects, Hitler made his first major mistake. He proceeded, in March 1939, to occupy all of what was left of Czechoslovakia, except the easternmost province of Ruthenia, which he tossed contemptuously to the Hungarians. He had delayed this move, which was bound to frighten the Poles, so long as there was a chance that Poland would give him what he wanted by peaceful agreement. Since the Poles proved obdurate, he petulantly went ahead to extinguish what was left of the Czechoslovak state.

By this move, Hitler placed himself on Poland's southern flank, and improved, of course, his position for further pressure against the Poles. But this represented a flagrant violation of the assurances he had given to the British at Munich; and it forced people in London and Paris to realize that even the ultimate act of appeasement involved

in the Munich settlement had been a failure—that Hitler
could not safely be permitted to gain any more bloodless
victories. The British reacted by summoning the Polish
Foreign Minister, Josef Beck, to London for negotiations,
and by proclaiming a British guarantee of the integrity of
the territory of Poland. Together with the French, they
also entered into negotiations with the Soviet government
to see whether a real and effective alliance against Hitler
could not at last be brought into being. These negotiations,
which began in the middle of April 1939, were pursued in
Moscow throughout the summer.

All this put Hitler in a difficult box. As things now stood,
he could not gain his objectives without an attack on Poland.
He was obliged to recognize that he could not attack
Poland, in the face of the British guarantee, without risk
of involving himself in a war wtih France and Britain. For
a time, he thought of attacking England and France first,
letting Poland go until later. But even this he could not
risk if there was any possibility that France and England
might be joined by Russia. Russia had, therefore, to be
neutralized. It had to be neutralized whatever he did, whether
he attacked Poland first or England and France. This
meant that the Soviet negotiations with the French and
British in Moscow had somehow to be spiked. If they could
be spiked, perhaps this would not only keep Russia out
of the conflict but England and France would then not dare
to fight at all. How could this be done? Only by a deal
with Stalin.

Hitler viewed only with deepest distaste and suspicion the
prospect of negotiating with the Russians. While he personally admired Stalin, he was sincere in his loathing for
Russian Communism. For some weeks, from mid-May to
early July, while permitting lower-level German representatives to take soundings of various sorts with their opposite
Soviet numbers, Hitler wrestled with this problem. For a
time he appears to have toyed, as an alternative, with the
idea of contenting himself for the moment with a bloodless
seizure of Danzig alone.

Stalin, meanwhile, sensing the approach of the final crisis,
convinced that Hitler was going to strike somewhere, and
determined to purchase his own safety, played his cards
with consummate skill. To the Germans he made absolutely
clear his willingness to discuss a deal. On March 10, 1939,
even before the German occupation of Bohemia and Moravia,

he had said, in a celebrated speech to the Eighteenth Party Congress in Moscow, that Russia did not propose to pull anybody else's chestnuts out of the fire for them. This was another way of saying that Russia was not going to fight Britain's or France's battles—that she would look after herself in her own way. A clearer hint to the Germans could scarcely have been devised. The Germans indicated that they understood and were interested. Six weeks later, Stalin removed Litvinov as foreign minister and turned the job over to Molotov. This was the first time since 1918 that the Foreign Affairs Ministry had been given to a member of the Politbureau. The change demonstrated that Stalin was preparing for major moves of foreign policy. At the same time, he continued to draw out the negotiations with the French and British, in order to have a second string to his bow and as a means of frightening the Germans into agreement.

For some reason—perhaps because he had become convinced that the Russians were serious in their desire for a deal, perhaps because the Poles had made it evident that they would regard even a bloodless seizure of Danzig as a *casus belli*—but certainly in any case, with the knowledge that the season was advancing and military decisions could no longer be postponed, Hitler, in early July, stopped his hesitation and made up his mind to attack Poland. Secret orders were at once issued to the armed forces to be prepared to launch the attack at the end of August. The all-clear signal was given, for the first time, for intensive, far-reaching negotiations with the Soviet government.

From now on, it was high politics, in the most dramatic and sinister sense of the term. On July 26, in the private dining room of a Berlin restaurant, Russian and German representatives got down to brass tacks. It was hinted to the Russians that Germany would be prepared to pay for Soviet neutrality, in the event of a German-Polish war, by turning over to the Soviet Union considerable areas of eastern Europe. Armed with this secret knowledge, Stalin and Molotov increased the pressure on the unsuspecting British and French negotiators in Moscow. In veiled terms the question was put to the French and British: would *they*, in the event of a war, be prepared to place large sections of eastern Europe at the mercy of Russia? Would *they*, for example, consent to regard Moscow as the guarantor of the three Baltic States, and entitled to do what it wanted

there? And would *they* compel the Poles and Rumanians to
accept Soviet troops on their territory in the event of an action
against Germany?

You can see what was going on. Stalin, with both sides
competing for his favor, was trying to find out who was
the highest bidder. Of the two bidders, only one, the Germans, knew that the other side was bidding; the other
bidder seems to have had no knowledge that any other bid
was being made. Faced with these demands, the French and
British temporized. They wanted Russian help against Germany, but they did not feel that they could buy it at the
price of the sacrifice of their Polish allies or of the Baltic
States. The Germans, of course, had not such inhibitions.
Hitler, calculating out of his own infinite cynicism and opportunism, figured that he could always handle the Russians
later; if he could be sure of getting his half of Poland
now, and getting it without great danger of a world war,
let the Russians, for the moment, have the rest, and certain
other parts of eastern Europe in the bargain.

Seeing that the Russians were inclining in this direction,
and with his own military deadline for the attack on Poland
crowding in on him, Hitler decided to force the issue. On
August 15 the Soviet government was informed that the
Germans were prepared to send their foreign minister,
Ribbentrop, to Moscow in the near future, "to lay the
foundations for a definite improvement in German-Soviet
relations."[76] This meant that the Germans were willing to do
business on the basis discussed in the secret talks. The
next day another message arrived asking that the date of
Ribbentrop's arrival be advanced to August 18, only two
days hence, on the grounds that

. . . in view of the present situation, and of the possibility of
the occurrence any day of serious incidents . . . , a basic and
rapid clarification of German-Russian relations and the mutual adjustment of the present questions are desirable.[77]

This meant that the German attack on Poland was only a
matter of days.

The moment of decision for Stalin had now arrived. The
Japanese had again been acting up. Major hostilities involving, in fact, several divisions—tanks, artillery, aircraft, the
entire paraphernalia of war—were just then in progress on
the Mongolian frontier. The British and French negotiators,

still in Moscow, suspected nothing. If Stalin turned down the German offer, he would of course have to come to some agreement with the British and French; he could not leave himself in a position of complete isolation in the face of the German attack on Poland. But he could then expect no mercy at the hands of Hitler; and if the British and French failed to engage Hitler's force in the West, Russia would be confronted at last by that war for which she was so ill-prepared: a war on two fronts, against both Germany and Japan. He would have to accept combat, furthermore, along the existing western Soviet frontiers, uncomfortably near to both the great cities of Leningrad and Moscow. If, on the other hand, he accepted Hitler's offer, he could not only remain aloof initially from the impending German-Polish conflict, with the possibility that Hitler might even become involved with the French and British, but he would be permitted, in the bargain, to take over a large area of eastern Europe. He could use this as a buffer zone in case Hitler attacked him at a later date. Meanwhile, the acquisition of it would be a great boon to his prestige.

To Stalin a bird in the hand was worth two in the bush. He chose, as he had perhaps secretly known all along that he would choose if he had the opportunity, for Hitler. The answer was given to send Ribbentrop along.

The Germans were mad with elation over the Soviet answer. They interpreted the negotiations which the French and British had been conducting so openly all summer with the Soviet government to mean that Britain and France, unless assured of Russian help, would never dare to oppose a German attack on Poland. Soviet acceptance of Ribbentrop's visit excluded even the possibility of the British and French going to war. Hitler it seemed had played, this time, for the highest stakes and had won. The last of his great objectives was about to be achieved; and it would be achieved, like the others, without bringing about the world war which the pessimists had always warned would be the result of his adventures.

You know the rest. On August 23, Ribbentrop flew to Moscow for twenty-four hours of hectic negotiation. That night, the German-Soviet Nonaggression Pact was signed. Its publication burst on the unsuspecting world like a bombshell, throwing consternation into the Western chanceries, bewilderment into the ranks of the Western liberal friends of the Soviet Union, and utter chaos into the foreign Communist parties which for six years, at Moscow's direction, had been following the most violent possible anti-Nazi line and denouncing anyone who as much as said a civil word in Hitler's direction.

Both sides, in signing this pact, were aware that it sealed the fate of Poland, that war—a German-Polish war, that is—would be only a matter of days. One week later, the Germans attacked. Contrary to the expectations entertained in Berlin when Ribbentrop signed the pact, the British and French did declare war. With this series of events, World War II had begun.

It had begun, let us note, with a situation similar to that of the period of Brest-Litovsk: namely, with the British and French facing a strong German enemy in the west, with Russia on the sidelines, and with a government in Moscow wishing for the warring powers nothing better than mutual exhaustion. "A plague on both your houses" was the sentiment with which Moscow had seen the old war out, in 1918; "a plague on both your houses" was the sentiment with which Moscow, in its innermost thoughts, saw the new one in, in 1939.

For a time, in the mid-Thirties, many people in the West had thought that it might be possible to have Soviet Russia as a voluntary partner in the effort to contain Hitler. Events had proved them wrong. A whole series of factors—Stalin's personal nature, his domestic-political predicament, the concern of his regime for the safety of Russia's Far Eastern frontiers, the inhibitions of the Poles and Rumanians, and the indecisive, timid policies of the Western powers themselves in their response to the Nazi danger —all these things had operated to keep Russia aloof from the war in its initial stages, and to leave the French and British face to face with a fanatical German opponent far stronger than themselves.

In 1917, the Western powers, in their determination to inflict total defeat on a Germany far less dangerous to them than that of Hitler, had pressed so unwisely for the continuation of Russia's help that they had consigned her to the arms of the Communists. Now, in 1939, they were paying the price for this folly.

In 1917, they had cultivated an image of the German Kaiser that was indistinguishable from the reality of the future Hitler. Now they had a real Hitler before them.

In 1917, they convinced themselves that Russia's help was

essential to their victory, though this was not really true. Now, they had a situation in which Russia's help was indeed essential but the Russia they needed was not there.

You see in this example what happens when people make policy on the basis of exaggerated fears and prejudices. Those dangers they conjure up in their own imagination eventually take on flesh and rise to assail them—or if not them, then their children. And they waste, in their over-anxiety before the fancied perils of the present, the assets they will need for the real ones of the future.

22   Before Germany Struck

I SHOULD like to describe in greater detail the visit of the German Foreign Minister, Ribbentrop, to Moscow on August 23, 1939, which I mentioned at the close of the last chapter. It was a very brief visit, lasting only twenty-four hours. Ribbentrop was wildly excited over the whole affair. He was a pompous, disagreeable man, a former wine merchant who had hitched his wagon to Hitler's star, a Nazi parvenu par excellence, bumptious, officious, bursting with energy, servile towards the Führer, arrogant to everyone else. He was attracted more by the trappings of statesmanship than by its substance. He wanted, no doubt, to be a great foreign minister, but he wanted even more to appear to be one. He wanted to walk in the image of Bismarck. One feels that he was always on stage—always playing the part. He was violently anti-British. He could never forgive the British for the chilly distaste with which they had received him in London as Hitler's ambassador in 1936-1937.

Hitler accepted the pact with the Russians out of cold, political calculation, and never denied or concealed his primary responsibility for it. But Ribbentrop had a real emotional interest in it. He regarded it as *his* personal triumph. This act, he felt, would take the wind out of the British sails. It would leave proud Anglia helpless and deflated in the face of Hitler's forthcoming attack on Poland.

It was therefore in a sort of frenzy of elation and self-importance that Ribbentrop rushed through the negotiations in the Kremlin on the night of August 23 to 24. Most of the points had already been settled by preliminary secret exchanges and little more remained to be done. The first of the results was a published treaty, the Nonaggression Pact, relatively innocuous in itself, although highly sensational as a political gesture. It provided for a mutual renunciation of aggression and for observation of neutrality by the unengaged side in case either side was attacked by a third party. Attached to it was a secret protocol, the effects of which were soon to become only too apparent to the waiting world. It provided in effect for the division of eastern Europe into spheres of influence. It defined the zones in which the respective parties were to take exclusive responsibility "in the event of a territorial and political rearrangement." By "a territorial and political rearrangement" was meant, quite simply, the pending destruction of the Polish state, the beginning of which, as both sides knew, was only a matter of days. When this destruction had been accomplished, each side was to be at liberty to do what it liked with the eastern European territories falling within its sphere. Under this arrangement the Soviet sphere of influence was to include Finland, the two Baltic States of Estonia and Latvia, and roughly the eastern half of Poland, as well as the Rumanian province of Bessarabia. Everything to the west of this line was to be Germany's.

One month later this line was somewhat modified, at Soviet request, on the occasion of a second visit by Ribbentrop to Moscow. Lithuania, like the other two Baltic States, was now assigned to Russia, whereas the Germans received a larger portion of Poland.

We cannot appreciate the full significance of this division of eastern Europe unless we visualize the extent of the catastrophe it spelled for the affected peoples. Delivery into the hands of either of these great powers, Nazi Germany or Stalinist Russia, was a calamity of the first order for almost everyone concerned. Acting from quite different ideological motives, both Germans and Russians perpetrated appalling cruelties in their respective spheres of influence. The Germans practiced their usual measures of sadism and extermination against the Jews and deliberately reduced the entire Polish population to a state of material misery and terror. The Russians took their customary reprisals against "class enemies," and deported innocent people to the interior of Russia in such numbers with such callous brutality that hundreds of thousands of them appear not to have survived the ordeal. For the three Baltic countries, this division eventually meant the end of national independence. In the case of the Estonians, in particular, it meant the deportation and permanent dispersal of a large portion of the population—the literal removal of much of a nation from its homeland. For the Finns, it meant a bloody and terrible war.

This was what was really implied by the Nonaggression Pact of August 1939; and it was with the security of this agreement that Germany attacked Poland one week later. Although it is doubtful whether Stalin had calculated that the British and French would go to war with Germany over this issue, he assuredly had no reason to be disappointed over the fact that they did. On the contrary, this was, for him, the best of all possible developments. As a statesman given to divisive policies, he seemed to have succeeded beyond his wildest dreams. Not only had a situation been produced in which Germany was formally involved with the Western powers in a war from which Russia could hope to remain indefinitely aloof, but he, Stalin, had contrived to regain in the bargain all those areas which had once been part of the Russian Empire but which had been detached from Russia at the end of World War I. Now, it seemed, there would be nothing more for him to do but to sit back and let Germany and the Western powers exhaust themselves in struggle against each other to Moscow's benefit, as Lenin had hoped they would do in 1918.

But the world of international affairs is full of surprises; and what must now be explained is how it came about that Stalin, contrary to his expectations, found it impossible to stay out of the Second World War.

This is, of course, a particular chapter in Soviet-German relations; and it is one which, for me, has always had a certain horrible fascination. Not only is it fascinating, but it is also at times deliciously comical—comical in the ironic, desperate way that only very tragic events can be, when the measure of their tragedy becomes too much for the mind to entertain, and man falls back on his ability to laugh at things, as the only respite from a total despair.

Consider the people most prominently involved in this

story. On the German side, in addition to Ribbentrop, whom
I have already mentioned, there was of course Hitler himself. It is often pointed out that history is generally written
by the victors and that it would look much different if it
were written by the vanquished. I have spoken of the tendency in the West, flowing from the anger and aversion
which Hitler aroused in the democracies, to dismiss him as
someone we all know was only a mad, vicious fool. Let me
reinforce what I said about the dangers of this impression.
Behind that Charlie Chaplin mustache and that truant lock
of hair that always covered his forehead, behind the tirades
and the sulky silences, the passionate orations and the
occasional dull, evasive stare, behind the prejudices, the cynicism, the total amorality of behavior, behind even the tendency to occasional great strategic mistakes, there lay a
statesman of no mean qualities: shrewd, calculating, in many
ways realistic, endowed—like Stalin—with considerable powers of dissimulation, capable of playing his cards very close
to his chest when he so desired, yet bold and resolute in
his decisions, and possessing one gift Stalin did not possess:
the ability to rouse men to fever pitch of personal devotion
and enthusiasm by the power of the spoken word. Hitler
was a dangerous man: fanatical, brutal, unreliable, capable
of the most breath-taking duplicity. But he was by no means
a mountebank; and if it be conceded that evil can be great,
then the quality of greatness cannot, I think, be denied him.

On the Russian side there was of course Stalin; and let
me call to mind once again his personality: cautious, secretive, hiding an iron ruthlessness under a mask of modest
affability, affected by a diseased suspiciousness toward those
who were his comrades and associates, but nevertheless capable
of the most coldblooded realism when it came to dealing with
those whom he recognized as ideological adversaries. Stalin,
curious as it sounds, was a man who was more comfortable
with avowed enemies than with avowed friends: he knew
better where he stood.

Finally, there was Stalin's wartime foreign minister, Molotov—this tremendous old workhorse of the Russian Communist movement, a man with the physique of the old-time
barroom bouncer, with iron nerves and poker face, imperturb-
able, stubborn, immovable in argument, and withal a master
chess player who never missed a move, who let nothing
escape him. There could have been no greater contrast than
Molotov and Ribbentrop. Molotov had no personal vanity;

there were no histrionics in his nature; it was a matter of indifference to him what those on the other side thought of him. He was the perfect tool of his master and of the Party, the nearest thing known to a human machine. Presumably, he had feelings—many years later he would be the only one among those who carried Stalin's body to the tomb who would be observed to weep on this occasion. But normally he knew how to conceal whatever feelings he had; and if those feelings ever had any bearing on his actions as a statesman, no one ever knew what it was.

All of these were the hardest, toughest sort of men imaginable. The game they played was the roughest of political games. They had all been engaged for years past in a brand of international politics beside which the activities of the Chicago gangsters of my youth looked like Sunday School picnics. Not only this, but for six long years they had been major ideological enemies; and each side had heaped upon the other, in incessant torrents, that reckless, endlessly malicious, propagandistic vilification of which only the totalitarian state, at its worst, is capable.

Yet here they suddenly were: thrown together in an association in which lip service had, after all, to be done to just those things which statesmen of the totalitarian world were supposed to be above: correctness, good faith, loyalty to engagements. The pretense to all these virtues, and to a certain dignity of statesmanship generally, had now to be outwardly maintained between them. And in the effort to maintain this pretense—in the effort of these men to behave as though they were not what they were—you had the *reductio ad absurdum* of political cynicism, the demonstration of the helplessness of people who have cut loose from every subjective obligation of decency, and have launched themselves into a stratosphere of unlimited opportunism where there is no moral gravity, nothing to hold on to, no point of orientation. One sees, in the record of their mutual dealings during these months of uneasy alliance, the most bizarre manifestations of this helplessness. One sees it in the pathetic understatement of Stalin's welcoming remark to Ribbentrop: "Well, we certainly did cuss each other out, didn't we?" One sees it in the preposterous fact that Stalin seems, believe it or not, to have conceived something in the nature of confidence in Hitler—of all people, Hitler. How wonderful it is, and yet in a way how logical, that this man Stalin, who was so abnormal, and so helpless in the problem of whom to trust, who mistrusted so many people unjustly and for the wrong reasons, who had so deeply mistrusted the French and British negotiators in that summer of 1939, should now for once, when it came to placing confidence, have made the greatest and wildest and most unbelievable of all possible mistakes.

You will remember that the French and British, despite their declaration of war in 1939, did not immediately undertake military operations against Germany. There ensued the so-called "phony war," during which the western front lay in a state of strange unreal inactivity. This endured through the autumn of 1939 and until the German attack on France and the Low Countries the following spring. During this interlude, the Germans were able to concentrate on Poland, and they succeeded in destroying the armed resistance of the Poles in the space of a few weeks.

The unexpected speed of the German victory in Poland was the first of Stalin's unpleasant surprises in the wake of the Nonaggression Pact. The Russians were beginning to learn what they had let themselves in for. They had been rushed into this pact faster than they liked by the stormy tempo of German diplomacy. Now the equally stormy tempo of German military victory gave them no peace. By mid-September, German forces had already crossed the demarcation line laid down in the secret protocol; and the Germans, plainly, were not prepared to stop until they had crushed completely the authority of the Polish government. It was clear that Russia had to move smartly if she was to assert her rights over what had been promised her in the pact.

To this situation, the Soviet government, startled, frightened, and poorly prepared, responded in two ways. First, it proceeded hastily to take under military occupation that half of Poland which had been assigned to it in the secret protocol. It being not possible to mention the protocol publicly, some other pretext had to be found for this bald invasion of the territory of a neighboring state. The best anyone in Moscow could think of was the flimsy and highly un-Marxist pretext of an alleged racial affinity between the peoples of this area and the people of the adjacent regions of the Soviet Union.

Secondly, a series of demands were issued to the governments of the three Baltic States and Finland for the acceptance of Soviet bases and garrisons on their respective territories. The three Baltic countries, seeing no alternative, being abandoned by the Germans and having no hope of Allied assistance, yielded peaceably to these demands, and admitted the Soviet troops. Finland refused to do so; and there ensued, during the following winter, the war between Russia and Finland which was generally referred to as the Winter War. This was a conflict in which the Russians, who had taken on the Finns much too lightheartedly, suffered heavily and spectacularly in the initial stages, until they were able to collect themselves and to mobilize their great superiority in man power and artillery.

The Germans were somewhat surprised and not particularly pleased by these Russian moves, particularly those in Finland and the Baltic. They, too, had a few things to learn about the people they were dealing with. When the decision was taken in Moscow to move into eastern Poland, the Russians made the astonishing proposal to the Germans that the action should be publicly explained on grounds of the need for protecting the people of this area from the advancing Germans. This proposal, to which the Germans objected vigorously, caused some sharply raised eyebrows in Berlin. But the Finnish war involved a much more serious strain on German patience. Started by the Russians without prior consultation with the Germans, this war was highly embarrassing to Hitler. It affected adversely Germany's vital supply of timber and nickel from Finland; it aroused intense sympathy for the Finns both in the Western countries and among the Germans themselves. It threatened for a time to produce an Allied intervention across northern Norway and Sweden for the support of the Finns—an intervention which would have cut the particularly vital German imports of iron ore from northern Sweden. In the face of this embarrassment, the Germans respected the terms of the Nonaggression Pact and did not interfere; but they did not like the Finnish-Soviet war one bit.

It is worth noting the Soviet reaction to the abundant talk, in February and March 1940, of a possible Allied intervention in Finland, for it illustrates very well Stalin's lively concern lest Russia should be drawn into the European war. Stalin had been glad to support Hitler diplomatically so long as he could hope that the war in the west would serve to absorb the attention of both Germans and British, and that Russia could remain outside the struggle. Only because of his confidence that this was the situation had he dared to

start the war with Finland. But if the British blow was going
to be directed towards the North Russian borders, this changed
everything. Immediately, though gradually and with that
cautious finesse which was the general mark of his statesmanship, Stalin proceeded to hedge in his relations with the
Germans, and to cover his flank by the cultivation of better
relations with England. It was probably these same considerations which led him to end the war with Finland, in March,
on terms relatively lenient to the Finns.

All this, however, was changed once more in April, when
Hitler took the bit into his teeth and proceeded to forestall
any possible Allied action in the north by successfully occupying Denmark and Norway. The Soviet leaders were obviously relieved by this turn of events, which placed German
forces firmly between England and Finland and obviated the
danger of any further British action east of Norway. With
this danger past, there was no longer any reason to be nice
to the British. Molotov hastened to congratulate Hitler on
this latest victory, and the Nazi-Soviet relationship settled
back once more—on the surface, but only on the surface—
to its original state of cordiality.

The next shock came with the unexpected speed of Hitler's
victory in his attack on France and the Low Countries in
May 1940. When this attack began, the Russians were once
more delighted. The failure of the Western powers to take
up active combat against Hitler in September 1939 had been
a constant source of worry to them. Now, it appeared, Hitler
would at last become involved in active and exhausting hostilities in the west. But once again, the tremendous speed of
the German advance shattered this pleasing prospect and
caused renewed alarm in Moscow. As the German victories reached their culmination point with the fall of France
in June 1940, it was hardly expected in Moscow that Britain could hold out. Stalin thus saw himself faced once again
with his familiar nightmare: the nightmare of a powerful
Germany, having disposed of England and France and with
its forces still intact, turning to the east to deal with the
Soviet Union.

Alarmed at this prospect, Stalin saw nothing better to do
than to tighten his hold on the sphere of influence he had
gained in 1939. In the preceding autumn, he had contented himself with putting military bases in the Baltic States.
In June 1940, he proceeded, with a brusqueness and brutality

that took even the Germans aback, to extinguish entirely the independence of these countries and to incorporate them into the Soviet Union. The Germans, again, were not asked for their views, and were given scant notice. At the same time, Molotov apprised the Germans of the Soviet intention to "solve"—this was the cynical euphemism of that day— the question of Bessarabia. This meant simply that it was proposed to invade Besarabia and to incorporate it, too, into the Soviet Union. And it was not only Bessarabia that Molotov mentioned in this connection, but also the Rumanian province of the Bukovina, which had not been mentioned at all in the original German-Soviet agreement.

All this came as a renewed shock to the Germans. It presaged an early attempt by the Russians to crush Rumanian independence by force of arms. It threatened to disrupt the very important wartime economic ties by which Germany and Rumania were united. Grudgingly, again, Berlin gave in and advised the Rumanian government not to resist the Russian demands. But this time the bad taste left in the German mouth was even greater than over Finland. Technically, the Germans had a poor case. They had indeed expressed, in the secret protocol to the Nonaggression Pact, their "complete political disinterestedness" in southeastern Europe and Bessarabia. The Russians were only taking them at their word. But it was amply clear that Hitler was beginning to regret some of these concessions of 1939. He felt, no doubt, that the spectacular nature of his military victories in Europe had created a new situation, and that the Russians, who had done very well by his victories at little cost to themselves, ought to recognize the change.

If these were Hitler's feelings at the beginning of the summer of 1940, how much more must he have felt this way as that summer drew to an end! The unexpected obduracy of England, which refused to surrender despite the clean Nazi sweep in France, and which now dug its toes in for a long war under the inspiring leadership of Winston Churchill; then the discovery that the German air force was unable, by its own efforts and without the support of an amphibious invasion, to compel a British surrender; finally, the failure of Hitler's effort to work out with Franco an arrangement whereby Germany could seize Gibraltar—these events greatly changed Hitler's whole situation. He was stymied in the Atlantic area. Strong as he was in land power, his sea and air power was not strong enough at that moment to permit the invasion

of England. The longer he waited, the harder this task
would be. He could strike England only in the eastern Mediterranean: through the Balkans, that is. But here the Russians were putting up rival claims; and even if they could
be persuaded to tolerate a German seizure of the Balkan
countries and a drive towards Constantinople and the Middle
East, which was not certain, they would still be hovering men-
acingly on Hitler's flank.

The growing German-Soviet rivalry over the Balkans was
heightened, in late summer, by the consequences of the Soviet
seizure of Bessarabia. The Hungarians, having their own
territorial grievances against Rumania, observed with keenest
pleasure and interest the plight of that country in the face
of Russian demands; and they concluded that the day had
come for them as well. They therefore staked out their own
claim for a sizable chunk of Rumanian territory, and threatened to take forcible action themselves if their demands were
not met. Both Hungarians and Rumanians appealed to Hitler
for his support; and the result was that the German and
Italian governments undertook to arbitrate the Hungarian-
Rumanian dispute. The two Axis foreign ministers, Ribbentrop and Ciano, met in Vienna and issued the so-called
Vienna Award, which tossed a very considerable piece of
Rumania to Hungary. Following with some relish the precedent the Russians themselves had established, the Germans
gave Moscow virtually no advance notice of this decision.
Not only this, but they followed it up by issuing a political
guarantee of what was left of Rumania, and sending a military mission to that country.

Now it was Stalin's turn to be furious. His Balkan ambitions had been growing day by day. He had staked out
Rumania and Bulgaria for his own. The Germans had not
only diminished the size of his prospective booty, but had
effectively denied to him what was left of it.

Aside from this, new questions, not envisaged in the 1939
agreements, now began to trouble the relations between the
two countries. Hitler's inability to crush Britain at home had
compelled him to seek for means of striking at the lifelines
of the British Empire. This in turn had given the war more
of a global quality and less of a European one than it had
had before. In particular, this widening of the theater of
struggle gave new importance to the orientation of the two
great uncommitted nations, Russia and the United States. Before he could approach with confidence the task of defeat-

ing Britain in this wider theater, Hitler was obliged to seek assurance that these two uncommitted forces would not join Britain against him.

Insofar as the United States was concerned, the means selected to provide this assurance was the so-called Three-Power Pact of Germany, Italy, and Japan, concluded in September 1940. "This alliance," Ribbentrop said to Molotov —in explaining the conclusion of the pact—

. . . is directed exclusively against the American warmongers. . . . The Treaty, of course, does not pursue any aggressive aims against America. Its exclusive purpose is rather to bring the elements pressing for America's entry into the war to their senses, by conclusively demonstrating to them that if they enter the present struggle, they will automatically have to deal with the three great powers as adversaries.[78]

But the question remained: How about Russia? Could she be safely left on the flank of a German move into the eastern Mediterranean? And could she be depended upon, in particular, not to take advantage of a possible Japanese embroilment with the United States in the Pacific? Would she not turn on Japan, and try to recoup the losses Russia had suffered thirty-five years earlier, in the Russo-Japanese War? These questions led Ribbentrop to probe the possibility of bringing Russia, too, into the Three-Power Pact. The idea was not to induce her to fight on Germany's side, but to bind her not to go over to the other one. Plainly, the time had arrived for a new clarification of German-Soviet relations.

On October 13, 1940, Ribbentrop therefore addressed a long letter to Stalin recapitulating German policy in matters of interest to Russia, expressing the view that it was now

. . . the historical mission of the Four Powers—the Soviet Union, Italy, Japan, and Germany—to adopt a long-range policy and to direct the future development of their peoples into the right channels by delimitation of their interests on a worldwide scale.[79]

For the discussion of this and other problems, he suggested that Molotov should be sent on a visit to Berlin.

This invitation was accepted, and on November 12 Molotov arrived in Berlin for a visit of forty-eight hours. Once again, the event was not without its incongruous side. It was the first visit of a Soviet statesman to Nazi Germany. The Germans were a bit startled when the cautious Molotov in-

sisted on bringing his own cook along and consuming, on
the German train, only that which had been prepared by
this reliable assistant. A crisis developed over what song the
German band should play at the railway station when Molotov emerged from the train. The Soviet anthem was at that
time the Internationale—the great old song of the European
revolutionary movement. Fears were expressed in the German
Foreign Office that if this tune were played the welcoming
Berliners would join enthusiastically in the singing. The decision was that neither national anthem should be played at
all. A further ironic touch was added by the activities of the
Royal Air Force. Ribbentrop throughout the talks kept stress-
ing the fact that England was finished—that the war was
really over—it was merely a question of getting the British
to admit it. Nevertheless, while the routine reception was
being given for Molotov, at the old Russian Embassy on
Unter den Linden, the British staged a raid over Berlin which
compelled the entire party to repair to the air raid shelter
underneath the adjacent Hotel Adlon. Stalin later told Churchill that as soon as the shelter door was shut, Ribbentrop
proposed that they continue the talks on the division of the
world. To this Molotov replied, "What will England say?"
"England," said Ribbentrop, "is finished. She is no more use
as a Power." "If that is so," said Molotov, "why are we in
this shelter, and whose are those bombs that fall?"[80]

However diverting these sidelights of Molotov's visit, what
was at stake could not have been more serious. This was,
in fact, the real turning point of World War II. Stalin, it
seems to me, must have been under a serious misapprehen-
sion as to the strength of his position. He was probably misled by the interest Ribbentrop had shown in trying to bind
Russia to the Axis side in the war. He evidently thought
this reflected a sense of weakness on the part of the Germans, and that this, in turn, increased Russia's bargaining
power. Molotov, in any case, arrived in Berlin with instructions
not only to pin the Germans down as to what they meant
when they talked about a new division of the world, but
also to demand very considerable concessions from the Germans in eastern Europe and the Balkans.

As the talks developed, Hitler, who viewed it as vitally
important at this time to keep Russia away from the Balkan
area, proposed to the Russians that they, as a substitute,
should regard the area south of the Caspian Sea in central
Asia—in other words, Persia, Afghanistan, and India—as

their natural field for expansion. Molotov smugly pocketed this suggestion without so much as a "thank you," and went on to insist, nevertheless, on the entire list of Soviet demands with respect to eastern Europe. He demanded the cessation of all German military activity in Finland, the recognition of Russian interests generally in the Balkans, Soviet bases on the Bosporus and the Dardanelles, virtually complete Soviet military control of Bulgaria and the entire area of the Straits. To these demands, which conflicted flatly with Germany's military interests, Molotov clung with that wooden stubbornness for which he came to be so well known in his later dealings with the United States. And this stiff position was reaffirmed, two weeks later, on November 26, 1940, in a diplomatic note to the German government. It is one of the most interesting documents in the history of Soviet foreign policy, showing clearly that Stalin still thought that he was in a position to exact a high price for lining up with the Axis in a four-power pact, and that all this palaver was only a form of preliminary bargaining.

In this, he grievously miscalculated. Hitler, whose head had now been turned by his series of brilliant military successes, was in no mood to trifle with Russia. To his various other anxieties and irritations, there was added the consideration that the German war economy was no longer able to provide the wherewithal to pay for the extensive imports of food and raw materials Germany was receiving from the Soviet Union. Germany could hope to continue to receive these deliveries only if she seized them by force. (Please note in passing that this was exactly the same motive which had moved the Germans to go into the Ukraine in 1918, at the time of the Treaty of Brest-Litovsk.)

Less than a month after the receipt of this note reaffirming the greedy Soviet demands, Hitler issued orders for the preparation of the so-called "Operation Barbarossa," designed— as was stated in the first sentence of the order—*"to crush Soviet Russia in a quick campaign . . .* even before the conclusion of the war against England."[81]

From this time on, the attack was a foregone conclusion. Whether Stalin realized this is uncertain. Churchill, in his history of the war, comments on the miscalculation and ignorance which Stalin displayed during that period, and describes him as being at that time "at once a callous, a crafty, and an ill-informed giant."[82] His behavior in those last months was certainly erratic. In some ways he went to great pains to appease the Germans, continuing liberal deliveries of raw materials and grain even at a time when the Germans had practically ceased to deliver any significant *quid pro quo.* There was also the extraordinary episode that occurred in early April 1941 on the occasion of the departure of the Japanese Foreign Minister, Matsuoka, from Moscow. After a gay farewell dinner in the Kremlin, Stalin, who normally never ventured out in public, accompanied the Japanese statesman to the station and appeared on the platform among the throng of astonished diplomats who had assembled to see Matsuoka off. He then astounded the company by asking where the German ambassador was and, on finding him, by going up to him, throwing his arm over his shoulders, and saying: "We must remain friends, and you must now do everything to that end." He then did the same thing with an utterly flabbergasted German acting military attaché, whom he had never seen before in his life.

In the remaining weeks before the German attack, Stalin consistently turned a deaf ear to the many people, including even some very bold Germans, who attempted to warn him of Hitler's developing intentions. On the other hand, he infuriated Hitler beyond words by interfering in Yugoslavia on the very eve of the German attack in that country. He just couldn't leave the Balkans alone.

The German attack was launched on the night of June 21-22. The unhappy German ambassador in Moscow, Count Schulenburg, a wise and able man who had attempted in vain to dissuade Hitler from this Russian adventure, and who was in fact destined to die, before the war was over, on a Nazi gallows, was obliged to visit Molotov in the middle of the night and to tell him of the German attack. Molotov's reply to this shattering news stands to me as an epitome of the weird hypocrisy by which this Russian-German relationship was marked throughout: "Can it really be"—said this iron-faced old representative of a regime which had only recently attacked its neighbor Finland, annexed three highly reluctant countries, and deported hundreds of thousands of the inhabitants of eastern Poland under conditions of shocking cruelty—"Can it really be that we have deserved this?"

I find this surpassed, if at all, only by Stalin's performance a year or two later at a banquet with Allied statesmen. Stalin, who loved to tease his own associates on such occasions, proposed a toast to Molotov, and then addressed him with the genial injunction: "Molotov, get up and tell them about your pact with the Germans."

The German attack signified the failure of the effort undertaken by Stalin, by concluding the Nonaggression Pact in 1939, to remain aloof from the European war—or to remain aloof from it at least until such time as the Germans and the Western powers should have exhausted their strength against each other. Why was it, then, that Stalin, contrary to his expectations, failed in the end to maintain his neutrality and to profit from the war as he had expected to do?

The first and main reason for this was the wholly unexpected course which the war took in the west. Here, by one of those curious contradictions with which history is so replete, it was both Western weakness and Western strength which turned Hitler's military power to the attack on Russia. It was Western weakness which made possible the ease of the German victory on the Continent and permitted Hitler to emerge from his conquest of France and the Low Countries with his ground forces almost unscathed. Had he suffered heavier losses in the west, he would never have courted the dangers of a two-front war—dangers which had caused Germany's failure in World War I, and of which he was very well aware. On the other hand, it was the moral strength of England under Churchill's leadership—the strength which dictated Britain's refusal to surrender even after the disaster of Dunkirk—which forced Hitler to widen the whole strategic theater of the war and persuaded him that he must attempt to eliminate by force of arms a Russia in the neutrality of which he had no confidence, and which refused to join the Axis except at an exorbitant price. Had France not fallen so easily, or had England not refused to fall at all, the German attack on Russia might never have occurred.

Neither of these developments could be foreseen in 1939; and Stalin hardly can be reproached, as a statesman, for failing to reckon with them at that time.

But there were other reasons as well for the failure of the Nonaggression Pact. One was the extreme distrust with which Hitler at all times regarded his Soviet associates in the pact. At no time had Hitler had any confidence in the durability of the arrangement. Only a few days after Ribbentrop's second trip to Moscow, in September 1939, Hitler expressed this lack of confidence very clearly in a directive to his mil-

itary leaders. The continued neutrality of Russia, he said,
could not be assured:

The trifling significance of treaties has been proved
on all sides in recent years. The greatest safeguard against
any Russian attack lies . . . in a prompt demonstration of German strength.[83]

You may well ask: Could this distrust be laid in any
way to the behavior of the Soviet government? Did this not
merely reflect Hitler's own unbounded cynicism—his distrust
of pacts in general? Would it have been any different had
this been a noncommunist Russia, or a differently behaved
one?

These are serious questions. It is impossible, of course,
to give definite answers to them, for they are hypothetical.
One can only note that there did crop out at every turn,
in Moscow's behavior towards the Nazis, the same negative
traits of Soviet diplomacy which subsequently became so apparent in the case of Russia's relations with the West: the
extreme secretiveness and slyness, the pervasive disingenuousness, the territorial and political greediness, and the addiction
to a diplomatic method characterized by the stubborn reiter-
ation of preconceived positions and demands rather than
by anything resembling a reasonable and flexible exchange
of opinions. That these traits of Soviet diplomacy irritated
the Germans, just as they later irritated the Allied governments, is clear. Whether the absence of such traits could have
deflected Hitler from his course is less certain. Moscow's
really impudent demands for control of the Balkans certainly
irritated Hitler and influenced importantly his calculations in
1941. But whether Moscow, by refraining from these demands, could have purchased immunity from the German
attack no one can say.

Only this is apparent: Stalin's Russia was not so constituted
as to be a very reliable or comfortable ally for any outside
force, whether it was the Western Allies or Nazi Germany
at the height of its wartime success. The ultimate aims of
Stalin's Russia were contrary to the wartime purposes of
both of the great warring parties in the West. Hitler, with
his brutal realism, recognized this, and was reconciled from
the start to the instability of the German-Soviet relationship
—to the fact that there would soon come a day when it
would have served its purpose and would have to end. The

Western democracies, also, had fair warning of this fact in their experience with Stalin's Russia throughout the 1930's, and even more in the behavior of Russia between 1939 and 1941. But by 1941 whatever sense of realism about Russia might once have resided in Western democratic opinion had once again been dimmed, as in World War I, by the emotionalism of the conflict with Germany. For this reason, Western opinion found it very easy to forget, after Hitler's attack on Russia, the lessons it should have learned about Stalin's qualifications as an ally.

23 Russia and the West as Allies

WHEN I think back on those years of World War II, when Russia and the West were associated in a common or at least a simultaneous military effort against Hitler, and when I reflect how much has happened since—how things have changed, how much that is now known was not known then—it seems to me that all this might have been a hundred years ago, so swiftly have the assumptions of that day been punctured and destroyed, so completely have its emotional and political currents disappeared into the past.

To do justice to this period, historically, it is not enough to look at the bare facts of the documentary record; one must also make an effort to conjure up the atmosphere of that day: the anxieties, the moods, the hopes, the illusions, the dreams, the seizures of bitterness, the strains of devoted wartime labor, the fixations and psychoses of militancy, by which the actors of the drama were animated. Unless one makes this effort—unless one shuts one's eyes and tries to re-create in memory and imagination this peculiar political-emotional climate, now so far behind us and so strange in retrospect—one cannot hope to be even reasonably just to the men involved.

There is nothing surprising about the fact that the diplo-

macy of the Western powers over these years should have
been subsequently the subject of much controversy. Russia
became involved in World War II, after all, in a manner
that would not have led one to assume automatically that
she would come out of it with any sensational diplomatic
or political successes. She had attempted to remain aloof from
the contest on the basis of a cynical deal with those
who caused it to break out in the first place—a deal
which in fact hastened and assured its beginning; a deal
which envisaged a sharing of the spoils with the aggressor,
as the reward for benevolent acquiescence in the aggression.
This deal had turned out badly; the assumptions on which it
was founded had failed to be substantiated; the aggressor
had turned on his would-be accomplices; Russia had herself
become the victim of attack. If, then, in 1941 she found herself unexpectedly fighting on the same side as the Western
Allies, this was certainly no doing of her political leaders.
They had not wanted it this way. It was a situation they
had done their best to avoid. *They* had not selected the
Western powers as allies; and indeed, in the months before
their own involuntary involvement, they had shown not only a
complete lack of concern but in some instances outright
hostility for the interests of the Western governments and
peoples. In such circumstances, one might have supposed,
they would have no particular claim on the gratitude or the
predisposition of those with whom they now found themselves accidentally associated in the military struggle against
Hitler, and no reason to expect that they should be particularly thanked or rewarded by those associates for such
military effort as they might be obliged to put forth in their
own defense. Nor would this situation appear to have been
affected in principle by the question as to whether this effort of defense on their part exceeded or did not exceed
the efforts being put forth simultaneously by the Western
Allies. There was, on the face of it, no obligation involved. There was no ostensible reason, surely, why in these
circumstances each party should not have been the exclusive arbiter of what its own interests required.

When one recalls all this, and then notes that Russia
emerged from this military contest in possession of half of
Europe, not to mention the gains in the Far East, and when
one reflects that all this occurred with the acquiescence, if
not the blessing, of the Western Allies at the moment, one

finds it not surprising that people in the West should subsequently have posed sharply and insistently the simple question: *Why?*

To answer this *Why?* it is not enough to look just at *Stalin's* diplomacy. People talk about Russia being an enigma wrapped in mystery, but I think this is overdone. The objectives of Soviet diplomacy, in the European theater at least, seem to me to have been simple and clear. They were almost precisely the same as they had been during the period of the Soviet-German Nonaggression Pact. Stalin wanted to retain the band of territory in eastern Europe which Hitler had tossed to him in 1939. In addition, he wanted all those things that Molotov had demanded of Hitler in November 1940: military and political control of Finland, Rumania, Bulgaria, and Turkey; influence in the Balkans generally—and so on. Only now it was the Allies, not Hitler, of whom these things were being demanded.

Soviet *methods*, too, were not really very complicated. There were two ways in which Stalin could hope to get the things he wanted. One was to seize them in the course of military operations and not to let go; the other was to induce the Allies to promise that they should be conceded to the Soviet Union in the future peace settlement. The first of these means depended on the course of military operations; the other depended directly on the disposition of the Allied governments. But actually, even the first was something which the Allied governments had it within their power to influence. They could influence it, to some extent, by their own military dispositions: by endeavoring to get to certain places with their forces before the Russians did. They could influence it by the nature of their strategic plans and by the emphasis they placed on various theaters of war. They could influence it by the shaping of their war aims and by the conditions which they were prepared to place on any termination of hostilities. The insistence, for example, on unconditional surrender and complete occupation of Germany implied, of course, that the Soviet military advance into Europe would proceed to the ultimate point of encounter with the forces of the Allies; a different policy would not necessarily have implied this. Please understand that I am not attempting to pass judgment at this point as to whether a different policy should have been followed. I am only saying that it was within the power of the Allies to influence these developments *to some extent* by their military and political decisions of the day.

Stalin and Molotov played their cards, throughout this period, in the customary Stalinist way: persistently, cautiously, slyly, taking good care to see that no card ever lay face-up on the table, following the game with the utmost seriousness, and viewing their adversaries, the Allied governments, without confidence, sympathy, or pity. In general, they played these cards ably and correctly—a minor mistake, perhaps, here and there, but basically a sound game. Nevertheless, theirs was, initially, the weaker hand. Had the other hand been played with equal coolness and skill and competitiveness of spirit, Soviet successes certainly would scarcely have been of this order.

I was serving in Berlin at the time of the German attack on Russia on June 22, 1941. We had seen evidence that something of this sort might be in the making; but we could not, of course, be sure until the news came through that it would actually occur. I was awakened with the news very early in the morning. Too excited to sleep, I went down to the office before breakfast. I can remember looking at the map and reflecting that the German troops were starting at precisely the same river—the Neman—and on almost precisely the same day of the year—June 22—that the forces of Napoleon began their advance in 1812. My head whirling with the realization of the implications of this development, I sat down and penned a little note to the head of the Russian division in the Department of State. What I said in it was nothing for which I wish to take any credit of hindsight. It was, I think, only what any American would have said who had lived long years in Russia and eastern Europe. Here we were, I wrote, and this thing about which all of us had been speculating had occurred. I realized that we would have no choice but to give Russia material aid, to enable her to defend her territory and to prevent a sweeping German victory in the east; but I did want to voice the hope that never would we associate ourselves with Russian purposes in the areas of eastern Europe beyond her own borders.

What I did not realize when I wrote those words was that it was already too late. One week earlier, aware of the German plans for attacking Russia, Churchill had wired Roosevelt that, should the German attack take place, the British would . . .

... of course, give all encouragement and any help we can spare to the Russians, following the principle that Hitler is the foe we have to beat.[84]

Roosevelt had replied that he would immediately support publicly "any announcement that the Prime Minister might make welcoming Russia as an ally."[85] On that very day of the German attack, while I penned my futile little note, Churchill was busily preparing a radio speech in which he would say:

... Any man or state who fights on against Nazidom will have our aid.... It follows, therefore, that we shall give whatever help we can to Russia and the Russian people....
The Russian danger is ... our danger, and the danger of the United States, just as the cause of any Russian fighting for his hearth and home is the cause of free men and free peoples in every quarter of the globe.[86]

In these statements, there were no reservations about Soviet ambitions beyond the Soviet borders.

I cite these things because to me they signify that the general nature of the Allied response to Stalin's wartime objectives was largely established by the time the German attack took place. It was not so much the decisions developed by the Allied statesmen *after* Russia became involved in the war which were determining: it was rather the attitudes and habits of mind with which they greeted the German attack on Russia, in the first instance. It was, in short, their concept of the war as a whole.

The view which Churchill expressed was, let us remember, not the only view one could have taken. One might very well have said to Stalin:

"Look here, old boy, our memories are no shorter than yours. We know very well how you tried to arrange your affairs in this war. We are perfectly aware of the feeling toward us by which your pact with Hitler was inspired. Now you have come a cropper in your effort to collaborate with Hitler, and that is your affair. If you are interested in receiving our material and military aid, we will give it to you precisely in the measure that we find suitable and for precisely so long as this suits our purposes. Meanwhile we want no sentimentality and no nonsense. You have revealed to us what your aims are in

Europe; and while we may help you to repel the German invaders, you may expect small comfort from us in those of your ambitions which extend beyond the territory that was recognized as yours up to 1938."

To understand why this was *not* said, you must remember a number of things. You must remember, above all, the tremendous strain and anxiety under which the Allied statesmen were then laboring, and particularly Churchill. Britain was fighting alone, against preposterous odds. The outbreak of war between Germany and Russia was the first ray of hope Englishmen had seen in this war. Our own country, while aiding Britain in various ways, was not yet participating militarily. Had it been doing so, England would presumably not have needed Russia so badly; and this is why any criticism from our side of Churchill's reaction of that moment comes with a certain ill grace. As it was, Western statesmen considered that the entire fate of the war depended on the readiness and ability of Russia to stand up to the German attack. A Western attitude which did not include the profession of a political sympathy for Russia could, they felt, bring discouragement to the Russian people—Russia's resistance might weaken; there might be a capitulation or a quick destruction of the Russian army comparable to what had occurred in France. Any words of warmth and support which could help to forestall or even delay such an eventuality ought, it was felt, to be given. Finally, I suspect, F.D.R. may also have felt that the American Congress would not be likely to support aid to Russia on a major scale unless an atmosphere of political intimacy with the Soviet government could be created and maintained.

Not all of these reasons were entirely sound. In particular, the picture Churchill painted of an aroused Russian people, heroically resisting the German invader and thirsting for the sympathy and companionship of the Allies in the cause, was—at the least—premature. This was a repetition of the persistent Allied error of World War I. Many hundreds of thousands of Russian soldiers would go over voluntarily to the Germans, and many Russian villages would welcome the Germans with hope and relief, before the Russian people generally could become convinced that the enemy they faced across the battle line was even uglier than the regime to which they had been obliged to adjust themselves at home. Even in later stages of the war, there were times when Russian discipline rested as much on fear of the threat from behind—the commissar's bullet in the back—as on righteous anger at the threat that lay before.

But the reasons given by Churchill for accepting Russia as a military ally were, if not founded on an accurate picture of the Russian scene, at least natural and understandable. The same cannot be said—at least, I cannot say it —about certain other of the components in the view taken of the Russians by the Allied chanceries in those wartime years. I have in mind here what seems to me to have been an inexcusable body of ignorance about the nature of the Russian Communist movement, about the history of its diplomacy, about what had happened in the purges, and about what had been going on in Poland and the Baltic States. I also have in mind F.D.R.'s evident conviction that Stalin, while perhaps a somewhat difficult customer, was only, after all, a person like any other person; that the reason we hadn't been able to get along with him in the past was that we had never really had anyone with the proper personality and the proper qualities of sympathy and imagination to deal with him, that he had been snubbed all along by the arrogant conservatives of the Western capitals; and that if only he could be exposed to the persuasive charm of someone like F.D.R. himself, ideological preconceptions would melt and Russia's co-operation with the West could be easily arranged. For these assumptions, there were no grounds whatsoever; and they were of a puerility that was unworthy of a statesman of F.D.R.'s stature.

These were, then, some of the feelings which caused both Washington and London to accept Russia gratefully and enthusiastically as an ally, or at least as a friendly associate, even before there had been any opportunity to test the temper of Soviet diplomacy in the light of the German attack. What ensued with regard to major political problems seems to me to have flowed naturally and logically from these background attitudes. Let us recall, in rough outline, the sequence of these events.

Stalin was not long in making known to his new associates his desire for those same extensions of Russian power in eastern Europe and the Balkans which he had either received from Hitler or vainly demanded of him. These desiderata were quite clearly stated to the British Foreign Secretary, Anthony Eden, when he visited Moscow at the end of 1941,

only six months after the German attack. They were not
very insistently or unpleasantly stated on this occasion. In
particular, they did not contain any hint of a determination
to unseat the Polish government-in-exile, which since the
beginning of the war had been functioning in London. On
the contrary, almost immediately after the German attack,
Stalin, evidently concerned at that moment not to sacrifice
needlessly any possible source of support against the rapidly
advancing Germans, had recognized the government-in-exile,
had established regular diplomatic relations with it, and had
concluded with it a far-reaching political agreement which
had clearly implied his acceptance of it as the legitimate
government of the postwar Poland. The agreement envisaged
the liberation of the hundreds of thousands of Polish citizens
then imprisoned or otherwise detained in Russia, and the
setting up on Soviet territory of a Polish armed force to
fight the Germans on the Soviet side. The agreement had
not, to be sure, disposed of the problem of the Polish-
Soviet border. To the Prime Minister of the Polish government-in-exile, General W. Sikorski, who had visited Moscow
just before Eden, Stalin had indicated that Russia would
expect to retain, at the end of the war, the major part of
the territory which had fallen to it by virtue of the
Nonaggression Pact agreements with Hitler in 1939. Sikorski
had evaded discussion of this subject, and nothing had been
agreed; but the very fact that Stalin was willing to discuss
it with Sikorski, and to pursue some sort of compromise
agreement about it, suggested a readiness on the Soviet side
to accept for the postwar period the principle of a genuinely
independent Poland, if not one quite within its old borders.

When these same Soviet desiderata concerning the Polish
border were voiced to Eden in December 1941, he asked
for time in order that he might consult the American government and the British dominions. He did not, however, turn
down out of hand the suggestion for border changes; and
this must have been taken by Stalin then and there as a
strong sign that something would be done, in the end, to
meet his territorial demands.

Initially, both London and Washington appeared to be
shocked at the suggestion that they should be asked to
guarantee to Stalin the fruits of his previous deal with the
Germans. But this resistance did not last long. As early as
March 1942, Churchill had come around to the belief that
one would, after all, have to give Stalin some satisfaction so

far as eastern Poland was concerned. He was not yet able to bring himself to a readiness to concede the Baltic States as well, which Stalin was also claiming. In Washington, Secretary of State Cordell Hull was strongly averse to making any concessions at all; and F.D.R. initially supported him. F.D.R.'s position was the one Americans customarily like to take in wartime: We don't make decisions about territorial questions while the fighting is going on; we concentrate on the total defeat of the enemy and leave political matters to the peace conference. But one does not get—at least I do not—the impression that Roosevelt had any substantive objections—any real political objections—to seeing these areas go to Russia, or indeed that he cared much about the issue for its own sake. One gets the impression that it seemed to him of little importance whether these areas were Polish or Russian. His anxiety was rather that he had a large body of voting constituents in this country of Polish or Baltic origin, and a further number who sympathized with the Poles, and he simply did not want this issue to become a factor in domestic politics which could make trouble for his wartime leadership of the country. Therefore, he opposed discussion of it at the moment.

During the first half of 1942, the question of future borders in eastern Europe was extensively fouled up with the question of a second front. Stalin was vehement and insistent in his demands that a second front be created at once in France, in order to relieve German military pressure on Russia. The American military leaders were very anxious that this be done. The British, on the other hand, with the lesson of Dunkirk still ringing in their ears, were equally determined not to become rashly or prematurely involved in this sort of venture. As the year developed the British had their way, and the plan for such an operation was abandoned; but not, unfortunately, before F.D.R. had gone very far, with Churchill's reluctant acquiescence, in encouraging the Russians and the world public to believe that such a second front would be created within the year. It was Churchill himself who finally, in August 1942, had to perform the unpleasant task of going to Moscow and apprising Stalin, with the German advance in Russia then at its maximum point and its maximum strength, that the Allies were not going to create a second front in Europe after all, during that particular year, though there would indeed be an attempt at a landing in North Africa.

Let me explain why these differences over a second front, which were much more tense and dramatic than I have been able to indicate here, were closely connected with the problem of Stalin's territorial demands in eastern Europe. One of the reasons why F.D.R. was so eager for a second front to be created was that he saw this as a means of placating Stalin and reconciling him to the postponement of the discussion of territorial problems until the peace conference. When it was finally recognized as impossible to create a second front at any early date, with the result that the Allies were obliged to sit by, month after month, in the European theater, while the Russian armies absorbed almost the entire impact of Hitler's vast war machine, this gave the Allied statesmen—naturally and inevitably, I am afraid—a pervasive feeling of guilt and inadequacy. The inability to open a second front heightened, in 1942, the fears that Stalin might be led to abandon the war in some way or other, thus permitting the Germans to turn against the West before the United States was prepared to assume its share of the burden of combat. People in London and Washington were inclined to feel that the only means available to them for decreasing this danger was the adoption of a reasonably sympathetic and encouraging attitude towards Soviet postwar aspirations. If they were still reluctant, at that early date, to make any firm promises in this regard, they were very reluctant to confront Stalin with anything so discouraging as a flat "no." They feared its effect on his willingness to continue the fight. Thus the natural distaste with which they first regarded these territorial demands was gradually eroded; and we must regard this erosion, I am afraid, as only another part of the great price the Western democracies were compelled to pay for their own military weakness in the initial phases of the war.

It would be wrong, of course, to assume that only military considerations entered into the tolerance the Western governments developed for Stalin's territorial demands. By 1942 and 1943, particularly, wartime emotionalism was beginning to take its toll. What memories there were of the Nonaggression Pact of 1939 began to fade. People who tried to point to unpleasant facts in the record of Soviet diplomacy, or to voice doubt about the political intentions of the Soviet leaders, were apt to find themselves brusquely put in their places—sometimes even charged with disrupting Allied unity and sabotaging the war effort.

So far as Poland was concerned (and Poland, remember, was at all times the center of the problem on the European side), the situation suffered a very serious deterioration in 1943, when the Germans triumphantly announced the discovery, on occupied Russian territory, in a place called the Katyn Forest, of mass graves containing the bodies of thousands of Polish officers who had been taken prisoner by the Russians in 1939. The men had obviously been cruelly executed, one by one, at the edge of the great pits, the bodies being then pushed in.

The Russians, at the time of their entry into eastern Poland in 1939, appear to have made it a policy to arrest and deport to Russia all Polish officers on whom they could lay hands. Three camps were originally established to house these prisoners. They had contained in all about 15,000 men. At the time the Germans announced their discovery, not one of these men had been heard of since April 1940, more than a year before the German attack on Russia. Ever since the resumption of their relations with the Soviet government in 1941, the London Poles had been bombarding Moscow with requests for information about the whereabouts or the fate of these men. They had received only evasive and wholly unsatisfactory replies. The graves discovered by the Germans, it soon developed, contained the bodies of men from one of the three camps. The fate of the inmates of the other two camps remains a mystery down to this day. The German government, in announcing the discovery, asked for an investigation by the International Red Cross. The Polish government-in-exile, after some anguish, associated itself with this request. The Allies were furious at them for doing this, correctly fearing that it would anger the Russians. It is hard, in retrospect, to see how the Poles could have done less.

The Soviet reaction, in any case, was violent. Moscow alleged that the men had been found alive by the advancing Germans, in 1941, and that it was the Germans themselves who had shot them. It savagely attacked the Poles for abetting German propaganda by agreeing to an investigation. Within a fortnight after the German announcement, the Soviet government broke relations entirely with the London Poles. From that moment on, Moscow applied itself to combating

the Polish government-in-exile with every means at its disposal, and to building up the nucleus of a new Polish Communist government which could take over after the liberation
of Poland. Stalin, plainly, was determined that the government of the future Poland should not be the sponsor of
charges that the Soviet government had deliberately murdered nearly 15,000 officer prisoners of war.

The Western governments never did willingly acquiesce in
this new Soviet bid to dominate entirely the political
life of the future Poland. They seem in fact never to
have realized how burning a challenge the Katyn charges
were for Moscow, or the effect they had on Soviet diplomacy.
To the end of the war, and for some time after, Washington
and London would profess themselves bewildered and somewhat hurt over Moscow's unwillingness to deal with the
London Poles, and its evident determination to control completely the future Poland.

All this, however, did not prevent the Allies from slipping still further into a position of acquiescence in Stalin's
territorial demands in Europe. Not only did they acquiesce,
but they were, by 1943, in some ways the moving spirits
in this development. At the Tehran Conference in November
1943 both Churchill and Roosevelt urged upon Stalin the
device that was eventually to be adopted: namely, that of
moving Poland bodily several hundred miles to the west,
thus making way for the satisfaction of Russian demands
in the east and letting the Germans pay the bill by turning
over to Poland extensive territories, going even as far as the
Oder, from which many millions of German inhabitants
would have to be displaced. It is hard for me now to understand—and it was hard at that time—how anyone could
fail to recognize that a Poland with borders so artificial,
ones which involved so staggering a dislocation of population,
would inevitably be dependent for its security on Soviet protection. To put Poland in such borders was to make it
perforce a Russian protectorate, whether its own government
was Communist or not. Whether Churchill or Roosevelt
realized this, I cannot say. In any case, this proposal for
moving Poland westward, with its utter lack of regard for
the future political stability of eastern Europe and with
its flagrant defiance of the principles of the Atlantic Charter
of which Roosevelt and Churchill were themselves the au-

thors, came—I am sorry to say—primarily from them rather
than from Stalin.

Outside of Poland, the satisfaction of Stalin's aspirations in
the European theater flowed almost automatically from the
course of military operations. The Western governments never
specifically sanctioned, I believe, the incorporation of the
Baltic States into the Soviet Union; and Stalin had, as it
turned out, no need to insist that they do so, since he ended
up in military control of these areas anyway, and had only
himself to consult about their disposition. The same applied
to the Balkan countries, with the exception of Turkey. At
the Yalta Conference, in January 1945, Roosevelt and
Churchill attempted to take some of the sting out of this
situation by binding Stalin to the terms of the so-called
Yalta Declaration on Liberated Europe, which said that the
three countries would concert their policies in order to assure to the liberated peoples of Europe representative and
democratic governments, responsive to the will of the people.
This was, of course, a futile gesture, and one which no
doubt would have been better avoided. Churchill and Roosevelt had no excuse for not knowing, by this time, that all
this vague and general political terminology had one meaning to them and an entirely different one to Stalin. To suggest,
however, as has been so frequently done in political debate in
the United States, that it was this declaration which delivered the respective peoples into Soviet hands, is wholly erroneous. The peoples in question had for the most
part already fallen into Communist hands at that time, or
would have done so anyway in the course of the military
operations of the war, even if this declaration had never
been devised; and once in control, Moscow would not have
dreamed of letting them go just because of a lack of
Allied approval. Aside from the question of Poland, it was
the course of military operations, not the futile efforts of the
Western statesmen to bind Stalin by public professions of
high ideals, which delivered eastern Europe into his hands.
And the only way this might conceivably have been prevented by the Western governments would have been either
the termination of the war on some basis other than unconditional surrender (for unconditional surrender was only
another way of saying that the war had to be fought until
the Allied and Russian armies met *somewhere*) or the creation of a successful second front in Europe at a much

earlier date, thus assuring that the Soviet and Allied armies would meet farther east than was actually the case.

Of all the motives I have mentioned to you for Western acquiescence in Soviet desiderata, the consciousness—up to 1944, at least—of the enormous military load the Russians were bearing and the fear that, if not treated sympathetically, they might attempt to lay this burden down were unquestionably the strongest. So much is this the case that even had Communist penetration in the United States government been as great as has sometimes been alleged, the historian would still have to say that in the United States the principal source of the policy of material aid and political concessions to Russia during the war was the Pentagon, as exemplified in the persons of the highest military leaders—men hardly to be suspected of Communist sympathies. There was indeed much error and misestimation behind the attitudes of Roosevelt and Churchill towards Russia during the war; but if one really wants to find a touchstone for the appraisal of their wartime policies, this touchstone will be found not in the field of political sympathy but in the soundness and accuracy of their fears with relation to the possibility of a separate German-Soviet peace.

This is a question which might well bear a great deal more study than I myself have been able to give it, and more than has been given to it, so far as I know, by anyone else to date. I felt personally at the time, and feel today, that this fear was greatly exaggerated; and that it would not have been nearly so great had those who entertained it taken greater pains to inform themselves of the history and the nature of the Soviet movement. I find it difficult to see at what stage anything of this sort—anything, that is, in the nature of a separate German-Soviet peace—could have occurred. During the first year and a half after the Soviet attack—up to the completion of the battle of Stalingrad, that is—Hitler would scarcely have been inclined to break off hostilities on any terms less than ones which would have required the complete dismantling of Russian military force, even beyond the final line of battle, and the extensive subordination of Russian political life to German military missions and advisers. The only conceivable purpose for which Hitler could have contemplated an interruption of hostilities in the east, during this period, would have been in order to turn his forces again westwards, against England. But to make this switch before he had achieved the complete destruction of Russian military power would have been to abandon the principal objective of the entire Russian campaign, which was to eliminate Russia as a factor in the war before tackling the problem of the reduction of the British Isles. To have interrupted the Russian campaign in this way, before it was completed, and to have attempted to turn the whole great German war machine around, while at the same time continuing some sort of defensive line in Russia, would have made no sense at all. If *this* was the necessity, then it would have been better never to have attacked Russia in the first place and to have rested on the far more easily defensible line in eastern Europe. For these reasons, it seems to me most unlikely that *Hitler* would have been inclined to break off the engagement on anything less than terms which would have assured the complete destruction of the Russian army and given him effective control of even those parts of Russia he did not yet occupy. He would have had to demand extensive sanctions: there could be no good faith between himself and Stalin.

But would Stalin have accepted such terms? In my opinion: never. Confronted with such demands he and his associates would, I am sure, have taken reference at once to the celebrated precedent of Brest-Litovsk. They would have remembered that while Lenin, in 1918, was willing to trade space for time and to consent to a great narrowing of the area to which Soviet power extended, with a view to turning the German thrust toward the west and thus achieving a breathing-space during which Germany and the Western powers might exhaust each other in mutual combat, he would never have accepted conditions which restricted the freedom of action of the Soviet government within such territory as was left to it, or which prevented it from doing what it could to build up an armed force for its own protection. Rather than accept such conditions, he would have retired to the most remote village of Siberia, thus imposing on his adversary the choice between desisting from the pursuit or attempting the genuinely impossible task of occupying all of Russia. Stalin, I am sure, would have reacted in exactly the same way. His military power might have been even more terribly destroyed than it was. He might have had to retire not only behind the Volga but even farther east. His regime might have become, momentarily, the government

only of the Urals and Siberia. This would still have been pref-
erable, in his eyes, to acceptance of German terms which
undermined in any way the plenitude of Soviet power in
such territories as were left to it. This was the lesson, incidentally, not only of Brest-Litovsk but also of Russian behavior in the war with Napoleon, in 1812.

After Stalingrad, of course, the shoe was on the other
foot. By this time the Germans were on the defensive. Hitler,
to be sure, might then have welcomed some sort of deal by
which he could have held the line and avoided losses in
the east in order to free his forces for the growing contest
in the west. But surely there was not the faintest prospect
that Stalin, at this stage of the game, could be interested
in such a deal. Why should he contemplate a deal with the
Germans when they were still on Soviet territory and when
he had them on the run? To have done this would have
been to invite one or the other of two most horrendous
eventualities. One was that the Allies might complete the
destruction of Germany's armed power, march deeply into
Europe, and emerge as occupiers in the east of the Continent
as well as in the west. The other was that the Allies, discouraged by Russia's departure from the struggle, might make a
compromise peace with Germany at Russia's expense.

Especially in the period following the Normandy landings
in 1944, there was not the faintest possibility of a unilateral
Russian withdrawal from the war. With Allied forces now on
the Continent, Stalin was passionately determined to get to
the center of Europe, and particularly to the center of
Germany, before the Allies did. At this time, surely, the
Allies had no further reason to reckon, in devising their
policies, with the possibility of a separate German-Soviet
peace.

Yet it was three months after the Normandy landings, at
a time when the second front was already a successful reality,
when Paris had already been liberated and Allied troops
were at the gates of Germany, and when the liberation of
Soviet territory itself—the Soviet territory of 1938, at any
rate—was no longer at stake, that there took place the
most arrogant and unmistakable demonstration of the Soviet
determination to control eastern Europe in the postwar
period: Stalin's reaction to the Warsaw uprising—a demonstration so revealing that no one in the West had the slightest
excuse for ignoring its lessons. You will recall what happened on this occasion: how the members of the Polish un-

derground, operated by the Polish government-in-exile, tried
to seize the city from the retreating Germans; how the Soviet
forces paused at the gates of Warsaw for many days, letting
the Germans make short shrift of this resistance; and how,
when the United States government asked permission to use
the facilities of the American air bases in Russia with a view
to dropping supplies by parachute to the beleaguered Poles,
Stalin's answer was a snarling no. How could it have been
more clearly demonstrated that Russia was claiming the future
Poland as its own and proposed to make no concessions to
the democratic forces in that country?

I can see that up to the establishment of the second front
a good case could have been made for letting military considerations dominate American policy, and even for attempting to avoid and delay a general political discussion with
the Soviet government. But from that time, and particularly
from the moment of the Warsaw uprising, I can see no
more justification for this whatsoever. We owed the Russians
nothing more, at this time, in the way of a second front.
Soviet territory had been almost completely liberated from
the German invaders. What was at stake from September
1944 on was only the question of Russian postwar aims
in eastern and central Europe; and on this subject we no
longer had the right to entertain any illusions.

Let us remember, in particular, that a considerable portion
of American Lend-Lease aid, particularly industrial equipment, reached Russia after this date. It was after this date
that both the Yalta and Potsdam conferences took place.
It was after this date that we decided to associate ourselves
with the Soviet armistice commissions in the Balkans. It was
after this date that we entered into the Declaration on Liberated Europe, made the unreal and unwise deal over
Poland, and exerted ourselves mightily to bring Russia into
the United Nations. Would it not have been better to have
paused at that time, to have had, then and there, the frank
and unsparing political clarification with Stalin which the
situation demanded? If that clarification did not give us real assurance of a basic alteration of Soviet behavior, then we
should have abandoned at once and for all the dangerous
dream of collaboration with Stalin's Russia in the postwar
era and have taken every conceivable measure to rescue
what could still be rescued. This might not have been much.
It would scarcely have been Poland. It might have been
Prague; and it might have been Berlin—Berlin in a sense

that would at least have spared us the embarrassment in which we find ourselves today.

One more afterthought. At the bottom of this whole subject lay the commitment of the Western Allies to the principle of unconditional surrender. It is idle, I think, to try to assign to either Churchill or Roosevelt the exclusive responsibility for this commitment. I cannot see that it was ever absent from the calculations of either government. England, after all, had bound herself as early as 1941 never to make a separate peace without Russia; and anyone who knows anything at all about military coalitions knows that the hardest thing in the world for such a coalition to do is to agree on the terms of anything as delicate as a compromise peace with the enemy. This was, as I said earlier, a commitment which would in any case have necessitated the carrying of the war to the bitter conclusion of a meeting of the Russian and Allied armies in the heart of Europe.

Could this have been otherwise? It is true that no useful purpose could have been served by any attempt to compromise with Hitler. From this standpoint, unconditional surrender made much more sense in World War II than it had made in World War I, when a compromise peace could presumably have been had, at one stage or another, on terms not wholly catastrophic, had one cared to pursue it.

But there was not only Hitler, in Germany. There was also the non-Communist German resistance. It was composed of men who were very brave and very lonely, and were so much closer to us in feeling and in ideals than they were to either Hitler or Stalin that the difference between them and us paled, comparatively, into insignificance. These men succeeded, at the cost of great personal and political danger, in establishing contact with the Allies during the war. They received literally no encouragement from the Allied side. They were obliged to carry out their tragic effort to unseat Hitler, on July 20, 1944, not only with the total absence of Allied support at that particular moment, but with no assurance of Allied support in future, or even of more lenient peace terms, in the event they should succeed and take Germany out of the war. The unconditional surrender policy, which implied that Germany would be treated with equal severity whether or not Hitler was overthrown, simply cut the ground out from under any moderate German opposition.

Would greater sympathy and helpfulness from the Allied

side have assured the success of these lonely conspirators? Who can say? They nearly succeeded as it was. One can say only that the effort, on the Allied side, was never made; and that seems to me a pity.

Roosevelt and Churchill did not like the German resistance movement. They did not understand it. One is depressed to observe, in their respective wartime statements, the extent to which they both carried into the Second World War all the prejudices of the first: how little they recognized the true lower-middle-class basis of the Nazi movement; how sure they both were that it was still the Prussian Junkers they were fighting—and how seriously they misjudged this conservative class itself; how little they realized what resources of courage and idealism the sons and daughters of just these people, scourged by the consciousness of Hitler's degradation of their country, would succeed in producing out of their bewildered midst.

And this leads me to the last thing I have to say. It is that the mistakes made in dealing with the Russians during World War II flowed not just from exaggerated military anxieties and from liberal illusions about the nature of *Soviet* society. A considerable importance must also be assigned to the seeming inability of a democratic state to cultivate and to hold in mind anything like a realistic image of a wartime adversary. The Nazi movement was in many ways a terrible thing: one of the most fearful manifestations modern history has to show of the delusions to which men are prone and the evil of which they are capable when they cut loose from all inhibitions of method and sell their souls to the pursuit of a total end. But this movement was not purely an act of God. It was not an evil miracle. It was a human tragedy, and one of which a great many German people were sufferers no less than others. No one would plead that the Allies should have blinded themselves to the danger of Hitler's ambitions or even to those deficiencies in the German experience and the German character which had made possible his rule. But had the statesmen of the West been able to look at Germany more thoughtfully and more dispassionately, to liberate themselves from the prejudices of World War I, to distinguish ruler from ruled, to search for the true origins of what had occurred, to recognize the measure of responisbility the Western democracies themselves had for the rise of Nazism in the first

place, and to remember that it was on the strength and hope
of the German people, along with the others, that any tolerable postwar future for Europe would have to be built—
had they been able to comprehend all this it would have
helped them to understand the relationship of Russia to
Germany in the war, to achieve a better balance in their dealings with both of these troublesome and problematical forces
and thus, perhaps, to avoid or mitigate some of the most
grievous of the war's political consequences.

In this day of another great political-emotional preoccupation, when the image of the Soviet leaders has replaced that
of Hitler in so many Western minds as the center and source
of all possible evil, it is perhaps particularly desirable that
we should remember these things. Let us not repeat the
mistake of believing that either good or evil is total. Let us
beware, in future, of wholly condemning an entire people
and wholly exculpating others. Let us remember that the
great moral issues, on which civilization is going to stand or
fall, cut across all military and ideological borders, across
peoples, classes, and regimes—across, in fact, the make-up of
the human individual himself. No other people, as a whole,
is entirely our enemy. No people at all—not even ourselves—
is entirely our friend.

24   Russia and the War in Asia

IT WILL be remembered that following the Russian Revolution, the Japanese took advantage of Russia's weakness to challenge the residual Russian positions in the Far
East. They first extorted from the Russians a number of
oil and coal concessions on northern Sakhalin. A decade
later they completed their domination of the Manchurian
area by invading northern Manchuria and creating there the
puppet state of Manchukuo. As I mentioned earlier, the
Soviet government saw itself obliged to sell the Chinese

Eastern Railway to this puppet government, thus liquidating all that was left of Russia's special position in Manchuria.

Down to the outbreak of war in Europe, the Japanese military pressure in Manchuria was so powerful that Stalin had his hands full just to keep the Japanese from crossing the border and seizing portions of the Soviet Far East and Outer Mongolia as well. By the time war broke out in Europe, a virtual war, undeclared but by no means trivial in scale, was already being waged between the Russians and the Japanese along the Manchurian-Mongolian frontier.

As part of the Nonaggression Pact of 1939, the Germans undertook to use their influence with the Japanese to get them to desist from further pressures of this sort on the Soviet frontiers in the Far East. Whether it was because of these German representations or because the Japanese calculated that more important things were in the wind, I do not know; but the Japanese did at once lay off. With the characteristic dialectical good sense of the East, they maintained this attitude throughout the period up to the German attack on Russia in 1941.

The German defeat of France and the Low Countries, in early 1940, and the difficulties which England was by this time suffering, were all—of course—of intense interest to the Japanese. The weakness of these mother countries rendered their colonial dependencies in southeastern Asia vulnerable and very tempting to Japanese seizure. Here were opportunities for Japanese expansion—opportunities, in particular, for assuring raw material supplies to Japanese industry—which overshadowed those implicit in a seizure of eastern Siberia. But the exploitation of these possibilities was dependent, of course, on a final German victory over the European mother countries. This, presumably, was one of the main reasons why Japan, in September 1940, joined the Axis and why she committed herself increasingly, from that time on, to the policy of expanding towards the south which was finally to lead her to war with the United States.

All of this was, of course, a great blessing to the Russians. When the Japanese Foreign Minister, Yosuke Matsuoka, visited Moscow shortly before the German attack in 1941 the two governments reached a compromise agreement, a Neutrality Pact, providing that either side would remain neutral if the other were attacked by third parties. Primarily, this pact was aimed at the United States. Stalin, by this means, encouraged Japan to move south and east, into the Pacific area. He promised, in effect, that if this led to war between Japan and the United States, Russia would not interfere or take advantage of Japan's situation. Japan, conversely, agreed in effect not to intervene if Russia became involved with Germany. Russia recognized Japan's hegemony in Manchuria; Japan recognized Russia's position in Outer Mongolia. The two countries, in other words—one being confronted with great opportunities, the other with great dangers, in other theaters—agreed for the moment on a moratorium in the rivalry over East Asia.

When the German attack on Russia came, a few weeks later, the Japanese respected this Neutrality Pact, and did not try to take advantage of Russia's plight. Instead, in December of the same year, they attacked the United States at Pearl Harbor, and the Pacific war was on. It was now the Russian turn to show forbearance. In other circumstances, they would have been delighted to take advantage of the Japanese preoccupation with the war in the Pacific and to seize the opportunity to improve their position in Manchuria. But their war with Germany left them no breath or resources for this purpose. Thus they, too, were content for the moment to remain faithful to the Neutrality Pact with Japan. In this sense, it may be said that if we failed to create a second front in Europe, the Russians also failed to create one in the Pacific.

We were, of course, extremely anxious from the start for the Russians to enter the Pacific war, and did not conceal this from them. But throughout 1942 and most of 1943, Stalin refused, in the light of his difficult military situation in the west, to discuss anything of this nature. By late 1943, however, as the turn of the tide in the European war became more clearly confirmed, and as the prospects for American victory over Japan became stronger, Stalin's mind must have been increasingly preoccupied with the thought that Japan's final defeat would present Russia with a magnificent opportunity for reversing all those gains the Japanese had made since the Russo-Japanese War, for taking back the assets of which Russia had been deprived, for gaining strategic control over the entrances of the Sea of Japan, and for replacing the Japanese, generally, as the dominant power in the Manchurian and Korean areas. The question was only how to go about this. To do it in collaboration with the United States, at the risk of having a lot of well-meaning and idealistic people breathing down your neck at the crucial moments, claiming a voice in your affairs, and enjoining you to restrain yourself in the name of the Atlantic Charter? Or to do it alone, at the moment of Japan's maximum weakness, without any prior agreement with the Americans? This last was fine in some ways; but you risked the chance that the Americans might get there first. You also risked the chance that you might get into a row with the Chinese —which, in view of the complicated political situation in China, could be troublesome if not dangerous.

This problem was both simplified and complicated for Stalin by conflicting American attitudes. Official Washington, in the first place, had no objection in principle to seeing outlying territories taken away from Japan. Considerations of self-determination and the terms of the Atlantic Charter, which had barred territorial changes that did not accord with the expressed wishes of the people affected, were evidently not regarded as relevant, in this instance. We were strongly for the dismemberment of the Japanese Empire and we had no objection to seeing these matters determined in advance. When it came to Europe, we were sternly insistent that there must be no discussion, while the war was on, of postwar political and territorial changes. But by virtue of that curious inconsistency which causes Americans to reverse so many principles when the gaze goes westward rather than eastward, all this seems not to have applied to the Far East.

In addition to having no obligation to seeing territories taken away from Japan, wartime Washington had no qualms, in principle, about seeing some of these acquisitions go to Russia. The Russians had been bravely resisting the Germans. We were sympathetic towards them, unhappy about our inability to create a second front in Europe, anxious to do what we could do to offset the resulting resentments and suspicions, and anxious to induce them to enter the Pacific war. If this purpose could be served by undertaking in advance to make Russia one of the beneficiaries of a breakup of the Japanese Empire, so much the better. If any consideration was given, in this connection, to the effects of such changes on the long-term strategic balance between Russia and Japan, and to the implications of this for long-range American interests, the record does not indicate it.

In the case of China, things were much more complicated. Since the beginning of this century, we Americans had tended to picture ourselves as the particular friends and patrons of the Chinese. This image was obviously gratifying to us; it enabled us to pose as the wise guardians and teachers of what we liked to think of as a childlike, innocent, and grateful people. It pleased us particularly to think of ourselves as the protectors of these people against the sinister designs of the other great powers, notably England and Japan. The satisfaction which Americans had always derived from the supposed success of John Hay's Open Door policy towards China was the embodiment of these feelings.

The concomitant of all this was a gross idealization of the Chinese themselves—a distortion which made itself felt with particular force during the Pacific war, when we and China were formally at war against a common enemy. In tune with the wartime psychology of democratic peoples, we assumed that since we were fighting against the same adversary, we were fighting in the same cause. Because China was partly occupied by Japan and because, again, it was hard for us to bring direct military aid to the Chinese government in this struggle, something of the same guilt complex entered into our feelings towards the Chinese which we have already noted with respect to Russia and the second front.

Out of all these ingredients there was brewed the curious view of China that seems to have animated American statesmanship during the war: the picture of a helpless, deserving nation, for whose virtues we alone, among the great powers, had understanding, whose interests we had to sponsor in the face of Japanese enmity and British callousness, and whose grateful support in the postwar period we could take for granted as a mainstay of the world position we hoped to occupy. China was, in fact, and on this we insisted with a most extraordinary vehemence, to be one of the future great powers—one of what F.D.R. called the "four world policemen."

In this highly subjective picture of the Chinese, there was no room for a whole series of historical and psychological realities. There was no room for the physical ruthlessness that had characterized Chinese political life generally in recent decades; for the formidable psychological and political powers of the Chinese people themselves; for the strong streak of xenophobia in their nature; for the lessons of the Boxer Rebellion; for the extraordinary exploitative talent shown by Chinese factions, of all times, in turning outside aid to domestic political advantage.

It was this idealized view of the Chinese, rather than any illusions about the relationship between the National Government and the Chinese Communists, which was most damaging to our Far Eastern policy. We did, to be sure, underrate the depth of the antagonism between these two elements. Our memories of what had transpired in 1927 were certainly shorter (if they existed at all) than were those of Mao and Chiang and Stalin. There also seems to me to have been a certain naïveté, but nothing worse, in our efforts to bring about a political compromise between these two factions, and to induce Stalin to join us in this effort. Why, in particular, General Patrick Hurley, of all people, should have been selected by F.D.R. as the man to take hold of this mediatory effort, remains a mystery to me. I have no doubt that General Hurley deserves well of the opinion of posterity for his previous services as a lawyer, a soldier, and a politician; but in the very suggestion that this leathery and picturesque product of the Choctaw Indian Territory in Oklahoma, with his violent personal prejudices, his sanguine disposition, and his fondness for uttering Indian war whoops at parties, should have been just the man to undertake the delicate task of reconciling the political ambitions of Mao and Chiang in a country where, so far as I am aware, he had never lived and of which he knew next to nothing—in this suggestion you have the epitome of that perverse dilettantism from which F.D.R. was no more immune than many another American statesman.

However that may be, our effort to mediate between the Communists and Chiang was, as I say, at the worst naïve; and I cannot see that its failure, or Chiang's subsequent failure to hold his own politically, were materially affected either by this effort or by the concessions we subsequently made to Stalin at Yalta. The reasons for these disasters ran deeper. They were present, as some of our more thoughtful and experienced observers in China attempted to point out, long before Hurley ever undertook his mission and long before anyone in China had any inkling of what would occur at Yalta. Our main mistake was to underrate the depth of the inner political differences which racked that country, and to assume throughout this period that whatever sort of China might emerge from the war, it would be one friendly to ourselves and prepared to join us in the pursuit of those liberal and democratic ideals to which we were attached.

This, then, was the complex of outlooks out of which

America's wartime diplomacy towards the Far East was concocted. What followed was not surprising. As early as March 1943, on the occasion of Anthony Eden's visit to Washington, F.D.R. was already voicing the view that Formosa and Manchuria ought to be returned to China (no one asked: What China?) and that Korea should be put under a trusteeship in which the Chinese and ourselves, and presumably the Russians as well, would have a part.

In the fall of 1943, as the Tehran Conference was in course of preparation, Stalin greatly pleased official Washington by giving several private intimations to American representatives that the Soviet Union would enter the Pacific war within a reasonable time after the defeat of Germany. This was before there had been any discussion of the possible terms of a Far Eastern settlement. Stalin must have come to this decision quite unilaterally, and he must have reckoned at that moment that it would be to his advantage to be in at the kill, whatever arrangements might or might not exist between him and the Allies. The limitation of time which he placed on this decision (that Russia would come into the Pacific war only some time after Germany's surrender) seems to have been well understood in Western circles; and there was never, so far as I can learn, any objection to this feature of his plans.

It was with these intimations on Stalin's part in mind that F.D.R. and Harry Hopkins met with Chiang Kai-shek in Cairo, on their way to the Tehran Conference; and it was on this occasion that there was drafted the so-called Cairo Declaration, promising that all territories "stolen" (as it was said) from China by Japan, including Manchuria, Formosa, and the Pescadores, should be returned to China. Japan, it was declared, was in fact to be striped of all territories acquired since 1914.

No one seems to know from what deliberations this declaration issued; it was apparently drafted, at the moment, by Harry Hopkins, after consultation only with the President and the Chinese visitors. Of all the acts of American statesmanship in this unhappy chapter, the issuance of this declaration, which is so rarely criticized, seems to me to have been the most unfortunate in its consequences. The other direct results of this phase of American statesmanship have either been erased by subsequent events or seem to have produced, at least, no wholly calamitous aftereffects to date; but this thoughtless tossing to China of a heavily inhabited and strategically important island which had not belonged to it in recent decades, and particularly the taking of this step before we had any idea of what the future China was going to be like, and without any consultation of the wishes of the inhabitants of the island, produced a situation which today represents a major embarrassment to United States policy, and constitutes one of the great danger spots of the postwar world.

What occurred at Tehran, immediately after the Cairo Conference, is something about which memories and records disagree. That Russia would enter the Pacific war after the defeat of Germany seems to have been tacitly understood and to have required no further discussion. The only thing about which all sources agree is that there was some vague talk about Russia having special privileges in the port of Dairen, a commercial port adjacent to Port Arthur on the Kwantung peninsula. Who initiated this discussion of Dairen is not clear—not to me, at any rate—but both Churchill and Roosevelt were evidently well disposed to the suggestion; and Stalin, though voicing a very sensible skepticism as to whether the Chinese would like the idea, showed no disinclination to take advantage of it. Port Arthur itself appears not to have been mentioned at all at that stage; and the records differ as to what else was discussed. Stalin later claimed that he had voiced at Tehran *all* the desiderata, with the exception of the recognition of the *status quo* in Outer Mongolia, which were later to be embodied in the Yalta settlement. This would then have included Port Arthur and a special Russian position in Manchuria. Whether this is true or not is probably not very important. There was at no time any strong objection in F.D.R.'s mind to giving him any of these things. It is probably safe to assume that Stalin came away from the Tehran Conference assured, at least, of F.D.R.'s general benevolence of outlook in these problems, and with the belief that the Americans were willing to guarantee him, in connection with Russia's eventual participation in the Pacific war, the recovery of at least a large portion of the losses sustained by Russia in the Peace of Portsmouth, at the end of the Russo-Japanese War in 1905. How he interpreted this disposition on the part of the Americans to reimburse him politically for something (namely, entering the Pacific war) which he had only recently stated his intention of doing anyway, without any reimbursement, we cannot know. I have a feeling there were many occasions when Stalin returned from discussions with our statesmen muttering to himself about the "inscrutable Americans," and assuring his associates that the motives of American policy were "a mystery wrapped in an enigma."

For this reason, perhaps, during the spring and summer of 1944 Stalin appears to have been somewhat suspicious of American intentions. He evaded a whole series of requests from our military authorities for the inauguration of military planning talks, looking to the co-ordination of a future Russian effort against Japan with our own. This worried the Allied military authorities, and particularly for the following reason.

At the Second Quebec Conference, in September 1944, where the Russians were not present but where the British and American leaders examined the future strategy of the war, the Combined Chiefs of Staff took as the target date for the Japanese surrender a time eighteen months after the end of the war with Germany. They overestimated, in other words, by just about one and a quarter years, the time it would take to defeat Japan after Germany had been defeated. This remained their estimate practically down to the time of Germany's defeat. I note this not in any sense of reproach to them. I have no doubt that the strictly military data before them at that time left room for no other prediction. I do find myself wondering whether on this occasion, as on others, they were not somewhat betrayed by their aversion to giving serious weight to psychological and political as well as to military factors. However that may be, this estimate of the duration of the Pacific war made it of course a matter of great importance, from the standpoint of saving American lives and facilitating our military effort, to assure Russian participation.

Still, let me just qualify this in one way. This was the implication which the estimate had *if* you were going to regard it as your wartime purpose merely to achieve total military defeat of the adversary by the most rapid and economical means, and if you were going to refuse to take into consideration, in devising your military plans, any political factors which might conflict with this military purpose. *If*, in other words, you said to yourself, as the Combined Chiefs of Staff no doubt did: "Our task is only to bring about Japan's total military defeat at the earliest possible moment and with the smallest possible losses, and nothing else

counts, or at least nothing else counts enough to enter into
the balance when it comes to drawing up strategic plans"—
then it made sense to try to get Russia into the Far Eastern
war and even, no doubt, measured against the military prospects of the moment, to pay her a price for entering it.
But if you conceived the war as only part of a complex of
long-term political problems—if you viewed the Soviet government coldly as a government no less hostile to ourselves
in ultimate political intent than the Japanese government of
1941—then you would have had to ask yourself to what
extent it was desirable to weaken Japan permanently to
the advantage of Russia; and the answer you would have
come up with about the desirability of Russia's participation in the Pacific war might have been a somewhat different
one.

There is, of course, no reason to suppose that either
F.D.R. or Harry Hopkins or the American military authorities
looked at things this way. A compromise peace with Japan
was a possibility that never entered into their calculations
at all. They were all imbued with the traditional American
attachment to the principle of unconditional surrender. This
meant, so far as they knew, fighting the war to the bitter
end of an invasion of the Japanese islands. Previous experience suggested that this would be a bloody and costly
exercise. Anything the Russians could do in the way of destroying the Japanese forces in Manchuria would presumably
facilitate this operation, and would perhaps save hundreds of
thousands of American lives. No one, certainly, can be blamed
for giving greatest possible weight to these considerations.
Harry Hopkins himself, let us remember, had already lost
one son, among the Marines at Kwajalein. No one, God
knows, could blame him for not wishing to see this tragedy
needlessly repeated an added hundred thousand times for
lack of military co-ordination with the Russians.

Advantage was therefore taken of Churchill's visit to Moscow, in October 1944, to go after Stalin once more about
the question of military collaboration in the Far East. The
head of our military mission in Moscow, General John R.
Deane, in reviewing for Stalin the course of the Pacific
war on this occasion, stressed that plans for further operations would depend partly on what Russia was willing to
do. Stalin, surprisingly, countered by asking whether we
were really sure we wanted Russia to participate. Would we

not prefer to finish off the Japanese alone? If so, this was all right with him.

I shall not speculate on the possible reasons for this change of attitude. They could have been many. Suffice it to note that it was a smart move on Stalin's part. It wiped out his previous statement of intention to enter the war anyway, wihout compensation, and it put us at once in the position of supplicants. The answer given was that of course we did want Russia to enter the Pacific war as soon as possible, and with all available strength. In particular, we wished the Russians to destroy the Japanese forces in Manchuria. This desire implied of course an initial Soviet occupation of the highly strategic Manchurian area which was formally part of China and in which Russia, as we knew, had been politically interested for a half-century past.

Stalin, in replying, said that the Soviet forces, in order to accomplish this mission, would have to carry out an out-flanking movement which would take them around to the south through the vicinities of Peking and Kalgan, and that an occupation of the North Korean ports would also be necessary. He futher observed that there were "certain political aspects that would have to be taken into consideration"[87] in connection with Russia's entry into the war. Please note that these operations he mentioned would obviously place Russia in complete military control of Manchuria and its railways as well as of the Kwantung peninsula. By virtue of these proposed operations alone, to which we gave enthusiastic assent, Stalin would be placed in a position to do what he liked with these areas, whether he was promised any special rights there or not. In these circumstances, an agreement on what special rights Russia was to have there after the war might, of course, serve rather to delimit and thus restrict Russian ambitions than to encourage them. This must be constantly borne in mind when one pursues the course of the further exchanges on this subject.

Two months later, in December 1944, our ambassador to Russia, Mr. Averell Harriman, sounded Stalin out, on the President's instructions, as to what he meant by the "political aspects" which he had said would have to be taken into consideration. Stalin replied by naming most of those things that formed the basis of the subsequent Yalta agreement. With a sweep of the hand against a map he indicated the southern part of the Kwantung peninsula. He wanted a lease on the Manchurian railways. He desired that southern Sakhalin and the Kurile Islands should be ceded to Russia.

Except for the Kurile Islands, these desiderata amounted to a restoration of what Russia had possessed in that area prior to the Russo-Japanese War. The Kuriles went beyond this. They had not been involved in the Peace of Portsmouth. They had been ceded to Japan by Russia, quite voluntarily, in an earlier settlement of 1875, in return for Japanese recognition of the Russian position in southern Sakhalin. Logically, if southern Sakhalin was to go back to Russia, the Kurile Islands should have been left with Japan.

Harriman reported these desiderata to F.D.R.; and at Yalta, less than two months later, the decisive discussion took place. Here Stalin upped the ante slightly, demanding Port Arthur, which he had not previously mentioned specifically, and insisting on language which recognized Russia's pre-eminent interest in Dairen and in the Manchurian railways. All of this was agreed to by a weary, overstrained F.D.R., who was within four months of his own death, who was obviously at that point not up to any detailed wrangling over the niceties of language, and who evidently never doubted that whatever disadvantages or embarrassments all this might subsequently involve would be a cheap price for Russia's participation in the Pacific war.

F.D.R. did insist that the agreement, insofar as it referred to Chinese ports and facilities, should require the concurrence of Chiang Kai-shek. It was further envisaged that the concessions in question should be the subject of a special bilateral agreement to be negotiated between the Soviet and Chinese governments. Their legal validity, in other words, was to rest not on the Yalta agreements but on a Sino-Soviet treaty yet to be negotiated.

The negotiations between Russians and Chinese were undertaken in Moscow, during the ensuing summer; and a treaty spelling out the respective arrangements was signed on August 14, 1945. The Chinese, certainly, did not regard this treaty as the ideal solution of the problem of their postwar relations with Russia; but I think they felt that it represented, on balance, a more favorable arrangement than they could have achieved without F.D.R.'s intercession. They had themselves solicited American assistance in composing their differences with the Soviet government. I know of no reason to doubt the sincerity of Chiang's statement to General Hurley, at the time, that he was "generally satisfied

with the treaty."[88] This conclusion is supported by the fact
that the treaty went in some respects further, in the way
of concessions to Russia, than the Yalta agreements had
envisaged; and this fact was drawn to the attention of the
Chinese before they set their final signature to the document.

Such are the facts about the Yalta agreement. Let us compare this set of circumstances with the concepts which
later became current in the United States and which underlay the posthumous attacks to which F.D.R. was subjected in
this connection. The charge was, of course, that the President, under the influence of the pro-Communist State Department—as represented at Yalta by Mr. Alger Hiss—
gratuitously had given to the Russians a wholly unearned
victory at the expense of our loyal and unsuspecting allies,
the Chinese, thus assuring the triumph of Communism in
China.

It is well to remember that Stalin, as it turned out, had
very little profit from those features of the Yalta agreement
which concerned China. He was as little prepared as we
were for a complete Communist take-over in that country.
It was, for him, an embarrassing consequence of that take-
over that within a few years he found himself obliged, in
the name of Chinese-Soviet friendship, to return these assets, almost without exception, to the Chinese. By the time
of Stalin's death, all that remained of the Yalta agreements,
from Russia's standpoint, was the possession of southern
Sakhalin and the Kuriles. The Kuriles were of minor importance. Southern Sakhalin could easily have been taken by
Russia at the close of the Pacific war had there been no
Yalta agreement at all. The truth is that the complete sweep
of Communist power in China, while in some ways advantageous to Russia, set back Russian interests in other
respects very seriously, and deprived Stalin of most of the
gains which, through all his tortuous diplomacy of the wartime period, he had hoped to extort from the confusions of
the Pacific war.

As for the Chinese, they had no means whatsoever of
preventing the military operations which Stalin proposed to
undertake in Manchuria and North China at the close of the
Pacific war and which he would surely have undertaken,

Yalta agreement or none. The agreement represented at least an attempt, backed by the prestige of the United States, to limit by definition the extent of the permanent gains Russia might make in China as a result of these operations. This was the best that the Chinese government of that day could expect. The decision to define these gains by agreement with Stalin was a military decision. It was made out of motives against which, in themselves, no criticism can be raised. The fact that this involved a gross overestimation of Japanese strength is one for which I, as a person not privy to the evidence then available, would not like to raise reproaches. The worst that can be said about these decisions is that they involved a somewhat overly rosy and naïve view of long-term Soviet intentions and of the possibilities for military collaboration with a government like that of Russia: a view that might have been corrected had the persons involved thought it worth while to go out of their immediate military circle and to take counsel with people who had had longer and deeper experience with Soviet diplomacy and with Russia generally.

If, in fact, you widen the inquiry from just the background of the Yalta agreements themselves and take under scrutiny the whole panorama of America's wartime diplomacy in the complex of problems commonly involving Russia, China, and Japan, you do indeed see certain serious deficiencies of concept and approach, but not at all the ones that have entered so prominently into political controversy in subsequent years. You see, first of all, and in a sense as the source of all other ills, the unshakeable American commitment to the principle of unconditional surrender: the tendency to view any war in which we might be involved not as a means of achieving limited objectives in the way of changes in a given *status quo* but as a struggle to the death between total virtue and total evil, with the result that the war had absolutely to be fought to the complete destruction of the enemy's power, no matter what disadvantages or complications this might involve for the more distant future. From this there flowed, of course, the congenital reluctance of American statesmen and military leaders to entertain the suggestion that there could be considerations of a political nature that could conceivably take precedence over those of military efficiency and advantage.

Added to this, there was the traditional American sentimentality about China: a prejudice which simply made it difficult for us to see things as clearly and coolly as we might otherwise have seen them.

Finally, there was a disposition on the part of the President and his advisers to disregard the obvious lessons of history in relation to this area—to assume that something had occurred during World War II which suddenly invalidated all the traditional concerns of the other powers involved and transformed their various statesmen from the hard, ruthless, and realistic figures they were into humane, enlightened people, no longer primarily concerned with the competitive political interests of their countries but guided by a new-found devotion to the principles of democratic self-government and a liberal world order. It may be said, in fact, that if the principal reason why the outcome of the Pacific war on the mainland of Asia was so contrary to our expectations lay in the spirit and manner in which Americans fight their wars, a scarcely less important reason could be found in their unwillingness to occupy themselves soberly and respectfully with the phenomenon of political power, with their failure to probe the depths of human motive that cause other governments to behave the way they do and to oppose one another at times with such uncompromising bitterness—in the complacent conviction that the common phenomena of strife, suspicion, and rivalry among nations exist only because people have failed to consult the American experience and to listen to the words of benevolent wisdom that flow so easily from the American tongue.

We who look back today on this phase of American statesmanship can well reproach ourselves, as a nation, for deficiencies in political philosophy and in historical understanding. We have no grounds to accept, and it would only blind us to our true faults if we did, that thesis which was so commonly invoked just in connection with Yalta: that our failures have come only from a treacherous conspiracy, operating in our own virtuous midst. The traits that betrayed us, in this chapter of our diplomacy, were not ones infused into us by internal subversion. They were ones to which respectable American political figures had long been prone, ones by which American statesmanship had been importantly affected long before there was an American Communist Party to operate among us, and ones which are by no means wholly eliminated from the outlooks that inspire our policies today.

25   Keeping a World Intact

WE HAVE followed Stalin's diplomacy, in its major outlines, up to the end of World War II. To continue the
story to his death in 1953 goes beyond the scope of these
discussions. But I might say a word about these final years,
in order that the story may not be left entirely in mid-air.

Stalin's ambitions in the final phases of the war ran, of
course, well beyond the objectives explicitly stated to the Allies
as the war came to an end, and beyond those that were implicit in the military advances of the Soviet armies at that
time. What Stalin was really after was the expulsion of A-
merican influence from the Eurasian land mass generally, and
its replacement by that of his own regime. In western Europe,
these ambitions were frustrated by the Marshall Plan and
the other measures taken to stiffen the independence of the
western European peoples in the post-hostilities period. In
Asia they came closer to realization; but even here unfore-
seen events—the precipitate sweep of the Chinese Revolution, the resistance of portions of southern Asia to Communist
pressures, and the unexpected American reaction to the launching of the civil war in Korea in 1950—all operated to complicate and disrupt the original Stalinist design.

In the face of these frustrations, Stalin's last years were
ones of increasing madness and sterility. His thoughts on
foreign policy tended to the reliving of old situations and to
the re-employment of old devices rather than to the recognition of the realities of a new day. The same was true in
domestic affairs. Stalin was a dangerous man to the end;
and almost to the end, he remained unchallenged in his
authority. But the men around him served him, throughout
those final years, in a sullen, guarded silence, expecting nothing and waiting only for the hand of Time to take him.
And when he went, he had consumed—almost to the last
crumb—those very prerequisites in Russian society on which

his fearful, jealous, totalitarian power had maintained itself. He had created a situation in which, fortunately for the Russian people, fortunately for us, it would have been very hard for any other Stalin to establish himself in his place.

So much for Stalin's diplomacy. I should like, in conclusion, to offer some reflections on the nature of the problem which Communist power in Russia has posed for the community of Western nations over these forty some years and on the nature of the responses by which a problem of this sort could—and could not—be met.

Let us go back to the situation with which the Western world was faced in 1921 and 1922, at the end of the process of original consolidation of the Soviet regime. The resources of the great Russian land and its people were now firmly commanded by a group of men who bore the most profound and preconceived hostility towards the social and political systems prevailing throughout the Western world. They did not only disapprove of these systems: they conceived it as their duty to collaborate actively in their destruction. In taking this attitude, they did not conceive it to be one of hostility towards the *peoples* of the West, or at least not towards that segment of the population they liked to speak of as the "toiling masses." But whether these same toiling masses, as they defined them, constituted majorities or minorities among the respective Western peoples was a question that apparently interested them little. Whatever the answer, it would not have affected their sense of obligation. The proletariat, in their view, deserved to rule, whether it constituted a majority or not. Beyond this, they persisted in viewing the parliamentary institutions of the West as shams and delusions, deserving to be overthrown by violent action. By this view alone they set themselves in opposition to that great majority of Western people, workers or otherwise, who saw in these institutions a more just and hopeful way of governing people than any other they knew, and for whom the political and social systems shaped by long series of parliamentary decisions represented something in the nature of a conscious choice. By this opposition to the very institutions of the West, the Russian Communists offered to the will of the Western peoples a species of defiance for which they have had no patent other than their own unlimited intellectual arrogance, and which was, in my view, quite inconsistent with their profession not to be hostile to the Western peoples.

On the face of it, this attitude was, in fact, little different from what we might call an attitude of war. To come along and tell another people how, on the basis of *your* ideas, it ought to be ruled, and to be prepared to back up this injunction by the encouragement of violent revolution within that country, by disaffecting numbers of its citizens and making them the agents of your own power, is of course something scarcely less offensive, scarcely less acceptable to ordinary standards of international intercourse, than the invasion of a country's territory. It was not surprising that numbers of people should have reacted, as did the English Tories of the early Twenties, by insisting that such an attitude was equivalent to the creation of a state of war, and that they should have wished to respond with comparable methods. This had been, indeed, a part of the rationale for the Allied intervention in 1918. It is a process of thought which still has considerable currency today. Many people, as you know, still raise the bewildered question: if Khrushchev and his associates want to rule the world, how *can* we have any satisfactory dealings with them? Must we not accept this attitude on their part as the manifestation of a state of war which they, not we, have created? And must we not then regard the antagonism as final and unbridgeable, and address ourselves, in the interests of our own safety, to the destruction of Soviet power? I should like to indicate to you why this line of reasoning, in my opinion, is not adequate, and why this is not the correct way of putting the question.

The fact is that while the relation to the Western world flowing from such an attitude was in many ways similar to what Western peoples had come to understand as a state of war, in other and very important ways it did *not* resemble the classic concept of a state of war, and was certainly not suitably to be met by the responses which—especially in our own century and with the Western democracies—a state of war has normally implied. Let us take note of these differences. They are essential to the understanding of our situation today.

If, first of all, the injury which the Soviet leaders wished to work upon the Western countries was as serious as many of the injuries nations have sought in the past to work on other nations by the normal devices of war (and we will not dispute this), it was not by these normal devices of war that Moscow itself set about to operate. The Marxist-Leninist ideology did not suggest that it was by a single grand military conflict between the world of Communism and the world of capitalism that these aims were to be achieved. I cannot think of a time when the Soviet government desired that there should be such a conflict, planned to launch it, or staked its hopes and expectations for the victory of world socialism on the effects of such an encounter. Central to the Soviet view of how socialism was to triumph on a world scale has always been the operation of social and political forces within the capitalist countries; and, while Moscow has always recognized that civil violence would have a legitimate place in the operation of these processess—while it has not hesitated in certain instances to promote or even to organize such civil violence; while it has even considered, in fact, that the use of the Soviet armies in a subsidiary capacity might be justified at one point or another as a means of hastening or completing an otherwise inevitable process—it has never regarded action by its own forces as the *main* agency for the spread of world revolution. It has not, in other words, sought to obtain its objectives by the traditional processes of open and outright warfare. In the course of the last twenty years, I have labored many hours to explain to other Americans the nature of the Soviet threat as I saw it; in no respect have I found it so difficult to obtain understanding as in the presentation of this one simple fact.

Secondly, if outright warfare has not been the means by which the Soviet leaders have sought to obtain their world objectives, it has also not presented to Western governments the most promising means of defense against the kind of attack which Moscow levied on their institutions and their independence. Precisely because the Soviet attack relied partly on the operation of indigenous forces within the respective capitalist countries, the governments of these countries have always been obliged to view this challenge as in part an internal one, and the responses to it have always had to lie partly in the field of domestic policy.

But beyond this, one has to ask: How could outright warfare serve to protect against this danger? What could be the specific objective of regular military operations undertaken to this end? To unseat the Soviet government? But how? By occupying *all* of Russia? I think military authorities would agree that this is not technically feasible even if it were worth one's while to make the staggering effort. And what would you expect to put in the place of the Soviet government? Do you have a ready substitute? Remember that one of the reasons for the failure of the intervention, in 1918 and 1919, was that there was no unity among the Russian opponents of Bolshevism, and not even any unity of opinion among the Western governments as to which of these opponents one would wish to see succeed. Would it be better today?

Besides, even if your military measures were directed, by intent, against the Soviet government, it would be the Russian people who would have to bear the brunt of them. Are you sure you wish to do this to them? Are you sure, in particular, that you wish to do this to them in the day of the horrors of the atom? The fact is that throughout all these years of anti-capitalist and anti-American propaganda in the Soviet Union, the Soviet peoples have remained touchingly well-inclined towards the United States, touchingly unwilling to accept the endless efforts of their government to persuade them that Americans meant them harm. You come here to the profound ambivalence in the relation between people and regime in such a country as Soviet Russia: to the fact that the interests and aspirations of these two entities in some ways differ but are in other ways identical, and that it is impossible to distinguish between the two when it comes to the hardships and injuries of war. Outright war is itself too unambivalent, too undiscriminating a device to be an appropriate means for effecting a mere change of regime in another country. You cannot logically inflict on another people the horrors of nuclear destruction in the name of what you believe to be its salvation, and expect it to share your enthusiasm for the exercise. Even if you were sure that the overwhelming majority of another people wished in theory to be freed by external intervention from a given situation of political subservience (and in the case of Russia I am not at all satisfied that this would be the case today), it would still be senseless to attempt to free it from the limited internal embarrassment of an unpopular regime (which still permits it, after all, the privilege of life in the physical sense) by subjecting it to the far more fearful destruction and hardships of modern war.

All these things, I may add, would have been true even had the atomic and other weapons of mass destruction never been invented. The existence of these weapons merely adds another dimension of absurdity to the idea that the devices of outright war would be a suitable means of

protecting the Western community from the kind of challenge with which Russian Communism has confronted it:
suitable, that is, in the sense of being a means to which
the Western community might rationally and voluntarily resort. The atom has simply served to make unavoidably
clear what has been true all along since the day of the
introduction of the machine gun and the internal-combustion
engine into the techniques of warfare—what should have
been clear to people during World War I and was not:
namely, that modern warfare in the grand manner, pursued
by all available means and aimed at the total destruction of
the enemy's capacity to resist, is, unless it proceeds very
rapidly and successfully, of such general destructiveness that
it ceases to be useful as an instrument for the achievement
of any coherent political purpose. Such warfare (and this
was true even in 1917) involves evils which far outweigh any
forward political purpose it might serve—any purpose at all,
in fact, short of sheer self-preservation, and perhaps not
even short of that. Even if warfare had been the answer
to Communism in a different stage of weaponry (and, mind
you, I do not think it would), it would certainly not be the
answer in the day of the atom.

There is more to it than this. We must remember that this
attitude on the part of the Russian Communists, which
seems to resemble the attitude we would associate with a
state of war, has always represented only one component in
the motivation of Soviet foreign policy. There are other
components which are quite different. Anyone who has looked
reasonably closely at political history will have had many
occasions to observe that the very experience of holding
and exercising supreme power in a country saddles any
ruler, whatever his original ideological motives, with most
of the traditional concerns of government in that country,
subjects him to the customary compulsions of statesmanship within that framework, makes him the protagonist of
the traditional interests and the guardian against the traditional dangers. He cannot free himself entirely from his
predecessors or his successors. However despotic he may
be, and however far his original ideas may have departed
from the interests of the people over whom he rules, his
position of power gives him, as Gibbon once pointed out,
a certain identity of interest with those who are ruled.
Their energies—and for this reason their lives, their health,

and their morale—are important to him even if their freedom and happiness are not; and he becomes *ipso facto* in many respects their guardian, their spokesman, and their champion vis-à-vis external forces. One cannot, therefore, just exploit one's power over a given people for the exclusive purpose of pursuing ideological aims unrelated to their interests and concerns. One is always to a degree the captive of one's own power, and is obliged, by the logic of one's position, to think partly in terms of the national interest on which that power is founded.

This began to happen to the Soviet government early in the day. As early as 1921, as we saw, it was obliged to shift the focus of its effort from world revolution to the building up of the physical strength of Russia itself. And if, after that time, world revolutionary motives—motives of ideological hostility to the capitalist West—continued always to be present to some extent in the pattern of Soviet statesmanship, many other motives were also present which did not have these connotations, and to which—again—war would have been no rational response.

Here we come to something which is vitally important but which, I think, is often lost sight of in the United States. This is the fact that international life normally has in it strong competitive elements. It did not take the challenge of Communism to produce this situation. Just as there is no uncomplicated personal relationship between individuals, so, I think, there is no international relationship between sovereign states which is without its elements of antagonism, its competitive aspects. Many of the present relationships of international life are only the eroded remnants of ones which, at one time, were relationships of most uncompromising hostility. Every government is in some respects a problem for every other government, and it will always be this way so long as the sovereign state, with its supremely self-centered rationale, remains the basis of international life. The variety of historical experience and geographic situation would assure the prevalence of this situation, even if such things as human error and ambition did not.

The result is that the relationship we have with the Soviet Union has to be compared, if we are to determine its real value, not with some nonexistent state of total harmony of interests but with what we might call the normal level of recalcitrance, of sheer orneriness and unreasonableness, which we encounter in the behavior of states anywhere, and which

I am sure we often manifest in our own. This, again, is largely
the product of the long-term factors affecting a nation's life.
Russian governments have always been difficult governments
to do business with. This is nothing new in kind—if anything
is new about it—it is only a matter of degree.

To satisfy yourselves of this, you have only to turn to
any epoch you like of Russia's past and consult the reports
of foreign diplomats and statesmen about their dealings with
the Russians. Take, for example, these words:

> Russia for a number of years has treated the United
> States as badly as she has treated England. . . . Her diploma-
> tists lied to us with brazen and contemptuous effrontery, and
> showed with cynical indifference their intention to organize
> China against our interests. . . . I should have liked to be
> friendly with her; but she simply would not permit it, and
> those responsible for managing her foreign policy be-
> trayed a brutality and ignorance, an arrogance and short-
> sightedness, which are not often combined.[89]

I could produce dozens of such statements. This one
happened to be made by President Theodore Roosevelt to
the British ambassador in Washington, during the Russo-
Japanese War.

Russia would have been a great military and industrial
power by mid-century, whatever regime she might have had.
This greater strength would certainly, in any circumstances,
have whetted her ambitions and stiffened her diplomacy.
Traditional, deeply ingrained traits of reaction and of
diplomatic methods would have made her, under any
government, a country difficult to deal with in the present mid-
century. It is against this reality, not against a state of blissful
conflictlessness, that Soviet recalcitrance and hostility have to
be measured. The result, as you will readily see, does not
justify us in the conclusion that we are facing a wholly new
and unprecedented situation.

Not only are these differences ones of degree but they
reflect factors which have been, are, and will continue to
be, in a state of constant flux and change. We have just
seen that Soviet statesmanship represents a mixture of some
elements which are ones of abnormal hostility towards us
and do indeed embody dangerous dreams of world hegemony, and of other elements which are indistinguishable
from the normal motivations of governments in a com-

petitive world. Let us now note, too, that the relationship between these elements is not a stable one. It is constantly changing; and if it is true that these changes have been erratic, that they have been in the nature of zigzags, with downs as well as ups, the general trend of them, especially in recent years, has been in the direction of normalcy—towards a preoccupation with internal and defensive interests in the Soviet state, away from the world revolutionary dreams of the early aftermath of the Revolution.

I feel it particularly important to stress, lest it be forgotten, that what I have been describing was the eras of Lenin and of Stalin, and not that of Khrushchev. The differences are of course relative; but they are not unimportant.

Let us not be put off by the angularities of Mr. Khrushchev's personality. Individuals are not so important here: they come and they go, sometimes faster than we expect. I am inclined to ascribe deep and encouraging significance to some of the changes in the character and structure of the Soviet regime that have taken place since Stalin's death. The drastic alteration in the role of the police has constituted a basic change in the nature and spirit of Soviet society. It has also altered somewhat the character of the political process, particularly in the senior echelons of the Party, away from the horror of unadulterated police intrigue, and in the direction of a rudimentary parliamentarianism, at least within the Central Committee. This is true despite the fact that it is a reform which could, theoretically, be reversed again at any time. The longer things go on this way, without a reversal, the harder any such reversal will be, in my opinion. The relaxation of the Iron Curtain has, to date, remained within modest limits. It obviously encounters deep inhibitions in the neo-Stalinist echelons of the regime. But I think it has gone so far that it would not be easy to bottle up again the intellectual and cultural life of this talented people as it was bottled up under Stalin.

Finally, we must note that the position of the Soviet regime has been fundamentally altered by the fact that for the last ten years it has not been alone within its own Communist community but has had, alongside it, one great associate to whom its relationship is partly that of ally and partly that of rival, and a number of other associates in eastern Europe whose interests it cannot treat quite as cavalierly as many people in this country seem to fancy. This means that it has passed from the relative simplicity of a bipolar world, in which the only issue was "we" and "they"—who-whom, *kto-kogo*, as Lenin put it—and has come into an international setting marked by real complications and contradictions. People who have only enemies don't know what complications are; for that, you have to have friends; and these, the Soviet government, thank God, now has.

If this is now a complicated world for the Soviet government, so it is for us. This, too, places limitations on our ability to treat Soviet hostility in the *simpliste* way that some of our people would like to see us treat it. When you have only *one* enemy, you can at least have some hope of doing this successfully. When you have more than one, and when they are too strong to be taken on all together, you cannot afford this luxury. We saw, in connection with the events of the 1930's, that when you were in this position, when you had two quite separate and unrelated adversaries: Nazi Germany and Soviet Russia—and when you were so weak that you could hope to cope with one of these adversaries only by collaboration with the other—then you could no longer cultivate the luxury of high moral attitudes. This, I fear, is our position again today, in the face of Russian and Chinese power, not to mention some of the other complexities of our international position.

Please do not think that in saying this I am entertaining dreams of setting the Russians at war with the Chinese. I don't want to see any great nation at war with any other great nation in this day of the atom. I think it naïve to suppose that Russian-Chinese relations could in any case be very different from what they are today, so long as the present world situation prevails. I am merely saying that it is incumbent on us, too, to recognize the existence of a complicated world, not a simple one; and that in the light of the duality which now marks the Communist orbit, we would be very foolish to overlook the differences in the nature of the challenge offered to us by these two great forces and to insist on having merely one adversary where we could, to our own benefit, have two.

I have two purposes in saying these things to you. The first is to assure that what I have said about the Stalin era does not unduly discourage us, and that we do not become the captives of this image when we consider our responses to the problem of Soviet power today. Remember that American public opinion has often been something like a decade behind the times, in devising these responses. Not until the late Twenties, a decade after the event, did it begin to be generally recognized in this country that a revolution had taken place in Russia of such strength and depth that it was destined to enter permanently into the fabric of our time. When F.D.R. recognized the Soviet government in 1933, he was acting largely on an image drawn from the Russia of Lenin's day; nothing was further from his powers of imagination than the Russia of the purges that was already then in the making. Even in World War II, Roosevelt's view of Russia, and that of many other Americans, was one that took little account of the purges, little account of the degree of commitment Stalin had incurred by virtue of his own crimes and excesses—a commitment which would have made it impossible for him to be a comfortable associate for the likes of ourselves, no matter how we had treated him. And when, in the late 1940's, numbers of worthy people in this country suddenly and belatedly discovered the rather normal phenomenon of foreign penetration and espionage, and set out frantically trying to persuade us that *we* ought to lose faith in *ourselves* because *they* had made this discovery, the evil of Communist subversion over which they were so excited was one which had actually reached its highest point several years earlier and was by that time definitely on the wane. Today, there are many equally worthy people who appear to be discovering for the first time that there was such a thing as the Stalin era, and who evidently have much difficulty in distinguishing it from what we have known since 1953. I could even name professional "sovietologists," private and governmental, who seem afraid to admit to themselves or to others that Stalin is really dead.

Let us not repeat these mistakes. Let us permit the image of Stalin's Russia to stand for us as a marker of the distance we have come, a reminder of how much worse things could be, and were—not as a specter whose vision blinds us to the Russia we have before us today.

My second purpose is to stress the necessity of an American outlook which accepts the obligations of maturity and consents to operate in a world of relative and unstable values. If we are to regard ourselves as a grown-up nation—and anything else will henceforth be mortally dangerous—then we must, as the Biblical phrase goes, put away childish things; and among these childish things the first to go, in my opinion,

should be self-idealization and the search for absolutes in
world affairs: for absolute security, absolute amity, absolute
harmony. We are a strong nation, wielding great power. We
cannot help wielding this power. It comes to us by virtue
of our sheer size and strength, whether we wish it or not.
But to wield power is always at best an ambivalent thing
—a sharing in the guilt taken upon themselves by all those
men who, over the course of the ages, have sought or consented to tell others what to do. There is no greater American error than the belief that liberal institutions and the
rule of law relieve a nation of the moral dilemma involved
in the exercise of power. Power, like sex, may be concealed
and outwardly ignored, and in our society it often is; but
neither in the one case nor in the other does this concealment
save us from the destruction of our innocence or from the
confrontation with the dilemmas these necessities imply. When
the ambivalence of one's virtue is recognized, the total
iniquity of one's opponent is also irreparably impaired.

The picture, then, which I hope I have presented is that
of an international life in which not only is there nothing
final in point of time, nothing not vulnerable to the law of
change, but also nothing absolute in itself: a life in which
there is no friendship without some element of antagonism;
no enmity without some rudimentary community of interest;
no benevolent intervention which is not also in part an
injury; no act of recalcitrance, no seeming evil, from
which—as Shakespeare put it—some "soul of goodness"
may not be distilled.

A world in which these things are true is, of course, not
the best of all conceivable worlds; but it *is* a tolerable one,
and it *is* worth living in. I think our foremost aim today
should be to keep it physically intact in an age when men
have acquired, for the first time, the technical means of
destroying it. To do this we shall have, above all, to avoid
petulance and self-indulgence: in our view of history, in
our view of ourselves, in our decisions, and in our behavior
as a nation. If this physical intactness of our environment
can be preserved, I am not too worried about our ability or
inability to find answers to the more traditional problems
of international life with which these lectures have grappled.
I am content to dismiss you, as Bismarck once did some of
the more curious and impatient of his junior associates,
with the words: "Let us leave a few problems for our children
to solve; otherwise they might be so bored."

Notes

[1] Ray Stannard Baker, *Woodrow Wilson, Life and Letters,* Vol. VII, p. 350. New York: Doubleday, Doran & Co., Inc., 1939.

[2] Maurice Paléologue, *La Russie des Tsars Pendant la Grande Guerre,* Vol. III, *19 Août–18 Septembre 1916,* p. 181. Paris: Librairie Plon, 1922.

[3] *Ibid.,* p. 188.

[4] *Ibid.,* p. 188.

[5] Georges Michon, *The Franco-Russian Alliance,* p. 299. London: 1929. (Cited in Robert D. Warth, *The Allies and the Russian Revolution,* p. 21. Durham, N.C.: Duke University Press, 1954.)

[6] Later Sir Robert Bruce Lockhart.

[7] *War Memoirs of David Lloyd George,* Vol. III, p. 1588. London: Ivor Nicholson & Watson, 1934.

[8] Paléologue (See Note 2), Vol. III, p. 226.

[9] *Ibid.,* p. 228.

[10] *Papers Relating to the Foreign Relations of the United States, 1917,* Supplement 1, *The World War,* p. 200. Washington: United States Government Printing Office, 1931. This series of publications of the Department of State will hereafter be referred to as *Foreign Relations.*

[11] Frederick L. Schuman, *Russia Since 1917: Four Decades of Soviet Politics,* p. 70. New York: Alfred A. Knopf, 1957.

[12] Paléologue (See Note 2), Vol. III, p. 313.

[13] *Soviet-American Relations, 1917-1920,* Vol. I, *Russia Leaves the War,* pp. 75-76. Princeton, N.J.: Princeton University Press, 1956.

[14] G. K. Seleznev, "Istoriya SSSR," pp. 196-201, *Voprosy Istorii,* No. 8 (August 1957).

[15] Albert Shaw, Editor, *The Messages and Papers of Woodrow Wilson,* Vol. 1, *March 4, 1913, to January 6, 1919,* p. 381. New York: George H. Doran Co., 1917.

[16] *Dokumenty vneshnei politiki SSSR* (Documents of the Foreign Policy of the U.S.S.R.), Vol. 1, p. 12. Moscow: State Publishing House for Political Literature, 1957.

[17] *War Memoirs of David Lloyd George,* Vol. V, pp. 2577-2578. London: Ivor Nicholson & Watson, 1936.

[18] *Ibid.,* p. 2571.

[19] New York: Boni and Liveright, 1919; Modern Library, 1935.

[20] New York and London: G. P. Putnam's Sons, 1933.

[21] V. I. Lenin, *Sochineniya* (Complete Works), Fourth ed., Vol. XXVII (1950), p. 520, n. 13. Moscow: State Publishing House for Political Literature, 1947-1952.

[22] David R. Francis Papers. St. Louis: Missouri Historical Society.

[23] *Bolshevik Propaganda, Hearings before a Subcommittee of the Committee on the Judiciary, United States Senate, Sixty-Fifth Congress,* p. 807. Washington: Government Printing Office, 1919.

[24] Lenin (See Note 21), Vol. XXVIII (1950), p. 49.

[25] *Bolshevik Propaganda* (See Note 23), p. 863.

[26] *Ibid.,* p. 828.

[27] *Pravda* (Moscow), September 15, 1957, p. 1.

[28] *Ibid.*

[29] Mikhail Sergeevich Kedrov, *Bez bolshevistskogo rukovodstva (iz istorii interventsii na Murmanye)* (Without Bolshevik Leadership [History of Intervention in Murmansk]), p. 28. Leningrad: Publishing House Krasnaya Gazeta, 1930.

[30] *Pravda,* February 21, 1935.

[31] Kedrov (See Note 29), p. 119.

[32] James Bunyan, *Intervention, Civil War, and Communism in Russia, April-December 1918, Documents and Materials,* pp. 133-134. Baltimore: The Johns Hopkins Press, 1936.

[33] Kedrov (See Note 29), pp. 130-132.

[34] Baker (See Note 1), Vol. VIII, p. 284 n.

[35] *Foreign Relations, 1918, Russia* (See Note 10), Vol. II, p. 289.

[36] Afterwards Field Marshal Lord Ironside.

[37] *Foreign Relations, The Lansing Papers, 1914-1920,* Vol. II, p. 365.

[38] *Foreign Relations, 1918, Russia* (See Note 10), Vol. II, p. 263.

[39] William S. Graves, *America's Siberian Adventure, 1918-1920,* p. 4. New York: Jonathan Cape and Harrison Smith, 1931.

[40] *Ibid.,* pp. 7-8.

[41] Frederick Palmer, *Newton D. Baker: America at War,* Vol. II, p. 394. New York: Dodd, Mead & Company, 1931.

[42] Graves (See Note 39), p. 328.

[43] *The Literary Digest,* September 6, 1919 (Vol. LXII), p. 60. Cited in Betty Miller Unterberger, *America's Siberian Expedition, 1918-1920: A Study of National Policy,* p. 183. Durham, N.C.: Duke University Press, 1956.

[44] Shaw (See Note 15), p. 352.

[45] *Ibid.,* p. 379.

[46] David Lloyd George, *The Truth About the Peace Treaties,* Vol. I, p. 315. London: Victor Gollancz Ltd., 1938.

[47] *Ibid.,* p. 331.

[48] *Ibid.,* p. 368.

[49] *The Bullitt Mission to Russia: Testimony Before the Committee on Foreign Relations, United States Senate, of William C. Bullitt,* p. 66. New York: B. W. Huebsch, 1919.

[50] *Ibid.,* p. 94.

[51] *Ibid.,* p. 97.

[52] Alexis de Tocqueville, *Democracy in America,* Vol. I, p. 235. New York: Alfred A. Knopf, 1948.

[53] *The Parliamentary Debates,* House of Commons, 5th Series, Vol. 114, col. 1351.

[54] *The Memoirs of Herbert Hoover,* Vol. I: *Years of Adventure, 1874-1920,* p. 416. London: Hollis & Carter, 1952.

[55] *Sunday Times,* October 10, 1920, as quoted in W. P. and Zelda K. Coates, *A History of Anglo-Soviet Relations,* Vol. I, p. 45. London: Lawrence and Wishart, 1943.

[56] *The Parliamentary Debates,* 5th Series, Vol. 125, cols. 43-45.

[57] Coates (See Note 55), pp. 26-27.

[58] Gustav Hilger and Alfred G. Meyer, *The Incompatible Allies, A Memoir-History of German-Soviet Relations 1918-1941,* pp. 58-59. New York: The Macmillan Company, 1953.

[59] See "Extracts from the Theses on the World Situation and the Tasks of the Comintern Adopted by the Third Comintern Congress," as given in *The Communist International, 1919-1943,* Vol. I, p. 238, selected and edited by Jane Degras. London: Oxford University Press under auspices of the Royal Institute of International Affairs, 1956.

[60] Degras, *The Communist International* (See Note 59), Vol. I, p. 229.

[61] From an ECCI statement on the Genoa Conference, of May 19, 1922. Degras, *The Communist International* (See Note 59), Vol. I, p. 348.

[62] *Ibid.*, pp. 253-254: Theses on Tactics, adopted by the III Comintern Congress, July 12, 1921.

[63] Kamenev's estimate of the world situation at the Tenth Party Congress, Moscow, March 15, 1921. Xenia Joukoff Eudin and Harold H. Fisher, *Soviet Russia and the West, 1920-1927*, p. 94. Stanford, California: Stanford University Press, 1957.

[64] Lenin's speech to a congress of metal workers, March 6, 1922. *Ibid.*, p. 100.

[65] *Pravda* (Moscow), No. 6, p. 2 (January 10, 1922). *Ibid.*, p. 125.

[66] E. A. Bond, Editor, *Russia at the Close of the Sixteenth Century*, Introduction, p. xvii. London: 1856.

[67] Lord Newton, *Lord Lansdowne: A Biography*, p. 467. London: Macmillan and Company, Ltd., 1929.

[68] *Foreign Relations, 1920* (See Note 10), Vol. III, pp. 466-468.

[69] Harold Nicolson, *Curzon: The Last Phase, 1919-1925; A Study in Post-War Diplomacy*, p. 245. New York: Harcourt, Brace and Company, 1929.

[70] Jane Degras, Editor, *Soviet Documents on Foreign Policy*, Vol. I, *1917-1924*, p. 298. London: Oxford University Press under the auspices of the Royal Institute of International Affairs, 1951.

[71] J. Ramsay MacDonald, *The Foreign Policy of the Labour Party*, pp. 47-49. London: Cecil Palmer, 1923.

[72] Bertram D. Wolfe, *Three Who Made a Revolution: A Biographic History*, p. 89. New York: The Dial Press, 1948.

[73] The document was published in *Life*, April 23, 1956, and was subsequently the subject of a book by Isaac Don Levine entitled *Stalin's Great Secret* (New York: Coward-McCann, Inc., 1956).

[74] *Stalin's Failure in China, 1924-1927*, p. 174. Cambridge, Massachusetts: Harvard University Press, 1958.

[75] New York: Harper and Brothers, 1953.

[76] *Nazi-Soviet Relations, 1939-1941, Documents from the Archives of the German Foreign Office* (Raymond J. Sontag and James S. Beddie, Editors), pp. 50-52. Washington, D.C.: Government Printing Office, 1948.

[77] *Ibid.*, p. 58.

[78] *Ibid.*, p. 195.

[79] *Nazi-Soviet Relations* (See Note 76), p. 213.

[80] Winston S. Churchill, *Their Finest Hour*, Volume II of *The Second World War*, p. 586. Boston: Houghton Mifflin Company, 1949.

[81] *Nazi-Soviet Relations* (See Note 76), p. 260.

[82] Churchill, Vol. II (See Note 80), p. 579.

[83] Telford Taylor, *The March of Conquest*, p. 44. New York: Simon and Schuster, 1958.

[84] Winston S. Churchill, *The Grand Alliance*, Volume III of *The Second World War*, p. 369. Boston: Houghton Mifflin Company, 1950.

[85] *Ibid.*

[86] *Ibid.*, pp. 372-373.

[87] As quoted by Herbert Feis, *Churchill-Roosevelt-Stalin, The War They Waged and the Peace They Sought*, p. 466. Princeton, N.J.: Princeton University Press, 1957.

[88] *United States Relations with China, with Special Reference to the Period 1944-1949*, p. 120. Washington, D.C.: Department of State Publication 3573, Far Eastern Series 30, released August 1949.

[89] Tyler Dennett, *Roosevelt and the Russo-Japanese War*, p. 47. New York: Doubleday Page and Company, 1925.

Index